BUSINESS POLICY AND ENVIRONMENT

[For B.Com./M.Com., and other Management Courses of All Universities]

By

R. Joseph

ANMOL PUBLICATIONS PVT. LTD.

NEW DELHI - 110 002 (INDIA)

ANMOL PUBLICATIONS PVT. LTD.
4374/4B, Ansari Road, Daryaganj
New Delhi - 110 002
Ph.: 23261597, 23278000
Visit us at: www.anmolpublications.com

Business Policy and Environment

First Published, 2005

PRINTED IN INDIA

Published by J.L. Kumar for Anmol Publications Pvt. Ltd., New Delhi - 110 002 and Printed at Mehra Offset Press, Delhi.

Contents

Preface

Business Policy and Environment as a paper is being taught at the graduate and post graduate level in B.Com., M.Com. and other Management courses syllabus in almost all the Indian Universities and Institutions. The various courses conducted by management institutions at the Central and State level too have been considered in respect of their syllabus, course contents and requirements. Thus the material presented here would be of interest as well as great use to the students of B.Com., M.Com. and other Management Courses. This book will provide complete knowledge of strategy and structure of business policy and environment, industrial growth, organisational objectives, social considerations, decision making, corporate policies in production, marketing personnel and financial management, foreign trade policies, socio-cultural, legal and technology environment and economic system.

The major topics dealt in this book are—Concept of Business Policy; Dynamic Setting of Organisational Objectives; Social Consideration in Business Policy; Business Policy in Foreign Collaboration; Decision Making in Business; Functional Strategies in Business; Corporate Policy for Production and Marketing; Corporate Policy in Personnel & Financial Management; Foreign Trade Policies; Industrial Growth and Policy in Business; Business Environment; Economic Reforms; Socio-Cultural Environment; Legal Environment; Technology Environment; Economic Systems and Environment.

Ved Prakash

1

Concept of Business Policy

It is necessary for the management to formulate policies for the achievement of organisational objectives. Policies are the guiding principles that govern human action usually of routine and repetitive nature. They are general statements which guide thinking and action of the company's official attitudes towards the range of behaviour within which it will permit or desire its employees to act. According to Koontz, O'Donnell and weihrich, "Policies are the general statements of understadings which guide or channel thinking and action in decision making. They limit the area within which decision is to be made and ensure that decisions will be consistent with and contribute to objectives." Thus, policies delimit the area within which decisions are to be made, and ensure that decisions will be consistent with the overall business objectives. A business policy is an established guiding canon premised on an objective devised to govern the activities of a business enterprise and from which the basic precepts of contact are derived. A policy is a steering mechanism used by the top management to ensure that activity proceeds in the desired direction. While objectives provide the ends which is management should try to achieve, the policies provide the goals which everybody should keep in mind while achieving the ends.

CHARACTERISTICS OF POLICY

A statement should have the following characteristics to be called a policy:

(1) **Consistency.** A policy should provide for consistency in operations of an organisation. The policy should not create

conflicts in the organisation. It should ensure uniformity of operations at various levels in the organisation.

(2) **Participation.** A policy should be developed with the active participation of top management. Policy formulation calls for serious thinking and participation of all the top level executives.

(3) **Written Form.** A policy should be in writing as far as possible. A policy takes concrete shape when it is be in writing. It will ensure uniformity of application at all times.

(4) **Clarity.** A policy should be clear, definite and explicit. It should leave no scope for misinterpretation.

(5) **Relationship to Objectives.** The policy should be derived from the objectives. It should faciliate the achieving of organisational objectives.

(6) **Expression of Intentions of Top Management.** A policy should be an expression of intentions of top management. It should present the principle that will guide the organisational actions.

(7) **Long Lasting.** A policy is a standing decision of the management. It should be long lasting. For this purpose, a policy should be formulated after taking into account the long-range plans and needs of the organisation.

(8) **Broad Definition.** A policy should be stated in broad terms. The purpose of policy statement is to serve as a guide to practice now and in future. So it should be stated in the broadest possible term.

Types of Policies. Policies may be classified into the following categories:

1. **General and Specific Policies.** As to the area of freedom policies may be classified as general and specific. General policies are stated in broad terms to give freedom to units

of the organisation. On the other hand, specific policies are intensively defined to restrict freedom of action.

2. **Written and Implied Policies.** Written policies are explicit declaration in writing. Implied policies are those inferred from the behaviour or conduct or organisational members, particularly of top executives. Where no written policy exists on a particular topic or the expressed policy is not enforced, subordinates interpret the actions of their superiors and make decisions accordingly. For instance, if promotions are made on the basis of seniority, there is an implied promotional policy, even though nothing is expressed in writing. Written policies are always.

3. **Orginiated, Appealed and Imposed Policies.** On the basis of origin, policies may be classified as Originaled, appealed and imposed policies. *Orginated policies* are deliberately formulated by top managers on their own initiative in order to guide the actions of their subordinates. They are generally put in writing and embodied in a policy manual. *Appealed policies* are formulated on the appeal or request of subordinates. Subordinates make an appeal to deal with a particular case which is not covered by earlier policies. *Imposed policies* arise from the influence of outside forces like government, trade unions, trade associations, etc. These forces either impose a policy or create conditions for the adoption of a particular policy.

4. **Organisational and functional policies.** In terms of scope, policies may be classified as organisational policies and departmental policies. Organisational policies are the overall policies of an organisation and they are formulated by top management. Departmental or functional policies are meant for specific functions or departments of business *e.g.*, sales policy, production policy, financial policy, personnel policy etc. They are derived from organisational policies to guide the efforts of people in particular

departments. Organisational or basic policies are used uniformly throughout the organisation whereas departmental policies are applied in particular departments.

ELEMENTS OF BUSINESS POLICY

(A) The Firm

The firm can be defined in a rather broad sense to mean a business entity (corporate or other form) or any other kind of entity (academic, military, government, religious). Within the firm it is useful to consider separately the resources, characteristics, capabilities, limitations, and organization, even though these overlap to some degree. Management can be viewed as within the firm and yet apart from it, in the sense that general managers are responsible not only for the firm but for all its relationships with other elements in the policy concpet. In this book, as in other literature, references to the company, the corporation, the firm, the enterprise, or the business are used somewhat interchangeable, and all refer to the business entity that is labled here as the firm.

Resources are defined here as those things under management's control that can be utilized to reach the firm's objectives. Resources in the classical economic sense are land, labour, and capital. Assets on the balance sheet are resources:

Money, on hand and due from others

Inventories of products and materials

Plant and equipment

Liability and equities on the balance sheet represent the ownership of the assets. the relationship and condition of these balance sheet items should be analyzed along with other factors as a parrt of policy or strategy evaluation.

Human resources, the people in the company, are an important resource not shown on balance sheets. Intangible resources are also valuable:

Patents, franchises, leases, and other contractual rights

Knowledge of the business and its environment

Goodwill and favourable relationships

Reputation of the firm and its leaders

Skills and capabilities of its people

Established sales routes

Dealer organisations

Sources of supply

Any other contractual or customary relationship important to the firm.

The organization of the firm (both structure and members) has a great deal to do with how the other resources are utilized. The choice of the firm's organisation form is a strategic kind of choice by management, because it will affect the way in which the firm achieves its objectives. But the existing oragnisation at any time of strategic analysis must be taken into consideration as a part of the firm that is supposed to follow some strategic path. Organisation structure and behaviour can usually be changed by strategic action. However, the organisation will influence the choice of objectives and strategies.

Experience and past performance can indicate capabilities and limitations of the firm. Performance, as shown in the financial statements and other available records, needs to be analyzed in detail along with the analysis of the current position of a firm. Experience and past performance, along with resources, should help to indicate what the firm is and the kind of business it is in.

The assessment of strengths and weaknesses is an important element of strategic planning, says. Howard Stevenson. Items for strategic evaluation include directions, strategies, overall policy commitments and past practices. This process enables managers to learn from their past successes and failures. To improve the process, Stevenson suggests that managers make measures and criteria (including goals) explicit, define attributes as well as strengths and weaknesses, and understand the difference in the use of strenths and weaknesses.

Experience can indicate something more than skill and knowledge: it should help identify what the firm does best-what has been called its "distinctive competence" (a term attributed to Philip Selznick). Distinctive competence is a crucial part of Andrews's definition of corporate strategy mentioned earlier, in which the focus of resources is the way in which to convert distinctive competence into market advantages.

In every business you must consider, "What does it take to win?" in the oil business you must drill. If you do not drill, you do not win. In construction you must bid to win. In every business you must be able to do something will in compete and succeed.

The precept that the best single indicator of probably for future behaviour is past behaviour may well just as true from a company as for an individual. Changes in behaviour can be made and often must be made, but the past force and direction of momentum can never be safely ignored.

(B) Time

Time, in the policy concept, has three components: *(a)* the pint in time when the analysis is made, *(b)* the point when the selected strategy is implemented, and *(c)* the time span, which is the period of implemnetation, performance toward objectives, and measurement of progress. In a sense, the illustration of the time span of a strategy may be partly artificial, because its visualization or establishment is not as final as the illustration would suggest. Changes take place, and new strategies and often employed before old ones are fulfilled. However, it is necessary to recognize the nature of the other elements of policy at a specific point in time (when formulating or reappraising any of the elements) and to designate the period of time (or continuity,

if a permanent objective is involved) for the employement of the strategic alternative considered.

Changes in any of the elements of policy may interrupt the time span that was intended origanally, making necessary a new appraisal with possible changes in the time period, the strategies, or even the objectives. Even without specific changes in conditions, managers need to periodically ressess their objectives and strategies and to continually monitor the environment and the performance and progress of the firm.

"Strategic issue management" (SIM) is a term used by Ansoff for a system to watch for early but weak signals to avoid strategic surprise. He emphasizes the real time character of SIM. "It follows no fixed planning calender; rather, the surveillance is continuous.

Timing is critical also in the sense of both the time when managers discern impending or actual changes in the environment and the time when they decide to make changes in objectives or strategies of their firm. Premature changes or initiatives can be as unsuccessful as changes made too late. For example, industry as a whole has been much more receptive to innovations in energy conservation since 1974 than was the case even a decade earlier.

(C) Opportunity

New opportunities abound in the changing environment and can also be created within the firm. Opportunity has a positive connotation, and we can differentiate the term "opportunity" form terms with negative connotations. such as "problem," distrubance," or "threat." Yet it requires attention, effort, and resources to respond to or create opportunities, and those commitments of resources are seldom made without some risk of loss or failure. At the very least, the choice of one alternative bears a price of alternative forgone (which is the way economists define cost). The risk of loss or failure associated with each strategic alternative should thus be weighed against its expected gain and success. Managers expect higher gain from higher risks, but other factors also enter into the assessment of risk and decisions about an acceptable level of risk. Flexbility to change from one strategy to another, when conditions en route to an objective indicate the need to consider changes, can help to reduce or control risk. Timing has an important effect upon risk. Long-term commitments of large amounts of resources involve substantial risk because of the uncertainty of the future and would therefore be expected to have a higher payoff than strategic alternatives offering more flexibility in the timing and use of resources.

Strategic alternatives include all the kinds of major strategic choices that need to be made toward the attainment of objectives. They may be functional as well as comprehensive, external, or internal. As in the case of objectives, however, it is useful to limit the extent of what we call strategy to a relatively few (compared with all the possible detail general means of attaining objectives or avenues toward objectives. Some typical strategic alternatives are discussed in Chapter 8. The details of breaking down major strategies into programmes, projects, plans, or tasks are part of the implementation of strategy and the on going management of the firm.

(D) Environment

Environment literally means the surroundings, external objects, influences or circumstances under which someone or something exists. The environment of any organisation is "the aggregate of all conditions, events and influences that surround and affect it." Since the environment influences an organisation in many ways, its understanding is of crucial importance. The concept of environment can be understood by looking at some of its characterstics.

Characteristics of Environment

Business environment (or simply environment) exhibits many characterstics. Some of the important—and obvious—characteristics are briefly described here.

1. **Environment has a far-reaching impact.** The environment has a far-reaching impact on organisations. The growth and profitability of an organisation depends critically

on the environment in which it exists. Any environment change has an impact on the organisation in several different ways.

2. **Environment is complex.** The environment consists of a number of factors, events conditions and influences arising from different sources. All these do not exist in isolation but interect with each other to create entirely new ses of influences. It is difficult to comprehend at once what factors constitute a given environment. All in all, environment is a complex phenomenon relatively easier to understand in parts but but difficult to grasp in its totality.

3. **Environment is dynamic.** The environment is constantly changing in nature. Due to the many and varied influences operating, there is dynamism in the environment causing it to continuously change its shape and character.

4. **Environment is multi-faceted.** What shape and character an environment assumes depends on that perception of the observer. A particular change in the different environment, or a new development may be viewed by different observers. This is frequently seen when the same development is welcomed as an opportunity by one company while another company perceives it as a threat.

   Since the environment is complex, dynamic multi-faceted and has a far reaching impact, dividing it into external and internal components enables us to understand it better.

TYPES OF ENVIRONMENT

The external environment includes all the factors outside the organisation which provide opportunities or pose threats to the organisation. The internal environment refers to all the factors within an organisation which impart strengths or cause weaknesses of a strategic nature.

The environment in which an organisation exists can, therefore, be described in terms of the opportunities and threats operating in the external environment apart from the strengths and weaknesses existing in the internal environment. The four environmental influences could be described as follows:

1. An opportunity is a favourable condition in the organisation's environment which enables it to consolidate and strengthen its position. An example of an opportunity is growing demand for the products or services that a company provides.

2. A threat is an unfavourable condition in the organisation's environment which creates a risk for, or causes demage to the organisation. An example of a threat is the emergence of strong new competitors who are likely to offer stiff competition to the existing companies in an industry.

3. A strength is an inherent capacity which an organisation can use to gain strategic advantage over its competitors. An example of a strength is superior research and development skills which can be used for new product development so that the company gains competitive advantages.

4. A weakness is an inherent limitation or constraint which creates a strategies disadvantage. An example of a weakness is overdependence on a single product line, which is potentially risky for a company in times of crisis.

IMPORTANCE OF POLICIES

Sound and clear-cut policies provide the following benefits:

1. Coordination. Sound policies facilitate unity of purpose by focussing attention on organisational objectives. They are helpful in securing uniformity of action throughout the organisation. Policies promote intelligent cooperation and initiative. They provide a guide for thinking in future planning and promote intelligent cooperation.

2. Quick Decisions. Policies ensure prompt action on the part of subordinates. They delimit the area within which a decision is to be made. Lower level executives can decide with confidence and need not consult their superiors again. Every policy sets forth the proper course of action to be followed in a given situation. It saves time and effort by pre-deciding recurring problems.

3. Effective Control. Policies provide the rational basis for evaluating performance. They help to ensure that actions are in accordance with the objectives and interests of the organsiation. They tend to prevent deviations from planned course of action. In the absence of clear-cut policies, management is prone to become lost in the maze of details to the extent that their overall efficiency is impared. Policies are derived from objectives but provide the frame work for procedure and programmes. They serve as ground rules for operating plans.

4. Better Decentralisation. By formulating policies top management can delegate authority for routine matters. Unless policy is clearly defined it is not possible to decentralise as excutive responsibilities and relationships are not clear. The executives to whom authority is delegated can act with effectiveness and coordination with the help policies. From the prescribed policies the necessary managerial practices and procedures can be derived. Policy avoids the need for repeated guidance and indicates expected behaviour. Policies foster an intelligent exercise. They facilitate delegation by providing "guidelines to the delegate in order to help him in determining what appropriate action to take and what action will be within the limits of the stated policies. In effect, a policy informs the delegatee what is trying to be attained by making known the general course of action to be followed."

In the words of Brech, "It is also important to appreciate that policy has considerable contribution to make to coordination, especially in the larger organisations, and to the maintenance of morale. Where policy is clearly defined in its general and sectional aspects, the organisation is already a long way advanced towards ensuring that its executive will in keep in step in the day-to-day discharge of their responsibilities." The policies give meaning to the overall objective by translating the same into comprehensible terms. In this way policies make the goals concrete and meaningful.

The entire process of management is coordinated and organised by means of management policies. The fabric of management is held together by the wrap and woof of policies. They make for uniformity of action and consistency in work. A policy reflects the intention and courses of management. Policies reduce the range of individual decisions and encourages management by exception. They set broad patterns of behaviour.

Sound policies prevent deviations from planned courses of action, make for consistency of action, promote intelligent co-operation, foster initiative and serve as guides to thinking for future.

Limitations of Policies

(1) Policies do not cover all the problems. Sometimes unforseen situations arise which are not covered by the existing policies.

(2) Policies are no substitute for human judgement. Policies only delimit the area within which decisions are to be made.

(3) Policies are not ever lasting.

(4) Policies are repeatedly used plans and bring about rigidity in operations. They leave no room for initiative by the subordinates.

PROCEDURE FOR FORMULATING BUSINESS POLICIES

Policy formulation refers to the designing of policies. The formulation of policies is generally a function of all managers. However, the higher a manager is in the organisation the more important is his role in policy-making. However, policies can be effective only when they are acceptable to those who are to use them. Therefore, the various functional and departmental executives should be actively involved in the formulation of policies. Contrary to popular impression policy-making is not reserved at the top, though higher level managers play a more important role in policy-making. Policy formulation is in effect planning. Policy-making is a vital phase of planning and is based upon the underlying objectives of the organisation. Policy formulation is largely an art as it involves the use of judement and experience. However, scientific analysis is helpful in generating and evaluating alternative. Policy-making is a highly skilled function requiring finest qualities of managerial talent. It is pervasive and far reaching in its effects on the affairs of the organisation. The formulation and administration of policies is one of the critical tasks of management. Only by thinking and deciding in terms of policy can executives successfully direct and control large organisations. The process of policy formulation consists of the following steps:

1. **Definition of Purpose.** The first step in policy formulation is to define clearly the objectives and philosophy of the company. A policy is a means towards the achievement of certain goals. Therefore, the basic concept of the business should be defined. For instance, the notion of an automobile manufacturing plant may be to develop a 'massclass automobile. In addition to such a conceptional idea, purpose needs to be defined in terms of relevant guidelines for measuring performance, and desired performance targets. If, for instance, a firm is interested in rapid sales growth, the relevant guideline may be total industry expansion and target may be to grow at the industry growth rate plus 5 per cent. The selection of specific targets and the appropriate base lines for measuring performance should be based upon an analysis of a firm's opportunities and risks, its available resources, and the performance of its various constients.

2. **Preparation of Strategic Intelligence.** The next step is to secure information—questions, insights, hypotheses, evidence relevant to policy. As a minimum, this intelligence

should consist of *(i)* detailed description of what the company is and how it defines its sphere of operations, *(ii)* a prediction of future environmental opportunities and risks and their likely impact on the company's competitive position, and *(iii)* an identification of corporate strengths and weaknesses and resources required to cope with future opportunities and risks. This step thus consists of an analysis and understanding of internal and external environment of the firm.

3. **Policy Alternatives.** Once objectives and a general philosophy of business have been defined, alternative operating policies need to be indentified and analysed. The policy maker should attempt a comprehensive overview of policy problem and alternative policies. This step is central to the task of policy formulation. Thus a comprehensive list of policy alternatives needs to be generated, the probabilities of the consequences of each alternative need to be assessed, and their consequences need to be evaluated in terms of satisfying corporate objectives. In indentifying the alternative policies, the relationships between goals and policies should be constantly kept in view.

4. **Policy Analysis.** After policy alternatives are indentified each of the alternative is examined in the light of its contributions to chosen objectives. Examination of alternative policies and evaluating the consequences of various alternatives and their effects on preferred values and norms are significant elements of the policy formulation process.

5. **Time Sequencing.** This step in formulation of policies involves the designation of timed sequence of conditional moves based upon price analysis of possible competitive responses and counter attack. The tentative policy may be tested to find out its impact on the organisation. The policy

finally selected is then communicated to all those involved in its execution.

6. **Strategic Choice.** The selection of consistent operating policies which, in the judgement of top management, best fit available resources and best serve the organisation's purpose, provides the basic guidelines for executive action. The establishment of specific policy represents the most visible evidence of strategic commitment.

7. **Policy Review.** Policy formulation also involves a periodic re-examination of the assumptions underlying current policies and an evaluation of organisational performance to date. A periodical review of policies is necessary to keep the policies up-to-date and useful.

OBJECTIVES OF STUDYING BUSINESS POLICY

As we know business policy focusses on top and general management, a basic question arises: Why should be study it particularly when not all of them are expected to reach at the top or perform general management functions? Normally, they start their career in a functional area; only very few start in corporate planning division. From this point of view, this question becomes quite important. This question can be solved only by analysing the basic objectives of business policy course. Policy course emphasises following aspects.

(a) Development of analytical and decision making skills through cases and other reading material which are multi-functional and multi-departmental in nature. Following are basic objectives of policy.

(b) Integration of the knowledge and the methods learned in previous courses, *e.g.*, statistics, economics, production, marketing, finance accounting and personnel.

I. (i) It helps in learning, understanding, and appreciating the knowledge research in other areas by integrating these together.

(ii) Business policy course provides understanding of uniqueness and setting of operations in different industries.

(iii) The policy study emphasises the limitations of specialised knowledge in solving complex business problems. Since a specialist looks at the problem from his own speciality, he is likely to overlook the total interest of the organisation. The policy study may provide him an understanding of how his knowledge can be integrated with others so that suitable decisions are made.

(iv) It emphasis undestanding of interrelationships among sub-systems in the organisation and problems top managers face in avoiding suboptimisation of parts.

(v) The study of policy enables students to understand how various steps of strategic management process can be carried on; how the strategies can be formulated and implemented; and how the organisation can overcome its weaknesses and emphasise its strengths.

(vi) The basic objective of any discipline is to impart knowiedge. Knowledge comes through the study of existing literature which provides base for further research. A considerable body of knowledge purporting to make general statements about policy course runs through several dimensions.

(vii) The basic objective is to gain knowledge and understand the central significance of policy and strategy to top management and its organisation. This means an understanding of how total enviornmental forces affect the functioning of the organisation. This is the basic core of systems approach in management also which is largely followed in management of large and complex organisations.

II. Top managers of the organisation have attitudes, values, and ways of thinking that are unique to them and which also have a distinctive impact on decision processes. Knowledge of policy inculcates these attitudes in the students. What a manager knows by way of policy course is quite helpful in developing the attitudes, values and aspirations which he brings to his tasks. There are several implications of developing attitudes appropriate for top management functions.

(a) Policy course also puts emphasis on innovation in management practices through creativity. Since the manager has to work in an environment of diversity and variability, he has to find out a way of lying in the world full of uncertainty. He develops such attidues through his learning by business policy.

(b) Business policy course tries to develop professional orientation among managers which is distinct from self-seeking contrives. The introduction of social responsibility and ethical consideration in policy formulation and implementation has put emphasis on looking organisational objectives in larger social perspective in larger social perspective. A generalist is, thus, required to focus more attention on his aspect as compared to specialists.

(c) A manager takes decisions on the basis of totality of factors involved in them because he takes a generalist's position. As compared to generalist, a specialist tends to look. As beyond his area of specialisation leaving many more things to be desired. A generalist, on the other hand, has a tendency to look at the problem from every corner. This attitude results in decision making on the basis of all relevant facts rather than on the basis of one discipline alone. This is likely to yield better result.

(d) A generalist develops the attitudes of making decisions under the condition of partial ignorance which is the reality of business system in any country. Thus he works on satisfying decisions rather than optimising decisions. He puts emphasis on cost traders in terms of the timing of decisions, the nature of the solution, problem implementation and so on.

III. Perhaps the major contribution of the policy course lies in developing appropriate skills necessary for viewing the total organisation. Effective managers need different skills and the relative importance of these skills may very with the level in the organisation Katz has identified three kinds of skills necessary for managers. These are technical skills, human or administrative skills, and conceptual skills. Their relative importance varies with the level of management.

(i) Human or administrative skills are concerned with how it is done. There skills are the ability to work with people effectively thereby getting their full support for achieving organisational effectiveness.

(ii) Technical skills are concerned with what is done. These pertain to knowledge and proficiency in activities involving methods, processes, and procedures. These involve working with tools and specific techniques. Such skills are learned by accountants, engineers, typists, and time-study men. These skills are the distinguishing features of job performance at the operative level. Such skills are developed by the actual practice on the jobs.

(iii) Conceptual skills or general management skills are concerned with why it is done. These skills refer to the ability to see the whole picture; to recognise signficant elements in a situation; and to understand the relationship among these elements. Such skills are necessary to deal with abstractions, to set models, and to set plans.

Thus technical skills deal with things, human skills deal with people, and conceptual skills deal with ideas. Since people in the organisation perform different kinds of job, they required different kinds of skill mix.

Business policy course tries to develop all these skills.

(a) The second type of skills which policy course tries to inclucate in the students relate to integration of various factors such as resources, times, goals, and so on, Integration of various subsystems of the organisations is also required. For this purpose, a manager has to treat an ogranisation as an organic entity comprising a system in itself, but related to the larger systems of its environment. In this process, a manager must pull the separate concepts he has studied in functional and basic discipline courses and to adapt them to a less structured set of problems.

(b) Administrative skills can be developed by policy course by providing an opportunity to students to judge the actions in the light of various objectives set. The strategies selected can be judged as consistent or inconsistent according to criteria which may be developed. The students can use their knowledge of other fields with balanced view to find out whether their strategies are able to achieve objectives.

(c) General management skills centre-upon relating the organisation with its environment and upon coordinating departmental specialities and their point of view, Knowledge of general management is needed not only by general or top managers but a sensitivity to these processes is helpful at various levels of organisation. The assential skills for strategy formulation and implementation which are concerned mostly with analytical and administrative processes make every manager more effective irrespective of his level in the organisation. However, it is more important at higher level where managers are directly responsible for strategy formulation. Policy course aims at developing these skills.

(d) A top manager requires analytical skills so as to size up quickly and accurately the situation presented in terms of identifying the core problems and issues involved, analysing the facts to identify opportunities and threats in the environment and identify the strengths and weaknesses of his organisation so that he integrates these with the environment. Though total management education tries to achieve this objective, the role business policy is crucial in this respect. It puts more emphasis on analytical aspect of the business problems and their solutions.

Business policy course, though focusses on top management point of view, is also important for other level managers and even functional managers in that it enables the participants to take total view of the organisation and the environment in which context they have to function. Business policy course may enable them to intepret the instructions they receive from above more broadly; perceive the significance of their own area's potential contribution as organisational priorities shift; and couch the recommendations or proposals they send upward in term that make sense to a general manager and are related to their conception of the organisational objectives. Such managers may not function as general managers but with a general management view point they can influence the strategic decisions. thus they need to develop their general management skills in order to become better subordinates.

COMPONENTS OF PLANNING

The scope of planning is very wide. An enterprise has several aims. Accordingly, it has to build up a hierarchy of plans. The various types of plans may be described as under:

1. *Objectives* are the goals or purposes towards which business operations are directed. They are the end points of planning as planning is done to achieve objectives. They are established to guide the efforts of an organisation and each of its constituents. Setting of objectives is the first step in planning. Objectives should be expressed clearly and precisely. Management cannot be effective without carefully defined objectives. Goals are broad statements while objectives are specific and in measureable terms objectives embody the broad goals towards which the group activity is directed. They are the building blocks to planning "Objectives are the goals, aims or purposes that organisations wish to achieve over verying periods of time." Objectives are often expressed in terms of standards, targets, quotas, dead lines, etc. Objectives are the key to sound and the basis of effective management.

An enterprise has multiple objectives: Long-term and short-term, organisational and departmental, internal and external, main and subsidiary, general or specific, economic and social etc. Different objectives should be properly integrated into a network or hierarchy. According to Drucker, "to manage a business is to balance a variety of needs and goals.....Objectives are needed in every are a where performance and results directly and vitally affect the survival and prosperity of the business. These areas are: market standing; innovation; productivity; physical and financial resources; profitability; manager performance and development; worker performance and attitude; public responsibility."

Objectives are very important as they provide a sense of purpose, serve as standards of performance, help in fixing responsibility, add to coordination, enable greater delegation of authority and serve as guides to action Objectives set up the framework for planning and, therefore, a meaningful formulation of enterprise objectives is a necessary first step in the planning process. They indicate the destination of an enterprise. Effective management is management by objectives. Objectives should be realistic rather than idealistic.

2. Policies are general statements of understandings created for the attainment of ojectives. They serve as broad guides to thinking and action on the part of members of an organisation. They indicate the manner in which particular situations should be handled by the organisational members. A policy can be defined as the guidelines or mode of action underlying certain operations. It is general guide to action. It does not tell a person exactly what to do, but it does point out the direction to go. In other words, "a policy is a verbal, written or implied statement outlining the guiding course adopted and followed by a manager. That is to say, a policy establishes the overall guides or boundaries which provide the general direction in which managerial action takes place. The guides provided by policies help to keep the activities moving along the routes intended by managers." A policy defines the area within which a decision is to be made. It expresses the intentions of the management and is a multi-purpose plant that continuously guides action. It is a standing answer to recurring problems; a continuing decision that applies to repetitive situations. They set up broad limits for decision making so that subordinates need not seek approval for every individual action. This saves time and effort. They help in ensuring that action conforms to objectives and there is harmony of effort. As a plan action, a policy relates efforts to objectives and helps in securing uniformity of action. A policy gives meaning to objectives, makes for stability and instills confidence in the employees. It helps delegation of authority and coordination. A good policy statement porivdes supervisors with guidelines for dealing in a consistent manner with issues which arise from time to time. Without policies each situation might to be rethought before action could be taken. Policies define limits within which executive discretion may be used. The application of policies requires initiative, and judgement. It also provides a yardistick for evaluation of alternative courses of action. "Policies tend to predecide issues, avoid repeated analysis and consideration of general courses of action and give a unified structure to other types of plans, thus permitting managers to delegate authority while maintaining control." Policies are the routes (means) for the achievement of a common objective. Objectives are the ultimate goals to be achieved while policies are the means to those ends.

Policies may be general or specific, functional or departmental, voluntry or imposed, written or implied, originated or appealed. They should always be clear, precise, flexible, consistent and integrated. They should be based on acts, resources and environments of the particular enterprise. They should be stated in broad terms to facilitate the organisation. They should be stated in broad terms to faciliate recurring use. Different policies should support one another and must reflect the internal and external environment of the organisation. To be effective, policies should be developed with the active coorperation of all concerned. All policies should be in writing and must be communicated to those who will use them so that they may be fully understood. The managerial policies should be revised from time to time to keep them up-to-date and effective. They should be precise yet flexible. They should be understood by all members of the organisation.

Policies are linked are linked to objectives yet differ from them. Objectives describe what is being sought after, policies describe how the objectives are to be accomplished. Both are equally important to effective action. A policy should be differentiated from practice which is the usual mode of handling a given problem. A practice stresses expediency and things as they are while a policy stresses direction and things as they should be.

DIFFERENCE BETWEEN POLICIES AND OBJECTIVES

Policies	*Objectives*
1. Policies are guidelines which faciliate the achieving of pre-determined objectives.	Objectives are the ends towards which all activities of of the enterprise are directed.
2. Policies determine how the work is to be done.	Objectives determine what is to be done.
3. Policies prescribe the mode and the manner in which objectives can be achieved.	Objectives are the end points of planning.
4. Policies are formulated at the top level, middle and lower level management.	Objectives are determined by the owners and top management of the business.

Distinction between Policies and Procedures

Policies are specific guidelines and constrains for managerial thinking and action. They are planned expressions of the organisation's official attitude towards certain issues. But procedures, on the other hand, are systematic ways of handling regular events. They involve chronological sequence of actions required to the particular tasks. They are operational guides to action and routinise the way certain recurring jobs are to be done. The other points of difference between policies and procedures are as follows:

(a) Policies are guides to decision-making while procedures are guides to action.

(b) Policies have some room for managerial thinking and discretion while procedures are generally detailed and rigid.

(c) Policies form part of strategies of the organisation while procedures are operational as tactical tools.

(d) Policies are generally framed by the top management and procedures are laid down at somewhat low-level in the light of policies.

The difference between policies and procedures can be further explained by means of an example. An industrial concern may adopt a policy of centralised recruitment and selection through the labour department. The labour department may then chalk out the procedure of recruitment and selection. This procedure may consist of several steps like inviting applications, preliminary interview aptitude and other tests, final interview, medical examination and issue of appointment letter. However, both policies and procedures can be termed as standing plans because they guide action.

3. Procedures. A procedure or routine is a chronological sequence of steps to be undertaken to enforce a policy and to attain an objective. It is a standard or uniform manner of doing repetitive work. It is more specific than policy and is a definite guide to action. It specifies the way in which particular work is to be performed so as to ensure that whoever performance it will do it the same way. A procedure emphasizes details while a policy concentrated on general approaches. For example, a company may have the policy of promoting employees on the basis of merit. In order to implement it, the procedure may consist of definition of merit, records of performance, tests and interview to identify the most meritorious. Similarly, there may be procedures for purchasing raw materials, selecting personnel, redressing grievances. In fact, a standard procedure is necessary for every repetitive activity. A procedure is different from a method which outlines the specific manner in which a particular step in the procedure is to be performed. For example, to measure merit employees may be compared in terms of punctuality, discipline, output and accidents. This is a method of merit rating. A procedure is also different from a schedule which specifies the time limit for each step in the procedure. Scheduling is the process of establishing a time sequence for the work to be done. It is essential to ensure continuity of operations to evaluate performance and to create order and regularity in executing policies and programmes. A policy delineates an area of operation, a procedure lays down the path through that area. A policy is guide to decision-making while a procedure is an operational guide to action. A procedure is a means of implementing policy. A policy is much wider in scope than a procedure. Both method and procedure simplefy efforts and make for uniformity of action. But a procedure is a series of steps while method is a single operation.

Procedure make for uniformity and consistency of action and coordination. They assist in efficient and cooperative effort. They save time involved in decision-making by standardising routine work and act as standards for performance appraisal under a particular situation. Rigid adherence to procedure may, however, stifle initiative and creativity in the organisation.

4. Rules. A rule is a rigid and definite plan that specifies what is to be done or not to be done in a given situation, without deviation. It allows to flexibility in dcision-making. Rules help in maintaining and enchancing efficiency. It is a specific guide to action and permits no discretion or judgement. No deviation is expected from the stated course of action. A rule does not lay down a sequance of steps. It may or may not be a part of of procedure. The rule "no smoking in the factory" is not a parrt of any procedure. On the other hand, the rule that "all orders must be acknowledged within 48 hours of their receipt" is a part of procedure. A rule reflects what a manager expects of his subordinates. A rule generally carries with it the penalty for violation.

5. Budgets are estimates or projections of expected results expressed in numerical terms. A budget is a financial plan. It establishes restrictions within goals are to be reached and serves as an yardstick of measuring performance. It may relate to income and expenses or production or sales. Budgeting is an element of planning but budgets serve as a means of coordination and control also. They express different plans into a common language (money) and serve as standards of evaluating performance. To be effective, a budget should be flexible and should provide for unforseen events.

6. Programmes. The planning process culminates with programmes and budgets. Programming helps to develop the most economical way of doing things in a uniform manner. A programme is a concrete scheme of action to accomplish a given task. It specifies the steps to be taken resources to be used, time limits for each step and the persons who are to carry it out. A programme is a sequence of activities designed to implement policies and accomplish objectives. A programme is thus a mixture of objectives, policies, procedures, rules etc. A major programme, *e.g.*, development of a new product may be supported by several derivative programmes concerning factory building, machinery, raw materials, technical personnel, etc. By establishing sequence and priority of work to be carried out all related efforts can be channelled. Scheduling helps to ensure availability of resources and to keep expenditures to reasonable levels.

7. Strategies. A strategy is a particular type of plan designed to intepret and adjust other plans. A strategy represents conscious decision to initiate certain actions directed towards specific purposes. It seeks to meet specific situations or crisis, *e.g.*, price reduction by competitors, strike by employees, etc. Plans and policies have to be changed according to changes in underlying conditions. Strategies help in adjusting and executing them. Competitive strategies are based on projected activities of competitors. Strategies are different from tactics which is a course of action designed to execute a strategy. A tactic designates policy in operation with respect to method and procedure.

Strategies are designed in response to phenomena occurring within and outside the firm. Strategies are formed in various functional areas *e.g.* product strategies, market strategies, financial strategies, etc. Strategy should be differentiated from policy. Policy is the general guideline while strategy is the course of action. Stretegy many exist without a policy. For instance, a supervisor may have a policy of enforcing discipline but his strategy may be to wait until enforcement is demanded by workers. The waiting strategy is not likely to be embodied in the policy. Policy and strategy may, at the time, be coextensive. For example, a business policy may be to distribute through retailers. The strategy is the same but it implies that action to implement policy will be taken at the right time.

Rudyard Kipling has summed up the elements of planning in the following lines:

"I keep six honest serving men

They taught me all I know;

Their names and why and who."

The determination of 'what must be done' also includes consideration of when and where the work is to be done, who is to do what and by what methods.

8. Projects. A project is a distinct cluster of functions and facilities for a definite purpose. It is a part of a general programme which can be designed and excuted as a distinct plan in itself. It is a time bound plan consistent of details, the time schedule, exact method of performing each step, provision for place and resources and special method designed for unique conditions. It is marked separate from normal operations because of its special significance. In a programme of developing a new product, for example, publicity may be a project Project help simplify coordiantion and control by identifying an integrated work package within a hetrogeneous mass of activities and resources.

Sometimes policy is confused with the term strategy. A policy is a guide to thinking and action on the part of executives. On the other hand, a strategy lays down the direction in which human and physical resources will be deloped and applied in order to maximise the chances of achieving a selected objective in the face of difficulties.

Plans are sometimes classified as single-use plans and multiuse plans. A *single-use plan* is designed to meet a specific situation or purpose. It is used up one for the particular task and has to be framed new for a different task. A *multi-use* plan or repeated use plan is designed to be used over and over again in recurring situations. It is a standing guide to thinking and action. Objectives, policies, rules procedures are 'multi-use plans while programmes, budgets, strategies, schedules, and projects are considered as single use plans.

A good plan must be simple, objective, logical, clear, precise, comprehensive, action oriented, economical, flexible and balanced. It must be based upon a clearly defined objective. It should permit optimum use of available resources. A good plan must be practicable and should be free from ambiguity. It should be developed through activie participation of all concerned and should lay down standards for evaluation of performance. It should provide for a proper analysis and classification of functions. Different types of plans must be tied together to ensure harmonious action. Efficient planning also requires adequate timing of plans. Effective planning also requires continuous checking on events and timely revision of plans. Flexibility in planning involves the ability to change a plant without undue cost or readjustment. Such flexibility or adaptability is needed due to uncertainty of the future.

STRATEGY & TACTICS

It is beneficial to make distinction between strategy and tactics so that managers can concentrate themselves on strategic functions rather than engaging in tactical functions. Organisational decisions range across a spectrum, having a broad master strategy at one end and minute tactics at the other. The major difference between strategy and tactics is that strategy determines what major plans are to be undertaken and allocates resources to them, while tactics, in contrast, is means by which previously determined plans are excuted. Beyond this, major difference, there may be some other differences which can be understood better by analysing military use of strategy and tactics.

Strategy is system of makeshifts. It is carrying through on originally considered plan under a constantly shifting set of circumstances. Strategy furnishes tactics with the opportunity to strike and with the prospect of success. It does this through its conduct of the armies and their concentration on the field of battle. On the other hand, however, strategy concept accepts the results or every single engagement and builds them. Strategy retires when a tactics victory is in the making in order later to exploit the newly created situation.

A basic objective of strategy accordingly is to 'break the will of the army, deprive him of the means to fight, occupy his territory, destroy or obtain control of his resources or otherwise made him submit.' The objective of tactics is success in a given action which is only one part in a group of related military action. A further distinction between strategy and tactics as used in Military Science is made on the basis of delegation of decision making authority. Strategy decisions are not delegated too low in the organisation. Normally the authority is not required for the most effective decisions.

Such a distinction between strategyand tactics is quite sharp. however, business is different than war in its true perspective not only in terms of its objectives vis-a-vis its competitors but also in terms of process of achievement of objectives. In business, there is seldom a win-lose situation as is the case with the way. Therefore, the distinction should be made between strategy and tactics in business terms. Such distinctions can be made as follow.

1. Strategy has a long-term perspective; specially the successful strategies are followed for quite long period. In occasional cases, it may have short-term duration. Thus depending on the nature and requirement; its time horizon is flexible, however, emphasis is put on long-term. On the other hand, time horizon of tactics is short-run and definite. The duration is uniform, for budget prepartion.

2. The formulation of strategy is affected considerably by the personal values of the person involved in the process. For example, the goals of an organisation is affected considerably by the personal values of the persons concerned. This aspect will be taken for further discussion in this later. On the other hand, tactics is normally free from such values because this is be taken within the context of strategic decisions.

3. Strategies are most important factors of organisation because they decide the future course of action for the organisation as a whole. On the other hand, tactics are of less importance because they are concerned with specific part of the organisation. This difference, though seems to be simple, becomes important form managerial action point of view.

(4) Generally separate group of managerial personnel are involved in strategy and tactics fourmulation and their implementation. As discussed earlier, strategic decisions are never delegated below a certain level in the managerial hierarchy. The basic principles in this context is not to delegate below the levels than those possess the perspective required for must effective strategic decisions. Tactical decisions can be taken by personnel at lower levels because these involve minute implementation of strategic decisions.

5. Element of uncertainty is higher in the case of strategy formulation and its implementation. In fact, strategic decisions are taken under the conditions of partial ignorance.

Tactical decisions are more certain as these are taken within the framework set by the strategy. Thus evaluation of tactics is easier as compared to evaluation of a strategy.

6. Total possible range of alternatives from which a manager can choose his strategic action is greater than tactics. A manager requires more information for arriving at strategic decision to its environment, this requires information about the various aspectss of environment. Naturally the collection of such information will be different. Tactical information is generated within the organisation particularly from accounting procedures and statistical sources.

7. The formulation of strategy is both continuous and irregular. The process is continuous but the timing of decision is irregular as it depends on the appearance of opportunities, new ideas, crises, management initiative, and other non-routine stimuli. Tactics is determined on a periodic basis by various organisation. A fixed time table may be followed for this purpose.

8. As discussed earlier, strategy is developed at the higher level of management either at the headquarter or at divisional offices and relates. Tactics is employed at and relates to lower levels of management.

❐

2

Dynamic Setting of Organisational Objectives

Organisational objectives seek to direct the efforts of all members of a team while personal goals are motives of people working in the team. Efficiency is high when two two types of objectives are mutually supportive or compatible. Organisational objectives are the goals established to guide the efforts of the company and each of its components. Objectives are variously referred to as purposes, goals, missions, or targets. The establishment of objectives is a very important step in planning. Planning can be effective only if objectives are carefully selected. A clear statement of purpose understood by one and all in the best guarantee of effective management. Objectives must be actionable, that is, meaningful to the manager who is to achieve them. Objectives or goals must be specific and capable of accomplishment. They must be identified in such a way that ultimate success of failure can be determined.

The foregoing description reveals the following characteristics of organisational objectives:

1. **Objectives are Multiple.** Every organisation has a number of economic, social and human objectives rather than a single aim. As stated earlier, objectives are required in every area of business where the success and survival of the business is important. Every department of division has its own objectives in addition to the overall objectives of the organisation. Different objectives should be balanced with one another. A business firm has both general and specific objectives. General objectives include survival,

growth, etc. while specific objectives are narrow in scope *e.g.*, to reduce absentecism. Organisational goals are sometimes divided into *(a)* maintenance goals, and *(b)* productivity goals. Maintenance goals are the expression of the desire to ensure the existence of the enterprise, while productivity goals aim at improvements in performance.

2. **Objectives are Basic Plans.** Objectives are the standing plans which recurringly guide action. They are the basis of other plans such as policies, procedures, programmes, etc.

   Objectives are the clear expression of the purpose of an enterprise. Primary or major objectives provide the principal reasons for the establishment of the enterprise while collateral objectives supplement and contribute to the primary objectives. Organisational objectives are the basis of long range planning whereas departmental objectives provide the basis for short range planning. Different organisations have different objectives and there is no universal set of objectives. Objectives must, however, he practicable, consistent and clear cut. There must be proper coordination between major and derivative goals and between long range and short range objectives. Objectives should be specific, verifiable and well planned. There must be active participation of all concerned in the determination of objectives.

3. **Objectives Very in Time Span.** Objectives may be long-term or short-term. Long term objectives refer to the objectives to be achieved over a long period of time while short-term objectives are to be achieved within a period of one to two years. Short-run objectives are steps towards long-term objectives.

4. **Objectives are the Ends.** Objectives are the ultimate ends or results towards which an organisation and its members

strive at all times. All activities and resources of an enterprise are directed towards the achievement of common and specified objectives.

5. **Objectives form a Chain.** Objectives are arranged in a hierarchy which is known as the 'Ends and Means Chain'. Objectives of a lower order act as the means for the achievement of higher level objectives. For instance, the organisational objectives are more basic than the departmental objectives.

Some of Examples of Objectives

Growth. The ensure a steady growth in business so as to fulfil national expectations from BHEL and expand international operations.

1. Continuity. To invest in human resource development, sustained research and development, strive for excellence in management and other long-range activities to ensure a leadership status for BHEL." *(Quoted from BHEL, Growth Perspective in the 80's.)*

2. Image. To build up a high degree of customer confidence by sustaining international standards of excellence in product quality, performance and service, particularly in regard to supply of spares and after-sales service. To fulfil the expectation which stakeholders like Government as owner, employees, customers and the country at large have from BHEL.

3. Profitability. To provide a reasonable and aequate return on capital employed pimarily through improvements in operational efficiency, capacity utilisation and productivity, and generate adequate internal resources to finance the company's growth.

The strategic objective formulated by another company have been stated as follows:

1. To employ the highest quality of people necessary to accomplish the prime objective and provide them with opportunities to development and apply their fullest abilities.

2. 'To ensure consistently increasing earnings per share to attain a satisfactory return on shareholders' equity on a continuing basis and to provide consistently increasing dividends (the prime objective).

3. To hae the company recognised as a dynamic, responsible, professionally managed, profit-oriented enterprise engaged in an important field of business with the ability to meet successfully the economic and social challenges of the future."

IMPORTANCE OF OBJECTIVES

Every rational human activity must have certain clear-cut objectives or goals. A manager, before performing his functions, must ask: What are the objectives of the activity he is going to manage? The answer to this question will serve many functions. The objectives provide orientation by depicting a future state of affairs which the organisation strives to realise. They set down guidelines for group activity. Objectives constitute a *sources of legitimacy* which justifies the activities of the organisational and indeed its very existence. Moreover, objectives serve as standards for assessing the success of the organisation. Thus, objectives will check the members of the organisation from deviating from the route they have set for themselves.

Objectives are key to effective planning which is an important function of every manager. Clear objectives encourage consistency in managerial planning and decision-making over a period of time.An organisation having well defined objectives will not give up long-range development programmes and policies for short-term monetary gains. Planning has no meaning if it is not related to certain objectives. It will be an empty mental exercise if it does ot determined what objectives are to be accomplished. Objectives represent not only the end-point of planning but also the end towards which other managerial activities like organising, directing and controlling are aimed. They provide direction not only to managerial activities but also to other activities. Purchasing, production, marketing and financıng are all directed towards the objectives of the enterprise.

The accomplishment of objectives is necessary for the survival of any business enterprise. The mangement must specify the objectives in all areas on which the survival of the business depends. Well defined objectives in major areas of the business will help in achieving the following benefits:

(a) Managerial work with appropriate authority and capacity for independent decision is shared by a large number of managers. This may lead to disintegration in place of decentralisation unless there is a common goal. The objectives guide to coordinate the remove conflicts or misunderstanding between various individuals.

(b) Objectives fit individual goals into overall organisation goals and make the job meaningful and worthwhile. This stimulated human motivation.

(c) Objectives provide the basis of control by clarifying the desired contribution of each job as well as each unit.

(d) All the managers at various levels make plans of their own planning may lose its consistency unless all plans have the same focus of action.

Guidelines Regarding Objectives

Peter Drucker has given the following guidelines regarding the objectives of a business organisation:

1. Objectives must be operational. They must be capable of being converted into specific targets and assignments. They must also be capable of becoming the basis, as well as the motivation, for work and achievement.

2. Objectives must make possible concentration of resources and efforts. They must win now out the fundamentals among the goals of a business so that they key resources

of men, money and physical resources can be concentrated. They must, therefore, be selecting rather than ecompass everything.

3. Objectives must be derived from what our business is what it will be and what it should be. They are not abstractions. They are the action commitments through which the mission of a business is to be carried out and the standards against which performance is to be measured. Objectives, in other words, are the fundamental strategy of a business.

4. Objectives are need in all areas on which the survival of the business depends. The specific targets, the goals in any objectives area, depend on the strategy of the individual business. But the areas in which objectives are needed are the same for all businesses, for all business depend on the same factors for their survival.

5. There must be multiple objectives rather than a single objective.

PURPOSE AND MISSION OF AN ORGANISATION

The purpose and mission of an organisation is a general enduring statement of the organisation the intent of which embodies the decision maker's business philosophy; it implies the image which the organisation seeks to projects.

An organisation's purpose and mission consist of a long-term vision of what it seeks to do and the reasons why it exists. Purpose is management's Concept of the organisation and its service mission to society. An organisation's purpose, when expressed in managerially meaningful terms, indicates exactly what activities the organisation intends to engage in now and in future. It suggests something specific about what kind of organisation it is and is to become. It depicts the organisation's business character and does so in ways that tend to distinguish the organisation from other organisations.

In this sense, purpose sets forth principles and conceptual fundation upon which the organisation rests the nature of the business in which it plans to participate, organisational mission, defined properly, offers guidance to managers in developing sharply focussed, result-oriented objectives, strategies, and policies. Therefore, a detailed understanding of organisational mission is the standing point for rational managerial action and for the design of organisation structure, processes, and procedures. Managerial effectiveness tends to begin with clarity of mission with an accurate, carefully delineated concept of just what the organisation is trying to do any why.

The concept of mission can be understood by taking the example mission of TICO.

The fundamental mission of TISCO (Tata Iron and Steel Company Limited) is to strengthen India's industrial base through increased productivity, effective utilisation of manpower and material resources, and continued application of modern scientific managerial methods as well as through systematic growth in keeping with national aspirations. The company recognises that while honesty and integrity are the essential ingredients of a strong and stable enterprise, profitability provides the main spark for economic activity. It affirms its faith in democratic values and in the importance of success of individuals, collective, and corporate enterprise for the economic emancipation and prosperity of the country. Guided by its basic philosophy, the company believes in discharging its responsibility towards:

1. Customers

(a) by products of proven quality at a fair price;

(b) by fulfilling its commitments impartially and courteously in accordance with sound and strightforward business principle; and

(c) by bearing their counting confidence in its productive ability and its technical competence to keep improving the quality of its products.

2. Community

(a) by assuming its proper share of social responsibilities in the community in which the company operates.

(b) by availing of opportunities to develop the democratic qualities involved in collective work undertaken in the interest of the community;

(c) by encouraging talent and promoting civic sense among members of the community;

(d) by respecting the dignity of the individual and acting according to the ideas of social justice.

3. Shareholders

(a) by protecting and safeguarding their investment; and

(b) by ensuring to them a fair return.

4. Employees

(a) by providing adequate wages, goods working conditions, job security, effective machinery for speedy redressal of grievances, and suitable opportuntieis for promotion and self-development.

(b) by promoting feelings of trust and loyalty through a human and purposeful awareness of their needs and aspiration;

(c) by creating a sense of belongingness and team-spirit through their closer association with management at various levles;

(d) by a realistic and general understanding and acceptance of their needs and rights and enlightened awarencess of the social responsibilities of industry.

The missions of the company are directed towards making the company:

(a) A leading company in the corporate field of the country,

(b) A reliable company to sell to,

(c) A good company to work for,

(d) A sound company to invest in.

The various points are indivisible. Together as a unit, they state the fundamental management philosophy of TISCO. However, most of the companies do not specify their purpose so clearly as TISCO has done. Nevertheless they do have certain purpose which is reflected in their specific objectives and actions.

A key feature of organisation's purpose in that its focus must be external rather than internal. For example, Drucker has the following suggestion:

To know what a business we have to start with it its purpose. Its purpose must lie outside the business itself. In fact, it must lie in society since business enterprise is an organ of society. There is only one valid definition of business purpose: to create a customer.

DIFFERENT OBJECTIVES OF BUSINESS

As we know, the business in an economic institution operating in a socio-economic system. Therefore, objectives of business should be defined keeping in view its prevailing environment and its needs for survival and growth. Like any other institution business has several rather than a single objective. Objectives of business are multi-dimensional in nature. Business is established and it exists to achieve multiple objectives. People enter into business and stay in business because they want to earn money, social power and prestige, joy of achievement and other goals. Generally, profit motive is considered to be the primary objective of business. But profit-making is not the sole or only objectives of a business. Every business enterprise has to lay down its multiple objectives to justify its existence.

The various objectives of business may broadly be classified as follows:

1. Economic Objectives
2. Social Objectives
3. Human Objectives
4. Organic Objectives
5. National Objectives

1. Economic Objectives. Business is an economic activity and, therefore, its major objectives are economic,. Economic objective refer to those goals which determine a person's conduct in the business part of life. Economic objectives of business are as follows:

(a) Creation of Customer. Business can earn profits only when it provides goods or services which people are able and willing to buy. Every business enterprise is conceived in terms of a product or service that meets the needs of public. A business enterprise cannot survive unless there are enough people to buy the products and services offered by it. Cusotmer is the generator of revenue for business. By paying for goods and services, customers determine what shall be produced and how much? In the words of Drucker, "There is only one valid definition to business purpose : to create a customer. It is the customer who determines what a business is... the customer is the fundation of business and keeps it in existence... and it is to supply the customer that society entrusts wealth-producing resources to a business enterprise." Customers can be created only when business supplies them what they want and at the price, place and time they desire. Business earns profits by satisfying the needs of the customers. Therefore, creation and satisfaction of customers is an important objective of business. Creating customers amounts to creating the market for goods and services.

(b) ***Innovation.*** Modern business is highly dynamic and an enterprise can continue to the successful only by adapting itself to changes in its environment. A successful firm has not only to adjust itself to chagning environment. It must on its own create conditions favourable to survival and growth. The highly competitive nature of modern business puts a premium on innovation and creativity which implies the introduction of new and better products, improved means of production and distribution, new technology, new methods and procedures of management, etc. To resist change is to court disaster profits are the result of efficient performanace in marketing, innovation and productivity. Innovation results in better and cheaper products and more employment for the society. Innovation is essential for the survival and growth of business. It is through innovations that business firms perform dynamic functions of growth, diversification and change in the economy. The most progressive or excellent companies allocate large amounts of money on research and development for achieving the objective of innovation.

2. Social Objectives. The economic objectives of business can be realised only by serving the society. Business is an organ of society and it draws its resources from the society. Therefore, it must satisfy the wants and aspirations of society. A business enterprise can survive and grow only when it caters to the needs of the society. A really sucessful business can be built on the foundation of social service. If a business enterprise serves the various sections of society, profits will follow automatically. Profits are, in other words, the reward which business receives by serving society. There is no conflict between profit-motive and service to society. It is through service that business earns profits.

Social objectives of business refer to the obligations of business towards customers, employees, investors, suppliers, government and the general public. The profits of business represent a social surplus in which all stockholders must share in proprotion to their contributions. The social objectives of business are as follow:

(a) ***Avoidance of Profiteering and Anti-social Practices.*** It is legitimate for a business enterprise to work legitimate profit. But it must not over-charge the customers or indulge in profiteering at their cost. It is the social obligation of a business concern not to indulge in hoarding, black-marketing, adulteration and other anti-social practices. In times of scarcity it should ensure fair and equitable distribution. Moreover, business enterprise is expected to adopt socially responsible and ethical behaviour with the suppliers, competitors, and other interacting groups of people. It should be fair in its dealings with all these groups.

(b) ***Providing Employment.*** Another social objective of business is to create opportunities for gainful employment of the people. Sometimes this objective may conflict with the economic objective of cutting down costs and improving profits by introducing mechanisation or automation. In a country like India, mechanisation may have to be deferred or implemented gradually into stages without causing loss of job to anyone.

(c) ***Quality Goods at Fair Prices.*** The first and foremost social objective of business is to provide regularly the goods and services of proper quality and quantity to consumers at reasonable prices. Today consumers are conscious of the quality of goods they buy. When goods are of sub-standard quality or adulterated, they stop patronising the enterprise and the enterprise faces eventual closure. Therefore, business units must always maintain a continuous and adequate supply of articles of standard quality. Businessmen who keep their customers satisfied are likely to earn profits.

3. Human Objectives. A business enterpise is an institution carried on by people (entrepreneurs and managers), through (employees) and for people (consumers and public). Therefore, human factor pervades all business activities. Business is not an end itself but a means towards human welfare. People are the most valuable assets of business and their well-being is its main concern. The success of a business depends upon the quality of people working in it. In order to win the co-operation of employees, business must fulfil their expectations. The human objectives of business arise from these expectations. The important human objectives of business are given below:

(a) ***Development of Human Resources.*** Business can accomplish its economic objectives of innovation and productivity only when the employees are given adequate opportunities for developing new skills and capabilities. Business should create a proper climate wherein the talents of workers are alllowed to growth and mature.

(b) ***Praticipation.*** Workers will put forth their best efforts only when they are given an opportunity to participate in making decisions which affect them. Workers participation in management facilitates redressal of employee grievances quickly and at the lowest possible level. Recognition of worker representatives and their legitimate activities helps to maintain healthy trade union practices and sound industrial relations.

(c) ***Job Satisfaction.*** It is the obligation of abusiness enterprise to make the jobs interesting and challenging so that employees may get job satisfaction while performing their jobs. Selection of right man for the right job and reducing unpleasantness of jobs help to offer job satisfaction which is turn ensures retention of an employee on the job for a long period. A business enterprise fulfils its human objective when it recognies the dignity of labour.

(d) ***Fair Deal to Employees.*** The first human objective of business is to pay fair wages, salaries and incentives to the employees at different levels. Fair working and living conditions and security of service are necessary for securing the whole-hearted efforts of the employees. Employee welfare is no less important than customer satisfaction.

The realisation of economic and organic objectives helps the business directly and immediately whereas the social, human and national objectives help the business indirectly and in the long run.

4. Organic Objectives. As an organic entity, a business enterprise has its own stages of infancy, childhood, adolescence, adulthood and maturity. Like a human being, the first concern of a business enterprise is to ensure its survival. When the enterprise is assured of its survival, it will aim at growth and expansion. The accomplish this objective, it will attempt to win prestige, recognition and goodwill from the society in which it operates. In order to pass through these stages in time and with strength, a business unit uses serveral methods, *e.g.*, ploughing back a part of its profits, attaining optimum size to avail of the economies of scale, etc. Organic objectives are the foundation for achieving all other objectives of business.

(a) ***Prestige and Recognition.*** Prestige and recognition help to ensure the survival and growth of a firm. A business enterprise with good image or goodwill can easily attract customers, investors and competent employees.

(b) ***Growth.*** Growth and diversification is one of the major objectives of business. Growth may be measured in terms of size, investment, market share, etc. Market share which a business enterprise commands reflects its standing in the market. A business enterprise may identify new customers, new products or new markets or increase its market share in the present market. Growth brings higher profits, economic and social power, etc.

(c) ***Survival.*** First of all a business enterprise tries to maintain its existence. Survival or stability objective implies the maintenance of a firm's competitive position or earning capacity or market standing. Unless an enterprise survives no other objective can be accomplished.

5. National Objectives. Present day business is expected to serve as an instrument for the fulfilment of national needs and aspirations and implementation of the national plans and policies in accordance with the accepted priorties. Keeping in view the overall national objective of establishing a democratic, secular and socialist society and fostering growth stability and social justice, business in India has to serve the following national objectives:

(a) ***Development of Skilled Personnel.*** Skill formation is essential for the economic growth of a country. Business can contribute to skill formation through training and development of managers and technicians.

In addition to the above objectives, business is also expected to promote national integration, balanced regional development, family planning, public health, education, sports, culture in the country.

The above description reveals that the operation of business requires reconciliation of serveral micro and macro level objectives.

(b) ***National Self-sufficiency and Export Promotion.*** In order to enable the country to become self-reliant, it is the responsibility of business to produce such articles as have hitherto been imported. Business should aim at import substitution, specially in the case of machinery, equipment and technology. Every business should take adequate steps to boost exports and thereby angment the foreign exchange reserves of the country.

(c) ***Production According to National Priorities.*** In keeping with national plan objectives, business enterprise should manufacture and supply goods necessary for the country's development. It is also the national objective of business to manufacture and distribute cheaper varieties of essential commodities like soap, cloth, edible oils, etc, so as to help the weaker sections of the society.

(d) ***Development of Small Enterprise.*** In tune with the national policy of decentralised development, large business houses are responsible for encouraging the growth and development of small scale and cottage indutries. Such indutries can be used as ancillary units and their products should be patronised. Large business concerns are expected to desist from assuming monopolistic position.

(e) ***Ensuring Social Justice.*** Asa responsible citizen a business enterprise is expected to remove inequalities of oppportunities and to provide a fair opportunity to all to work and progress. For this purpose special attention must be given to the neglected, weaker and backward sections of the society.

OBJECTIONS AGAINST PROFIT-MAXIMISATION OBJECTIVE

Despite their indispensable role in business, profit cannot be the he all and end-all of business. The profit-maximisation objective is undesirable on account of the following reasons:

1. Profit-maximisation is inconsistent with the modern trends in business. Diffusion of share ownership, professionalisation of management, growth of institutional shareholding and the emergence of a distinctive techno-structure are some of these trends. The main goal of the techno-structure (control by managers and technologists) is survival and growth of business. Profit-maximisation may endanger long-term growth and, therefore, the techno-structure prefers long-term growth. These professionals regard profit-maximisation as unrealistic, inappropriate and even immoral.

2. Profit-maximisation has capitalistic overtones. The adcocates of socialism decry the goal of profit-maximisation on the ground that profit-maximisation results in the exploitation of poor by the rich. It also accentuates inequalities in the distribution of income and wealth.

3. Profit-maximisation misguides managers to the point where they may endanger the survival of the business in order to maximise current profits, managers may undermine the firm's future. They may ignore research and development, executive development, pushing of the most easily saleable products, and other long-term investments. Such activities threaten the long-term success of the enterprise.

4. Profit-maximisation overstresses the reward for owners and ignores the interests of other stockholders. Profit is the reward for capital and profit-maximisation gives the impression that a business concern is the domain only of owners. In reality, no business can succeed without the fullest co-operation of labour, consumers, Government and the community at large. Profit-maximisation objective overlooks the sake of these groups in business.

5. Profit-maximisation overstresses the end result and overlooks the means employed to achieve the profits. It considers profit as the ultimate goal of business rather than a means to the real end. The ultimate aim to business should be social welfare. It profit-maximisation is considered as the ultimate aim of business, the businessmen might try to maximise profits by socially undersirable means such as profiteering, black-marketing, hoarding, exploitation of workers and consumers etc.

A truly successful business can be built only if the objective of "service to the society" is constantly followed. If this is done profits will come automatically, but if the whole emphasis is on making money business may not survive and succeed for a long period. The guiding principles of business should be 'profit through service'. Every business should provide a proper balance between profit motive and social service.

Why Mission and Objectives Change

As strategists define their mission, they are usually urged to seek a common thread to which activities can be related. The common thread is often stated in terms of the scope of products, but markets of technologies in the domain of the enterprise are also used. The problem is that the firm might define the scope so broadly that strategic decisions or objectives tied to the mission become meaningless. On the other hand, an overly narrow mission definition can lead to the oversight of factors that are potentially important to the success of the enterprise.

If the domain of TWA is defined too narrowly, executives may miss important technological or competitive activities occuring outside the more limited domain of "other air carriers." As a result, the firm may risk the potential loss of a large part of its customer base.

Thus the domain must be sufficiently board so that decision makers will be sensitive to important issues it may face in the future. Of course, overgeneralization, the opposite of myopia, may lead to a lack of focus on relevant issues as well. Should an airline view itself as being in the vacation business it should lose sight of its basic mission. Paper Mate now views itself as in "office products" with the acquisition of Liquid Paper. A radio is product, but manufacturers of radios are in the business of providing a means of delivering audio information and or entertainment. The Bostan Consulting Group statement on this issue is instructive:

Unfortunately, there is a prevalent notion that if one merely defines one's business in increasingly general terms—such as transportation rather than railroading—the road to successful competitive strategy will be clear. Actually, that is hardly ever the case. More often the opposite is true. For example, in the case of the railroads, passengers and freight represent very different problems, and short haul *vs.* longer haul are completely different strategic issues. Indeed as the unit train demonstrates, just coal handling is a meaningful strategic issue.

Thus perhaps on of the best ways to determine a common thread is to seek out synergies which could be obtained between old and new activities. "Synergy" refers to the idea that the whole is greater than the sum of its parts (2 + 2 = 5). Here if a firm can find new activities which utilize the strengths or benefits of old activities it is likely to create more value for all activities. As noted in Exhibit 2, 4. Hallman Found synergy in its markets, products, and technologies. Another suggestion is to give careful attention to the *utilities* provided for customers (*e.g.*,cost, time, location convenience) by the functions performed by the enterprise. Careful attention to categories of goods and services (rather than "product") and synergies can lead to more useful definitions of the organization's mission and domain. For instance, Sears began its move into providing financial services to complement its existing insurance business by using its broad base of retail outlets and large number of charge customers as a point of must be periodically evaluated as part of the strategic management process.

A final point before turning to the specificity of objectives is the idea that these issues of domain definition are stated in different terms at different levels of the organization, but similar question emerge. For instance, the scope question at the coporate level implies issues concerning the overall degree of diversification in the portfolio of business operations. At the SBU levels, the breadth of the product market scope or degree of vertical integration (technology scope) is debated in terms of product-market segments. Although organizations tend toward stability, mission and objectives change over time As discussed before, objectives could change on the basis of a rational analysis of a gap between expected and desired states. That is a normative approach. But what might lead to the determination of the different perceptions regarding the gaps between goals and how the future goal states might be arrived at?

On the basis of the foregoing discussion of how mission and objectives are formulated, we can present some descriptive reasons why mission or objectives might change.

1. **The Aspiration Levels of Managers could Alter Goal Orientations.** They may begin to extrapolate past achievements and say that the enterprise can do more. They may look at what relevant competitors or other enterprises have achieved and decide to match or exceed these levels. The arival of a new CEO from outside the organization is the most prevalent condition under which mission and goals are reconsidered. New managers from the outside who are not tied or committed to past strategy and ideology are more likely to alter the mission, objectives, and strategies of an organization than are new CEOs from the inside.

2. **The Mission can Change in Crisis.** When a firm's market disapears, for example, or its reason for being cease a crisis exists. Some firms supplying equipments to the oil industry discovered this in 1974 and again in 1982 and 1986. Faced will an uncertain future, their objectives have begun to focus on flexibility. When the cure for polio was found, the mission of the National Foundation for Infantile Paralysis changed. So the attainment of objectives can also lead to a crisis. Or, new opportunities can create an indentity crisis if a firm seeks to take advantage of them.

3. **Demands from Coalition Groups that Make up the Enterprise can Change.** This often occurs as the memebership or leadership of groups changes or as internal power groups change. For instance, new government or labour leaders or new competition can alter the way a business sets its goal-priorities. Similarly, if the comptroller becomes more powerful internally, the firm might begin to stress shorter-term financial goals.

4. **Normal Life-cycle Changes may Occur Which Alter Goal Orientations.** Though the alalogy with humans can be taken too far, there may be changes in objectives or strategies which "naturally occur in the aging process. Of course, organisation may have more control over the

sequencing and timing of these stages than humans. Yet it is often difficult for an organization to know what stage it is in. And we're not sure what might precipitate organization again or movement. We do know that commitment to the past may hinder change, and new agents in coalition groups are likely to hasten it.

These four classes of factors-aspirations, crisis, demands, and development can be used to predict the likelihood that mission and objectives will remain similar to those of the past or be subject to redefinition. Thus in considering how mission and objectives are formulated, we must examine various pressures for stability or change before a gap analysis can be effectively done.

FORMULATION OF MISSION AND OBJECTIVE

We believe that mission and objectives are formulated by the corporate level strategist. But these executives do not make choices in a vacuum. Their choices affected by several factors: the realities of theexternal environment and external power relationship, the realities of the enterprise's resources and internal power relationship, the value systems and goals of the top executives, and past strategy and development of the enterprise. Let us discuss each of these influencing factors then summarize.

The first factor affecting the fomulation of mission and objectives is forces in the environment. As discussed in Chapter I, the stakeholders with whom the organisation has an exchange relationship will present demands or claims. These can be thought of as constraints on objectives. The stakeholders may vary. The nature of their constraints can change, and their power *vis-a-vis* the organization and one another may change. Taken together, they represent one set of forces within which managerial objectives must be established. The claims of the most powerful stakeholders will be met, so long as the entire set of objectives falls within the constraints imposed by the set of stakeholders.

Suppose that managers want to choose maximization of sales as an objective. They may have to modify this objective becuase of governmental regulations regarding excess profit, antitrust legislation, consumer labeling, and so on. Trade unions may require higher-than-market wage rates or fringe benefits which lead to higher costs (possible reducing sales). Competitors may sell other products or services at unrealistically low prices and spend excessive amounts on advertising. Suppliers may become monopolized and charge outrageous prices. If the organization is more dependent on suppliers than on any other stakeholder, the operative objective may very well be limited by the availability and cost of supplies. As discussed in Chapter 1, then the political-behaviour realities of the situation influence the chocice of objectives.

So the prudent strategist will ask a variety of questions when establishing mission objectives, and strategy: who are the critical stakeholders? What are our critical assumptions about each shakeholders? How do stakeholders affect each division, business, or function at various points in time. And what changes can be expected among the stakeholder groups in the future?

The second factor affecting the formulation of mission and *objectives is the realities of the enterprise's resources and internal power relationships*. Larger and more profitable firms have more resources with which to respond to forces in the environment than do smaller or poorer firms.

In addition to this, the internal political relationship affect mission and objectives. First, how much support does management have relative of others in the organization? Does the management have the full support of the stockholders? For example, Paul Smucker has the support of the Smucker family stockholder to emphasize quality as an objective for his jam and preserves firm. If the management has developed the support of employees and key employees groups like the professional employees' lower and middle management, then it can set higher objectives that employees will help achieve.

Mission and objective are also inflenced by the power relationship among the strategists either as individuals or as representatives of units within the organization. Thus if there is a difference of opinion or which objectives to seek or the trade-offs among them, power relationships may help settle the difference.

A final internal factor is the potential power of lower-level participants to withhold information and ideas. To the extent that this occurs the evaluation of past goal attainment and expectation about the future can be affected. For instance, consider the sales manager who tries to hide the fact that a competitor's new product is starting to hurt sales. This might be an attempt to protect the unit, but it could mislead top managers regarding future goals and strategies. Or lower-level managers might decide whether or not to forward a proposal which could lead to goal changes on the basis of what they think top management is (or is not) ready to accept. Thus the exercise of this type of informal power can play a role in the slection of objectives.

Mintzberg has advanced a theory about formulation of objectives that combines the stakeholder forces described earlier with the internal power relationships. He believes that power plays result from interactions of internal and external coalitions.

SIX PURE POWER CONFIGURATIONS AFFECTING OBJECTIVES FORMULATION

External	*Internal*	*Power*
Coalition	Coalition	Configuration
Dominated	Bureaucratic	The Instrument
Passive	Bureaucratic	The Closed System
Passive	Personalized	The Autocracy
Passive	Ideologic	The Missionary
Passive	Professional	The Meritocracy
Divided	Politicized	The Political Arena

Source: Henry Mintzberg, Power in the Around Organizations (Englewood Cliffs. NJ. : Prentice-Hall, 1983) p. 307

The external coalition includes owners, suppliers, unions, and the public. These groups influence the firm through social normal specific constraints, pressure campaigns, direct controls, and membership on the board of directors. Mintzberg specifies three types of external coalition.

The internal includes top management, middle-line managers, operators analysts, and support staff. These groups influence the firm through the personnel control system, the bureaucratic control system, the political system, and the system of ideology. Mintzberg specifies 5 types of internal coalitions.

Mintzbergy says that there are six basic power configurations, as shown is above fig. In the instrument power configuration, one external influence with clear objectives typically the owner, is able to strongly influence objectives through the top manager. In a closed-system power configuration, power to set objectives rests with the top manager, who sets the objectives. This is also true in the autocracy power configuration. In the missionary power configuration, objectives are strongly influenced by past ideology and a charismastic leader. Ideology tends to dictate the objectives. In the meritocracy power configuration, the objectives are set by a census of the members, most of whom are professionals.

Thus the formulation of mission and objectives can be a simple process: the top manager sets them subjects to the environment. Or, more frequently, they are by a complex interplay of past and present, internal and external role players.

The third factor affecting the formulation of mission and objectives is the value system of the top executives. Enterprises with strong value systems or ideologies will attract and retain managers whose values are similar. These values are essentially a set of attitudes about what is good or bad, desirable or undersirable. These in turn will influence the percption of the advantages and disadvantages of strategic action and the choice of objectives.Let's look at each of these to see how they might affect objectives.

VALUES TOWARD VARIOUS GROUPS IN THE STRATEGIC SITUATION

1. Very innovative	Noninnovative
2. Risk-oriented	Risk-aversive
3. Autocratic	Participative
4. Personal goals	Shareholder goals
5. Quality	Quantity
6. Very combative	Very passive

The following list corresponds to the continuum in Exhibit the above Each dimension is explained below:

1. Some executive believes that to succeed a firm must innovate. Others prefer to "let others make the mistakes first."
2. Some executives know that to "win big, you must take big risks."
3. Some executives believe that one should treat employees in a manner that makes them know who the boss is. Others believe that cooperation comes from a participative style.
4. Some executives believe that they should be primary beneficiaries of corporate success while others think the business is operated for the benefit of stockholders.
5. Some executives believe that one becomes successful by producing quality. Others go for volume.
6. Some executives believe that to be successful a firm must attack in the market place. Others believe that you "go along to get along."

Prescriptively, from a "maximizing" decision perspective, these and other kinds of values *ought not* be considered when goals are being established. Yet some believe that it is better to recognize the inevitability of their influence on decision makers. That is, even if they are not explicitly stated, value assumptions will be implicit in decision premises and the types and forms of data collected. Consequently, stating these values in the form of assumptions is one technique recommended to force these values explicitly into the open. If they are included, the bases upon which decisions are made can be considered "more rational" than if decision makers pretended that thee factors don't exist. Exhibit 2.9 suggests that value shifts do affect the mission and goals of a business.

The fourth factor affecting the formulation of mission and objectives is the *awareness by management of the past development of the firm*. Management does not begin from scratch each year. It begins with the most recent mission and objectives. These may have been set by strong leaders in the past. The leaders consider incremental changes from the present, given the current environment and current demands of the conflicting groups. The managers have developed aspiration levels of what the objective ought to be in a future period. But by mudding through, they set the current set of objectives to satisfy as many of the demands and their wishes as they can. The momentum of thelarge organization and its strategies and policies are all designed to accomplish the existing mission and objectives. Just as it takes time to turn a large ship around, it usually takes time to make major corporate changes.

Let's summarize what has been paid so far on how mission and objectives are established. The factors are shown in Mission and objectives are not the result of managerial power alone. These result from the managers' trying to satisfy the needs of all groups involved with the enterprise. These coalitions of interests (stockholders, employees, suppliers, customers, and others) sometimes have conflicting interests. As the strongest coalition group, managers try to reconcile the conflicts. Management cannot settle them once and for all. Management "bargains" with the various groups and tries to produce a set of objectives and a mission which can satisfy the groups at that time. The goals of these groups are considered in relation to past goals. This is a very complicated, largely consensus-building process with no precise beginning or end. And at any given time, only a few specific goals can be grasped and comprehended by any single executive. Thus there appears to be a need for same grander vision as expressed by a mission definition.

Mission and objectives will become a meaning part of the strategic management process only if corporate strategists formulate them well and communicate them and reinforce them throughout the enterprise. The strategic management process will be successful to the extent that general managers participate in formulating the mission and objectives and to the extent that these reflect the values of management and the realities of the organization's situation. These factors also play a role in strategic choice.

How are Goals Actually Set?

In practice, goals are set by way of a complicated power-play involving various individuals and groups within the organisation and by reference to values which govern behaviour in general and the specific behaviour of the relevant individuals and groups. Goal-settling, in other words, involves a process of reconcilisation of diverse needs of interest groups-coalitions of interests or stakeholders in the organisation including the owners (shareholders), employees, suppliers, customers, Government and others. The respective stakeholders often have conflicting objectives which management as the strongest coalition of interests has to resolve. The process of reconciliation is a continuous one, for conflicting group interest cannot be resolved once and for all. The acceptable set of objectives which management arrive at is the result of bargaining between the various groups at a certain point of time, but then revisions take place and incremental changes are made; the current set of objectives are derived by management so as to satisfy as far as possible the current demands of the interest groups in the light of the existing environment and aspirations of the management about what the objective ought to be.

Examples of Good Objective Setting

Below are given certain examples as how the organisations should define their objectives so as to provide direction for their course of action.

(1) "We strive to become leader in product innovation in our field by investing five per cent of our sales revenue on research and development." This provides direction to management about what the organisation wants to do in the field of innovation and how it can be achieved.

(2) "We want to make our product the number one selling brand in its field in terms of units sold." This leaves little doubt about the intended sales objectives and market standing.

(3) "We seek to produce the most durable, maintenance-free product that money can buy." This obviously focusses on the organisation striving to become leader in respect to high quality product.

(4) "Our profit objective is to increase the earning so that we earn 12 per cent post tax return on the net worth of the company." This is very clear objective, easily measurable and providing direction about the quantum of profit for the organisation.

Examples of Poor Objective Setting

Some organisations do not define their objectives as sharply as above statements suggest. Their objective setting is quite poor and may not provide clear direction. Following are some example of such objective setting.

(1) "We will go to great leangth to develop new ideas." This is not very precise and clear, hence fails to provide direction.

(2) "Our objective is to maximise our profit." This statement of objective is not subject to measurement because it does not provide any yardstick for that. Therefore, the organisation can not know whether it is achieving its objective or not. Further it does not spell out the way in which the objective can be achieved. Therefore, it does not spell our commitment on the part of the management.

(3) "Our objective is to offer best and cheapest product." This statement does not provide yardstick for measuring cheapest and best product, hence fails to provide direction.

AREAS OF OBJECTIVE SETTING

As discussed earlier, organisational objectives are the multiple character. Even major objectives are multiple in nature. Thus an organisation has to set objectives in many areas. However, what objectives should be selected must meet three criteria *(i)* They must be in consistent with the values of the management in the organisation. They must pinpoint the organisational strengths and weaknesses. *(ii)* They must satisfy the external environmental forces. From these points of view, the organisation will set its objectives in several areas. For example, Peter Drucker has emphasised eight areas which an organisation must emphasise as its objectives. These are:

Physical financial resources, profitability, manager performance and development, worker performance and attitude, and public responsibility, market standing, innovation, productivity.

England and dent have give a wide range of such objectives. These are:

1. maximise net profit over a short period of time,
2. maximise the company's net assets and reserves,
3. maximise net profit over a long period,
4. maximise the dividends for the shareholders,
5. run a stable organisation,
6. maximise the company's prestige,
7. be influencial in local community decisions,
8. have satisfied employees,
9. survive,
10. create a friendly and pleasant workplace,

11. provide high rewards and benefits to the employees,
12. be a socially responsible company,
13. be the leading innovator in the community,
14. be of service to the community,
15. maximise the rate of innovation of products or services,
16. have the most satisfied customers,
17. be a market leader, *e.g.,* first in market with new products or services,
18. provide the best quality products or services possible,
19. increase sales growth,
20. maximise the company's rate of growth,
21. maximise the market share,
22. keep tax payments to a minimum,
23. keep the government out of the business,
24. provide income or jobs for owning family members,
25. present unionisation or further unionisation,
26. be themost efficient firm in the industry.

MANAGING BY OBJECTIVE (MBO)

John Humble defined managing by objectives as a dynamic system which integrate the company's need to achieve its goals for profit and growth with the manager's need to contribute and develop himself. According to Georgre S. Ordiorne the system of Management by Objectives can be described as a process whereby the superior and subordinate managers of an organisation jointly identify its common goals, define each individual's major areas of responsibility in terms of results expected of him, and use these measures as guides for operating the unit and assessing the contribution of each of its members. Ordiorne also stressed that MBO is not merely a set of rules, a series of procedures or even a set method of managing, but it is a way of thinking about management.

Management by objectives is also known as management by results and goal setting approach. Dale D. McConkey has preferred the term management by results and has defined it is an approach to management planning and evaluationin which specific targets for a year, or some other length or time, are established for each manager, on the basis of the results which each must achieve if the overall objectives of the company are to be realised. At the end of this period, the actual results achived are measured against the original goals, *i.e.,* against the expected results which each manager knows he is responsible for achieveing.

Management by objectives has become a comprehensive management planning and control technique and is bound to affect the entire organisational structure, culture and style. Management by objectives calls for regulating the entire process of managing in terms of meaningful, specific and variable objectives at different levels of management hierarchy. Management by objectives moulds planning, organising, directing and controlling in number of ways. It stimulates meaningful action for better performance and higher accomplishment. It is closely associated with the concept of decentralisation because decentralisation cannot work without the support of management by objectives.

THE PROCESS OF MBO

The process of managing by objectives revolves around the setting up of organisational goals and the goals of various divisions and subdivisions. It is anever ending process. The continuous nature of the process of MBO not only ensures sustained concentration of efforts towards organisational objectives, but also helps in modifying objectives to suit the changed situation.

Managing by Objective

(a) Setting of Objectives. The first step while installing the system of 'Management by Objectives' in an organisation is to establish verifiable objectives for the organisation and for varous portion at various levels. In order to set objectives of the enterprise, a detailed assessment has to be made of the various resources at its disposal. A market survey must be conducted to know what types of goods and services are required by the community. Proper forecasts should be made to estimate the demand and the business conditions in the country. This detailed analysis would lead to highlighting of desirable objectives, both long-range and short-range. An attempt should be made to set specific goals ın various key areas on which the survival and growth of the business depends. These are the objectives which the top management will tend to achieve.

The major activities of every enterprise are divided on some basis of departmentalisation. The top management must determine the objectives of every department. At this stage, the top management should discuss the objectives with the departmental managers so that a statement of agreed objectives may be evolved. Each department sets its both long-range and short-range objectives with the approval of top management. This process of setting objectives is repeated at lower levels of management. At each level, objectives are set in verifiable units so that performance of every department and individual may be reviewed after the end of a particular period. Once this process is complete, there will exist a meeting of minds of each superior and his subordinates as to what is to be accomplished and why it is to be accomplished.

(b) Revision of Organisation Structure. When the goals for each individual are set under MBO, there is a considerable change in the job description of various positions. This may call for a revision of the existing organisation structure. The organisation charts and manuals should be suitably amended to depict the change brought by the introduction of management by objectives. The job descriptions of various jobs must defined their objectives, responsibilities and authority. They must clearly lay down the relationship with other job positions in the organisation.

(c) Establishing Check Points. Management by objectives ensures periodic meetings between the superior and the subordinate to review the progress towards the accomplishment of targets of the subordinate. For this, the superior must establish check points or standards of performance for evaluating the progress of the subordinate. The standards should be defined quantitatively as far as possible and the subordinate must understand them fully. This practice should be followed by every superior for each of his subordinates and it should lead to key result analysis as targets or goals are represented in terms of results. The key result analysis should be reduced into writing. It should contain the following information:

(i) The overall objectives of the job of the subordinate.

(ii) The key result he must achieve to fulfil his objectives.

(iii) The long-term and short-term priorities to tasks he must adhere to.

(iv) The scope and extent of assistance he may expect from his superior and related departmental managers and the assistance he must extend to other departments.

(v) The nature of information and reports he will receive to carry out self-evaluation.

(vi) The standards by which his performance shall be evaluated.

(d) Appraisal of Performance. While informal performance appraisal of a subordinate is done by his immediate superior almost everyday, formal appraisal at periodic intervals, usually once or twice a year, does ensure that a thorough evaluation of a manager's performance is being done at least once or twice a year when the achievements are carefully analysed against the background of prevailing circumstances and given objectives. The design and format of the Performance Review Form will depend on the nature of an enterprise.

The important benefit of MBO is that it does away with the judgemental role of the supervisor. The performance of every individual is evaluated in terms of the standards or end-results clearly agreed to by the superior and the subordinate. Whenever MBO has been introduced, it has led to greater satisfaction, more agreement, greater comfort and less tension and hostility between the superiors and the subordinates. Under MBO, the superior does not evaluate the individual concerned but his performance in terms of the standards set in advance. Moreover, the performance review is aimed to assist the subordinate to improve his performance in the future. It also helps in setting goals for the next period.

BENEFITS OF MBO

Management by objectives is being increasingly recognised not merely as a philosophy of management but also as a system which aims at synchronising the objectives of the individuals with the objectives of the organisation. When applied consciously and systematically, it leads to the following benefits:

1. Providing a realistic means of analysing training needs and opportunities for growth on the basis of measurement of performance against accepted standards.
2. Stimulating the subordinates' motivation.
3. Serving as a device for organisational control and integration.
4. Improved communication and organisation structure which help in locating weak and problem areas.
5. A grater sense of identification by the management team with the objectives of the enterprise wherein controls are reckoned as tools of 'self-control' rather than devices to the used against managers.
6. Improvement in productivity due to the fact that management team concentrates on the important task of reducing costs and harnessing opportunities rather than dissipating energies on less important matters.

Following are the difficulties which make the implementation of MBO difficult:

1. **Inflexibility.** Management by objectives may tend to introduce inflexibility in the organisation. Since goals are set after every six months or one year, the superior may not like to modify them in between because of fear of resistance from the subordinate. There may arise a need to revise the goals at lower levels to achieve the long-range objectives of the enterprise. The manager must handle such a situation properly. Some managers give more emphasis on goal setting. But they should remember that they are also to perform other functions of management like organising, directing and control.

2. **Lack of Follow-up.** Lack of follow-up by the superior at the appropriate time is another hurdle in the successful implementation of MBO. In practice, superiors have many things to do. It is most easy to procrastinate. The superior must get with the subordinate at the appropriate time. The subordinate is prepared to tell the boss exactly what has been accomplished and how. If the superior delays the meeting, the subordinate will think this is just one of the those management programmes that everyone got so held up over and has now gone down the drain. Job efforts probably will be relaxed since the superior does not appear to attach much importance to a review of results. Needless to say, this may affect his performance in a negative way.

3. **Lack of Training.** There is generally lack of training and knowledge on the part of the supervisor in implementing the programme. Many are prone to sit down with the subordinate, dictate the goals and targets with no input permitted from the subordinate, and then demand they be met in a specified time. Whether they are realistic goals or not does not enter the picture. No consideration is given to any outside factors over which the subordinate has no control or influence. In this type of environment, there can be no two-way communication because of the outer-imposed objective. This stab at MBO will destroy morale,

initiative and goods results faster than anything else in an enterprise.

4. **Poor Planning.** One of the major weaknesses often seen in MBO is poor planning of the programme prior to implementation. Implementors must be well-trained. They must know how to involve all levels of management and obtain their support.

   Despite various difficulties and shortcomings in management by objectives, it is an efficient way of managing as it emphasizes in practice the setting of objectives as the logic of planning and control. In order to achieve all the advantages of managing by objectives, it is essential that it should start at the top of the organisation. The active participation of top management to this programme is essential for its implementation. If the top manager uses the objectives as an instrument for managing his subordinates, this practice will be followed down in the organisation.

It is also essential that goals should be set by participation with the subordinate. There should be face-to-face communication between the superior and the subordinate for setting the goals, discussing the subordinate's problems and for reviewing his performance. Thus, there must be effective two-way communication in the organisation. Lastly, a greater degree of decentralisation of authority is required for the success of MBO. The subordinates who have accepted the challenging assignments through discussion with the superior, must be given adequate authority to accomplish their goals. MBO will not work if subordinates as the subordinates will not be willing to accept new assignments and they will resist the setting of clearly defined goals.

MANAGEMENT BY EXCEPTION

Management by exception is an important principle of organisational control put forward by the classical management writers. This principle holds that only significant deviations (*i.e.,* exceptions) from standards of performance should be brought to the management's attention. If actual performance is according to the planned performance (*i.e.,* standards already laid down), it need not be brought to the attention of the concerned manager as no follow-up action is necessary. But if there is a major deviation from the standard, it should be reported to the manager. For example, suppose a manager establishes a quality control standard which lays down that five defects per 100 units produced are permissible. Under the management by exception principle, only significant deviations from the standard-six or more defects per 100 units in this case-should be brought to the notice of the manager concerned.

Minor deviations from the standards are usually given less attention. But in some cases, small deviations may mean a great deal and have greater significance than large deviations in other cases. For instance, management will be more concerned if the cost of labour is five per cent more than the budgeted labour-cost as compared to cost of postage stamps which is fifteen per cent more than the budgeted one. So the principle of management by exception must be practised in conjunction with the principle of critical point control. Management should be selective in exercising control. It should select key areas of activity on which the preformance of the entire organisation depends and concentrate more on those areas. The exception principle logically refers to the size of deviations from the standards only in the critical control points or areas. It has been devised to conserve managerial time, effort and talent and apply these in more important areas. It is a technique of separating important information from the unimportant information. Only such information which is critical for managerial control actions is sent to the management. This facilitates the installing of an effective control system.

❐

3

Social Consideration in Business Policy

A large number of significant changes have taken place in social, polical, economic and other aspects of modern culture. These changes make it appropriate to re-examine the role of modern business. It is common today to hear speeches or read articles calling for more social consciounsess on the part of the business organisations. The demand for greater social awareness from the business organisations is a move and an important part of the society's attempt to make them more responsive to the need of mankind. It is heartening to note that society's changing values and needs are being given due importance by the leading business houses of the world. This is obvious from the fact that the business houses are carrying on research and development activities and producing goods and services to provide greater satisfaction to the economic and social developent of their nation.

The phrase 'social responsibility' is widely used in the literature of sociology, anthropology, economics, politics and business management. H.R. Bowen has defined the concept of social responsibility as "obligation (of manager) to pursue those policies, to make those decisions, or to follow those lines of action which are desirable of the objectives and values of our society. According to George A. Steiner, "In the real sense, the assumption of social responsibilities implies recognition and understanding of the aspirations of the society and determination to contribute to its achievement." Both these definitions contain vague phrases and assume every-one knows those to whom an obligation is owed and the meaning of social values.

Since an obligation can be owed only by one person to another, social responsibility is an interpresonal relationship that exists when people are continuously dependent upon one another in both organised, and unorganised way. As a working definition, *"Social responsibility may be regarded as the personal obligation of people as they act in their own interests to assure that the rights and ligitimate interests of others are not impinged, "said Harold Koontz and Cyril O. Donnel.* Thus, the busines managers must assess the implications and effects of their decisions and policies on the other components of the society and to ensure, that the interests are not adversely affected by their actions.

Social responsibility may also refer to an obligation, a liability, social conse ousness, corporate legitimacy, charitable contribution, "do goodism, "managerial enlightement, and so on. Most businessmen prefer words other than social responsibility because these words connote a social obligation with unclear commitments. They prefer such synonyms as social concern, social programmes, social challenge, social commitment, or concern with public problems. Social responsibility of business can be better appreciated if we move away from abstract to concrete specific responsibilities to be pursued by the business. A brief review of social obligations towards different groups has been given later in this chapter.

AREAS OF SOCIAL RESPONSIBILITY

Social responsibilities of management can be studied under two headings: *(i)* Internal social responsibilities, and *(ii)* External social responsibilities, Internal social responsibilities are concerned with assuring due process, justice, equity and morality in employee selection, training, promotion, and hiring, or they may relate to such things as increasing employee productivity, or improving employee physical environment. External social responsibilities refer to such actions as stimulating minority enterpreneurship, improving the balance of payments, or training and hiring hard-core unemployed. Thus, management owes social obligations to two major groups, namely, *Insider*—Shareholders and employees, and *Outsiders*-Customers, supplies, government and the society as a whole. The responsibilities of management towards these groups are discussed below:

A. Responsibility Towards Customers

Customer satisfaction is the ultimate aim of all economic activities. This involves more than the offer of products at the lowest possible price. Adulteration of goods, poor quality, failure to give fair measure, lack of service and courtesy to the customers, misleading or dishonest advertising are some of the examples of violation by business of its obligation towards the customers of its products. Therefore, it is the duty of management to take care of the following points:

1. **Fair Trade Practices.** The management should not indulge in unfair and unethical practices such as black marketing hoarding. adulteration etc. The goods and services should be distributed properly so that the customers do not face any difficulty in purchasing them.

2. **Regular Flow of Goods.** It is the duty of management to make goods of the right quality available to the right people at the right time and place and at reasonable prices.

3. **Need Satisfaction.** The company should produce those goods which meet the needs of the consumers of different classes, tastes and with different purchasing power.

4. **Right Information.** The management should ensure that advertisements and other statements issued by the business are true and fair.

5. **Courteous Service.** The business should provide a prompt, adequate and courteous service to customers, and to handle their grievances carefully.

B. Responsibility Towards Shareholders or Owners

There is a separation of ownership and management in the case of joint stock companies. The shareholders are emplowered to appoint directors on the Board of Directors and seek regularly accurate and full financial information about the company. The management or the directors of the company are responsibility for safeguarding the intrests of the shareholders. But in case of sole tradership and partnership concerns, the owners can lookafter their interest themselves.

The management of a company has the following responsibilities towards the shareholders:

1. **Information.** It is the responsibility of the management to keep the shareholders well informed about the progress and financial position of the company.
2. **Protection of Assets.** The assets of the company are purchased with the funds provided by the shareholders. The management is responsible to safeguard these assets.
3. **Soundness.** It is the duty of management to see that financial position of the company is sound and the company always looks for growth.
4. **Reasonable Dividend.** Shareholders are a source of funds for the company. They expect a high rate of dividend on the money invested by them and also the maximisation of the value of their investment in the company.

C. Responsibility Towards Workers/Employees

The employees should be treated as human beings and their cooperation must be achieved for the realisation of organisational goals. The management of a business should fulfil the following obligations towards its employees:

1. **Good Working Conditions.** Since workers spend about eight hours one every working day at their place, they

must be provided with good working conditions. Good working conditions are necessary to maintain the health of the workers.

2. **Opportunity for Growth.** The workers should be helped by training and other means to improve their skills. Management should give the workers adequate opportunities to develop their capabilities through training, education and the enjoyment of freedom to the greatest possible extent.

3. **Recognition of Workers Right.** The management should recognise the workers' rights to fair wage, to participate in desicions affecting their working life, to form trade unions, to collective bargaining and to go on strike if their demands are not accepted.

4. **Cooperation.** It is the responsibility of the management to win the cooperation of the workers by creating the conditions in which workers are willing to put forward their best efforts towards the common goals of the business.

5. **Adequate Service Benefits.** Workers should be provided service benefits such as housing and medical facilities, insurance cover and retirement benefits. These will make them feel secure.

6. **Fair Wages.** Every business should pay reasonable wages and salaries to its employees so that they may satisfy their needs and lead a good life.

D. Responsibility Towards Society/Community

Peter Drucker suggested that the business should be so managed as to make the public good the private good of the enterprise. Thus, every business owes and obligation to the society at large. The specific responsibilities of business towards the society are discussed below:

1. **Improvement of Local Environment.** Good management can contribute to the advancement of local amenties where

the enterprise functions. It can develop the surrounding area for the well-being of the workers and the general public. Management has certainly great responsibility to keep the healthy environmental conditions where the production is being carried on. It should take preventive measures against water and air pollution, and should contribute to the community development activities. If the management fails to discharge its responsibility, the Government will interfere to prevent the enterprise from pulluting the environment.

2. **Employment Opportunities.** It is the responsibility of management to help increase direct and indirect employment in the ara where it is functioning.

3. **Socio-economic Objectives.** Management must be guided by the socio-economic objectives of the society. It should not indulge in any practice which is not fair from social point of view. Society expects that the business uses the factors of production effectively and efficiently for the satisfaction of the needs of the society. If the business fulfills these expectations, its goodwill and reputation wil increase.

4. **Efficient Use of Resources.** The resources at the command of business belong to the society. Therefore, the management should make the best possible use of capital, raw materials, machines, technical knowledge and other resources for the well-being of the society.

5. **Business Ethics.** The business should not indulge in anti-social and unfair trade practices such as adulteration, hoarding and black marketing. It should not issue misleading advertisements.

6. **Welfare Activities.** The business should contribute towards the upliftment of the weaker section of the society. It should cooperate in the welfare activites of the community.

D. Responsibilities Towards Government

Every business enterprise is governed by various laws. It is the duty of the management of every enterprise to manage its affairs according to the laws affecting it. Management's policies should be laid down taking into consideration the provision of various legislations and guidelines issued by the Government. Management should follow fair trade practices. It should pay taxes and other Government dues honestly, fully and promptly. It should not encourage corruption, black marketing and other social evils.

The specific responsibilities of business towards government may be enumerated as follows:

1. To avoid corrupting government employees.
2. To discourage the tendencies of concentration of economic power and monopoly.
3. To encourage fair trade practices.
4. To pay government taxes honestly and in time.
5. To abide by the laws of the nation.

E. Responsibility Towards Suppliers

Management should deal with the suppliers judiciously. It should try for fair terms and conditions regarding price, quality, delivery of goods and payment. Their dealings with the suppliers should be based on integrity and courtesy in the absence of which the suppliers will not supply them the goods on credit. It short, management must create healthy relations with the suppliers.

We have observed that the interest of various groups or constiuents of the society are not indentical. Owners of a business want the highest wages and best working conditions, the consumers the best quality goods at the lowest possible price and the Government wants the highest revenue. According to the Committee or Economic Development (Social Responsibilities of Business

Corporation. (Washington, 1971), the responsibilities of business are four fold:

1. To preserve financial well-being and profit making capacity of the firm in order to provide a fair return on its capital to the owners.
2. To continue to provide useful goods and services to the consumers at a price they are willing to pay.
3. To exercise its economic functions with a sensitive awarness of changing social values and priorities.
4. To continue to provide employees with jobs at an appropriate level of compensation.

The task of management is to reconcile and balance the conflicting interests. As a matter of fact, management is an arbiter among the various interests. It is worthwhile to quote Ernest Dale. "The manager sees himself as an arbiter among the many interests of 'publics' affected by the business : the stockholders, the employees, the suppliers, the local community and the customer. It is his duty to divide the returns from the business equitably by providing a 'fair' return to the 'shareholders', 'fair' working conditions and pay for the employees 'fair' prices to the suppliers and customers and to make the business, in the general, an asset to the community and the nation."

ARGUMENTS OFFERED IN FAVOUR OF SOCIAL RESPONSIBILITIES

Since long there has been controversy whether business should assume social responsibilities, or it has no such obligations to fulfil. It would be worthwhile to analyse the arguments offered both in favour and against assumption of social responsibilities by business. First of all we shall begin with the analysis of arguments in favour.

The important arguments offered in favour of business assuming social responsibilities ar as follows:

1. Emergence of strong trade unions compel the business organisations to safeguard the interests of workers.
2. Social responsibilities must be assumed by the business to achieve good public image.
3. The long-term self-interest of business are best served when business assumes social responsibilities; and
4. If the business does not assume social responsibilities voluntarily, the government will intervene.
5. Consumers' movement is spreading at a fast rate to take action against the dishonest businessmen.
6. Socio-cultural norms of the society require the business to fulfil their their social obligations.
7. Business is the creation of society, hence should respond to the demands of the society.

These arguments have been further elaborated below:

1. Strong Trade Unions. The level of education among the workers has been increasing. They understand the need of organising themselves into unions to advance their economic and social interests. The government has also enacted social security measures due to which it has become difficult for the business houses to ignore the interests of the workforce.

2. Public Image. The antennas of business managers are turned to the public opinion as good public opinion is a precondition to the success of any business. Therefore, they seek to maintain a proper image of their business in the public mind by assuming social responsibilities.

3. Long-term Self-interest of Business. There is a growing realisation on the part of the enlightened businessmen that it will be in their self-interest to fulfil the demands and the aspirations of the society. People who have a good enivornment, education, and opportunity make better employees, customers and neighbours for business than those who are poor, ignorant and oppressed to quote Arjay Miller : "Under current conditions, management cannot effectively discharge its long-run responsibilities to shareholders unless it also behaves responsibility towards employees, customers, government, education and the public at large. The ability of a corporation to protect and enahance the stockholders equally depends crucially upon the prosperity, goodwill and confidence of the larger community. Acceptance of a large measure of responsibility towards the community is, therefore, good business as well as good citizenship."

4. Conciousness Among Consumers. The consumers to today are well informed. They accept higher quality products at reasonable rates from the business. They can organise themselves in case a business resort to malpractices such as adulteration and black marketing.

5. Government Intervention. If the businessmen do not rise to the occasion in meeting the social responsibility, the Government will step in and make them assume such responsibilities through legislation. Such legislative regulaton is expensive for business and stand in the way of flexibility and freedom in making decisions and meeting competition. Hence, it would again be in the interest of business community to voluntarily undertake to fulfil the social responsibilities. In doing so the business will also retain the needed credibility with the public pressure.

6. Response to Social Demand. It is a well know fact that buiness is set up to earn profit by producing goods or rendering services to the members of the society. Thus, the business is the creation of the society in the sense that its primary objective is to fulfil the needs of the members of the society. In case the business fails to do so, the society through people's representatives in Government will either force them to do so through laws or may no longer permit them to survive.

7. Socio-cultural Norms. A business operates within a set-up of socio-cultural norms and restraints. No society will allow a business to maximise its profits at the cost of the society. It requires the business to respond to social obligations. It may even resort to legal means to enforce discipline among the businessmen.

CASE AGAINST ASSUMING SOCIAL OBLIGATIONS

The classical view has been against the business assuming social responsibilities. It is argued that business is an economic institution and as such *its primary responsibility is to produce goods and services efficiently and to earn profits for its owner.* Milton Friedman, a noted world economist and Nobel laureate supports the view of the classists in this regard. Friedman argues that "in a free enterprise, private property system, a manager is an employee of the owners of the business and directly responsible to them as his employers. Since stockholders want to make as much profit as possible, the manager's sole objective should be to try to do this. If a manager spends stockholder's money in the public interest, he is spending stockholder's money without their approval and perhaps in ways stockholders would oppose. Similarly, if the cost of social action is passed on to consumers in the form of higher prices the manager is spending their money also. This is taxation without representation." He further goes on to observe that "there is one and only social responsibility of business to use its resources and engage in activities designed to increase its profits so long as it stays within the rules of the game which is to say, engages in open and free competition, without deception or fraud."

In addition to the observations made by Milton Friedman, some more agruments are advanced opposing the idea of business assuming social responsibilities. These arguments are as follows:

1. **Burden on Consumers.** If the market price of a product does not truly reflect the relative costs of producting it, but includes costs for social actions, the allocative mechanism of the market place will be distorted. The customer will have to pay a higher price than necessary to call the goods into the market because the business is spending funds on social responsibilities.

2. **Lack of Social Skills.** Businessmen do not necessarily have social skills. Because of this they may not be able to solve social problems even though they spend a large amount for this purpose.

3. **Violation of Rule of Profit Maximisation.** As a businessman moves away from the simple rule of profit maximisation that guides his actions into the social and political realm, he has two guides to help him know what social responsibilities he should assume in the public interest. The businessmen should nottry to determine what is the public interest because "the economic system is not a playground on which businessmen may exercise their peculiar preferences."

4. **Lack of Self-interest.** There is no substitute for the power of self interest to get people to act. Assumption of social responsibilities will hinder the achievement of self interest of businessmen. Any replacement of the altruism for self-interest will, therefore, be fatal to the efficiency of the business system.

5. **Less Efficient use of Resouces.** The doctrine of social responsibility implies acceptance of socialist view that political mechanism rather than market mechanisms are the appropriate ways to allocate scare resources to alternative case. As this process evolves, there will be an erosion of the drive to use resource efficiently and a loss of the greater productivity of the present economic mechanism.

SOCIAL RESPONSIBILITY OF BUSINESS IN INDIA

Since 1947, Government, educationists, political parties, labour unions and various other groups in our society have brought about tremendous changes in the minds of the people about aims and values of life. In our present society, people are now anxious to have equality of opportunities for their growth and development within the framework of their working spheres and political institutions.

The Government is eager to see that the rate of our national income is increased so that people may have better standard. Unless Indian business makes full use of modern technology and science, and encourages the development of innovational personnel within, there will be no impetus for economic growth. Our entrepreneurs must develop values and aims conducive to the increase in the rate of economic growth. When these characteristics do not appear in their personalities, they are taken as moving time. It is obvious that one social responsibility of our business entrepreneurs is to help the country in raising its national income.

Increasing the rate of new jobs to absorb persens is another social responsibility. The development plans which the country has undertaken since independence should normally create new jobs for engineers, technologists, scientists and personnel. Technical and engineering institutions are training such young men. The absorptive capacity of business, however, has not increased in proportion to the supply of trained personnel. Already, there is considerable interest among thousands of trained young men who are still unemployed.

While no country can possibly solve its unemployment problem through reliance on business sector only, Indian entrepreneurs must understand the implication of the expensive development of higher education in that society looks to them for the absorption of a large segment of educated people. It is not enough that only the present employees should get the benefits from the productivity of enterprise; equally important is to provide additional jobs for new personnel every year. A large amount of nation's capital is being spent for developing human resources in schools, colleges and universities. Whether or not the policy-makers of education are giving a rational and correct approach to our educational development, the pressure from society for immediate planning manpower development, the planners depend heavily on the possible expansion of industrial enterprises. The creation of new jobs is not a problem but a challenge which business must accept. The immediate entrepreneurial group will have have to think of capital investment and industries in the light of human resources which they can utilise on increasing rate, without affecting business purpose. Business cannot perform its social responsibility without developing an organisational culture of its own which will aim at giving a unity of character in thinking and action among all its members and which adapts itself to the changes made necessary by other cultures. Today it is the enterpreneurial culture with its distinct aims about ownership exercise of authority, control and sharing of gains which dominates business. Authority, control and gains are desired by all employees. The contract with enterpreneurial culture naturally brings these desires in these employees, more so when they are competent in their functional areas.

Organisational culture in business must have a unity of purpose. Unity of purpose should also have the recognition of society. It is not merely the problem of human relations but of integration of aims and beliefs of every member in business with business purpose. This integration will lead to the formation of organisational culture strong enough to influence other communities and to be influenced by them. Such a culture will make it possible for all members to respond to all human situations in society, to foster spirit of service in its members towards communities, to develop habit of thinking from the point of view of society, to offer a fellowship to members in which their life assumes new meaning and direction, and to appreciate desires and aspirations of men who have the abilities. Developing an organisational culture in business is the responsibility of the entrepreneurs. If entrepreneurs do not become alert in understanding the implications of social changes in business in time and continue to remain indifferent to designing and developing orgaisational culture acceptable in society, the quantum of animadversions of business on social purpose will increase and gather momentum to force society to thing of "other ways" in exercising control and making an enterprise socially responsible. What these "other ways" will be and whether they will be better and more rational both for business and social purpose, no one can hazard to make a prophecy at this stage.

A new social phenomenon in India is the slow alienation of the public from the problems and difficulties of big enterprises in the private sector because of latter's lack of social purpose. The image of a big business is that of a class of men on the top level of management which is concerned with making profit rather than the image of a company, genuinely interested in the needs of society. Some imponderable factors are also responsible for the impression the public has made on the private sector in India. The alignment of politicians with the trade unions, the shrinkage in the philangthropic activities of the top management people and the occasional outbursts of Chambers of Commerce in favour of private sector and against the government policies inspite of their assoication with latter are doing in no small measure positive injury to the business class in its relation with the public. The business class can bring a considerable change in the attitude of the public if it can devise suitable measures.

Fortunately, the enterprises in the public sector have become acutely aware of the urgent need of an organisation culture. The delay in developing organisation culture so far has not been due to any lack of faith or obduracy of the top management. It is rather because the public sector in its present form is a recent development in India. The task is most exciting and exacting, and yet most urgent. Since the top management in the private sector has not given its best efforts to this task, it should do well to emulate the public sector for organisation culture.

SOCIAL AUDIT AND SOCIAL ACCOUNTING

The concepts of social accounting and social audit are sometimes used to convey the same ideas. But from the operational point of view one should make a distinction between the two terms. Social accounting is the process of selecting firm level performance variables, measures and measurement procedures; systematically developing information useful for evaluating the firm's social performance to concerned social groups, both within and outside the firm." Social audit, on the other hand, refers to the evaluation or assessment of a company's performance against planned goals in the areas of social responsibility. The assessment may be carried out by internal or external bodies for internal or external use.

According to Clark Abt, a social audit should as far as possible be approximated to an ordinary commercial audit; it should be based on a social balance sheet with a 'credit' side and a 'debit' side (inputs' and 'outputs' or 'costs' and 'benefits')

1. The first approach to social accounting and social audit is as follows:

Social Accounting refers to the indentification, measurement, recording and reporting to the internal and external users relevant information that is generated with respect to the social activities of a firm. It is a "systematic assessment and reporting on those parts of a company's activities that have a social impact-the impact of corporate decisions on environmental pollution, consumption of nonrenewable resources, and ecological factors; on the rights of individuals and groups; maintenance of public services; on public safety; on health and education and many other social concerns."

Social Audit, on the other hand, refers to "a retrospective review of the impact or contribution of a company in the recognised social dimensions; a tool of the socially responsible company undertaken by itself or admitted groups, for the purpose of planning control and accountability.

METHODS OF SOCIAL AUDIT & SOCIAL ACCOUNTING

The financial costs of social activities can be computed by any trained finance manager, but the valuation of social costs and benefits is a difficult task for corporate executives to undertake unless they are trained in social science. The socio-economic impact of public projects on health, education, welfare, housing, transportation, etc. are often analysed by Government agencies in term of benefit cost ratios. Total benefits are estimated in money terms, total costs are substracted from total benefits, or benefit/cost ratio is estimated for comparison with other projects. This approach involves the use of shadow prices in respect of those inputs and outputs for which market prices do not reflect the real economic or social worth. Likewise, social costs and benefits may be discounted at the social discount rate to determine their social net present value.

A second approach suggested by Eichhorn is that of social reporting by way of social profit and loss account and a social balance sheet, the former listing the producers' surplus and consumer's surplus as well as the positive and negative external effects of corportae activities so as to arrive at net social costs, and the latter listing the social assets and social debts. Eichhorn's method is similar to that suggested by Abt, Bauer and Gastil.

Third method of determing the worth of social investments is to estimate the 'market worth' of the expected benefits to the people affected. This approach is based on the assumption that consumer preferences are most signficant in the valuation of social goods and services as in the case of economic goods. Thus, to apply this measurement technique, it is necessary to identify the population who are likely to be affected by a particular social activity. A sample survey or interviews should be carried out to ascertain whether the social activity is perceived as a benefit or cost by the affected population. The degree or amount of benefit or cost as perceived by the people should then be determined as the average unit cost or unit benefit per person affected and expressed in money terms. This may require the use of shadow prices. Finally, the unit cost or benefit is to be multiplied by the number of persons affected to arrive at the total benefit/cost measure.

Fourth method based on the concept of 'social goal accounting and reporting' is considered superior to the social indicator approach inasmuch as it requires the indicator to be derived from the societal goals and objectives set by the company rather than the indicators being arbitrarily chosen. Corporate management is thus required in this approach to select its 'social market' by reference to its own study of the environment, and then choose those areas of social activities in which it believes it can contribute effectively by reducing the social costs or increasing the social benefits. The corporate social reporting therefore focuses on the objectives for a performance period, resources allocated for the purpose, achievements made in the area, and problems left to be resolved. Through this process, management may also find it possible to integrate financial reporting and social reporting, and get the evaluation of economic and social achievements carried out externally or internally so as to enable a balanced view to be taken by the stakeholders from their respective viewpoints. However, Developing a comprehensive statement of socio-economic objectives and specifying the corresponding operational tasks for each period is an elaborate and time-consuming process.

Fifth method is David Linowes' concept of 'socio-economic operating statement' provides to social reporting which aims at focusing on 'what a corporation has done for society on the one hand, and what it has failed to do on the other'. Linowes suggested that the 'socio-economic operating statement', to be prepared along with the company's financial statement, should include expenses incurred voluntarily by the company aimed at improving the welfare of the employees and/or public safety of the product and/or conditions of the environment, and offset against those expenses the costs of items which have been brought to the attention of management-items that would improve the welfare of the people, safety to the product and/or environmental conditions, etc.-that a reasonably prudent, modern socially conscious management would be expected to undertake but which the management of the particular company ignored.

Last method is to the measurement of social performance consists of developing 'social indicators' and measurement of the firm' contribution to the overall quality of life in different areas. According to Brumet, the possible areas in which the contributions of corporate social activities may be measured and reported are:

(1) Human resource contribution (Development of system of human resource accouting which sould measure the impact of organisational decision on human asset values);

(2) Public contribution (Creation of jobs and providing employment opportunities to backward and socially handicapped population, contributing towards educational development, relief to people in distress caused by natural calamities, rural uplifitment, etc.);

(3) Product or service contribution (Ensuring quality, durability, safety and servicebility of products, customer satisfaction, truthfulness in advertising etc.)

(4) Environmental contribution (Environmental improvement through pollution abatement, conservation of scarce natural resources, maintenance ecological balance, and so on);

(5) Net income contribution (A corporation must earn enough to provide for the present and future costs of its continuned existence but it should be limited to legitimate socially desirable profits).

❐

4

Business Policy in Foreign Collaboration

Collaboration with foreign companies has been found to have special appeal as a growth strategy particularly in developing countries. Depending on the purpose in view, such collaborations may be classified as: Managerial, Technical and Financial. There are many advantages which a firm in the host country can derive from the collaboration deal:

1. Improving competitive abilities for domestic and export marketing;
2. Enlarging the scale of operations and reducing costs;
3. Developing indigenous production of components and spare parts;
4. Upgradation of existing technology or introduction of advanced technology, acquiring technical know-how, and facilitating transfer of technology;
5. Fostering cultural changes with respect to work ethos, attitude towards discipline, etc.;
6. Securing foreign equity investment as a part of risk capital and enhancing the potential ability to raise necessary funds from the domestic capital market;
7. Deriving the benefits of import substitution and increased foreign exchange earning;
8. Developing the brand image of products more quickly.

Benefits which may accrue to the foreign collaborators are:

1. Return on financial outlay;
2. Earnings by way of royalty and fees for technological collaboration, supply of drawings and documents technical and managerial know-how;
3. Tax benefits derived in low-tax host countries. Royalties, technical fees, and service charges are taxed at a lower rate than profits;
4. Market expansion in countries restricting hard currency imports.

Examples of Foreign Collaborations in India

The growth of many enterprises in India is attributable to the strategy of foreign collaboration. In recent years, a number of companies have decided to join hands with foreign companies providing for technical financial and managerial collaboration. Some of these are mentioned below:

Maruti Udyog tie up with Suzuki of Japan for the manufacture of passenger cars and vans;

Technical collaboration of Nirup Synchrome Ltd., with Acna Chimica Organica S.P A., a division of Montedison, Italy, for the manufacture of synthetic dyes;

Hindustan Teleprinters Ltd., tie up with Olivetti of Italy to make electro-mechanical teleprinters and electric typewriters. Financial and technical collaboration of TISCO. UK promoting Tata Robins-Fraser Ltd., a company manufacturing material handling equipments of various kinds and undertaking 'system contracts' for such equipments.

Financial and technical collaboration of Bajaj Tempo Ltd., with West German Daimler-Benz AG;

Joint ventures promoted during the last four years by DCM, Hyderabad Allwyn, Punjab Tractors, and Eicher Motors in collaboration with Japanese companies—Toyota, Nissan, Mazda, and Missubishi respectively, to manufacture light commercial vehicles;

Technical collaboration of Noduran Founders Maharashtra Ltd., with SKF-GISAG of East Germany (GDR).

In addition to this 'orientation' of foreign collaborations, they also suffered from a number of other disadvantages.

1. The practice of multiple collaborations led to the introduction of standards of various countries (in raw materials, spare parts, designs, specifications, and even terms of measurement) into the Indian industry even for very similar products or within the same firm. This multiplicity led to large inventory accumulation and uneconomic locking up of working capital. It also hindered standardisation and variety reduction which are so essential for raising industrial productivity;

2. Foreign collaborations have helped the growth of monopolies and concentration. They joined hands with the big business houses and the latter were only too eager to enter into understanding with them since the presence of foreign links often conferred certain strategic advantages (patent, resources, foreign exchange, etc.) enabling the big business houses to diversify and expand;

3. The government permitted multiple collaborations, *i.e.* repetitive import of the same or similar technology. This resulted in repetitive payments without additing to the stock of technical knowledge in the country;

4. The most important part related to the presence of various restrictive clauses in the agreements. Some restrictions imposed were: *(i)* the technology cannot be passed on to anyone else, in some cases even after the expiry of the

agreement; *(ii)* manufacturing is to be carried out according to the specifications laid down by the collaborator and no local adaptations can be made; *(iii)* control over overseas purchase was exercised through the provision that it had to be made directly or indirectly through the collaborator; *(iv)* production was tightly controlled at times through the posting of foreign technicians; *(v)* controls over the pricing and marketing of the products were exercised by requiring that a part of the production was to be sold to the collaborator's subsidiary in India at a fixed commission or that specified firms were to be made the sole selling agents; and *(vi)* right to export was also restricted by provision that exports could be done only to specific countries or on certain preconditions.

5. The terms of agreements were mostly weighted in favour of the foreign collaborators and were against Indian interests. This arose on account of the lack of bargaining power in the Indian side and the government's eagerness to acquire foreign participation in the face of foreign exchange shortage;

6. The terms of payment were also drawn up so as to squeeze out the maximum payment under one head or other. Generally 5 per cent of the annual turnover for 10 years as royalty plus 5 per cent of the imported plant cost as technical fees in the case of royality-cum-technical fees, or 10 per cent of the issued capital as lumpsum payment for technical fees alone, were the limits of official policy. However, these tended to become routine;

7. Since the responsibility of specification and supply of equipment was entrusted to the foreign collaborators, there was close tie-up between the designers and suppliers resulting not only in price mark-up but also in over-import of equipment. Sometimes equipments were imported even when they were available locally, sometimes they remained idle for want of spares.

REGULATORY CONDITIONS GOVERNING THE SETTING UP OR INDIAN JOINT VENTURE ABROAD

(A) Formation of a limited company is a must for participation in a joint venture abroad; only corporate bodies are allowed such participation as per the Guidelines of the Government of India.

Under Sec. 27 of the Foreign Exchange Regulation Act, 1973 (FERA) approval is required to be obtained for the proposed venture *(a)* from the Ministry of Commerce, GOI, in Case of industrial joint ventures, *(b)* from the Ministry of Finance (Deptt. of Economic Affairs) in the case of non-industrial joint ventures.

After approval of the Ministry concerned a formal approval for the project is to be obtained from the Reserve Bank of India (Exchange Control Deptt.) Application for this purpose should be accompanied by: *(i)* Copies of the application with annexures submitted to the Ministry and approval received; *(ii)* Copy of the project/feasibility study report of the project: and *(iii)* Copies of the Memorandum and Articles of Association as well as of the Certificate of Registration of the overseas joint venture company.

Also under Sec. 27 of FERA, permission must be obtained by Indian residents to accept appointment as Directors on the Board of the joint venture company, for which application has to be made to the Ministry of Finance (Deptt. of Economic Affairs). Approval is generally given for a period of two years, which may be renewed on application. The permission so granted is to be submitted for approval of the Reserve Bank of India.

(B) The joint venture agreement finalised and executed on consultation with the solicitors should be submitted to the Ministry of Commerce for approval: and a copy of the agreement, as approved by the Ministry, submitted to the concerned office of the Reserve Bank.

(C) For entitlement of deduction of certain payments received from the overseas joint venture company u/s 80-O of the Income Tax Act, 1961, an application in the prescribed form along with the copy of joint venture agreement has to be submitted to the Central Broad of Direct Taxes, New Delhi, on or before the last day of October of the relevant assessment year.

(D) Prior approval has to be obtained front the Ministry of Industry (Deptt. of Company Affairs) for investment in the shares of the overseas joint venture company under Sec. 372 (4) of the Companies Act. The time specified in the approval for such investment must be adhered to, and if it is likely to be delayed suitable extension of times should be applied.

(E) Permission for export of machinery to the joint venture company against equity participation has to be obtained from the Commerce Ministry. On application .giving details of each item of such machinery including FOB value in Indian Rupees price in foreign currency break up of FOB value against a lakh shares will be issued by the joint venture company and the balance value if any, to be received by the Indian company.

(F) Registration with the related Export Promotion Council to avail of export incentive, excise duty concession, etc., and enrolment with the Regional JCCI & E for cash compensatory support and REP licence the also necessary.

(G) Half yearly progress reports have to be submitted to the Ministry of Commerce till the project is fully implemented and a copy of the same submitted to the RBI.

(H) After the project is fully implemented, annual performance report in the prescribed format is to be submitted every year to the Ministry of Commerce together with the copy of audited Balance Sheet and Profit and Loss Account of the joint-venture company, and a copy of the report with annexures is to be sent to RBI.

INDIAN GOVT. POLICY ON FOREIGN COLLABORATION

The inflow of foreign private investment and the import of foreign technology have been subject to Government regulation in most developing countries. This has been so essentially for two reasons.

(A) To ensure industrial growth in conformity with national priorities. The contribution of foreign capital and foreign technical collaboration in different respects having been found to be of significance also prompted governments in third world countries to be less enthusiastic about foreign participation. Indian Government policy in this respect has changed over time.

(B) To prevent the continuation and emergence of foreign vested interests.

The regulatory framework and Government policy with respect to foreign investment and collaboration were spelt out in July 1980 along with the industrial policy statement presented in Parliament. The policy was modified in May 1990, and a new policy initiative announced in July 1980.

Policy Statement, July 1980

Advanced Technology for Economics of Scale: In a number of cases Indian industry has not been able to compete in markets abroad because the scale of output which is related to the level of domestic demand is too small to give them the advantage of modem technology and economies of scale. In cases where a larger production base would increase the competitiveness of Indian industry abroad, Government will consider favourably the induction of advanced technology, and will permit creation of capcity large enough to make it competitive in world fiarkets.Provided substantial exports are likely. The purpose of introducing such a policy would be not only to encourage exports but also to enable industry to produce better quality products at lower cost which will ultimately benefit the consumer in terms of price and quality.

The Indian industry must earmark substantial resources for R & D to constantly update technologies with a view to optional utilisation of scarce resources, better service to the consumer achieving greater exports. We also have to lay greater emphasis on bringing the benefit of the latest R & D to the medium and small Units.

There has already been considerable simplification and streamlining of licensing procedures. Nevertheless, there is scope for further improvement in reducing the period of time taken for disposal of applications for the creation of new capacities, proposals for substantial expansion and the production of new items. It is proposed to speed up the processes of examination and decision-making and also to examine the possibilities of further rationalisation and simplification of the system of industrial licensing.

The industries where no foreign collaboration, is considered necessary are specified. The import of technology may be considered by Government even in these fields if they conform to the guidelines referred to in the statement on Industrial Policy.

Government will take active measures to facilitate the transfer of technology from efficiently operating units to new units. Companies which have well established R & D organisations, and have demonstrated their ability to absorb, adapt and disseminate Modern technology will be permitted to import such technology, as will increase their efficiency and cost effectiveness. This will not only lead to saving of foreign exchange but would also ensure self-sufficiency and higher exchange earnings.

Guidelines for Approval. The following are some of the important guidelines for approval of proposals for foreign collaboration (financial and or technical):

1. ***Equity Participation.*** Government's policy towards permitting foreign equity participation will continue to be selective. Such participation has to be justified having regard to factors such as the priority of the industry, the nature of the technology involved, whether it will enable or promote exports which may not otherwise take place, and the alternative terms available for securing the same or similar technological transfer. The ceiling for foreign equity participation is 40 per cent although exceptions can be considered on merit.

   The foreign share capital should be by way of cash without being linked to tied imports of machinery and equipment or to payment for know-blow, trade marks, brand names, etc.

   Keeping in view the need to provide additional facilities to promote investment in the country from Oil Exporting, Developing countries, which have large financial resources but not the type of technology that the country needs, it base been decided that foreign proposals from these countries need not be associated with transfer of technology from the equity holders, and that such investment may be of a portfolio nature. Within the framework of the investment policy of the Government, it has been decided to provide the following facilities:

   (a) Investment of the aforesaid pattern may be allowed in hotels.

   (b) Investment may also be allowed in new hospital projects and such hospitals should have adequate provision for outdoor and emergency medical service to the general public, and also for a minimum percentage of occupancy by Indian public.

   (c) Loans should also be allowed to be raised abroad for such joint ventures provided the terms are reasonable.

(d) Investment from oil-exporting developing countries may be permitted in new companies even if it is in the nature of portfolio investment.

(e) Such investments should not exceed 40 per cent in the equity.

(f) The new companies should be export-oriented or should undertake manufacturing activities covered under Appendix-I of the press Note of 2nd February, 1973.

2. ***Renewal of Collaboration Agreement.*** Applications for extension of collaboration agreements are scrutinised carefully and extensions are agreed to only in those cases where Government is satisfied that there is need for them. Application for extension may be considered in the following circumstances:

(a) If the collaboration agreement involves the manufacture of a large number of items and the Indian party could start manufacturing some of the items only at a later stage. In such cases, extension is granted only in respect of these few items the manufacture of which started later;

(b) If the item of manufacture is sophisticated and it is necessary that the period of collaboration should be extended for a short period to enable the Indian party to fully absorb the know-how;

(c) If it is felt that such extension would be in the interest of exports of the manufactured products. Even where extensions are considered and granted, every effort is made to reduce the rate of royalty payable, with regard to the nature of the product and the period of extension.

3. ***Technical Collaboration.*** Technical collaborations are considered on the basis of annual royalty payments, which are linked with the value of actual production. The percentage of royalty will depend on the nature of technology but should not ordinarily exceed 5 per cent. Royalty is calculated on the basis of ex-factory selling price of the product net of excise duties minus the cost of standard bought out components and landed cost of imported components. Royalty payments are subject to Indian taxes. Wherever appropriate, payment of a fixed amount of royalty per unit of production will be preferred.

   Lumpsum payments may also be considered in appropriate cases for the import of drawings, documentation and other forms of know-how. In deciding on the reasonableness of such payments, account will be taken of the value of production so that the lumpsum and the recurring royalty, if any, is an acceptable proportion of the value of production. Such payments will be subject to applicable Indian taxes. The lumpsum payments should be phased out as follows:

   1/3rd after agreement has been taken Oil record,

   1/3rd to be paid on the transfer of documentation, etc., and 1/3rd to be paid at the commencement of production or after completion of 48 months of the signing of the foreign collaboration agreement whichever is earlier.

Policy, May 1990

While making certain changes in the industrial licensing policy in May 1990, the government also announced certain decision with respect to foreign investment and collaborations with the object of attracting inflow of technology more effectively. Foreign investment up to 40 p.c. equity was decided to be allowed on an automatic basis. The landed value of imported capital goods in such cases was to be allowed up to 30 p.c. of the value of plant and machinery. As regards transfer of technology, if import of technology was considered essential they would be free to conclude an agreement with the foreign collaborator without obtaining any clearnance from the Government. Two conditions were laid down in that connection; *(i)* Royalty payment should not exceed 5 p.c. on domestic sales and 8 p.c. on exports; *(ii)* If lumpsum payment was involved in technology import, the proposal must be submitted for clearance lay Government, but decisions would be communicated to the entrepreneur within 30 days.

ACQUISITION OF TECHNOLOGY THROUGH FOREIGN COLLABORATION

Foreign technical collaboration may involve agreement for supply of technical know-how, engineering services in respect of specific projects, patent or trade mark agreement, and agreement for supply of plant, machinery and other equipment. The technology policy of the Government of India announced on 3rd January 1983 envisaged import of technology in selected areas for its efficient absorption and adaptation appropriate to national priorities and research. In accordance with this policy, acquisition of technical know-how or services is governed by the following principles:

(i) There shall be a firm commitment for absorption, adaptation and subsequent development of imported know-how through adequate investment in R and D by importers of technology.

(ii) The collaboration agreement should necessarily provide for horizontal transfer of technology.

(iii) The company importing technology trust built up its engineering and R and D centre to assimilate, update and indigenise the technology in defect improvements as required within the shortest possible time.

To give effect to the objectives underlying its technology policy, the Government passed the Research and Development Cess Act, 1986, and notified the Rules framed thereunder in October 1987 to be effective from 1st December 1987. The Act and. Rules provide for the levy and collection of a cess at the rate of 5% on all payments made for the import of technology with a view to encouraging the commercial application of indigenously developed technology and adapting imported technology wider domestic application. The cess is payable on payments for import of technology, including:

(i) Payments made towards the cost of drawings and designs, publications and services of technical personnel.

(ii) Payments made towards import of technical know-how approved by Central Government in terms of any foreign collaboration agreement.

(iii) Payments made to foreign collaborators or to any other person for or in connection with deportation of technical personnel to India in accordance with the approval granted by the Central Government or the Reserve Bank of India. If the technology package includes supply of plant and machinery, and acquisition of patent and trade marks, payment for the same will also be regarded as payment towards or in connection with import of technology and hence will be liable to the levy of cess.

HARMFUL EFFECT'S OF THE OPERATIONS OF MNCs ON INDIAN ECONOMY

The operations of MNCs open up the possibilities of interference in the industrial (and other) activities of the recipient country and are thus resented by the 'nationalist' thinkers. Their arguments against the operations of. MNCs can be summed up as follow:

1. **Payment of Dividends and Royalty.** A large sum of money flow out of the country in terms of payment of dividends, profits, royalties, technical fees and interest to the foreign investors. For instance, remittance made abroad by private sector companies stood at Rs. 72.26 crores in 1969-70. This rose to Rs. 398.9 crores in 1981-82 and further to Rs. 8135 crores.

It would be revealing to point out that Caltex which had a total investment of Rs. 16.92 crores in India, remitted profits, amounting to Rs. 43 crores in the period 1968-70. ESSO with a total investment of Rs. 29.58 crores remitted profits totaling Rs. 83 crores during the same period.

2. **Political Interference.** Because of their immense financial technical power, the MNCs have gained the necessary strength to influence the decision making processes in underdeveloped countries. Though they do help in transferring technology to underdeveloped countries, it has been often found that models and patterns of industrial development and technologies transferred are not in harmony with the interests of the host countries. The governments of underdeveloped countries have also felt threatened by the direct and indirect interference of MNCs in their internal affairs. The autonomy and sovereignty of the host countries is in danger. Because of these reasons, the governments of various countries have sought to restrict the activities of MNCs in their economies through a battery of administrative controls and legal provisions.

3. **Technology Transfer not Necessarily Conducive to Development.** As far as transfer of technology to underdeveloped countries is concerned, the behaviour pattern of MNCs reveals that they do not engage in R and D activities within the underdeveloped countries. Their R and D efforts are concentrated in laboratories in the home country or in other industrialised countries. Though R and D activities continue to be centralized in the parent country, the host countries have to bear the bulk of their costs since the affiliates of the MNCs in these countries remit payments on this account generally in relation to their sales volume. Such payments by the affiliates are generally over and above those remitted in the form of royalties and technical fees to the parent firm. The satisfaction expressed on technology transfer is partly misconceived also on account

of the fact that MNCs which generally command a semi-monopolistic position in their product lines do not transfer their first-line or most advanced technology until foreign firms compel them to do so. In many cases, the technology transferred is of a capital-intensive nature which is not useful from the point of view of a labour surplus economy. In fact, continued insistence on the import of such technology can have serious consequences for the economy of the host country since unemployment will increase. Also, market will fail to grow and this constraint alone would suffice to restrain the rate of growth from increasing.

4. **Distortion of Economic Structure.** MNCs can inflict heavy damage on the host country in various forms such as suppression of domestic entrepreneurship, extension of oligopolistic practices (such as unnecessary product differentiation, heavy advertising, or excessive profit taking), supplying the economy with unsuitable technology and unsuitable products, worsening of income distribution by distorting the production structure to meet the requirements of high-income elites, etc. Modern Marxist economists (Paul Baran, for example) argue that foreign investment (especially through multinational corporations) opens up the doors of 'neoimperialism' and 'exploitation'.

CONCESSIONS GRANTED BY GOVT. TO FOREIGN COLLBORATION

Policy Initiative, July 1991

As a part of the changes in industrial policy announced on 24 July 1991, the Government also initiated changes in its policy relating to foreign investment and foreign collaboration agreements. In sum the decisions are as follows:

1. In respect of industries other than the high priority industries, automatic permission would be given subject to the same guidelines as above if no free foreign exchange is required for any payments.

2. All other proposals will need specific approval under the general procedures in force.

3. No permission would be necessary for hiring of foreign technicians, foreign testing of indigeneously developed technologies. Payment may be made from blanket permits or free foreign exchange according to RBI guidelines.

4. To provide access to international markets, majority of foreign equity holding up to 51 p.c. equity would be allowed for trading companies primarily engaged in export activities. While the thrust would be on export activities, such trading houses shall be at par with domestic trading and export houses in accordance with the Import-Export policy.

5. Automatic permission would be given for foreign technology agreements in high priority industries up to a lumpsum payment of Rs. 1 crore, 5 p.c. royalty for domestic sales and 8 p.c. for exports, to total payment of 8 p.c. of sales over a 10 year period from date of agreement or 7 years from commencement of production. The prescribed royalty rates are net of taxes and would be calculated according to standard procedures.

6. Approval would be given for direct foreign investment upto 51 p.c. foreign equity in high priority industries There shall be no bottlenecks of any kind in this process. Such clearance would be available if foreign equity covers the foreign exchange requirement for imported capital goods.

7. While the import of components, raw materials and intermediate goods, and payment of know how fees and royalties would be governed by the general policy applicable to other domestic units, the payment of dividends would be monitored through the Reserve Bank of India so as to ensure that outflows on account of dividend payments are balanced by export earnings over a period of time.

8. Other foreign equity proposals, including proposals involving 51 p.c. foreign equity which do not meet the criteria under *(i)* above, will continue to need prior clearance. Foreign equity proposals need not necessarily be accompanied by foreign technology agreements.

FOREIGN COLLABORATION AND MNCs

A common form of MNC participation in Indian industry is through entering into collaboration with Indian industrialists. Foreign collaboration agreements are made between Indian companies and foreign parties, involving sale of technology, as well as use of foreign brand names for the final products. The enormity of Foreign collaborations entered into by the Indian companies would be clear from the fact that in nearly all of the new industries in the large or medium size group, privately or publicly owned, set up after independence, some collaboration agreement was present. Trends of liberalisation in the 1980s' gave substantial spurt to foreign collaborations. This would be clear from the fact that the annual average number of foreign collaboration approvals by the Government witnessed a big jump from 319 during the period 1975 to 1980 to over 771 between 1981 and 1988. In fact, of the total 12,760 foreign collaboration agreements approved in 40 years between 1948 and 1988. As many as 6,165 (*i.e.* 48.3 per cent) have been approved during the eight years between 1981 and 1988. This is a direct result of the liberal policy on technology imports being pursued by the government in recent years.

While there have been collaboration agreements with a number of countries, the largest number of collaborations has been with the U.S.A. followed by the West Germany and the U.K. In recent years there has been a spurt in collaboration agreements with Japan. Of the total of 6,165 collaborations approved between 1981 and 1988, the USA accounted for 1,245 followed by West Germany 997, the UK 963 and Japan 600. The other important countries are France (315), Switzerland (265), Italy (232), Sweden (155) and Neatherlands (130).

Study of these foreign collaborations reveals certain interesting results. Thus, a large number of agreements were concluded for the manufacture of products which were non-essential or which could be produced with help of local technology. These items included vaccum flasks, lipstick, toothpaste, cosmetics, brassiers, ice-cream, gin, beer, biscuits, dry batteries and readymade garments. Not only were collaborations granted for these products, they were often in multiple numbers and were renewed on expiry. Clearly such collaborations were often directed to serve the needs of high income groups and to take advantage of a foreign brand name.

Characteristics of Multinational Corporations

The MNCs have certain characteristics, among which the more important are as follows:

1. ***Giant Size.*** The assets and sales of MNCs run into billions of dollars and they also make supernormal profits. For example, the General Motors' yearly operating revenues exceed gross national product of all but a dozen or so countries. It has more than 40 subsidiaries in 26 countries, with its centralised decision-making apparatus being located in the United States. The IBM's physical assets are worth round 7 billion dollars. ITT has 708 subsidiaries in 67 countries on 6 continents. It is the biggest multinational, accounting for USA's one-third balance of payments. Such is the enormous size of MNCs.

2. ***International Operations.*** In such a corporation control resides in the hands of a single institution. But its interests and operations sprawl across national boundaries. An MNC operates through a parent corporation in the home country. It may assume the form of a branch or a subsidiary in the home country. If it is a branch, it acts for the parent corporation without any local capital or management assistance. If it is a subsiiliary, the majority control is still exercised by the foreign parent company, although it is incorporated in the home country. The foreign control

may range anywhere between the minimum of 51 per cent to the full 100 per cent. An MNC thus combines ownership with control The branches and subsidiaries of an MNC operate under the united control of the parent company.

3. ***Spontaneous Evolution.*** MNCs usually grow in a spontaneous and unconscious manner. Very often they develop through creeping incrementalism. Many films have become international by accident. At times, firms have also established subsidiaries abroad due to wage differentials and better opportunities prevailing in the home country.

4. ***Oligopolistic Structure.*** Through the process of merger- and takeover, etc., in course of time an MNC acquires awesome power. This coupled with its giant size make it oligopolistic in character.

5. ***Collective Transfer of Resources.*** An MNC facilitates a multilateral transfer of resources. Usually this transfer takes place in the form of a "package" which includes technical know-how, equipments and machinery, raw materials, finished product, managerial services, and so on. MNCs are composed of a complex of wodely varied modern technology ranging from protraction and marketing to management and finance.

Regulation or Multinational Corporations

In view of that fact the MNCs do possess a potential that can be gainfully exploited, most of the underdeveloped economics have chosen to regulate their activities rather than to dispense with them altogether.

1. The government may allow collaboration in certain selected industries or certain selected regions where the operations of MNC is felt highly suitable.
2. The threat of nationalisation is an effective tool of regulation. Although nationalisation should be resorted to only its the

extreme situations, the very fact that it on be exercised makes the corporations act in a disciplined manner.

3. The host country may lay down certain export criteria.
4. A multi-tax system may be followed by the government. The MNCs be taxed at a higher rate.
5. MNCs may be allowed to invest for specific periods. Thus, after a certain period of time restrictions may be imposed on foreign holdings, or there may be provision for gradual disinvestment.

Finally, MNCs may be asked to carry out a minimum fixed share of their total research and development activities within the host countries.

Reasons for the growth of multinationals are manifold, the important ones being as follows:

1. **Technological Superiorities.** The main reason why MNCs have been encouraged by the underdeveloped countries to participate in their industrial development is on account of the technological superiorities which these firms possess as compared to national companies. The underdeveloped countries regard transfer of technology from MNCs useful on account of the following reasons: *(a)* Industrialization represents the most important way out of underdevelopment and the resources of these countries are insufficient to sustain the industrial progress on their own; *(b)* Local manpower rematerials local capital equipment etc. have to be optimally exploited and these countries are unable to accomplish this; *(c)* Depending totally on local companies would require heavy imports of raw materials capital equipment machinery and technical knowledge whereas MNCs bring these on their own; and *(d)* The underdeveloped countries have to face stiff competition for selling their products in international markets. Unless their goods meet

international standards and quality specifications, they cannot sell. MNCs help them in producing such goods.

2. **Product Innovations.** MNCs have Research Development Departments engaged in the task of developing new products and superior designs of existing products. Therefore their production opportunities are far greater as compared to national companies.

3. **Marketing Superiorities.** A multinational firm enjoys a number of marketing superiorities over the national firms: *(a)* It possesses a more reliable and uptodate market information system; *(b)* It enjoys market reputation and faces less difficulty in selling its products; *(c)* It adopts more effective advertising and sales promotion techniques; and *(d)* It has efficient warehousing facilities due to lower inventory requirements.

4. **Financial Superiorties.** A multinational firm enjoys the following financial superiorities over the national firm: *(a)* It has change financial resources with which it can easily turn all circumstances in its favour; *(b)* It maintains a high level of funds utilization by generating funds in one country and using them in another; *(c)* It has easier access to external capital markets; and *(d)* Because of its international reputation it is able to raise more international resources. Even investors and banks of the host country are eager to invest in it.

5. **Expansion of Market Territory.** As the operations of a large-sized firm expand and as its international image builds up it seeks more and more extension of its activities beyond the physical boundaries of the country in which it is incorporated.

FOREIGN COLLABORATION IN FOREIGN TRADE

Foreign trade or international trade refers to the exchange of goods and services between two nations. The whole volume of foreign trade of a country consists of its purchases from, and sales to, other countries during a particular period. Purchase of goods from a foreign country is known as 'import trade' and sale of goods to another country is known as 'export trade'. But when goods are imported from a country with the objective of exporting them to some other country, it is known as '*entrepot trade*'.

Foreign trade can be bilateral or multilateral. Where trade is between any two nations, it is bilateral. Foreign trade is multilateral when a country buys from and sells to more than one country. Foreign trade is more complicated as compared to the internal trade of a country. An important reason for this is that each country has it's own currency system and the currency of one country is not acceptable in another country. Therefore, foreign trade invo!ves the exchange of currency first and the exchange of goods afterwards. There are many difficulties in the foreign trade because of geographical distance, physical barriers and lack of personal contacts between exporters and importers. Moreover, foreign trade is also subject to certain restrictions by the Government of the country concerned. No trader is free to export or import goods without the prior permission of the Government.

ADVANTAGES OF FOREIGN TRADE

Foreign Trade offers the following advantages:

(a) Better Use of Resources. Foreign trade facilitates international division of labour and specialisation. It permits different countries of the world to manufacture or produce those products which they can manufacture or produce economically. It reduces waste of resources in the production of uneconomical goods.

(b) Equalisation of Prices Between Countries. Foreign trade leads to enqualise the prices of various commodities throughout the world. Whenever the prices of commodity are rising in a country, it can increase the level of its import to check the rise in prices. Similarly, a commodity in abundance can be exported to avoid situation of glut in which the commodity will fetch an unreasonably low price.

(c) Economic Growth. Foreign trade helps in the growth of under-developed or developing economies. Such countries can import machines and equipments, technical know-how, etc., from the developed countries and utilise them to exploit their natural resources.

(d) Economies of Large Scale. Because of specialisation brought about by foreign trade, economies of large scale can be achieved. Foreign trade helps in carrying production or manufacture not only for home consumption but also for external consumption. This generates several economies of large scale production.

(e) Higher Standard of Living. Most of the countries do not have resources to produce everything they require. In the absence of foreign trade, the citizens of a country would not be able to consume those products which are not produced there. Foreign trade provides such products and increases their standard of living.

(f) Employment. Foreign trade facilitates the growth of industries engaged in manufacturing goods for export purposes. This generates greater employment.

(g) International Brotherhood. Because of foreign trade, different countries are dependent upon one another. Each country can have access to the goods that it does not produce itself. Similarly, a country with surplus of certain goods can make them available to the countries facing their shortage. This promotes goodwill and cordial relation among various nations.

PROBLEMS OF FOREIGN TRADE

Foreign trade gives birth to a large number of problems in the exchange of commodities between different nations. Some of the important problems are as under:

(a) Currency. Every country has its own currency system and the currency of one country is not in circulation in the other country. This creates a problem in the foreign trade. The traders have to fix the rate of exchange between two currencies before they enter into any foreign trade transaction.

(b) Credit Worthiness of Dealers. The value of goods involved in foreign trade in fairly high. Every exporter is interested to know the credit worthiness of the importer and every importer wants to know reliability of the exporter. It takes a long time to verify from references given by the parties to the foreign trade transactions.

(c) Language. Each country has its own language and also often its own script this creates a problem of communication between dealers of different countries knowing different languages.

(d) Rules and Regulations. Every country has imposed restrictions in the import and export of goods to protect its economic and political interests. These restrictions are created by various laws, regulations and customs formalities enforced by the governments of different countries.

(e) Time Lag. Since there is a wide gap between the time the goods are despatched by the exporter and the time when they are received and paid for by the importer the capital of the exporter is blocked for along period.

(f) Transport and Risk. Because of distance between the countries and the physical barrier, there is a problem of transportation of the good. The risk to the goods during transit is also higher.

EXPORT TRADE PROCEDURE

In India exports are regulated by the Central Government under the provisions of the Imports and Exports Control Act, 1947. The Central Government announces rules and regulations and procedures to be valid for export of goods from time to time. The general procedure for exporting the goods involves the following steps:

1. Receipt of Enquiry. The first step in the export trade is the receipt of an enquiry from an importer or his agent by the exporter. An enquiry is a request by a prospective purchaser regarding price, quantity and quality of goods which he intends to purchase: The reply of such an enquiry is in the form of quotation. Both enquiry and quotation should contain the full details of the goods required, their description, catalogue number, Sizes, rates or other distinguishing features, the number or quantity, time and method of delivery, method of packing, and in case of a quotation the price and terms of sale.

2. Enquiry about Credit. After accepting the order of the importer the exporter will proceed to find out the credit-worthiness of the importer. The exporter will like to satisfy himself about the credit other buyer from various sources before despatching him the goods. Generally, the exporter asks the importer to send a letter of credit to him. The importer will open an account with his banker and get a letter of credit in favour of the exporter of the banker of the exporter.

3. Receipt of Order. When the importer accept a quotation he will place an order with the exporter either directly or through some specialised agency known as indent house. The order or indent contains the importers instructions concerning the goods to be exported. It gives full particulars of goods with regard to size, quality, shipment required, etc., and also states the price, the importer is willing to pay. An indent may be open or close. An open indent leaves the selection of goods to the agent while a close indent gives full particulars of the goods required.

4. Obtaining the Licence. As said earlier exports are subjects to the provisions of Imports and Export Control Act, 1947. In exercise of the power granted by the Act, the Central Government issues from time to time, an export control order bringing various items under control. The goods covered by such order cannot be exported unless an export licence is secured, The goods liable to export control are listed in the schedule attached to the Export Control Order, 1962 issued by the Central Government.

In order to obtain export licence, the exporter has to apply to the controller of export in a prescribed form. He has also to submit a challan to be obtained from a Government Treasury on payment of the prescribed free under the head export licence fee and an income tax verification declaring that the exporter is paying income tax regularly. After the controller of exports is satisfied, the exporter will be issued an export certificate on licence which is normally valid for a period of three months from the date of issue.

5. Compliance with the Exchange Regulations. The exporter has to make a declaration that he, will surrender the foreign exchange to the extent of full value of the export of goods to the Reserve Bank of India within a prescribed period. This declarations necessary under the Foreign Exchange Regulations Act, 1947. A prescribed form of declaration is used for this purpose. The exporter should specify the full particulars of the value of the goods, method by which payment is expected and name of the dealer in the foreign exchange through whom the documents are to be negotiated.

6. Securing the Shipping Order. The exporter has to enter into an agreement with a shipping company or its agent for hiring space in a ship for transporting the goods to the importer. The shipping company will give a shipping order which contains instructions to the. Captain of the ship to receive the specified quantity of goods from the exporter mentioned therein. Sometimes the consignment is very big the exporter may charter a whole ship or a major part of ship. Such all agreement is known as a Charter Party. The Charter Party may be of two types—Voyage Charter Party and Time Charter Party.

7. Fixation of Exchange Rate. The rate at which the currency of one country is exchanged for the currency of another country is called the exchange rate. The exchange rate keeps on fluctuating. Since there is a good time gap between the despatch of goods by exporter and the receipt of payment, it is necessary that the exchange rate at which the payment would be made by the importer should be fixed before hand so that variations in the exchange rate do not affect adversely the interest of either the importer or the exporter.

8. Packing ana Marking. Packing may be under taken by the exporter or by a firm of packing agents. It is an extremely part of the export procedure and should receive careful attention of the exporter. While packing the goods, it should be ensured that all the instructions given by the importer in this regard are strictly followed. Packages should not be too bulky to be handled. A package must be compact so that the cargo occupies the minimum space and facilitates convenient handling. It should be noted that the shipping company charges freight not only for the weight of the cargo but also the space occupied. So care should be taken to pack the maximum of cargo in the minimum of space. Packing should also ensure safety of the goods during the process of handling and transportation.

9. Mate's Receipt. Goods may be delivered to the dock or the ship. When delivery is made to the dock, a dock receipt or wharfinger receipt is issued to the exporter. But when the goods are directly handed over to the Captain of the ship or his assistant, called the 'Mate' the exporter will get a Mate's Receipt. The exporter has to hand over a copy of the shipping bill and the shipping order to the Captain of the ship who will inspect the goods and will issue a clean receipt if he is satisfied with the packing of the goods. If the packing is defective, the Captain of the ship issues a receipt to the exporter which will specify the defect in packing.

10. Customs Formalities. The exporter has to observe certain customs formalities before the goods can leave the country. He has to prepare the shipping bill in triplicate and an application to export in duplicate. The shipping bill is a printed form in which the exporter is required to mention his name, description of goods, name of the ship which is to carry goods, the port of destination and the name of the importer it is available from the customs office. There are different forms for different classes of goods, namely, free goods, dutiable goods and bonded goods. There is also a specified form of application to export which is available with the Landing and Shipping Dues Office of the Port Trust. The exporter presents both the forms to the Landing and Shipping Dues Office. He also pays the shipping charges that he is called upon to pay. The shipping bill and a copy of the application to export duly endorsed for payment for shipping charges are returned to the exporter who will present them to the customs office. The customs authorities scrutinise the documents and ask the exporter to pay the duty, if any. Two copies of the shipping bill are returned to the exporter.

11. Bill of Lading. A Bill of lading is a document by which the shipping company acknowledges the receipt of goods expected to be carried in its ship to the port of destination specified therein in return for the payment of freight. It serves three purposes. Firstly, it is a quasi negotiable documents of title to the goods. It can be transferred to another person by endorsement and delivery. Secondly, it acknowledges receipt of goods on board. Thirdly, it is an evidence of the terms of contract of affreightment between the shipper and the ship owner. The bill of lading is issued by the shipping company on presentation of the mate's receipt at the shipping company's office. If the Mate's Receipt contains any remark regarding any defect in the packing of the goods, the same is noted in the bill of lading.

12. Certificate of Origin. As the name implies the certificate indicates the origin of the exports and is issued by a Trade Consul or some other authorised persons or by the Secretary of a Chamber of Commerce. This certificate is required for purpose of calculation of import duties. Some countries give preferential treatment of certain friendly nations in the matter of payment of customs duties under trade agreements.

13. Insurance. Before the goods are despatched, they are insured against sea peril. The insurance policy is also to be sent to the importer along with the bill of lading. Generally, the shipping companies refuse to carry the goods unless they are insured and the commercial banks also refuse to discount the documentary bills of exchange unless they are accompanied by the insurance policies.

The marine policy is a document setting out the contract for insuring the goods against the perils of sea. It can be made out in favour of one person and may be assigned to another by simple endorsement and delivery.

14. Invoice and Consular Invoice. The exporter prepares invoice in triplicate showing the quantity, quality, description and price of the goods and sends two copies to the importer. The invoice is prepared according to the terms and conditions of the agreement between the exporter and the importer. For instance, if the goods are sold on C.I.F. basis, no separate mention will be made regarding the insurance and freight charges paid by the exporter. The value of the goods itself includes these charges. The exporter is also required to obtain the Consular Invoice for the purpose of clearance of goods at the port of destination. The Consular Invoice is issued by the Trade Consul of the importing country stationed in the exporting country. The Consular Invoice is also sent to the importer. It is very useful particularly when the goods are subject to ad valorem duty, *i.e.*, duty on the basis of value of goods.

15. Securing Payment. When the shipment has been despatched, the exporter takes steps to secure payment from the importer. He can secure payment in either of the following three methods. First, the exporter can draw the bill of exchange on the importer, ordering payment to be made to the exporter's order to his bank, attach to it the bill of lading, marine insurance policy, invoice, certificate of origin and other documents. Such a bill is known as 'documentary bill' and is handed over to the exporter's bank for collection. The bank will send the bill and other documents to its branch or agent in the importer's country for presenting it to the importer. If the bill is marked D/A (Documents against Acceptance), documents will be handed over to the importer or his bank immediately after the acceptance of the bill by the importer or his bank.

Second, the exporter can discount the documentary bill of exchange with a bank. For this purpose, he will have to sign a letter of hypothecation and give it to the bank. The letter of hypo the cation entitles the bank to take delivery of the goods and dispose them of in case the importer fails to make payment or take delivery of the documents.

❐

5

Decision Making in Business

Etymologically, the verb decide is derived from the Latin prefix 'de' meaning 'off, and the word 'caedo', meaning 'to cut'. In this sense, some cognitive process cuts off as preferred, selects, a particular alternative action among a set of possible alternatives. In decision-making, totality of human mind is involved. Therefore, three aspects of human behaviour are involved in decision-making.

(a) affectation, the aspects of the mind identified with emotion, feeling mood, and temperament. Based on these facts, decision-making has been defined as 'a conscious and human process, involving both individual and social phenomena, based upon factual and value premises, which concludes with a choise of one behavioural activity from among one or more aliternatives with the intention of moving toward some state of affairs.' Thus decision-making involves, essentially, the selection from among several alternatives.

(b) conation, the action of the mind implied by such words as 'willing' 'desire', and aversion.

(c) cognition, those activities of the mind associated with knowledge.

The definition of decision has following characteristics:

1. Decision-making involves a certain commitment. This commitment may be for short run or long run depending upon the type of decision.

2. It also involves the evaluation of available alternatives because only throuh this evaluation one can know the best alternative.

3. Decision involves rationality because through decisions, one tries to better one's happiness.
4. Decision is aimed at achieving the objectives of the organisation if it is made in organisational context.
5. Decision-making is a mental process because the final selection is made after thoughful consideration.
6. Decision-making is a process of selection and the aim is to select the best alternative.

Decision making is a *process of selection* from a set of *alternative courses of action* which is thought to fulfil the objective of the decision problem *more satisfactorily than others*. It is a course of action which is consciously chosen for achieving a desired result. To state this in terms of managerial decision making, it is an act of choice wherein a manager selects a particular course of action from the available alternatives in a given situation. Managerial decision making involves establishing goals, defining tasks, searching for alternatives and developing plans in order to find the answer to the decision problem. The process of *decision making* involves following characteristics:

1. It always has a purpose. Keeping this in view, there may just be a decision not to decide.
2. It is a process of choosing a course of action from among the alternative course of action from among the alternative courses of action.
3. It is always related to the situation. A manager may take one decision in a particular set of circumstances and another in a different set of circumstances.
4. It is the end process proceeded by deliberation and reasoning i.e., it is a rational process.
5. It is a human process involving to a great extent the application of *intellectual* abilities. And hence subjective values may also go in decision-making process.

Types of Decisions

There are various ways of classifying decisions in an organisation. These bases give five sets of decisions.

A. Individual and Group Decisions. The classification is based on the basis of persons involved in the decision-making process. Individual decisions are taken by a single individual. These are taken in the context of routine of programmed decisions where the analysis of various variables is simple and for which broad policies are already provided. Sometimes, important decisions are taken by single individual also.

Group decisions are taken by a group constituted for this specific purpose or by a standing committee. These decisions are generally very important for the organisation. Group decisions have certain positive value such as greater participation of individuals and quality in decisions, and certain negative values such as delay in decision-making process and difficulty in fixing the responsibility of decisions.

B. Programmed and Non-Programmed Decisions. Such classification of decisions is made on the basis of the use of operations research. Prgrammed decisions are normally of repetitive nature and are taken within the broad policy structure. These generally have short-run impact and are taken by lower level managers, such as, granting leave to an employee, purchase of materials in normal routine, etc.

Non-programmed decisions are of non-repetitive nature. The necessity of such decisions arises because of some specific circumstances. Thus, these are very important for the organisation, such as, opening of a new branch at a new place, introducing a new product in the market, etc.

C. Organisational and Personal Decisions. In an organisation, When an individual takes decisions as an executive for the organisation, these are known as organisational decisions. The authority for taking such decisions can be delegated from a superior to a subordinate. Such decisions affect organisational functioning directly.

An executive can take decisions about himself which are personal decisions normally affect personal life of the decisions-maker, though at many times they may affect organisation also, such as, leaving of the organisation by an individual. Decision-making power cannot be delegated to any one else in the case of personal decisions.

D. Policy and Operative Decisions. Policy decisions are taken by top management in the organisation which determines the basic policies. The policy decisions are very important and have long-term impact. These decision provide help in establishing the business such as deciding location of plant, volume of production, sale and purchase decisions, policy decisions regarding the employees, etc. Policy decisions are sometimes published as policy manual which become the basis for other operative decisions.

Operative decisions are related with the the day-to-day operation of the business. These are taken generally by middle and lower managers who are more closely related with the suervision of actual operations. These decisons may be written or otherwise.

E. Routine and Strategic Decisions. Routine decisions are taken in the context of day-to-day operation of the organisation. Mostly, they are of repetitive nature and related with the general functioning. They do not require much analysis and evaluation and can be made quickly. Authority for taking these decisions is generally delegated to lower levels in the organisation because these are taken within the broad context of policy prescribed in this respect.

Strategic decisions are those which are taken during the current time period, but whose primary effect is felt during some future period. Strategic decisions affect organisational structures, objectives, facilities, and finances. These decisions are mostly non repetitive in nature. Since they have fundamental effects on the organisation, they are taken careful analysis and evaluation of various alternatives. These decisions are taken compartively at higher level of management.

IMPORTANCE OF DECISION MAKING

"Whatever a manager does, he does through decision making", Peter Drucker. Decision making lies deeply embedded in the process of management. It is the foremost function of the manager. The manager has to take a decision before acting. Whether consciously or unconsciously, every manager is engaged in decision making or determining what is to be done. Some of the decisions are of routine nature and it might be that the manager does not feel that he is taking decisions. Other decisions are of strategic nature which may require a lot of systematic and scientific analysis. Whatever may be the case, it cannot be denined that management is always deision making process-Decision making spreads over all the managerial function and covers all the areas of business. The management has to take a large number of decisions while performing its functions of planning, organising, staffing, directing and controlling. Decisions making involves thinking and deciding before doing and is a part of every managerial function. In fact, the very determination of objectives, policies programmes, strategies, etc. of the enterprise is a decision making process.

Management of an enterprise has to take a series of decisions every day. Let us-take the case of a textile mill which has decided to manufacture shirt pieces. Deciding to manufacture shirt pieces is not an insolated decision, it will be followed by many other decisions such as : What design, size, weight, colour and texture of the shirt piece wil be? what materials are to be used? From where and when to purchase the materials? When will the production process start? How will the final product be stored and marketed? What will be its sale price? All these questions are to be answered in order to implement the decision of initiating production of shirt pieces. In addition to the above listed decisions, management may be confronted with a large number of decision problems before the goods are marketed to the consumers.

This function is performed by managers at al levels though the nature of decisons differs with each level. According to John McDonald. The business executive is by profession a decision maker. Uncertainty is his opponent, overcoming it his mission. Whether the outcome is a consequences of luck or wisdom, the moment of decision is without doubt the creative event in the life of the executive." Every manager has to take decisions constantly for his better performance. He has also to decide whether to stick to an old decision or to revise it. Thus, it is obvious that management is essentially a decision making process.

ELEMENTS OF STRATEGIC DECISIONS

Strategic decision is a major choice of actions concerning allocation of resources and contribution to the achievement of organisational objectives directly. Though the various characteristics of strategic decision, as identified earlier, may very from organisation to organisation because of their different nature, the elements of strategic decision are somewhat common to all the organsitions. The strategic decision normally has three elements :

A. Commitment which directs some part of organisation to undertake the course of action, makes the personel involved responsible for attaining the objective and allocates to them the resources necessary for the same, the commitment element.

B. Desired result or objective to be achieved through the implementation of the decision, the result elements; and

C. Course of action or plan which specifies the work to be done to achieve the result, the action element.

Thus a strategy requires that a desired result and course of action be paired to the extent that they become completely interelated. Since business realities are quite complex, the decision making in strategic management goes through a complex process. However, a detailed description of the various elements of strategic decision may make the points clear.

(A) Result. Organisation are goal-directed and any organisational process, including decision making should also be goal-directed to meet the organisational objectives. Naturally, the value of a decision and the associated action is related to the dispatch with which the goal is achieved. The result element of strategic decision is a specially defined objective or statement of desired future accomplishment which will contribute to the company's overall purpose. Subsequently this becomes the basis for measuring the effectiveness of the strategy. The first test of completeness for a strategy, therefore, is whether a pertient result element has been clearly specified. It forces the clear specification of a matching action element so that the objectives are achieved. It is quite a normal practice to express the result or objective in quantitative terms, such as, sales volume, market share, profit margin, expense reduction by certain percentage, etc. These are needed for the people at lower levels in the organisation but they do not reflect why a matching action element is to be undertaken. As such the result is not related specifically to the action element of the strategic decision. The result element of strategic decision must specify what specific result is to be achieved and why. Thus the result element in strategic decision may be defined in terms of purpose that the organisation may adopt and the relationships which exist between these purpose and the various sphers of interest in organisation's business environment. Such result elements may be expressed in the form of technological leadership, market leadership, profitability, social contribution, employment, strengthening the national economy, and so on.

(B) Action. A stated result or objectives does not become a useful element of a strategic decision until it is paired with a pertinent action programme. Strategic decision is action oriented and directed towards the controlling aspect of the environment. A decision may be interpreted as the intervening variable which may ultimately lead to the end result variables. The action element of strategic decision specifies what work must be done and how, in order to accomplish its matching set of results. Though there may be many alternative opened to the organisation concerned the various alternatives may be described in two forms: *(i)* those strategies and actions which define what type of business the organisation is to be in particularly in terms of its products and markets; and *(ii)* those startegies and actions which specify how the particular type of business is to be established, maintained and developed. These may result into a number of grand and functional strategies depending on the nature of organisation in terms of its size, age, area of operations, type of environment and management approach towards strategic management. The organisation may adopt a number of alternative strategies, such as growth strategy, stability strategy, or retrenchment strategy as grand strategies and market development, product development, financial and administration, and personnel as functional strategies depending on the situation.

(C) Commitment. A management decision is not strategic unless it has been translated into a set of action decision whereby the organisation's resources are committed for a particular course of action. Committing decision relates to both present competitive actions and the assignment of development work leading to future. Commitment of resources includes the allocation of resources on various actions and since these resources are utilised for the actions concerned, these can not be got back except in the form of their result. Since the commitment of resources involves future period, the appropriate commitment period should be selected. What the commitment principle implies is that long term planning is not really planning for future decisions but rather planning for future impact of today's decisions. Thus a decision is a commitment, normally of funds, direction of action, or reputation. The commitment element of the strategic decision relates to who, where, and when with respect to the proposed action. These three Ws determine the asignment of responsibility, locus of action, and timing of action.

(i) Timing element is the most important element of commitment principle and deevlopment and implementation of strategy. This relates to the timing of taking of taking action so that the organisation stands to certain benefits as compared to its competitors.

(ii) Decision regarding who will be taking up the jobs or actions is an important aspect of commitment element of strategic decision.

Sometimes, this is not given adequate attention on the presumption that either organisational plan or past precedent will provide answer for the problem. However, adequate care must be taken that new strategic assignments are clarified. Such an exercise is specially required when there is: *(i)* entirely new jobs requirement calling for specialised skills not previously needed; *(ii)* creation of separate operation whose personnel would devote full time to the new strategy area; and *(iii)* need for creating internal competition as a basis for sharper evaluation of strategy.

(iii) The commitment decision should also specify where and under what circumstances implementation is to be effected. Thus lcans of action element of commitment relates to what action is to be taken, who will do the work, and what are the competitive and other environment circumstances of the strategy.

ISSUES IN STRATEGIC DECISION MAKING

Being a complex process, strategic decision-making is difficult to perform. It is incomeprehensible; it cannot be analysed and explained easily. Decision makers are unable to describe the exact manner in which strategic decisions are made. Like the working of the human mind, strategy decisiön making is fathomless. And rightly so, for it is based on complex mental process which are not exposed to view.

For these reasons, no theoretical model, however, painstakingly formulated, can adequately represent the different dimensions of the process of strategic decision-making. Despite these limitations, we can still attempt to understand strategic decision-making by considering some important issues related to it. Following are these issues.

(1) Rationality. Rationality, in the context of strategic decision making, means exercising a choice from among various alternative courses of action in such a way that it leads to the achievement of objectives in the best possible manner. The economists who support the maximising criterion consider a decision to be rational if it leads to profit maximisation. Behaviourists, who are the proponents of the satisfying concept, believe that rationality takes into account the constraints under which a decision maker operates. Incrementalists are of the opinion that the achievement of objectives depends on the bargaining process between different interested coalition groups existing in an organisation and therefore, a rational decision making process should take all these interests into consideration.

(2) Criteria for. The process of decision-making requires objective-setting. These objectives serve as yardistick to measure the efficiency and effectiveness of the decision-making process. In this way, objective serve as criteria for decision-making. There are three major viewpoints regarding setting criteria for decision-making.

(a) **The First is the Concept of Maximisation.** It is based on the thinking of economists who consider objectives as those attributes which are set at the highest point. The behaviour of the firm is oriented towards achieving these objectives and, in the process, maximising its returns.

(b) **The Second View is Based on the Concept of Satisfying.** This envisages setting objectives in such a manner that the firm can achieve them realistically through a process of optimisation.

(c) **The Third View Point is that of the Concept of Incrementalism.** According to this, the behaviour of the firm is complex and the process of decision-making, which includes objective-setting, is essentially a continually-evolving political concensus-building. Through such an approach, the firm moves towards its objectives in small, logical and incremental steps.

(3) Individual Versus Group. Owing to the person-related factors, there are individual differences among decision makers. These differences matter in strategic decision-making. An organisation, possessing special characteristics, operates in a unique environment. Decision makers who understand an organisation's characteristics and its environment are in a vantage position to undertake strategic decision-making. Individuals such as Chief excutives or entrepreneurs play the most important role as strategic decision makers. But as organisation become bigger and more complex and face an increasingly turbulent environment, individuals come together in groups for the purpose of strategic decision-making.

(4) Creativity. To be creative, a decision must be original and different. A creative strategic decision-making process may considerably affect the search for alternatives where novel and untried means may be looked for and adopted to achieve objectives in an exceptional manner Creativity, as a trait, is normally associated with individuals and is sought to be developed through techniques such as *brainstorming*. Readers may recal that one of the attitudinal objectives of a business policy course is to development the ability to *go beyond and think*, which in other words, is using creativity in strategic decision-making.

(5) Variability. It is a common observation that, given an indentical set of conditions, two decision makers may totally different conclusions. This often happens during case discussion also. A case may be analysed differently by individuals in a group of learners and, depending on the differing perceptions of the problem and its solutions, they may arrive at different conclusion. Such things happen due to variability in decision-making. It also suggests that every situation in unique and there are no set formulas that can be applied in strategic decision-making.

(6) Person-related Factors. There are a host of person related factors that play a role in decision-making. Some of these are age, education, intelligence, personal values, cognitive styles, risk-taking ability, and creativity. Attributes like age, knowledge, intelligence, risk-taking ability and creativity are generally supposed to play a positive role in strategic decision making. A cognitive style which enables a person to assimilate a lot of information, interrelate complex variables and develop an integrated view of the situation is specially helpful in strategic decision-making. Values, as enduring prescriptive beliefs, are culture-specific and important in matters of social responsibility and business ethics; issues that are important to strategic management.

DIFFERENT APPROACHES TO STRATEGIC DECISION MAKING

As we know that strategic decision-making process is complex and intriguing. Various researchers and authors have studied and described the manner in which such decision-making takes place. These different approaches have also been categorised by a few authors. We here attempt to understand the different approaches to strategic making.

(1) Intuitive-anticipatory. This approach is based on the intuition of, usually, a single person who is the promoter or chief executive of an organisation. He anticipates the future and takes strategic decisions accordingly. The process is implicit in the sense that the mental processes involved in decision-making are not readily evident. The basis of decision-making is intuition, judgement or hunch, which are the result of long years of experience in dealing with a variety of stategic problems. A few authors, including Herbert Simon, Rechard Cyert James March and Henry Mintzberg have contributed to an understanding of this approach. It is difficult to provide an illustration of this approach. Owing to its incherent nature, the process of decision-making adopted under this approach is not clear and inexplicable and, therefore, cannot be reported.

(2) Formal-structured. This approach involves systematic planning and set procedures. Since it is formal and structured, strategic problems are dealt with by a designated group of planners who follow a set procedure to arrive at decisions. Different types of planning systems such as strategic planning, corporate planning or long-range planning are used. Most authors in strategic management use the formal-structured approach framework in their texts. This book is also based on a systematic approach to strategic decision-making. As an illustration, we may consider the example of Larsen & Toubro (L & T), which adopts a formal strategic planning system. In essence, the company follows a three-stage process. The first stage is the *diagnostic phase* involving the setting of corporate mission, objectives and goals, and SWOT (strengths, weaknesses, opportunities and threats) analysis by each of the seven business group in the company. The second stage deals with providing *directions through the choice of alternative strategics* to be adopted. The last phase is the *implementation phase* where the action plan is put into action.

(3) Adaptive. The essence of the adaptive approach is on taking strategic decision on the basis of how a change is perceived at a given point of time. With changing circumstances, the decisions are also reviewed. The gap between the current position of the company and its objectives. Strategic decisions are meant to reduce such a gap. Circumstances are defined in terms of the environment. For an environment that is perceived to be stable, strategic decision are based on certainty decision are based on certainty. Where stability is less, and the future is risky, contingency planning systems are adopted. In an uncertain environment, the emphasis is on building up adaptive capability to respond to changes as and when they occur. This approach has been dealt with by authors like H. Igor Ansoff and Russell L. Ackoff. Many organisations exhibit the adoption of such an approach in the Indian business environment.

Mintzberg's classification of the modes of strategy making as *entrepreneurial, adaptive,* and *planning*, offers another theoretical framework which aids the understading of the strategic decision-making process.

According to Mintzberg, three pure modes of strategy making could be defined. The entrepreneurial mode envisages an active search for opporrtunities by a person, usually the entrepreneur or chief executive, who takes bold and risky decisions and rapidily moves the organisation towards its objectives. In the adaptive mode, the emphasis is on solving short-term problems by adopting a reactive attitude and decisions are made in incremental steps based on negotiated settlement among different interest groups. The planning involves a systematic appraisal of the environment, assessment of internal capability and choosing courses of action in the form of meticulously formulated strategies. These three pure modes could be combined to form mixed modes like adaptive-entrepreneurial, adaptive-planning or entrepreneurial-planning modes. The method of strategy making may also differ with respect to different functional areas. Organisations may also adopt different modes at successive stages of their development.

Thus, there could be many different approaches to strategic decision-making. But to state that an organisation follows only a single approach at a time or only one approach all the time would be unrealistic Real-life business situations offer countless examples of organisations and decision makers who adopt a combination of approaches.

(4) Incremental. The incremental or, colloquially, the *mudding through* approach involves limiting the focus of strategic decision-making to a few alternatives at a time, that differ only marginally from one another. The choice of the best alternative is based on an interative process of continually redefining problems so as to make them manageable. The end result is a negotiated settlement between different interest groups. Charles Lindblom has explained this approach through the concept of *disjointed incrementalism*. Most public sector companies in India, in their strategic decision-making, exihibit the adoption of an incremental approach. Owing to the various pulls and pressures between which public sector companies typically operate with regard to their objectives and goals, the strategic decision-making is based on negotiated settlement among different groups.

E. Entrepreneurial-opportunistic

This approach is characterised by a constant search for opportunities and exploiting them for the benefit of the organisation. Entrepreneurial strategic decision-making is based on the perception of opportunities diagnosing them for the generation of alternatives, analysing the consequences and selecting the course of action that would best meet the objectives. Such an approach is generally adopted by entrepreneurs and family-business executives but may also be adopted by managers in organisations. Henry Mintzberg has dealt with the entrepreneurial mode of strategy making which we shortly refer to below.

Many examples can be provided in the Indian context where this approach is adopted for strategic decision-making. The illustration of Dhirubhai Ambani, the founder-chairman of the Reliance group of companies typifies the adoption of the entrepreneurial-opportunistic approach. Starting as a humble office member of staff in Burmah Shell, Ambani moved into spices exports and then to nylon yarn trading. It is in this business that he, in the early sixties, realised the importance of synthetic fabrics. Seizing upon the opportunity, Ambani laid the foundation of Reliance Textiles Ltd. a gaint multi-product and multi-location company.

CONDITIONS FOR EFFECTIVE DECISION MAKING

Decision-making involves the selection of an alternative out of the several available alternatives. Thus alternative is put into action which will take place in future period. Thus, a manager is taking a decision for future conditions. In fact, long-range action is not a process of making the future decisions but a means of reflecting the future in today's decision. Conditions under which managers make decisions vary along a continuum from those of perfect certainty to those of complete uncertainty. This continuum may have three possible points depending upon the degree of certainty in the decision-making conditions ; risk, uncertainty and certainty.

(A) Risk. Most of the organisational decisions are made under the conditions of risk, is some information is available but these are not sufficient to answer all questions about the outcome of the decision. However, he has sufficient information for estimating the probability of outcomes. Probability can be defined as the percentage of times in which a particular outcome would occur if any action were repeated a very large number of times. There are three methods of estimating the probability under conditions of risk.

(i) Empirical probability is based on recording actual experience over a period of time and computing the percentage of times that each event has becurred. Managers can calculate this probability on the basis of various data available either with them or with outside the organisation. Life insurance companies generally compute probability of death on this basis.

(ii) *A priori* probability is obtained through deductions from assumed conditions. For example, the probability of getting a head is 0.5 when a coin is tossed. Through the knowledge of the nature of coin, one can know the probability of results, though it is not possible to predict with certainty the outcome of any single toss.

(iii) When the manager does not have sufficient data to calculate either a *priori* or empirical probability, he may estimate probability by his own judgment. This is called subjective probability. This probability is less exact as compared to others. However, it is better to use subjective probability than just completely ignoring the probability of occurrence associated with various alternatives.

The assignment of probability is never so simple as it might appear. The decision-making who finalises the assignment is the ultimate arbiter and different managers may assign varying estimates for various reasons. The risk preference of a manager may play key role in probability assignment. Various techniques have been developed to make decisions under the conditions of risk. Some of these are decision tree, payoff table, simulation, etc., which will be discussed later in this chapter.

(B) Uncertanity. Uncertainty conditions are those for which the manager feels he cannot develop probability estimates because he has no way of gauging the likehood of the various alternatives. Though managers assign probability to various alternative based upon past knowledge and experience there may be conditions where such probability assignment is not possible. In such cases, the conditional probability is assigned which sugests that the assigned probability holds true only when certain events happen.

(i) There are various alternatives for making decisions in such cases. Since the occurrence of the events is not known, the manager can apply equal probability to all states of nature of events. This is called the Laplace criterion.

(ii) Maxmin approach can be applied which is based on pessimism and the manager may ascertain the worst condition for each alternative.

(iii) He may use optimism criterion commonly known as maximax. The manager may be optimistic in assigning the probability to various alternatives. Dealing with decisions under uncertainty is not an easy task. In the three approaches, a different strategy emerges as most favourable each time.

(C) Centainty. If the manager has sufficient information about the elements affecting the outcomes of the decision, so that he can predict the outcomes 100 per cent of time, the conditions of certainty exist. Such conditions exist when decisions involve actions in immediate future, and the manager has made such decisions a number of times with the results. Under such conditions, he can use a deterministic model, the one in which all factors are assumed exact, with chance playing no role. Under such conditions of certainty, he does not need to analyese the chance elements.

Conditions for certainty exist in case of routine type of decisions in the organisation. Routine type of decisions are made in the context of day-to-day operations of the organisation. Mostly they are of repetitive type and relate to general functioning. Such decisions are taken in the conditions of certainty. For example, the allocation of resources to various product lines constitutes decision under certainty because the manager knows his resources and the amount of time it will take to process them into finished product. However, the conditions of certainty do not exist for most of the organisational decisions.

PROCESSES FOR STRATEGIC DECISION MAKING

Various theories have been suggested about how decisions are made. Let us examine these first. Most writers focus on three approaches: Intuitive-emotional, rational-analytical and behavioural-political.

(A) Intuitive-Emotional. The opposite of the rational decision maker is the intuitive decision maker. This decision maker prefers habit or experience, gut feeling, reflective thinking, and instinct, using the unconscious mental processes. Intuitive decision makers consider a number of alternatives and options, simultaneously jumping from one step in analysis or search to another and back again.

Some who prescribe intuition or judgement as the preferred approach point out that in many cases, judgement may lead to "better" decisions than "otimizing" techniques. For example, consider senstivity analysis on a tool such as the economic order quantity. EOQ models suggest that there is an optimal order quantity considering trade-offs of ordering and holding costs. Yet you can stray far from optimal in most cases without a very signficant impact on total cost differentials. Here, then, judgement concerning other factors in the deision situation could lead to a better decision about order quantities, rather than holding fast to deciding what the rational model prescribes. In fact, the timing of when to implement a decision based on the analysis may require an intuitive feel for what the dates are telling you. In many cases, judgement such as this might be prefer stockable to relying on the analysis. Recognize, then, that analytical models are tools to help the decisions maker in improving judgement.

Those opposed to this approach argue that

(a) The rational approach ensures that adequate attention is given to consequences of decisions before big miskakes are made.

(b) It does not effectively use all the tools available to modern decision makers.

(B) Rational-Analytical. In this model, the decision maker is a unique actor whose behaviour is intelligent and rational. The decision is the choice this actor makes, in full awareness of all available feasible alternatives, to maximize advantage. The decision maker therefore considers all the alternatives as well as the consequences of all the possible choice orders these consequences in the light of a fixed scale of preferences, and chooses the alternative that procers the maximum gain.

This is the oldest decision theory. It prescribes a rational, conscious, systematic, and analytical approach. It has been criticized because.

(1) Decision makers make decisions with more than a maximization of objectives in mind. They tend to "satisfice", that is, make a decision expected to yield a satisfactory, as opposed to an "optimal".

(2) The decision maker is often not a unique actor but part of a multiparty decision situation.

(3) Decision makers are not rational enough or informed enough to consider all alternatives or know all the consequences. And information is costly.

(C) Political-Behavioral. A third model suggests that real decision makers must consider a veriety of pressures from other people affected by their decisions. An organization interacts with a variety of stakeholders in series of interdependent exchange relationships. Unions exchange labour for decent wages and job security. Customers exchange money for products and services. Owners exchange capital for expected returns on investment. Suppliers exchange inputs for money and continued business. Government exchanges protection and economic security for taxes. Even conpetitors exchange information with one another through trade associations or other contacts. The list of agents and expectation goes on.

Each shareholder gives the organization something and expects something in return. To the extent an organization has favourable exchange relationship gets a bit more than given compared with other organization and stockholders. It more power. More powerful stackholdeɪs have more influence over decisions because the organization is more dependent on these stockholders. A majority stockholder can have a greater influence on decisions about reinvestment versus dividend payout than if stock is widely held by many small owners. If the firm is labour intensive more attention may be paid to union leaders demands for better wages than to the desires of stockholders for more profit, beceause the union might shut the firm down. Given these realities, decision makers to a juggling act to meet the demands of the various stockholders. Through political compromise they attempt to merge competing demands so that a coalition of interests emerges that will support the decision.

The mode of decision making is descriptive theory suggesting that the organization in which the decision maker works limits the choices available. Decisions are made when the several people involved in the process agree that they have found a solution. They do this is mutual adjustment and negotiation following the rules of the game the way decisions have been made in the organisation in the past. The decision maker must consider whether the decision can be implemented politically.

❐

6

Functional Strategies in Business

All organisations, irrespective of their size, nature and scope of business must perform the functions like production/operations, finance, marketing, human resource and research and development. Careful planning, execution and coordination of these functions are highly essential for efficient strategic planning, implementation and control. The strategic managers at functional level should understand the interrelationship of these functions in formulation of the strategies at functional levels. The activities of all the functional areas are interwoven in attaining their purposes as well as the purpose of the total firm as shown in fig given below. In fact, these functional areas of a firm are like different organs of a human body. Therefore, it is needless to say that the organisational strategies are implemented at the functional levels.

1. Production/Operations. The basic objectives of production/operations management is to ensure that the outputs produced have a value that exceeds the combined costs of the inputs and the transformation process. In other words, it should added the value to the inputs in the process of transformation.

STRATEGIES FOR SMALL BUSINESS UNITS

(i) Small business units that complete with the niche-low-cost strategy go for low initial investments in their plant, equipment, building outlets etc.

(ii) These business units also go for low investments in semi-variable and variable costs.

(iii) Small business units that adopt the niche-differentiation strategy select strategies that yeild superior quality. These units, in some situation may go for hand-crafting processes to differentiate the product and produce according to the customer's preferences.

(iv) Small business units adopting niche-low-cost/differentiation strategy go for strategies that simultaneously lower costs and increase differentiation. This strategy, though, initially involves higher costs, it will result in cost savings and quality improvement in the long-run.

STRATEGIES FOR LARGE BUSINESS UNITS

Large business units can take advantage of a number of factors. The major advantage is the reduction in cost per unit of output that occurs as a firm gains experience in producing a product or rendering a service. Production/operations costs may be systematically reduced through larger sales volume. The experience curve concept is based on three variables *viz.*, learning, economies of scale and capital labour substitution possibilities. Learning refers to the idea of specialisation and its advantages. Economies of scale refer to reductions in costs per unit of output as volume of output increases. Capital-labour substitution is substituting capital for labour and *vice versa*. This is possible with the increase in the volume of operations, the three variables, put together, will result in decrease in cost per unit as business gains greater market share as it takes the advantages of experience curve.

The business with low cost strategy are prticularly vulnerable to business units that are also able to attain quality in addition to low cost.

Adopters of differentiation as a generic strategy are vulnerable to competition that offer alternative products, but at lower, or even predatory prices. However, managers of the business units that adopt differentiation strategy do not actively capiatalise on the opportunities presented by lower costs.

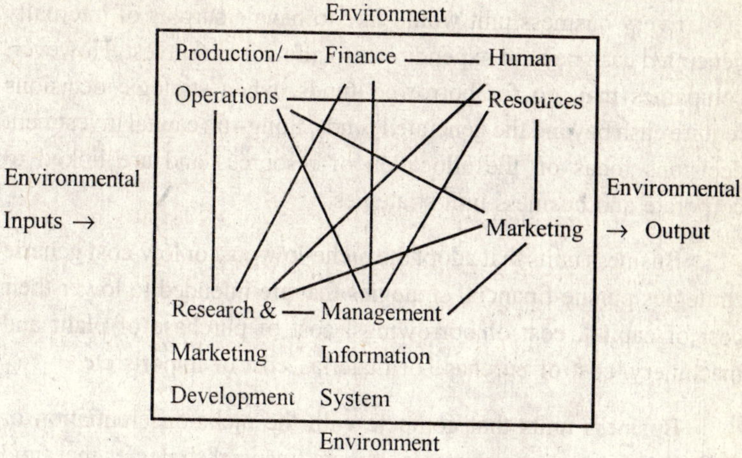

Fig. Interrelationships Among Functional Areas

Regardless of the generic strategy adopted, large business units may have to bear the risk of experience curve. These risks are due to technological innovations. Consequently, plant and machinery will be obsolete. Crores of rupees of investment may have to be written off.

1. Quality Considerations. Maintenance of superior and total quality brings the advantages as follows:

(a) Producing a quality product reduces the quantity of defects, which causes yeild to increase.

(b) Producing product right the first time reduces the number of rejects and time and money spent on network.

(c) Making the operative employees responsible for quality eliminates the need for inspection.

(d) Improvement of quality converts the waste of employee hours and machine time into the manufacture of good product and better service. Improvement in quality naturally and inevitably begets improvement of productivity. This process is essential for business unit adopting the niche-low-cost/differentiator or low-cost-differentiation generic strategies.

Every business unit would like to have a surplus of internally generated cash beyond expenditure, to allow it to reinvest. However, companies may go for borrowed funds, when strategic decisions require cash beyond the generated funds. Long-run capital investment decisions focus on the allocation of resources and are linked to corporate and business unit strategies.

Business units that adopt the niche-low-cost or low-cost generic strategies pursue financial strategies that are intended to lower their cost of capital, cost of borrowings, cost of purchase of plant and machinery, cost of purchase of material, cost of imports etc.

Business units that compete with the niche-differentiation or differentiation generic strategies pursue financial strategies that fund quality improvements. They upgrade their plants, machinery, production processes to maintain the quality above the level of the competitors and invest finances in these areas. These businesses place the top strategic priority on quality maintenance and improvements.

The businesses that compete with the niche-low-cost differentiation, low-cost-differentiation, or multiple strategies use their financial function to lower costs, on one hand, and promote quality improvements on the other hand.

2. Research and Development. The two basic areas of research and development are: *(i)* product/service R & D, and *(ii)* process R & D. Product/service R & D refers to efforts that ultimately lead to improvements or innovations in the firms products/services. Process R & D refers to reducing the costs of operations and making them more efficient.

Business units that adopt the niche-low-cost and low-cost strategies emphasise process R & D with a view to reduce the cost of operation. Business units that adopt the niche-differentiation and differentiation strategies give emphasis on product/service R & D to produce improved and innovative product models. Businesses that adopt niche-low-cost/differentiation, low-cost differentiation, and multiple strategies simultaneously emphasise both on product/service R & D and process R & D.

3. Marketing. The strategic considerations of marketing are: products/services, place of markets/location of outlets, channels of distribution, price and promotional activities. The business units that adopt the niche-low-cost and low-cost generic strategic produce no-frills products/services. Business units that adopt generic strategies of differentiation and low-cost differentiation pursue different marketing strategies. Marketing unique, quality products/services that are distinguishable from that of competitors are some of the strategies followed by these businesses.

The business units with compete with niche-differentiation and niche-low-cost/differentiation strategies tend to offer specialised, high quality to highest products to meet the particular needs of a relatively small market.

4. Human Resources. Human resources management function includes the major activities like designing and analysing jobs based on the future organisational needs, planning for future human resource needs, recruiting, selecting and employing people based on the needs of the organisation, training and developing employees to develop their human resources, appraising their performance and move the employees among different levels based on organisational needs and employee career goals, fixing and maintaining the compensation package, maintaining conducive human relations, and creating and maintaining high quality of work life.

In addition to these activities the firm adopting growth strategies go for the human resource development, creating and maintaining harmonious organisational climate, team building organisational development, empowering the employees, management of diversified cultures and the like. Companies adopting stability strategy do not bring signficant changes in human resources management. Companies adopting retrenchment strategies cut the size of human resources, cut the compensation package etc.

5. Information Systems. All functional areas of the business can be benefited by a well designed information system. A computer-based decision support system that contains a central data base permits each functional area to access information its need and to communicate electronically with the other functional departments as necessary. This facility helps each department to keep abreast of what other departments are doing and coordinate its efforts accordingly.

Information systems of most organisations evolve through four stages of growth. At the first stage, companies use electronic data for cost reduction, accounting applications, etc. Computer applications, in the second stage spread into all functional areas. The activities include: forecasting, inventory control, cash flow, personnel records and sales analyses. The third stage focuses on certain control activities such as in purchasing and scheduling. The final stage is the most sophisticated, involving decision support applications such as planning models, simulations, and on-line uses in human resources, cost analyses and order entries. This stage, enables management to develop competitive advantages.

MARKETING POLICY

From a practical point of view, marketing includes activities through which an organisation tries to satisfy the needs of human beings through exchange process. Organisations come into existence and grow as a result of their ability to satisfy the needs of their customers. They must be able to identify and satisfy these needs by producing the required goods and services. This process involves large number of activities which require policy decisions. Below is given a list of such activities and factors determining the performance of each which will help managers to develop policies in marketing area.

1. **Inventory Levels.** Demand pattern, customer service level, plant and warehouse location, production planning and scheduling, financial strengths.

2. **Credit and Discount.** Channel intermediaries requirements, cash flow requiements.
3. **Physical distribution.** Plant location, transportation mode, customers location, customer geographic distribution service level requirements.
4. **Marketing Research and Information System.** Financial strengths, production equipment and facilities, financial and accounting information.
5. **Promotion.** Promotion capacity, financial strengths, channel intermediaries capacity, availability of promotional avenues.
6. **Price.** Cost structure, product quality, stage of product life cycle, nature of competition, target market share, functional discounts, quality discounts, return on investment objectives.
7. **Product Packaging.** Product characteristics material and product handling equipment, middlemen needs, transportation modes.
8. **Distribution Channel Structure.** Nature of market, product characteristics, availability of middlemen and other channel specialists, financial requirements, firm's market position.
9. **Product Research and Development.** Financial strengths of the organisation, marketing feasibility, product technology.

Thus major policy issues in the area of marketing include the competitive tactics to be used in the marketing mix.

Whether a firm will sell its product or service directly to the consumers or make use of intermediaries (middlemen) for the purpose constitutes a major policy issue. For certain service service organisations, direct sale to consumers is invariably called for, like, for instance, civil airways, banks, consultancy firms, passenger and freight transport services. But for most manufactures of goods, selection of the channel of distribution involves a choice of great significance. For one thing, on channel decisions depend the firm's pricing decisions, advertising decision and sales force decisions. Pricing decisions depend upon whether it chooses wholesalers or retailers for distribution of its products; the firm's advertising decision depend upon the degree of co-operation from the agencies in the channel of distribution; the sales force decisions also depend upon whether the firm choose to sell to retailers or uses its own representatives. Secondly, the significance of channel decisions lies in that they involve long-term commitments to and dependence on other firms.

Channel decisions refer to the managerial decision on the selection of he most suitable route for distribution of goods from the producers to the users. Following are the important reasons which place channel decision in policy decision areas:

(a) If the choice of channels is proper, fluctuations in production may be reduced. The manufacturer can obtain date regarding sales and stock of the middlemen and exercise control wherever he feels necessary. The stability of production will help to ensure steady employment and proper budgetary control.

(b) The channels chosen involve the firm in relatively long-term commitments to other firms or middlemen. The relations between the manufacturer and the middlemen depend mainly on the choice of appropriate channels of distribution. Therefore, it is necessary that channel decisions are taken with great care.

(c) The channels selected for the firm's product affect every other marketing decision like pricing, promotion, physical distribution and the cost involved in the use of trade channels enter the price of the product that the ultimate consumer has to pay. If the costs of trade channels are very high the firm may draw public criticism.

The choice of the appropriate channels of distribution is not a simple job. While taking a decision in this regard, management should carefully consider the following factors:

(1) Market Considerations. The nature of the market is a key factors influencing the choice of channels of distribution. The following features of the market should be analysed to determine the channels:

(a) Consumer or industrial market.

(b) Number of potential customers.

(c) Size of order.

(d) Customer buying habits and expectations.

(e) Geographical concentration of market.

(2) Product Consideration. The type and naure of the product influences the number and type of middlmen to be chosen for distributing the product. The important factors with regard to the product are as follows:

(i) Product line.

(ii) Standardised product.

(iii) Unit value.

(iv) Persihability.

(v) Bulk and weight.

(vi) Technical nature.

(3) Company Considerations. The nature and size of the business firm have an important impact on the selection of channels of distribution. Following factors are important in this regard:

(i) Services provided by sellers

(ii) Experience and competence of management.

(iii) Financial resources.

(iv) Volume of production.

(v) Desire for control of channels.

A manufacturer who wants to control the distribution of his product will select a short channel of distribution. He may do so even though the distribution cost is higher if he feels that he can give his product more aggressive promotion.

(4) Middlemen Considerations. Certain factors related to the middlemen which influence the channel selection are as follows:

(i) Competition and legal constraints.

(ii) Cost.

(iii) Sale potential.

(iv) Attitude of middlemen.

(v) Financial ability.

(vi) Availability of desired middlemen.

PRODUCTION POLICY

Production functions involve the transformation of a set of inputs to predetermined outputs in accordance with objectives of the organisation. Production management encompasses the design, implementation, operation and control of system made up of workers, materials, capital equipment, information and money to accomplish some set of objectives. Following are the major production/operations policy decisions with their determinants:

1. **Process Planning and Job Design.** Forecast of demand, product engineering, product technology, labour force, design stability.

2. **Raw Material and Work-in-progress Inventory.** Forecast of demand, cash flow, supplier reliability.

3. **Facilities Layout.** Medium and long-term forecast of demand and stability of product line. Production technology physical facilities constraints, safety considerations.

4. **Planning of Aggregate Output.** Short-range forecast of demand finished goods inventory level, cash flow, employment policy, plant capacity, state of production/ operation system at the time of decision.

5. **Plant Location and Capacity.** Long-range forecast of the size and location of the market, capital structure, environmental conditions, state of operations and logistic system production technology.

The basic objective of policy decision in the area of production operations is the effective utilisation of organisational resources.

Alongwith the policy decisions on production activity policies need to be formulated also on production processes. Following are different aspects of the choice *viz.*,

(A) Division of Labour. The volume of production and the extent of standardisation of products determine whether and how far line operations could be sub-divided and entrusted to different operatives. Division of labour has been the characteristic features of large-scale manufacturing works since the industrial revolution. Routinisation of operations is known to produce monotony, boredom, lack of motivation and low morale due to 'anomie' (aloneness among many). Job enlargement is recognised now as a superior means of securing higher productivity and efficiency.

(B) Choice of Technology. The technology to be used is uniquely given in the case of certain industries (products). Airlines may use aircrafts of different types to service particular regions. On the choice of technology depends the divisions regarding equipment, personnel, methods of operation and organisation. In the service organisations, too, the process to be used may require a choice to be made out of different alternatives.

(C) ***Policy on Mechanisation and Automation.*** Technological advances over the last half a century have enlarged the scope of mechanisation and automation in many industries, *e.g.*, the use of tractor and harvesters in agriculture, automatic spinning and weaving in textile mills, packing and packaging of products, loading and unloading of cargo, automatic signalling in the railways, assembly line operations, etc.

(D) Size and Location of Production Units. For large enterprise, the decision with respect to the size of plant needs to be examined with two alternatives in view, *viz.*,

(i) Large size with centralised location, and

(ii) Dispersal of operating units with small size of plan capacity.

Most consumer goods as well as industrial goods are procured or produced in anticipation of demand. Sales are made out of stocks carried. On the other hand, in some industries, procurement and production take place on the basis of order booked. Manufacture of heavy mechinary, quality furniture, aircrafts, ships and trawlers, indeed all products to be supplied according to customer specifications fall in this category. However, even in these cases, it may be possible to carry standard parts and components in stock, and only the final assembly operations may be done on the basis of orders received. It is sure that holding inventories in anticipation of customer demand involve certain risks, *e.g.*, the risk of obsolesence, demange and deterioration; it also involves locking up of capital, and incurring storage costs. Procuring inventories in accordance with sales orders may reduce the risks and costs involved. However, procurement of inventories for stock may enable managment to take advantage of the economy of large-scale operations, quantity discounts, and prompt delivery, as well as to avail of the vendor's services. Contrarily, purchasing small lots corresponding to orders booked may result in slow delivery and higher costs.

Thus, the coordination of purchasing and production with sales is essentially related to the timing of procurement. It is not a question of either buying in anticipation or oders or wating until orders are in hand. Rather it is a question of the extent to which procurement for stock should be combined with procurement 'to order'. The policy on this issue depends on the following considerations:

(a) **Minimum Inventory of Raw Materials and Finished Goods that is to be Carried.** This should be adequate to meet unforeseen contingencies like delay in getting supply from the vendor, or the actual use being more than the anticipated requirement, or any possible delay in production operations. The level of finished goods inventory at which replenishment should be ordered, *i.e.*, the re-ordering point, must take care of the sales during the lead time (or period required for replacement). In the case of raw materials, orders should be placed for replenishment of stock at that point where the level of inventory is adequate to meet the production requirements during the period which the vendor may take to execute the order.

(b) **Recorder Quantity.** The size of the purchase order for replenishment of stocks is primarily dependent on the economical production runs which can be estimated in terms of the number of days or weeks or months' requirement. On the other hand, there are cost implications of buying large lots and small lots. With large order size the number of purchase orders is likely to be fewer and hence clerical expenses (ordering costs) may be lower; freight charges and handling costs are also likely to be less; further, quantity discount may reduce the cost of purchase. But large order size also involves corresponding large investment in working capital and interest obligations, as also higher carrying costs (cost of storage space, insurance, damage and deterioration, if not obsolescence). Ordering small quantities will imply a larger number of orders. Hence higher ordering costs (clerical expenses), but reduced capital investment and interest, freight charges and handling costs, as well as lower carrying costs. The concept of 'economic lot size' or 'economic order quantity' may be used to resolve the question or order size. The most economical lot size or reorder quantity should be that which minimises the average cost taking into account the aggregate of carrying costs and ordering costs. With different order sizes, the ordering costs will tend to decline and carrying costs go up as the order size is increased. The aggregate cost would be minimum when the two types of costs are going up and the other coming down) are equal. Thus, the most economical order size is given by the equation.

$$Q = \sqrt{\frac{2AS}{i}}$$

Where a company decides to make or produce rather than buy material/components, the total cost of inventory can be minimised by modifying the EOQ (Economic Order Quantity) formula to take into account the fact that only a part of the production goes into inventory while the remaining part is used concurrently in the production process or sold. It is assumed that the production rate may be equal to a greater extent than the consumption or demand rate. The 'Economic Run Length' (ERL) which is a modified form of EOQ is thus calculated wherein the 'ordering cost' is replaced by 'product set-up cost'. The set up cost is the fixed cost representing one-time cost of machine adjustment, work scheduling, etc. ERL is calculated by using the formula:

$$ERL = \sqrt{\frac{2cs}{I\left(1 - \frac{d}{p}\right)}}$$

c where, c is the annual consumption in units

s is the set-up cost (Rs. per set-up)

I is the carrying cost per unit

d is the consumption/demand rate in units per day

p is the production rate in units per day.

(c) **Fluctuations in Sales.** Purchase and production in the face of seasonal and cyclical fluctuation in the volume of sales may lead to over-stocking or under-stocking of inventory at different times.

The problem can be overcome by *(i)* adjusting purchases and production in harmony with sales volume, *(ii)* maintaining a level rate of production, purchasing and producing for stock during the slack period and using the same to meet peak demand, or *(iii)* sub-contracting instead of expanding production during periods of peak demand, or *(iv)* levelling out the impact of periodic fluctuations in demand.

The first option, that is, adjusting purchase and production in accordance with the sales volume, is found useful in the case of products which are subject to periodic changes in customer tastes and fashions, *e.g.*, ready-made garments, ladies handbags, footwear, etc. In these cases, it may be advisable not to carry inventories in excess of the sales needs. But it implies higher costs on account of ideal facilities and plant capacity, loss of skilled personnel, and discontinuity of operations. Level production (the second option) involves production in excess of demand during slack periods and building up inventory to be available for sale during peak demand. The policy may help the company to retain skilled personnel and enable full use of the production facilities, plant and equipment throughout the year. But it involves additional financial and storage costs to be incurred during the slack season, along with the risks of obsolescene and deterioration. In industries subject to rapid technological changes, level production may lead to a competitive disadvantage for the company. Moreover, it may not be easy to predict the extent of fluctuations in demand. The third option of subcontracting may not permit procurement of adequate quantities during the busy season and hence lead to loss of customers. The fourth option (levelling out the impact of fluctuating demand) may be acted upon in different ways, *e.g.*, adding new products that have complementary seasonal fluctuations. Allowing off-season discounts on sale, or by changing the time of introducing new models as was done by automobile manufactures in the United States.

(d) **Fluctuation in Prices.** Should the reorder quantity be adjusted in anticipation of price changes? One normally expects that order quantity should be currently increased if prices are likely to rise, and correspondingly it should be reduced if prices are expected to fall. In other words. stocks should be built up in anticipation of a price rise, and cut down in anticipation of a decline in prices. But there are two problems to be taken care of. One is that of forecasting price changes. The other relates to the availability of supply. With anticipatory rise of prices and brisk business conditions procurement is likely to take longer time in view of higher demand. It may be easier to redcue order quantities in anticipation of fall of prices. Besides speculative buying, *i.e.*, building up stocks in anticipation of a price rise is risky, particularly on account of the difficulty of accurately forecasting price trends. The policy of adjusting the size of purchase orders and timing thereof should therefore be governed by two considerations: *(a)* predictability of price changes, and *(b)* estimation in advance of volume of demand of particular items of inventory.

Just-in-time (JIT) Inventory System

Just-in-time inventory system is a cost saving mechanism relevant to organisations where materials are purchased and finished goods delivered without any waiting time. It involves materials being procured more frequently and in small lots 'just-in-time' to be used, and finished produce being turned out 'just-in-time' to be sold. Thus, if a situation prevails where goods are produced at the time when needed and in the quantity that is needed, the inventories of work in process and finished goods would be almost nil. Likewise if supplies of raw materials can be obtained just at the time and in the quantities required, there will be virtually zero inventory. Actually JIT system does not require storage of materials as the materials procured lie on the shop in between the consecutive manufacturing operations.

The concept of JIT inventory was originally introduced in Toyata Motor Company, Japan, and later adopted by many American companies producing automotive and electronics goods. The system may result in considerable savings in cost. But its application to be fruitful need two pre-conditions to be satisfied: *(1)* There has to be close rapport between workers and management as well as between suppliers and the company; *(2)* There has to be strict self-discipline.

NATURE OF PERSONNEL POLICY

Personnel management is primarily concerned with human resources with the organisation. Therefore, policy issues in the areas of personnel management should be concerned with *(a)* manpower planning, recruitment, selection and placement *(b)* training and developments of manpower *(c)* transfer, promotion, demotion, and separation; *(d)* working conditions and employee service; *(e)* communication, consultation and negotiation; *(f)* human and social implications of change in the internal organisation and methods of working of economic and social change in the community at large. The basic objectives of personnel policies is to ensure adequate and effective manpower at the right to implement the strategy. Besides the organisation has to forumulate policies in other areas which can support the implementation of basic strategy through the performance of main functions. Such areas may be research and development, legal, and public relations. *(g)* terms of employment, methods and standard of remuneration.

The signficance of personnel policy in strategy implementation hardly needs any elaboration. Both physical and human resources are crucial to the achievement of strategic goals. The basic objective of personnel policy in an organisation is to ensure consistency of action and equity in its relations with employees. These policies constitute the basis for sound personnel practices. They provide the yardstisk by which implementation of strategic plans and programmes can be appraised. Besides, personnel policies are an integral part of the whole policy structure of an enterprise. Any weakness in personnel policy may thus weaken the other functional policies.

The close interrelation between the quality of personnel and strategic managment requires the top executives to be concerned with the following policy issues.

Recruitment Policy. The appropriate match between strategic goals to be achieved and the kind of people employed require two different but related aspects of staffing to be examined.

On the one hand, there is the necessity of recruiting and maintaining the required number of work people and on the other it is retired, experienced persons available for employment and others employed in other organisation but seeking a change for better prospects. External recruitment obviously provides a wider choice from among personnel to select those with skill, training, education and experience required by the firm. For a firm which needs personnel for implementing growth strategy, the process of recruitment from external sources must be planned well in advance. The problems of external recruitment consists of the relatively higher turnover of new recruits and the demoralising effect of outside recruitment on the existing work organisation.

Sources of Recruitment

A. Internal Sources

Internal sources refer to the employees currently working in an enterprise. As and when a post falls vacant, someone already working in the enterprise is transferred or promoted to it.

While a promotion or transfer does not result in any increase or decrease in the number and kinds of persons working in the enterprise, it may leave a significant effect on this working of the departments effected by it.

B. External Sources

(i) Advertisements, Personnel Consultants, and Jobbers and Contractors.

(ii) Employement Exchange and Educational Institutions.

(iii) Field Trips, Miscellaneous.

CHARACTERSTICS OF A GOOD TRAINING AND DVELOPMENT POLICY

A good training policy must be based on the following principles:

(1) ***Relevance to Job Requirements.*** To be effective, a training programme must be related to the requirements of the job for which it is intended. For this, a thorough analysis of each job is essential.

(2) ***Allowance for Individual Difference.*** A good training programme should take into account the difference in ability, learning capacity, interests and temperamental and emotional make-up of trainees.

(3) ***Management Support.*** Top managers should actively support all training programmes. It is the nature of subordinates to look to their superiors for an indication on what to support and what to ignore. It is futile to expect

subordinates to be serious about their training of their bosses themselves because they are indifferent about it.

(4) ***Suitable Incentives.*** There should be provision for suitable monetary and non-monetary incentives to motivate trainee, so that they take training seriously.

(5) ***Determination of Training Needs.*** Training needs of employees should be determined carefully and the methods chosen for the purpose should be effective.

(6) ***Compensation and Supplementary Benefits.*** Policies with regard to wage and salary administration and policy on supplementary benefits are vital components of personnel policy because it is mainly on the basis of satisfactory compensation schemes that company is able to attract and retain capable personnel. In the absence of sound policy with respect to the compensation structure, wages and salaries are likely to be based on personalised arbitrary decisions and thus fall short of the essential elements of adequacy and equity in compensation plans. A satisfactory policy frame is invariably conducive to high morale and minimum frictions among individuals and groups of employees. For apart from the adequacy of the level of compensation, inequities in the pay structure happen to be the most common causes of dissatisfaction and grievances among employees.

The basic issues to be resolved while formulating the compensation policy are those relating to:

(a) Incentive pay

(b) Recognition or relative efficiency of performance;

(c) The internal structure of compensation or internal alignment of pay for different job so as to ensure that pay rates are equitable;

(d) The level of pay and its adequacy.

PROMOTION POLICY

Promotion refers to the advancement of an employee to a higher job involving greater responsibility, more pay and better status. It is the movement of an employee to a position of better remuneration, higher status and greater responsibility. A mere increase in pay or working conditions without an increase in status and responsibility is called upgrading or dry promotion. Demotion is the opposite of promotion.

The policy of filling vacancies at higher levels through promotion of lower level employees has several advantages: *(a)* Employees have an opportunity for improving their status and earnings. Promotion, therefore, improves he motivation and morale of employees. *(b)* It creates sense of royalty among employees. By satisfying the basic urge for advancement, it reduces industrial disputes, labour turnover and absenteeism *(c)* It improves the quality of performance. Reduction in waste and indiscipline results in lower costs. "The company that has no recognised promotion policy likely to have frustrated and restless employees as they have no opportunity for advancement."

However, all higher level vacancies need not necessarily be filled through promotion. Sometimes, lower level staff may be fit for promotion. Moreover, recruitment from outside brings new blood and independent thinking. The basic aim should be to obtain the best possible personnel irrespective of wherefrom they come.

BASIS OF PROMOTION—MERIT *VS.* SENIORITY

There are two bases of promotion, *i.e.*, seniority and merit. Employees generally favour merit, while employees and their unions prefer seniority as the basis of promotion.

Seniority means length of recognised service. It is counted from the date of joining the organisation or from the date of confirmation. Seniority can be calculated in several ways. It is lost due to certain events. *e.g.*, frequent absence from duty.

Seniority is the oldest and most widely used basis of promotion. Promotion on the basis of seniority is justified on following grounds:

(a) It is an objective basis. It prevents favouritism and arbitrary action as there is no room for discretion or prejudices.

(b) It is very simple and practicable as seniority can be measured easily and accurately.

(c) It reduces labour turnover as employees try to remain in the firm to accumulate seniority,

(d) Every employee has a definite idea at all times of his place in the group. He feels secured and develops a sense of loyalty to the organisation. Promotion based on seniority is reward for loyalty.

(e) Length of service is an approximate measure of experience and ability.

(f) Seniority is acceptable to trade unions and gives a feeling of satisfaction to employees.

If a man has been in service for a long time he ought to be better than a newcomer, unless he has been dodging work. Seniority also fits with the cultural expectations for social customs of India.

Seniority as the sole basis of promotion has, however, the following demerits:

(a) Rules for the accumulation of seniority have to be laid down with particular reference to the impact of suspension, lay-off, strike, discharge, etc.

(b) Rigid adherence to seniority makes it difficult to recruit and retain capable personnel.

(c) Employees with longer service are not necessarily more competent. Seniority overvalues experience and premium on merit.

(d) The quality and quanity of work suffers as employees try to stick around and do not make full use of their capabilities.

(e) It lowers the morale of ambitious and meritiorius employees as they get no recognition. When less competent lose interest in efficiency.

(f) Seniority provides performance and inefficiency, as no differentiation is made beween efficient and inefficient employees.

Advantages refer to the efficiency and ability of an employee. Promotion on the basis of merit has following advantages: *(a)* It provides a powerful incentive to work hard and make continuous improvement in efficiency *(b)* There is an overall improvement in operations and the profit of the enterprise. *(c)* Ambitious and hard working employees are duty rewarded. They feel satisfied and contributed maximum to the success of the organisation.

Merit has been criticised due to following limitations: *(a)* Employees feel insecure and become discontented. *(b)* The morale of employees is low when they find that their juniors are promoted before them it causes frustration and loss of interest and loyalty for the organisation. Moreover, merit does not indicate an employee's promotability. An individual may be quite competent for the present job, but his overall personality may not be suitable for higher positions.

Thus, neither absolute seniority nor exclusive merit is a sound basis of promotion. A sound promotion policy should be based on a judicious balance between the two in practice, seniority is given more weightage but merit should also be given due consideration. None of two should be exclusive criterion for promotion. Seniroity can be the deciding factors when two persons are equally meritiorious. Similarly, out the two equally senior employees the more competent one should be promoted first. If senior-most employee is incompetent to do the job well junior employees with merit should be promoted.

Essentials of a Sound Promotion Policy

A sound systematic promotion policy should consist of the following:

(1) The report of each employee should be prepared by his superior but subject to the approval of the departmental head.

(2) The policy management regarding filling of vacancies through promotion or from outside should be clearly stated.

(3) Accurate and uptodate records of seniority and merit should be kept. All employees should be kept informed of their record and opening for promotion.

(4) Promotion policy should be based on job analysis to define job requirement. Employees should know clearly what is expected of them in higher jobs, so that they can prepare themselves for advancement.

(5) Objective and systematic plans of performance appraisal should be set up to identify promotable employees. This is necessary to avoid unfairness in promotions.

(6) Lines of promotion should be clearly defined. For each job a schedule of jobs to which promotion can be made should be prepared.

(7) The basis of promotion should be clearly defined. The relative weight to be given to merit and seniority should be specified.

Industrial Relations Policy

The personnel policies and practices of a firm in many ways are influenced by the state of union-management relations. To what extent the basic philosophy of top management *vis-a-vis* their human resources is subordinated to the bargaining power of employee union depends upon the company's policy with regard to the nature of relation with the union, recognition the support of the union organisatin, the scope of collective bargaining and settlement of industrial disputes. Ideally, harmonous relation between management and employee union should develop on the basis of mutual co-operation. But company executive are often inclined to adopt a policy of belligerency toward union activities. This approach is born out of strong dislike and mistrust of the union by the executives, who refuse to recognise the union as a bargaining agent of when forced to negotiate, do it grudgingly with a house-trading approach. With a hostile attitude to management toward the union, the relationship is inevitably vitiated by mutual suspicion, and there is increasing militancy on the part of the union leaders.

CHARACTERISTICS OF A GOOD TRANSFER POLICY

To be effective, the transfer policy should possess the following characteristics:

(1) If a transfer is going to result in any change in the rate of remuneration this should be made sufficiently clear.

(2) How a transfer is going to affect the seniority of the person concerned should be spelt out in clear terms.

(3) It is quite likely that requests for transfer to the same job, or to the same shift, are received from many employees. In such cases, a decision should be taken in keeping with the predetermined policy.

(4) The deparments or units within which transfers have to be made should be decided in advance.

(5) If transfers become necessary because there is surplus of labour force in one department of unit and shortage in another it should be ensured that workers in their new positions are not given completely new kinds of jobs.

(6) There should be accurate and complete job description of the jobs to which transfers are under consideration. Requirements as to training of the new jobs should be clearly laid down. Also, the workers to be transferred should be clarly informed about the time during which they are supposed to adjust themselves to the requirements of their new jobs.

(7) Responsibility for recommending and approving transfer should be clearly defined.

FEATURES OF A GOOD PERSONNEL POLICY

Every enterprise should relate its personnel policy to the economic legal, social and technological factors present in the society in which it operates. This means it has to keep on adjusting and adpating personnel policy to suit and change in these factors.

A good personnel policy should possess the following features:

(1) **Proper Communication.** It should enjoy acceptability among the people for whom it has been formulated.

(2) **Acceptability.** It should enjoy acceptability among the people for whom it has been formulated.

(3) **Integrative.** It must fully take into account the differing amenities, capabilities, interests, desires, aspirations, beliefs and temperamental make-up of the people for whom it is intended.

(4) **Uniformity.** It should be uniformly applicable to all members and units of the enterprise.

(5) **Stability.** Even though personnel policy has to be consistently adjusted and adapted to suit any changes in economic, legal, and technology factors, it should be reasonably stable and permanent.

(6) **Flexibility.** It should not be so rigid and inflexible that it can not be adjusted and adapted to changes in economic, legal, social and technological factors.

(7) **Responsiveness to Prevailing Trends.** Personnel policy should be adjusted to the prevailing norms and trends in ways. For example, if the current thinking is in favour of involving the management process, the policy should be against.

(8) **Precision and Certainty.** It should be clear to the point and complete in every respect. It should not lead to varying and conflicting inerpretations.

(9) **Promotion of Enterprise Policies.** It should fit into the basis of overall policies of the enterprise.

(10) **Protection of the Interests of All Parties.** It should take into account the interests of all parties associated with the enterprise, *i.e.*, workers enrepreneurs, consumers, government and the community.

NEED FOR FUNCTIONAL POLICIES

For effective implementation, strategists have to provide direction to functional managers regarding the plans and policies to be adopted. In fact, the effectiveness of strategic management depends critically on the manner in which strategies are implemented. In this section, we see the nature of functional plans and policies, why they are needed, and how they are developed.

In terms of the levels of strategy formulation functional strategies operate below the SBU or business-level strategies. Within functional strategies there might be several sub-functional areas. Thus, a company might have a textile division among its several SBU or business areas. Within the textile division, there might be functional areas such as marketing, production, research and development, etc. Further, the functional area of marketing may have sub-functions such as product development, advertising and sales promotion, marketing research, etc.

Functional strategies, or more appropriately, functional plans and policies as they actually are plans or tactics to implement businesss strategies—are made within the guidelines set at higher levels. Plans are made to select a course of action while policies are required to act as guidelines to action. Functional plans and policies, therefore are operational plans and tactics to make a strategy work.

Functional managers need guidance from the business strategy in order to make decisions. Operational plans tell the functional managers what has to be done while policies state how the plans are to be implemented.

Glueck suggests five reasons why functional plans and policies are needed. Functional plans and policies are developed to ensure that:

1. There is a basis available for controlling activities in the different functional areas of business:
2. Similar situations occurring in different functional areas are handled in a consistent manner by the functional managers;
3. The time spent by functional managers in decision-making is reduced as plans lay down clearly what is to be done and policies provide the discretionary framework within which decisions need to be taken; and
4. Coordination acorss the different functions take place where necessary.

Development of Functional Policies

The development of functional plans is aimed at making the strategies—formulated at the top management level practically feasible at the functional level. Strategies need to be segregated into viable functional plans and policies that are compatible with each other in this way, strategies can be implemented by the functional managers.

The process of development of functional policies may range from the formal to informal. Larger and more complex organisations may be several hundred policies related to every major aspect. Many of these policies could have been formulated through the formal process and laid down in company manuals and documents. Smaller organisations with simpler businesses may operate with a few policies most of which could be informal and understood rather than written down.

The process of development of functional policies—whether formal or informal—is similar to that for strategy formulation. Environmental factors relevant to each functional area have an impact of the choice of plans and policies. Organisation plans and policies affect the choice of functional plans and policies. Finally, the actual process of choice is influenced by objective as well as subjective factors. Functional plans and policies affect, and are affected by the resource allocation decisions.

PREPARING A PRODUCT STRATEGIES

One of the most important areas is new products or services since these, more than any other single factor, will determine what a company or other enterprise is or will be. The key questions in this area may be summarized as follows:

1. What do Our Customers Want? An effective strategy must be based on knowning what customers want. Do they want price, value, quality, availability, service? The success of the Hughes Tool Company, for example, has been based largely on making a shrewd analysis of what oil-and gas-well drillers wanted and furnishing them the exact drill but they wanted, of a high quality, in the place the bit was needed, and with adequate service to support the product. Likewise, International Business Machines (IBM) leadership in business computers has in large part been due to knowing what its customers wanted and needed, supplying it, maintaining advancement of product design, having a family of computers, and running a strong service organisation.

2. What is Our Business? This classic question might also be phrased in terms of what is not our business. It is also well to ask. What is our industry? Are we a single product-line industry, such as shoes or furniture? Or are we a process industry, such as chemicals or electronic components? Or are we an end-use indutry, such as transportation or retailing?

3. Who are Our Customers? To furher identify what kinds of business we are in and to give meaning to a product or service strategy, this is an especially key question. Peter Drucker has long said that the purpose of a business is to "create a customer," although he could hardly have meant to create customers without regard to profits. In answering this question, it is important to avoid too great an attachment to present customers and products.

4. What is Existing and Potential Competition? In deciding on a product strategy, it is important to assess realistically the nature and strength of existing competition. If a competitor in a field has tremendous strength in new products, marketing, and service, as IBM has had in the computer field, a company should carefully consider whether it has a change to enter the field effectively.

5. How far can we go in Serving Customer Needs? Product strategy formulation must consider this question. There are ofen important limitations. One is, of course, financial, and company must consider whether it has the financial resources to support necessary product research, manufacturing facilities, inventory and receivables, advertising and marketing, and a requisite service competence.

Legal limitations may also be important, as Procter and Gamble found when it was forced by the antirust laws to divest itself cf its acquisition of the Clorox Company (makers of household bleach).

6. What Profit Margins can we Expect? A company naturally wants to be in a business where it can make an attractive profit. One of the keys is the gross profit margin, that profit above operating expenses which will carry overhead and administrative expenses and yield a desired profit before taxes.

7. What Basic form should Our Strategy Take? In formulating a product or service strategy, a company should determine the direction it wishes to go in terms of intensive or extensive product diversification. If it follows an intensive strategy, it might move in the direction of market penetration—going further in present product markets. Or it might decide on one of market development—going into markets it has not been in.

H. What Advantages do we have in Serving Customer Needs? This is a difficult and important question. Most companies like to have a product or service that competitors cannot very easily duplicate. Some larger companies look only for products that require a high capital investment in tooling and machinery, heavy advertising, strong engineering, expensive service organisations, and similar characteristics that tend to discourage the entry of smaller competitors into a market.

9. Do we Wish to Develop Our Own New Product? Here again, a company must address itself to the question of whether it is better for it to develop its own new products, whether it should rely on innovation by competitors to show the way, or whether it should lean heavily on product development by materials suppliers.

10. Do we Wish to be a Product Leader? This may seem to be a question with an obvious answer. Bu it is not, developing and marketing their products, some companies owe their success to being a close second in product leadership. The product leader will often have an advantage in reaching a market firm, but such a company may incur heavy costs of developing and attemtping to market products which do not become commercial successes as well as those which do. One of the major airlines, for exmple, prided itself for years on being the leader in acquiring and putting into service new aircraft. But after undergoing extensive "debugging" of several new planes, and suffering financial losses as a result, the company adopted the strategy of letting someone else be the leader and of becoming a close second.

11. How Much will not Customers Buy at What Price? This is a matter of what customers think they are buying; what they consider value, and what they will pay for it will determine what a business is, what it should produce, and whether it will prosper. Being able to answer this kind of question, particularly after identifying a business and who its customers really are, will be a major key to a product or service strategy.

THE FACTORS CONSIDERED IN FORMULATING MARKETING STRATEGY

Marketing as a body of resources allocated to the process of sale and distribution of product or services is not an end in itself. On the other hand, it is a means to an end, *i.e.*, obtaining the objectives of the firm. To contribute substantially to the firm's objectives, it is very necessary for marketing executives to chalk out their markeing programme and marketing policies well in advance. But the field of marketing is very sensitive and responsive to the environment. If a market fails to understand the realities of the particular environment he will make poor—perhaps disastrous—decisions and performance. Departure from convention, experimentation and innovation are frequently essential to business success, and even survival. Likewise, grasp of his marketing environment must underlie that marketer's decisions. Hence, adjustment in marketing programme and policies from time to time is a must. A firm can react to market environment in two ways: by adopting a natural policy of showing indifference to the changes or by adjusting its own marketing policy to the changed circumstances. An efficient manager who is desrious of success in future will always prefer the latter alternative. Hence, the need for marketing strategy arises in this context.

In the words of Philip Kotler. "Marketing strategy is the technique which a firm adopts to contract market changes. Thus, marketing strategy is a changing variable which changes according to market environment. It is the heart core of a marketing plan. Marketing strategy is a functional strategy and a part of grand corporate strategy. It is a consistent appropriate and feasible set of principles through which a particular company hopes to achieve its long-term marketing objective and profitability". In other words, markting strategy is a comprehensive plan of action design to meet the needs of the certain enterprise operating in a particular environment. It is based on overall corporate marekting objectives and is implemented by a co-ordinate marketing programme through the firm's marketing-mix the ideal marketing strategy would achieve optimum utilisation of all resources of the firm.

Factors

1. Synergistic Potential of Marketing Inputs. Some marketing inputs have mutually reinforcing power and this fact should be taken into account while working out an optimum overall marketing strategy. For example, advertising and displays repeat the advertising message at the time when the consumer is an outlet where the product is on sale.

2. Input Elasticity. Different marketing inputs vary in their effects on demand which should be considered in selecting the bet combination of marketing inputs. For example, a marketer may have to make several pricing decisions for a single product and his choice of the best combination depends partly on his analysis of price elasticity and demand. This will be possibly only through repeated tests and exercises.

3. Productivity of Marketing Inputs. The marketing executives should also recognise that all marketing inputs have equal productivity at various levels of use before they begin to have noticeable effects. So marketer should have an optimum combination of marketing inputs.

4. Substitutability of Marketing Inputs. Various marketing inputs can be mutually substituted by one another. This attribute brings flexibility and utility in marketing strategy. Hence, this factor should also be taken into account while considering marketing strategy.

5. Competitor's Counter Moves. The company has to estimate and forecast the competitor's counter moves with different marketing inputs and has to assess the relative effectiveness of those counter-moves. Price reduction, attractive gift schemes, improvement in packing may be an example of such countermoves. According to Coundiff and Still, "A marketer desiring to improve the 'hitting power' of his marketing strategy should give first consideration to those moves involving inputs that are least subject to effective retaliatory actions of competitors."

FINANCIAL MANAGEMENT

Financial management is concerned with managerial activities related to procurement and utilisation of funds for business purposes. It deals with planning, organisation, directing and controlling financial activities of the enterprise. Financial activities should not be merely restricted to raising of capital, but also to other aspects of financing like assessing the needs for capital, raising sufficient funds, cost of financing, budgeting, maintaining liquidity, lending and borrowing policies and distribution of profits.

In order to ensure the continuous availability of sufficient finance, financial management assesses the needs of the business in advance and then sets itself into motion to procure funds. Procurement of funds is a complex problem as choice of sources of finance is based on complex factors like risk, period, control and cost. Various sources of finance like shares, debentures, banks and other financial institutions, public deposits, etc., have to be compared in the light of these factors. After the funds have been procured, their effective utilisation is another major task of financial management. Funds should not be allowed to remain idle as they involve many costs. Funds should be put into those channels which generate an income higher than the costs of procuring them.

Since financing is one of the functional areas of any business enterprise, the objectives of financial management should be in tune with the overall objectives of the enterprise. The main objectives of a business enterprise is to earn sufficient profits so that a reasonable rate of return is paid on the capital employed and a part of the profit is ploughed back into the business to make it a stronger enterprise so that it may bear all the ups and downs in the business. The finance department can play an important role for the realisation of this objective. The objective of the finance department should be so devised that they contribute directly towards the achievement of the overall organisational objectives. Following is the list of the objectives of financial management of big enterprises:

(i) Ensuring better utilisation of capital by following the principles of liquidity, profitability and safety;

(ii) Ensuring regular and sufficient supply of capital to the business;

(iii) Co-ordinating the activities of the finance department with those of the other departments of the enterprise;

(iv) Ensuring a fair rate of return to the suppliers of capital.

Maximisation of profits is generally regarded as the objective of a business undertaking. Should this objective be followed in financial decision making? Modern authors on financial management have criticised the goal of profit maximisation and have advocated 'wealth maximisation' as the goal of financial decision making. Any financial action which creates wealth or which has a net worth above zero is a desirable one and should be undertaken. The rationale is using wealth maximisation concept as an operating financial management goal is that it reflects the most efficient use of society's economic resources and thus leads to maximisation of society's economic wealth.

The objections raised against profit maximisation as an objective of financial management are listed below:

(a) It does not consider the risk or uncertainty or prospective earnings stream. The prospective earnings stream would be more uncertain if the investment projects undertaken are more risky as compared to others.

(b) It does not specify the timing of expected returns. Few shareholders may like to invest in a project that promises its first return after 25 years or so. For most of the shareholders, the size of the total returns is not as important as the time patterns of returns.

(c) It does not take into consideration the interest of workers, consumers, government and other segments of the society. Thus, it is too narrowly centred. In practice, the goal of a business enterprise cannot be to maximise profits but to attain a certain level of profit, holding a certain share of the market or a certain volume of sales. The concept of social responsibility has also gained wide acceptance by the business houses these days.

(d) It does not allow for the effect of dividend policy on the market price of the share. The goal of profit maximisation prevents management to pay dividends so as to maximise earnings. "To the extent payment of dividends can affect the market price of the stock (or share), the maximisation of earnings per share will not be a satisfactory objective by itself", said Ezra Solomon. It should also be noted that the objectives of maximising earnings per share may not be the same as maximising market price per share.

The above mentioned reasons show that the objective of 'profit maximisation' or maximisation of earning per share' does not take care of the investment, financing and dividend decisions of the business. Ezra Solomon has made a good case for the adoption of the objective of "wealth maximisation." He has pleaded for a distinction between profit and profitability. Maximisation of profits in the sense of maximising shareholders' wealth is clearly an unreal objective. But profitability maximisation in the sense of using resources to yield economic values higher than the joint values of inputs required is a useful objective and it involves a 'different set of considerations. "In fact, achievement of wealth maximisation also maximises the achievement of the other objectives. To conclude, therefore, maximisation of wealth is the operating objective by which financial decisions should be guided."

SCOPE OF FINANCIAL MANAGEMENT

In order to realise the objective of financial management, the finance manager of a business enterprise has to manage various aspects of finance function which determine the scope of his duties. These aspects are explained below:

(a) Determining the Structure of Capital. By capital structure we mean the kind and proportion of different securities for raising finance for the business. Once the requirement of capital funds has been determined, a decision regarding the kind and proportion of various sources of capital has to be taken. For this, financial manager has to determine the proper mix of equity and debt and short-term and long-term debt ratio. These decisions have to be taken in the light of costs of raising finance from different sources, period for which funds are required and several other factors.

(b) Estimating the Requirements of Capital. The requirements of capital must be carefully estimated. A business requires funds both for long-term and for short-term. Estimating the requirements of funds involves the use of techniques of long-range planning. The financial management must also prepare budget of various activities to estimate the financial requirements of the business. If proper thought is not given to the financial requirements of the business, there will be either deficiency or surplus of funds. If the business has insufficiency of capital, it will not be able to meet its commitments in time. And if it has surplus funds, the management may become extravagant in spending.

(c) Investment decisions. The funds procured from various sources are to be prudently invested in various assets so as to optimise the return on investment. The investment of long-term funds requires a careful assessment of various alternatives through capital budgeting and opportunity cost analysis. A part of the long-term funds has to be invested in the working capital of the company.

(d) Choice of Sources of Finance. The management can raise finance from various sources like shareholders, debentureholders, banks and other financial institutions, public deposits, etc. The choice of the source or sources of finance should be done very carefully as they involve different costs and conditions. For instance, public deposits, though carry higher rates of interest than on debentures, do not involve any security of the assets of the company. A company may like this source if it does not want to create a change over its assets.

(e) Disposal of Surplus. The management has to decide how much to retain for ploughing back and how much to distribute as dividend to shareholders out of the surplus of the company. The factors which influence these decisions include the trend of earnings of the company, the trend of the market price of its shares, the requirements of funds for self-financing, the future prospects and so on.

(f) Management of Cash Flow. Cash is required to pay off creditors, purchase stock of materials, pay to labour and to meet day-to-day expenses. These should not be shortage of cash any time as it will damage credit-worthiness of the enterprise. It is also to be seen that there is no excess cash. Excess cash may be invested in near-cash assets which may be converted into cash quickly when needed.

Role of the Financial Management

Recent developments in business have placed the financial manager in a central position in the business enterprise. Financial manager is incharge of the management of the funds of the enterprise. He is concerned with the determination of requirements of funds, selecting and tapping various sources of funds and allocation of funds to particular assets—fixed and current.

Financial management is concerned with three types of decisions: *(i)* investment decisions—financial plan, capital budgeting, etc., *(ii)* financing decision—formulations of capital structure of financing mix; and *(iii)* dividend decision—dividend policy. Since most business activities involve the use of funds, financial management has come to occupy an important place in the modern business enterprises. Ezra Solomon has summed up the role of financial management in the following words: "Financial management is properly viewed as an integral part of overall management rather than as a staff specially concerned with fund raising operations. In this broader view, the central issue of financial policy is the wise use of funds and the central process involved is a rational matching of the advantage of potential uses against the cost of alternative potential sources so as to achieve the broad financial goals which an enterprise sets for itself."

FINANCIAL PLANNING

Financial planning is an important part of the overall planning of any business enterprise. This task is done by the promoters at the time of floating the business and by the financial manager and the top management after that. A considerable thought has to be given to evolve a financial plan for any business venture. If a business is started with inadequate capital, it may not be able to function smoothly because of its inability to meet its commitments in time. Thus, survival of the business may be in danger. If, on the other hand, it has more capital than is required, the earnings will have to be spread over an unnecessarily greater amount of capital and there may be a temptation of wasteful expenditure.

Financial planning involves three functions which are as follows:

(a) Determination of capital structure or form and proportion of different types of secuirities, namely, equity share, preference shares and debentures.

(b) Determination of amount of capital required. This depends upon many factors like promotional expenses, cost of fixed and current assets, cost of raising finance, and future needs.

(c) Laying down the financial policies in regard to cash control, borrowing and lending, and other areas of financial management.

FACTORS IN FINANCIAL PLANNING

At the time of formulating the financial plans, the following points should be given due consideration:

(a) **Present and Future Requirements.** A good financial planning system should be based on imagination and foresightedness. It should take care of not only the present requirements of the business but also the future requirements of the business. It should also make a provision for various contingencies which may arise in future.

(b) **Objectives.** The objectives of financial management should be consistent with the objectives of the enterprise. The main objectives of the financial department are raising of funds at the cheapest cost and utilisation of funds in the best possible manner.

(c) **Independence.** Financial planning should aim at sufficient return on investment so that the business enterprise may retain a part of earnings for ploughing back into the business every year. This will enable it to reduce dependence on outsiders which is necessary if the management does not want any interference by the outsiders with the internal working of the company.

(d) **Solvency and Liquidity.** The financial plans should be so devised that they do not jeoparadise the survival of the enterprise. The enterprise should be solvent and liquid both in the short and long-run. The funds should be invested in those ventures which are likely to give sufficient return on investment. At the same time, it is also essential that adequate cash is always available with the business to purchase the current assets and meet the current expenses.

(e) **Flexibility.** Many times, business conditions change drastically and financial readjusments become essential. The financial plans must be easily adjustable to such changes. Thus, financial planning should be flexible to allow the diversion of funds into more profitable channels. It should also make provision for raising more funds at a short notice.

CHARACTERISTICS OF A SOUND FINANCIAL PLAN

Second financial planning is essential for the success of any business enterprise. It will provide policies and procedures to achieve closer coordination between the various functional areas of business. This will lead to minimisation of waste of resources. Management can follow an integrated approach to financial policies, procedures and programmes only if there is a sound financial plan. While preparing the plan of capitalisation in a company, the following factors should be given due consideration:

(a) **Flexibility.** Financial re-adjustments become necessary quite often. The financial plan must be easily adjustable to them. A rigid capital structure will limit the scope of initiative by the management. The company should be in a position to finance its expansion programmes without much difficulty. This can be achieved only when the financial plan is dynamic in nature.

(b) **Foresight.** Financial planning should be based on vision and foresightendness of the management. These should be systematic forecasting of various contingencies. It should be decided well in advance the level of liquidity to be maintained in the enterprise.

(c) **Simplicity.** A sound financial plan should provide simple financial structure which could be managed easily. It is not always necessary to include all type of securities in the capital structure.

(d) **Optimum Use of Funds.** It may prove very costly to keep idle funds. These should be optimum utilisation of available financial resources. If this is not done, the profitability will suffer. There should be a proper balance between the fixed capital and the working capital.

(e) **Liquidity.** The financial plan must provide sufficient financial liquidity. This will be possible only when there is adequate net working capital a major portion of which is represented usually by share capital, reserves and long-term loans. The degree of liquidity to be maintained is determined by the size of the company, its age, its credit standing, nature of its business, etc.

(f) **Anticipation of Contingencies.** The finance department should anticipate various contingencies which it may have to face. This may lead to keeping the same idle capital for meeting some unforeseen events. It will be much better if these contingencies are anticipated in advance.

Financial aspect of business activities deals primarily with raising, administering and distribution of funds by the organisation for the purpose of business operations. Thus financial policies have three major dimensions: *(i)* determination of the total amount of funds to be used by the organisation; *(ii)* determination of what specific assets the organisation should acquire, or allocation of funds among various assets in an efficient manner; and *(iii)* determination of how the needed funds should be financed or obtained the best mix of financing with relation to the overall valuation of the organisation. Accounting policies will be established to deal with questions as how to treat inventories, which accounts to capitalise, and how to treat expenses and cost. These policies affect the organisation's appearance of success or failure. Thus major policy decisions in the area of finance and accounting are as follows:

1. **Level of Dividend Payment.** Dividend payment history, the stability of earnings, rate of growth and profit levels, liquidity positions, ability to borrow, debt contract restrictions, legal constraints.
2. **Capital Structure.** Nature of business operations, nature of capital market, cash generation capacity, tax savings.
3. **Level of Working Capital.** Uncertainty of cash receipts and disbursements, borrowing capacity, efficiency of cash management, volume of credit sales, reasonability of sales, credit policies.

The basic criterion in financial policies is that the funds needed are available at the right time and at the lowest possible costs.

SOURCES OF POLICIES AND STRATEGIES

To understand how strategies and policies come about in a typical organisation, it might be well to review their major sources. These may be classified as follows:

1. Externally Imposed. To a rapidly increasing extent, strategy or policy is being externally imposed by government, trade unions, and trade associations. Whether in the form of direct regulation, the competition of government-owned or government-supported business, or the many conditions for accepting government aids or contracts, the result is to circumscribe and dictate many aspects of strategy or policy. Strong national unions, operating through collection bargaining and detailed labour contracts, have also imposed policy upon managers. Besides, thousands of local, regional, and national associations have their effect in varying degrees on policy. Other social group-such as church, school, fraternal, social, and charitable organisation-may also mould or dictate an entrprise's strategy or policy.

2. Implied. It is not unusual for policy and even strategy to develop from actions which people see about them and believe to constitute them. Employees will readily understand what is real policy if they work for an enterprise that has published policies to product high-quality goods, to maintain plant cleanliness, or to promote from within, and yet permits contrary actions. Its real policies, or the lack of them, are implied.

For example, the top managers of a certain company earnestly solicited new product ideas, especially from its marketing and engineering groups. The response was generous. Each idea was subjected to complex investigatory procedures and was judged by conservative standards. Most were rejected, and no explanations were made. Even key people in the firm came to believe that it was company's policy to confine new products to low-risk items. This imputed policy, which was quite contrary to what the firm really wanted, became the guideline for new product decisions.

3. Originated. The most logical source of strategy or policy is top management, which originates it for the express purpose of guiding subordinates in the their operations. Originated strategy or policy flows from the objectives of the enterprise, as these are defined by the top executive authority. These may be broad in scope, allowing key subordinates to give them clearer definition, or they may be promulgated so completely as to leave little room for defintion and interpretation. The extent to which they are centralized or decentralized is obviously dependent upon the extent to which authority is concentrated or dispersed.

Characterizing a strategy or policy as originated does not necessarily imply that it is imposed by command. Many are the adroit managers who originate them and obtain compliance by making unobtrusive suggestions. In fact, some skillful managers originate strategy or policy and secure compliance by allowing subordinate managers to leave a conference believing that they themselves originated it. But often a strategy or policy is imposed upon subordinates with a force and clarity that permit no deviation. Thus, a company president might originate a policy of using sales agents on a commission basis, rather than full-time sales people, by merely making indirect suggestions along this line to a sales manager, or, in another instance, the president might be positive and blunt in stating a policy that the company will not engage in price-cutting to make a sale.

4. Appealed. Second source is appeal. In practice, perhaps most policy and even some strategies stem from appeal of exceptional cases up the hierarchy of managerial authority. If occasions for decision arise for executives who do not know whether they have sufficient authority or how the matter should be handled, they may appeal to their superior. As appeals are taken upward and decisions are made on them, a kind of common law is established. Precedents develop and become guides for future managerial action.

Policies or strategies developed from appeals are sometimes incomplete, uncoordinated, and confused. If decisions are made on a given set of facts without regard for their possible effects on other aspects of the operations, or if unintended precedents develop from them, the resulting policies may not guide the thought and action of subordinates as really desired by top managers. Moreover, policies, or even strategies, may be formulated that the top executives do not even know about. For example, in one company there existed a long-time strategy of marketing strictly on a quality basis and never engaging in price-cutting. In a particularly strong competitive period, the chief executive gave the sales manager the right to cut price to meet some aggressive competition. After permitting this on several occasions, he found that he had, for all intents and purposes, changed the company's marketing strategy to that of being an industry price-cutter.

TYPES OF PLANS

Basically plans are of two types: formal and informal. Formal planning is comprehensive and rational. Informal planning is exclusive to managers who develop plans, but they never formally put them on paper and may not even communicate them to others. The informal planning remains only within the minds of the managers as an image of what should or shall be done. It lacks definiteness, expression and even rationality in the sense that it is instinctive in nature and not systematic. However, it is interesting to note that at times informal plans are more significant than formal ones.

Formal plan can be further classified into several categories:

(i) Strategic and Functional Planning. In strategic planning, the top managers determine the general objectives of the enterprise and the steps to accomplish them in the light of resources currently available and likely to be available in future. Functional planning, on the other hand, is planning that covers some functional areas like production, marketing, finance and purchasing.

(ii) Long-range and Short-range Planning. Long-range planning sets long-term goals for the enterprise and formulates specific plans for attaining these goals. It involves an attempt to anticipate, analyse and make decisions about basic problems which have significant reaching well beyond the present operating horizon of the enterprise. Short-range planning, on the other hand, is concerned with the determination of short-term activities to accomplish long-term objectives. Short-range planning relates to a relatively short period and has to be consistent with the long-range plans.

(iii) Administrative and Operational Planning. Administrative planning is done by the middle-level managers and it provides the foundation for the operative plans. Operative plans are made by the lower level managers to put the administrative plans into practice.

(iv) Ad hoc and Standing Planning. Ad hoc plans are made for certain specific matters. But standing plans are designed to be used over and over again. They include organisational structure, standard procedures and standard methods.

PLANNING PROCESS OR TECHNIQUE

It was observed earlier that planning is basically an exercise in determining the ends (*i.e.*, objectives) and means to achieve them. Thus, planning process involves basically two phases, namely;

(1) Determination of objectives.

(2) Setting up of plans to achieve the determined objectives.

Objectives

Objectives are the ends towards which the activities of an enterprise are directed. They provide direction to various activities of the enterprise. They depict a future state of affairs which an organisation strives to realise. They lay down guidelines for various activities and also constitute a source of legitimacy which justify the various activities of an organisation and also its very existence. Objectives serve as bench-mark of measuring the performance of various people working in the organisation and the overall efffectiveness and efficiency of the organisation.

Objectives are key to effective planning in any business organisation. In fact, planning has no meaning unless it is related to certain well-defined objectives or goals. Objectives are not only useful in planning but also in other managerial functions like organising, directing and controlling. They are an important aid in decision-making in any area of business. Clear-cut objectives encourage consistency in decision-making in the long-run.

On the basis of above discussion, we can define objective as follows:

It is an end (purpose, mission, result, or goal) the organisation is expected to achieve, acquire, create, preserve or distribute and towards which managers direct their efforts. The achievement of objectives is a must for the survival and growth of any business organisation. Peter F. Drucker has suggested that objectives must be set up in the following key areas of business: marketing, innovation, human organisation, financial resources, physical resources, productivity, social responsibility and profit resources.

Significance of Objectives

The importance of clearly defined objectives is generally recognised as contributing to management function in a variety of ways:

(1) Objectives serve as reference point for keeping the efforts of the organisation on proper lines.

(2) Continuous reviewing of objectives helps the organisation to compete effectively with the rival firms.

(3) They are helpful in co-ordinating the activities undertaken by the organisation.

(4) Clearly defined objectives are analogous to the star system which acts as a watch-word for managers just as it is used by ships for navigation.

(5) Objectives serve as prerequisites to determine effective policies, procedures, methods, strategies and rules.

Well-defined and integrated objectives for various units and functional areas within the organisation have numerous advantages which are as follows:

(i) Unity of Planning. Managers at various levels in the organisation make plans of their own. Planning may lose its consistency unless plans have the same focus of attention.

(ii) Means of Decentralisation. Managerial work with appropriate authority and capacity for independent decision is shared by a large number of managers. This may lead to disintegration in place of decentralisation unless there is a comman goal. The objectives guide to coordinate and remove conflicts or misunderstanding between various individuals.

(iii) Basis of Control. Objectives provide the basis of control by clarifying the contribution of each position as well as each unit.

(iv) Stimulate Motivation. Objectives fit individual goals into overall organisation goals and make the job meaningful and worth-while and stimulate human motivation.

NATURE OF OBJECTIVES

Objectives are the action commitments through which the mission of a business organisation is to be carried out and the standards against which performance is to be measured. Effective objectives have the following characteristics:

(i) Objectives are Realistic and Operational. Objectives must be derived from "what our business is, what it will be and what it should be". They must be capable of being converted into specific targets and assignments, They must be capable of becoming the basis as well as the motivation for work.

(ii) Objectives may be Long-range or Short-range. Since a business organisation is a continuous entity, it must have both long-range and short-range objectives. Short-range objectives normally cover a period up to two years and long-range objectvies are to be achieved in the long-run. There must be an integral relationship between the short-range and long-range objectives of the enterprise.

(iii) Objectives are Multiple in Nature. There must be multiple objectives rather than a single objective. Objectives are needed in all areas of business on which its survival depends. Every department should have specific objectives which are directed towards the achievement of overall business objectives. Similarly, every position has certain objectives which are derived from the departmental objectives.

(iv) Objectives Follow a Hierarchy. The objectives of the organisation must have a hierarchy. A convenient way of structuring the objectives is first to view the organisation as a total entity with overall global goals. These goals provide the basis for setting them at the second level which in turn becomes the basis for goals of the third level and so on. The goals at the second level are the means used for achieving the goals or ends set at the level, and similarly, goals at third level become means to attain the objectives of second level. Thus, goals at various levels of organisation form an 'end-means' chain.

ORGANISATIONAL LEVEL	PARTIAL FUNCTIONAL ORGANISATION CHART		
TOP	MANAGING DIRECTOR		
FIRST	PRODUCATION	FINANCE	SALES
SECOND	PRODUCT A	PRODUCT B	PRODUCT C
THIRD	SHOP 1	SHOP 2	SHOP 3
LOWEST	OPERATIVE	OPERATIVE	OPERATIVE

This 'end-means' chain continues throughout the organistional structure. The goals at each level are derived more or less logically, from the levels immediately above, and they collectively form a hierarchy. The above figure illustrates the idea of goals following the hierarchy, through 'end-means' chain. The hierarchy of goals following the 'end-means' chain highlights two important aspects of the nature of objectives:

(1) Movement to lower levels of organisational hierarchy, results in narrowing the scope for goal setting at successive levels;

(2) The time perspective kept in view similarly shrinks as we move down to lower levels of the organisational hierarchy. While an operative worker may have goals for each day, say, the number of units to be produced, the time perspective of a departmental head, say Production Manager may be a year or so.

FEATURES OF VALID OBJECTIVES

If objectives are to serve as effective guides to action they must possess the following characteristics:

(1) **Objectives Must be Concrete, Specific and Particular.** If stated in the too general terms they may not successfully direct the efforts constructively. A company may say that it is in the business of producing air conditioners. However, since it will be in entirely different business if it chooses to make air conditioners for office buildings, or for home cooling, or for automobiles, the company must specify the kind of air conditioners it will produce.

(2) **Objective Should be Verifiable.** If progress cannot be measured against specific standards or goals they lose their value from the standponit of controlling. A goal 'to increase profits' is measurable in general sense but whether the increase is of 5 percent or 50 percent both will meet the goal. If, however, it is set " increase porfits by 10 percent," 'progress is measurable with greater specificity.

(3) **Objectives Should Encourage Higher Performance yet be Realistic.** The objectives should have an orientation towards bringing about growth, developement and improvement of the organisational performance at all levels, but they must not be set at so high a level that they discourage even a try on the part of the members of organisation not to talk of achieving them.

(4) **Objectives Should be Result-centred.** Goals should focus on results and not on activity. Activity is only a means to achieve the results or objectives. Taking the above example, if the management decides to increase sales by 20%, it is an activity in terms of increasing the sales. This activity may or may not achieve the results of realising 10% increase in profits because of increase in cost of distribution and taxes. Thus, increasing sales is a means and not an end in itself.

(5) **Objectives Must be Balanced.** Once a hierarchy of objectives has been established, there may be tendency for certain objectives to claim undue emphasis. Part of managers's role is to make sure that each objective gets only the due share of activity and resources.

(6) **Objectives Must Form a 'Network'.** They must be interconnected and mutually supportive, and cannot exist in isolation. For example, suppose that one unit of the company has the objective that will increase costs at the same time there is in effect a 'cost saving' programme, the two objectives will become conflicting, and obviously, such a situation will not work.

MANAGEMENT BY OBJECTIVES

A method of implementing compatible objectives at all organisational levels is management by objectives (M.B.O.). The thrust of MBO is on what must be accomplished (goals) rather than how it is to be accomplished (methods). Fundamental to the MBO is the mutual setting of objectives between each subordinate and his superior. It allows the subordinate plenty of room to make creative decisions on his own. The supervisor is available for advice, counsel, and direction, should the subordinate seek his assistance.These objectives are then used as standards for evaluating the performance of subordinates. Ideally, the process should begin at the top of the organisational hierarchy.These objectives are then used as guides to set goals at second level and so on. This process works in the fashion of 'end-means' chain discussed above. But, goal setting under MBO differs from other approaches because of its emphasis on measurable objectives, the specification of time period for the completion of objectives, and participation by superior and subordinate in goal setting process and the evaluation of performance. The process seems deceptively simple; in reality, it requires careful analysis of each position and its necessary contribution to overall organisational objectives. Moreover, it requires that top management makes special efforts to determine measurable objectives at all levels.

MBO has several advantages:

(1) It provides greater employee involvement and commitment. One works one's best to achieve goals set by self.

(2) Under M.B.O. objectives are more realistic because they are set by those who have to carry them out.

DEVELOPMENT OF PLANS

Once objectives are established, the logical sequence is to develop the plans to achieve them. The plans shall be developed along three lines:

(1) Establishing policies and strategies.

(2) Developing medium-range and short-range plans to implement the policies and strategies.

(3) Laying down procedures, schedules for carrying out the medium and short-term plans.

Before we detail the process how each of these three is shaped it is important to know the framwork within which they are to be developed:

(i) **Developing the Planning Premises.** It is important to identify the assumption on which plans will be based. Assumptions are the expected future setting on which all planning depends. As a matter of fact, each of us makes assumptions for everything we plan. For instance, we either take packed lunch or money to buy lunch even though we are not hungry when we leave for work in the morning.We do so on the simple assumption that we will be hungry again by noon. Similarly, managers draw up plans based on their assumptions or beliefs about the future events. It is important to point out that these assumptions need revision with the change in situation.

(ii) **Reviewing Limitations.** There is always the possibility of existence of certain limitations that could affect the ability of the work-group to reach its objectives. An intelligent manager must make plans anticipating the conditions of limitations that might restrict the smooth operation of the plans. Key areas for anticipation are power, machinery, inventories of material and parts, finance and labour availability. There are some of the important areas which must be given due weightage while making plans. A good manager must consider combinations of all possible limitations and make provisions for them.

(iii) Developing Alternatives. The planner must try to find all the possible alternatives plans of action. Without resorting to such a search, he is likely to be guided by his limited imagination. Usually, there are several alternatives for any problem. The planner should try to screen out the most unviable alternatives so that he has a limited number of alternatives for final choice. Contingency plans should also be developed in order to smooth out the effects of deviations in the original plan.

(iv) Evaluating Alternatives. The alternatives must be evaluated in terms of various factors like cost, risk, availability of funds etc. to choose the most feasible alternative.The reason for considering many alternatives is to know which plan offers the greatest chance of success in reaching the predetermined objectives. The planner may take the help of various quantitative techniques to evaluate the available alternatives. This exercise may lead to the conclusion that no one course of action is optimum; so the planner may decide to select two or more alternatives and combine them to have the most feasible plan.

The purpose of listing these steps is that before the managers set themselves to formulate plans they should do so with reference to the framework provided by these steps.

After the objectives have been laid, the formulation of policies and strategies constitutes the next step. Policies are broad guides to action. They prescribe the most desirable ways and means for the accomplishment of a given objective. For example, to meet the objectives of 'making prompt collections from creditors' the policy statement may be: "To extend credit after satisfactory investigation, in line with sound credit principles, and pursue the creditor delaying the payment beyond credit period".

Policies generally deal with recurring problems. They may apply to entire institution or to specific functional areas or to both. Policies may extend over long or short periods of time. They may be either broad or limited in scope. A policy simply sets guidelines or boundaries within which subsequent decisions are made. The purpose of policies is not to achieve absolute uniformity of action but to guide people who have to take decision in that connection. While objectives provide the end which a manager should try to achieve, the policies provide the guidelines which he should keep in mind while achieving the ends. Policies tend to predecide to avoid repeated analysis and give a unified structure to various types of planning.

PROCESS OF FORMULATING POLICIES

In formulating business policy, the first step is to specify clearly the areas needing policies. Relevant information should then be collected. The sources of information are past practices, stated objectives, government requirements, trade associations, unions and other sources. Once the information is collected, the top management should work on deciding the policies in consultation with the different levels of the organisation. The responsibility of laying down policies though lies with top management, the lower levels must be consulted and due weightage given to their advice. Participation by subordinates would ensure that policies are realistic because they possess the first hand knowledge of organisational climate. Secondly, since policies are to be used by subordinates, their participation in formulation process would encourage ready acceptance of these by them. While laying down the policy statements the management should take care that policies laid down possess following features:

(1) The policy should express the intention of management.

(2) The policy must be preceded by a brief description of subject-matter so that there may be a common understanding of what policy covers.

(3) The policy must be laid by top management only. It is only at this level that a total view of organisation can be taken.

(4) The policy must be broad, general and flexible. To be a guide to action or decision "generality" is necessary, or else it would become a decision in itself.

(5) The policy must be translated in writing; two reasons may be advanced for this:

Firstly, a policy will be vague unless it is written down. Secondly, if a policy is in writing, it will reveal the intentions of the top management clearly. Special skill is required to select and adhere to policy language which will state and synthesize the general principles and the scope for discretion. A policy should be finalised after consulting the persons who are supposed to use it. The reaction of such people should be analysed carefully. After a policy is framed it must be properly communicated to the people who are expected to use it. It is also necessary to appraise the policies after a certain period of time to know their effectiveness.

Kinds of Policies

Policies may be set up in the key areas of the enterprise like production, purchase, finance, personnel and marketing. If this is done, the policies will be classified by major functions of an enterprise. Policies may also be classified on the basis of source of the policy, *i.e.*, *(i)* internal, *(ii)* external, and *(iii)* appealed. Internal policies include those initiated by managers at various levels to guide the subordinates. External policies include those policies arising to meet the various pressures and requests of forces outside the enterprise, such as government, trade unions and trade associations. Appealed policies come into existence from the appeal of an exceptional problem by a subordinate to his superior regarding how to handle the problem.

There is one more classification of policies based on the organisational levels of managers. There may be policies which are used primarily by the top managers, other policies by the middle managers and still other policies which are applicable chiefly to the first line managers. The policies at these three levels may be termed as basic, general and departmental policies. Basic policies affect and relate to the topmost level of managerial hierarchy. General policies affect the middle level managers and are more specific than the basic policies. Departmental policies are highly specific and are applicable at the lowest level of management.

Benefits of Policies

Policies are set up to achieve the following benefits:

(i) By making policy decisions on frequently recurring problems the top management provides the guidelines to lower level managers. It will permit decisions to be made in case of similar problems without repeating the reasoning and expensive analysis required initially to state the policy or make the decision.

(ii) Policies help managers at various levels to act with confidence without the need for consulting the superiors every time. This will also ensure promptness of action.

(iii) Policies facilitate better administrative control. Policies provide the rational basis of evaluating the results. By setting up policies, the management ensures that decisions made will be consistent and in keeping with the objectives and interests of the enterprise.

Strategy

Having laid the policies, the other related task is to choose strategies. Strategy involves as to how available resources will be used to achieve objective, in the face of obstacles, which may be in form of competitive forces, government regulations, technical upheavals, social change etc. That is to say, the strategic planning pays special attention to relatively uncontrollable external factors. Emphasis is placed on predicting the future behaviour of external variables and the formulations of alternative courses of action in the light of future events. As such, the manager has to do a lot of forceasting before laying down the strategy. To illustrate the view point, in view of changing consumer tastes and technology the company may decide to change its product line. This decision would be termed as strategic. This illustration points to how the organisation is irrevocably committed to large expenditures once the decision is taken. A mistake in strategic planning may be disastrous.

Once the policies and strategies have been decided upon, the management's task is to specify the medium-range and short-range plans. Medium-range planning is the process whereby specific functional plans are laid for specific number of years incorporating the details of how strategies are to be carried out to achieve the long-range objectives. Normally, the planning period is five years. Medium range plans generally cover major functions only and are translated into financial term in the form of a proforma Balance Sheets and profoma Profit and Loss Statement.

The short-range plans are one or two year plans to carry on the actual work. They are very detailed and include budgets and programmes. These are explained below:

Programme

A Programme is a sequence of activities designed to implement policies directed towards the achievement of objectives. A programme lays down the definite steps which will be taken to accomplish a given task. It also lays down the time to be taken for the completion of each step. A programme might include such general activities as purchasing new machines that will enable to increase output or hiring work-force to operate new equipment or introduction of a new product in the market. Thus, a programme is a complex of objectives, policies, procedures, task assignments, steps to be taken, resources to be employed and other elements necessary to carry out a given course of action. The managers at different levels chalk out programmes describing the contents, and actions in their spheres of responsibility to contribute towards organisational objectives.

Budgets

A budget is a statement of expected results expressed in numerical terms like rupees, product units, and man hours. Since it is a statement of expected results it is also used as an instrument of managerial control. It provides a standard by which actual operations can be measured and by which variations can be checked. But it should not be forgotten that making a budget is clearly planning. A budget forces an enterprise to make in advance a numerical compilation of expected cash flow, expenses and revenues, capital outlays or machine hour utilisation. Budgeting is essential for control, but it cannot mechanise unless it reflects plans. As a means of effective planning, the process of budgeting may involve the preparation of budgets of sales, purchase, materials, labour and manufacturing expenses.

Budegting coordinates the activities of various departments of a business enterprise by adjusting the departmental budgets into the master budget. Every departmental head consciously plans the future operations of his department in tangible terms. Since budget portray verifiable and measurable goals to be reached within a period of one year, they inject a sense of clarity, direction and purpose in the activities of the organisation. However, to be effective means of planning, budgets should have functional flexibility. They should not be rigid instruments. They should be able to cope with unforeseen circumstances within a predictable range of activities.

Schedules and Procedures

The final step in planning process is to develop schedules and procedures to put into operation the short-range plans. Schedules are the timings fixed for completing the programmed operations. They lay down the timings when each step in a programme will be executed. Schedules are a necessary part of planning in order to ensure continuity in production to secure constant flow of product into the market and to avoid delay in various operations.

The procedures are sequence of steps in implementing various plans. According to G. R. Terry, a procedure is a series of related tasks that make up the chronological sequence and the established way of performing the work to be accomplished. It is a list of systematic steps for handling events that occur regularly. Procedures involve planned sequence of operations for handling recurring business operations uniformly and consistently. Procedures are genarally set up for processing an order, shipping the goods, handling claims, collection of payments and so forth.

Procedures should be distinguished from policies. A policy is a guide to thinking. But a procedure is a guide to action and it hardly leaves any room for judegment. Policies are specific guide-lines for managerial thinking towards certain issues. But procedures are systematic ways of handling regular events. They are operational guides to action and routinise the performance of repetitive jobs. Every procedure consists of various methods to accomplish each phase of work. A method is the manual or mechanical way by which each operation is performed. A method is more limited in scope than a procedure because it deals with a task that is only one step of a procedure.

❒

7

Corporate Policy For Production and Marketing

Companies make locational decisions after considering following factors.

1. Availability of Raw Materials. The availability of the required quantity of raw materials at a reasonable cost is an important factor for determining the location of an industrial unit. In most of the industries, the cost of raw materials forms more than 50% of the total cost of their products. The impact of raw materials on location depends upon their nature and the source of their deposits. Weber classified raw materials into ubiquities and localised materials. Generally, ubiquities like water, clay, and sand which are found at all places have very little influence on location. That means the place of production would be fixed independently. But in some cases materials of ubiquitous nature may so vary in quantity and, quality that they are in fact regarded as fixed.

Localised raw materials may be further sub-divided into pure materials such as raw cotton and wool and gross materials such as sugarcane, iron ore and coal. The latter type of materials lose their weight in the process of production, it is better to locate the plant near the source of material because there will be greater savings of transportation costs. For instance, iron and steel industry which uses coal and iron ore as raw materials has localised near the coal and iron are mines.

2. Proximity to the Market. Industrial units using non-weight losing raw materials tend to locate near the markets because of so many advantages. A manufacturer can improve his customers relations and render rapid services to his customers. Industries producing perishable commodities and those producing for a local market are also drawn towards the market because it would reduce the cost of transport in distributing the finished products. The Industrial units tend to disperse only if they find a new market for their product.

3. Transport and Communication Facilities. Transport services are required for assembling of material and distribution of products. While selecting the location it should be seen that transportation facilities are easily available at reasonable rates. The junction points of water ways roadways and railways have the tendency to become industrial centres because of this reason only. If an industrial unit is directly linked with the means of transportation, its transportation costs are lower. Besides transportation, communication services also play an important role in the location of industrial units. Every business firm requires information as regards raw materials, finished goods and market price which can be made available only when there are communication facilities. Since transport and communication facilities are not adequately available in rural areas, entrepreneurs are reluctant to start their operations in those areas.

4. Power and Fuel. An adequate supply of power and fuel is an important factor for the un-interrupted operations of any enterprise. In the initial days of industrial revolution, industrial units were located near coal deposits because coal was the major source of power and fuel and was of weight losing nature and quite bulky. But with .the introduction of other sources of power like electricity, gas, oil etc., the power factor has become more mobile. This has helped in dispersal of industries. The industrial units which mainly depend on the electric power tend to shift from a place if they do not get its regular supply. But iron and steel industry where coal is still the major source of fuel, is located near the coal mines.

5. Labour Supply. Every plant requires an adequate supply of labour with appropriate skills. Weber deduced that an industrial unit will deviate from the point of minimum transportation cost to the cheaper about centre if the additional cost of transportation at the new centre is more than compensated by the savings in labour cost. But this hypothesis has lost its significance in the recent years because of many reasons. Labour is easily mobile and there is a level of minimum wages fixed by law below which an industrial concern cannot go. Morecver, certain industries are capital intensive and they require less labour. Therefore, it can be said that supply of labour, particularly in country where there is large scale unemployment is not as important as it used to be half a century ago.

6. Supply of Capital. Finance is the life-blood of any industrial venture. Availability of adequate funds at low rates of interests is an important factor influencing industrial location. But in these days capital has become a highly mobile factor of production. Despite this fact, availability of funds at cheaper prices—is an important consideration. For instance, there are State Financial Corporations in various states which offer loans at a very low rate of interest if the entrepreneurs start their projects in the specified areas. Similarly, technocrat entrepreneurs who do not have sufficient capital to implement their projects will naturally be attracted towards these areas where they can get sufficient supply of finance.

7. Climate Considerations. Natural and climatic considerations like level of ground, topography (hilly and rocky surface) of a region, and drainage facilities influence the location of industries in certain cases. For example, cotton textile must require a humid climate. The humid climate of Bombay offered greater scope for the development of cotton textile industry. But the development of artificial humidification and air-conditioning has reduced the importance of climate to some-extent. Entrepreneurs do not prefer to locate their units in hilly and rocky are because of increase in transport cost. Similarly, regions which are subject to frequent floods, earth-quakes etc. do not attract industrial units.

8. External Economies. Sometimes industrial units are located in those centres where other industrial units area already located. It is because of the fact that transportation, warehousing, banking, communication and other services are easily available. Secondly, the raw materials may be easily available at cheaper rates. For instance, by-product of one unit may be the raw material for another. Distilleries are located near sugar factories because molasses which is the by-product of sugar industry is the raw material for distilleries.

9. Government Policy. In planned economies, the role of government policy with respect to location of industry is crucial. In India, the Central Government follows the policy of balanced regional development of the country which is necessary from the point of view of defence and social problems like slum, disparity of income and wealth and optimum use of resources. In order to implement this policy, the Government encourages industrialists to invest their money in backward areas by giving various tax incentives in the form of remission of excise duty or sales tax. Government also offers certain non-tax incentives like loan at cheaper: rates, factory sheds, etc. to attract the entrepreneurs. The Government has also announced that in future generally no license will be given to industries to be set up in metropolitan cities with a population of more than 10 lakhs and urban areas with more than 5 lakhs population as per 1971 census.

10. Personal Factor. Personal preference and prejudice of an entrepreneur may also play an important role in the choice of location. For instance, Mr. Ford started manufacturing motor cars in Detroit because it was his home town, and Lord Nuffield selected Cowley because the school in which his father was educated happened to be for sale. The success of the entrepreneur in such a location depends upon his extra personal efforts.

11. Strategic Considerations. Strategic considerations like law and order; political stability and safety also influence location. Naturally, entrepreneurs will like to locate their units in those areas which are safe and where there are least disturbances on account of law and order problems.

12. Miscellaneous Factors. Miscellaneous factors like historical incidents and attitude of the community also influence location of industries. In Mughal days, cottage industries thrived near the courts of rulers due to the patronage of State. Industrial relations atmosphere also affects the location. Facilities like housing, medical, recreation, banking and credit also attract the location of certain industrial units.

PRODUCTION POLICIES

Production functions involve the transformation of a set of inputs to predetermined outputs in accordance with the objectives of the organisation. Production management encompasses the design, implementation, operation and control of system made up of workers, materials, capital equipment, information and money to accomplish some set of objectives. Following are the major production/operations policy decisions with their determinants:

1. **Process Planning and Job Design.** Forecast of demand, product engineering, production technology, labour force, design stability.

2. **Raw Material and Work-in-progress Inventory.** Forecast of demand, cash flow, supplier reliability.

3. **Facilities Layout.** Medium and long-range forecast of demand and stability of product line production technology physical facilities constraints, safety considerations.

4. **Planning of Aggregate Output.** Short-range forecast of demand finished goods inventory level, cash flow, employment policy, plant capacity, state of production/operation system at the time of decision.

5. **Plant Location and Capacity.** Long-range forecast of the size and location of the market, capital structure, environmental conditions, state of operations and logistic system production technology.

The basic objective of policy decision in the area of production operations is the effective utilisation of organisational resources.

PURCHASING POLICY ISSUES

Having discussed the production policies bearing on vertical integration, production process, plant size and capacity and maintenance of facilities, we may now turn to the basic purchasing policy matters. While examining the question of vertical integration we have already explained the relevant factors that may influence decisions to produce raw materials, components and, parts for the final product, and the extent of backward vertical integration possible under various circumstances. What about supplies and services? Should a company make or buy its requirements of containers, stationery, transport services, water and power supply and such other items? Secondly, how should vendors be selected for procuring the supplies? Thirdly, what kind of policy decisions should govern the coordination of production purchasing and sales?

Policy on Vendor Selection

All companies regardless of the extent of vertical integration have to make purchases of certain materials and supplies as well as services. This is because of the various constraints—mainly financial and managerial—which make downstream integration impracticable beyond a stage. Wholesalers have to buy the factory stores and supplies, if not raw materials, for the final product, or for components and parts to be produced. Assuming that a number of dependable outside sources of supply exist, it needs to be decided:

(a) by what criteria should the company choose the suppliers to deal with?

(b) how many suppliers (vendors) should a company make purchases from-several of them, or one or two of them.

Maintenance and Replacement Policy

If the existing plant capacity and service facilities are well maintained, there are distinct advantages, and management can accordingly decide on plant capacity to be initially created. Depending on personal preferences of the executives and the philosophy of management, determining the attitude toward up-keep and maintenance, the policy may be one of high level conditioning of work environment, or a discriminating policy with deliberate decisions to provide for proper maintenance of only those facilities which are of critical importance like production, and stores. But just fixing things up is not good maintenance. Machines and equipments, plant services (power, gas, water, swears, pumps, fire protection), transportation facilities, and buildings (roofs, walls; floors, fixtures and fittings) need repairs. The importance of preventive maintenance is recognised in all workplaces for several reasons. Breakdowns stop production, make men and machine idle, cause lost production, and put orders behind schedule. It helps to reduce repairs, particularly those caused by breakdown of machines in use. The cost of maintenance cannot be kept too low. Preventive maintenance cost may be fairly high but the corresponding pay-off may justify the same. One way of holding down maintenance costs it to have trouble-free machines-machines that are designed to be trouble free, or which provide for built in detectors and gauges to reveal trouble spots before failures occur. Operations Research techniques like the 'queuing or waiting line theory' may also be useful to balance the need for maintenance staff and the maintenance work involved.

Whether to repair or replace machine parts and equipments which have worn out is a decision related to the maintenance of facilities. Obviously it should depend on the cast involved.

GOVERNMENTS APPROACH TO LOCATION

The Government can tackle the problem of concentration of industry by following two approaches:

(i) Positive approach-encouraging establishment of industrial units in the backward areas; and

(ii) Positive approach restraining the establishment of industrial units in the concentrated areas.

Negative Approach. The negative approach includes certain deterrents (*i.e.*, restrictions and disincentives) designated to prevent establishment of new units in concentrated areas. The State may introduce the following deterrents:

(a) Absolute prohibition to set up new industries in particular areas may be followed. For instance, the Industrial Policy, 1977 stated that no more licenses should be issued to new industrial units within certain limits of the cities having a population of more than ten lakhs and urban areas with a population of more than 5 lakhs.

(b) Enhanced rates of local taxes may be introduced. A levy may be imposed on the industrial units in the concentrated areas which may be spent for the benefit of units in the backward areas.

(c) Licensing policy may be so designed that it discourages new units in highely developed regions.

Positive Approach. The adaptation of positive approach is likely to give more satisfactory results as compared to the negative-approach. Under this approach, the State provides certain incentives for the establishement of industrial units in the selected areas. These incentives may take the following forms:

(a) Provision of public utility services in selected areas. These services include electricity, water, gas, transport and provision of socio-economic lamenities like recreation, education, health, etc. In addition, the Government has also extended certain ancillary economic facilities in these areas like institutions for importing technical knowledge to the workers.

(b) Providing adequate and cheap financial facilities directly by the Government or through the financial institutions. Establishment of industrial estates in industrially backward regions and liberal issue of licenses on a preferential basis for industrial units in backward areas.

(c) Granting of direct and indirect subsidies, granting of income tax exemption to the units set-up in backward areas and giving assurance by the State to purchase the products of the industrial units established in backward areas.

CONSIDERATIONS REGARDING BUY DECISIONS

Research studies have shown that make-or-buy decisions are sometimes made on the basis of insufficient data and faulty evaluation of implications resulting in huge wastes from making what could be more advantageously bought. Whether it is the production of containers and packing materials, or printing of forms, circulars and notices, or securing factory and office supplies, or transportation service, if there is no dependable source of procuring the items, obviously the buying option is ruled out. Dependability or reliability of supply should be naturally considered in terms of quantity, quality and timeliness of availability. Thus, for instance, the inadequacy of public power supply has led to the installation of power generators by many companies in certain States.

In general, a decision to make should follow whenever the expected cost savings provide higher return on the required capital investment than can be obtained from employing the funds in an alternative investment bearing the same risk. Thus, few firms, if any, consider making the items of office stationery (pencils, writing paper, and hundred other items) worthwhile. Likewise, setting up of printing press to print office forms, circulars and notices may not be worthwhile for most firms since there may not be enough printing work to ensure economic use of the printing machine. But intuitive decisions may not be possible in all cases particularly when differential costs are of major significance.

Identifying and estimating the relevant costs of manufacturing a product or creating a service facility require the following aspects to be noted:

1. Labour costs should be projected the light of such factors as the effect on the existing labour force, availability of the type of labour needed, probable labour cost trends, etc.

2. Imputed interest costs have to be taken into account when large investment are involved, which can be done by discounting the future cash flows;

3. Sunk cost (*i.e.*, costs otherwise incurred on creating facilities) have a value depending on whether the same can be utilised by the firm for other internal purposes rented, or disposed of;

4. While calculating the differential cost of making and buying, the purchase cost should include the net supply price plus freight and incremental handling cost;

5. Fixed costs seldom remain unaffected, particularly the managerial costs. The planning and supervision of any new operation may divert present managers from other responsibilities or require additional supervisory personnel. These costs are somewhat difficult to measure and are often ignored;

6. Risk of long-term investment creates a bias in favour of buying. The risk element may be recognised by adding a premium to the rate of expected return;

7. Projecting the cost of raw materials needs consideration of the type and quantity of materials required, probable market trends, availability of reliable suppliers, freight, order size, discount, etc.

Apart from the saving in cost and return on capital investment, there are several non-cost factors that also need to be considered. In favour of making, there may be such factors as:

(a) maintenance of labour already employed,

(b) idle facilities,

(c) tax considerations,

(d) desire to maintain secrecy of process,

(e) poor quality of supply,

(f) instability of supply.

On the other hand, in favour of buying there may be considerations, such as:

(A) special services rendered by outside suppliers,

(B) scope of wider selection,

(C) fluctuation in requirements due to uneven production of end products,

(D) lack of managerial experience,

(E) possibility of passing on the risk of investment to suppliers,

(F) lack of capita.

CHOICE OF PRODUCTION PROCESSES

Along with the policy decisions on production activities policies need to be formulated also on production processes. Following are different aspects of the choice, *viz.*,

(1) Division of Labour. The volume of production and the extent of standardisation of products determine whether and how far line operations could be sub-divided and entrusted to different operatives. Divisions of labour has been the characteristic features of large-scale manufacturing works since the industrial revolution. Routinisation of operations is known to produce monotony, boredom, lack of motivation and low morale due to 'anomie' (aloneness among many). Job enlargement is recognised now as a superior means of securing higher productivity and efficiency.

(2) Policy on Mechanisation and Automation. Technological advances over the last half a century have enlarged the scope of mechanisation and automation in many industries; *e.g.*, the use of tractors and harvesters in agriculture, automatic spinning and weaving in textile mills, packing and packaging of products, loading and unloading of cargo, automatic signalling in the railways, assembly line operations, etc.

(3) Choice of Technology. The technology to be used is uniquely given in the case of certain industries (products). Airlines may use aircrafts of different types to service particular regions. On the choice of technology depends the devisions regarding equipment, personnel methods of operation and organisation. In the service organisations, too, the process to be used may require a choice to be made out of different alternatives.

(4) Size and Location of Production Units. For large enterprises, the decision with respect to the size of plant needs to be examined with two alternatives in view, *viz.*,

(i) Large size with centralised location, and

(ii) Dispersal of operating units with small size of plant capacity.

MARKETING STRATEGIES OR LEADING INDIAN COMPANIES

Plans and policies related to marketing have to be formulated and implemented on the basis of the 4 Ps of the marketing mix, *i.e.* product, pricing, place (distribution), and promotion. The major issues and decisions relate to these marketing mix factors. Questions such as; what types of products to offer? to offer at what prices? through which distribution channel? and, by the use of which promotional tool? have to be answered. We discuss each of the marketing mix factors below.

(A) Product Policy

Product denotes the goods and services that an organisation-offers to its target markets. Plans and policies related to the product and market need to be formulated and implemented on the basis of characteristics such as quality, features, choice of models, brand name, packaging, etc. Strategies dictate the manner in which product and market characteristics would be defined. Thus, competitive strategic may be implemented by stressing on high quality, better and more features. The growth strategy of Bajaj Auto has the quality of its vehicles as a prominent factor. The product policy of Reliance is to offer high fashion fabrics of new varieties and design. Not only consumer goods companies but industrial products manufactures may also have to consider the product characteristics, as mentioned above, to set marketing plans and policies. Thermax offers a service franchise scheme to implement its marketing policy for boilers. This policy is based on the thinking that if service is assured in a competitive market, sales will follow. In this manner, product and service characteristics help a company in implementing its strategy just like a strategy guides the formulation and implementation of product plans and policies.

(B) Place (Channels of Distribution Policy)

Place (or distribution) is the process by which goods or services are made available to the customers. Distribution plans and policies address themselves to issues such as, the channels to be used; transportation, logistics, and inventory storage management; coverage of markets; etc

The use of distribution plans and policies in the marketing function as well as strategy implementation is important. The success of market-oriented strategies, specially in competitive environment, rests on the efficiency and activeness of the distribution system. Several companies realise this importance and make efforts to use their distribution systems strategically. For instance, Foods Specialities Ltd. (FSL) has a conscious policy of regarding the retailer as an important link in the distribution system. It offers better margins, facilities support to its retailers. In contrast, Glaxo-its competitor in the baby foods market-failed to react favourably to retailers demand for better margins during the 1970s as a result of which its popular brand Farex lost out to Nestle's (now FSL) brand Cerelac, a competitive disadvantage that still exists.

Marketing Plans and Policies at Atlas Cycles

Atlas Cycles, traditionally for over three decades, had relied on a marketing policy built around the product attributes of durability and reliability. But during the 1980s, its leadership position was seriously threatened by competitors, mainly Hero Cycles, which offered their products with new features and lower prices. Since 1985, Atlas Cycles has had to rethink its marketing plans and policies as it has decided to adopt a growth strategy.

The major aspects of marketing plans and policies are described below:

Product. Based on stringent quality control newer models such as Atlas Goldline, Atlas Goldline Super, Funfleet (in the sports cycles category), and Atlas Concorde Pro.-10 have been introduced, Several new features, such as front wheel reflector, better handle, new chain cover, and mascot on front mudguard were added to create Atlas Goldline. Atlas Concorde Pro-l0 is a high-tech model with an imported 10-gear system and a new set of seats, handle grips, reflectors, etc..

Pricing. Atlas Cycles markets its products on the basis of a premium pricing policy, *i.e.* its models are priced higher than those of its competitors. All the marketing policies revolve around the question: how to maintain competitiveness, market share, and leadership position with higher-priced products?

Distribution. Dealers in the bicycle industry-like those in several other industries-have a major influence on the brand choice. Distribution policies at Atlas Cycles are centred on the approach of maintaining a close relationship with dealers arid convincing them of the high quality of products that justifies a premium pricing policy.

Promotion. The advertising policy at Atlas Cycles is built on two central tasks to adopt a proactive approach to highlight the genuine "quality" leadership of Atlas products; and to find ways to project the market leadership of the company through contemporary and technologically superior products.

In this manner, Atlas Cycles attempts to implement its strategies of modernisation and competitive stability in a market which is increasingly becoming more quality and status conscious.

(C) Promotion Policy

Promotion deals with marketing communication intended to convey the company, and product or service image to prospective buyers. The promotional mix consists of four activities: advertising, personal selling, sales promotion, and publicity.

Promotional plans and policies have to consider the basic question of what promotional mix to adopt so that promotional activities can be used to implement strategies.

The increasing competitiveness in several industries in India has prompted companies to adopt promotion as a strategic tool. The availability of the medium of television has encouraged small companies making products like Vicco creams, Lijjat Papad, Pan Parag, Promise toothpaste, Nirma and several others to adopt a promotional policy of using TV advertising extensively., The nature of product/industry also determines the type of promotional tool used. The promotional policy of Lohia Machines for LML Vespa Scooters currently rests on using safety as a unique selling proposition as scooters are considered as vehicles mainly for the middle class men. Eureka Forbes has adopted a deliberate sales promotion policy of door-to-door selling, and demonstrations at exhibitions for its home improvement products.

(D) Pricing Policy

Price denotes the money that customers pay in exchange for goods and services. It is important to the seller because it represents the returns of efforts. To a buyer, price is the value that is assigned For instance, HCL has based its marketing policy on low-priced copiers and competes with its rivals, mainly Modi Xerox, by claiming a better price-performance relationship of its products. This is done through a promotional policy of comparative advertising. Prices are often used as a determinant of market segmentation, which in turn becomes the basis for creating different models of the same product. The market for soaps, for instance, is divided into premium and popular segments representing the high-priced and low-priced soaps. A segmentation of this type has implications for all the factors in the marketing mix, apart from pricing and helps in implementing marketing policies such as market penetration or partial retrenchment from markets.

PRODUCT LIFE CYCLE

Marketing managers plan for creating new products and recreating the image of existing products. The question is why they do so? Product life cycle concept provides the answer. The concept informs the managers that sooner or later a product will die. If a business enterprise is to be an ongoing entity, it must develop new products or improve on its established ones. What is product life cycle, then? Product life cycle refers to the stages from conception to death in the life of a product. William Shakespear spoke of seven ages of man from birth to death. Like human beings, products also pass through several distinct life stages, each of which generates unique problems and opportunities and calls for special strategies.

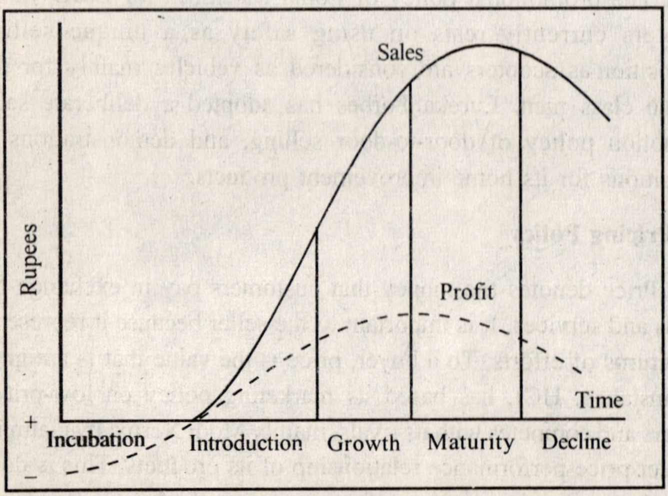

The Product Life Cycle

The product life cycle is made up of five phases: incubation, introduction, growth, maturity and decline. These phases are depicted in the following figure in terms of the sales and profit of a typical product.

(1) Incubation. In this phase, a rum conceives the idea of a product, develops the 'Product on a limited scale and tests its profitability before finally deciding to introduce it in the market-place. Conception of ideas, Creation or development and testing of the product involves huge investments in Research and Development (R & D). Therefore, at this stage of a product's life, the firm will have lots of expenses to incur but no profits. The diagram shows that in incubation phase, the profit line is sinking below the axis.

(2) Introduction. After testing, a product enters the introduction, stage during which the public is acquainted with the merits of the new product and acceptance is gained. Since the product is new to the public and customers take time to shift from the existing products, sales and profits are at a low level. Sales begin to build up as the prospective customers learn of the product from advertising and other promotional avenues. The rum may even incur losses at introduction stage since heavy expenses in overheads are involved and also because of the risk attached with product's acceptability in the market.

(3) Growth. If the product is accepted by potential buyers, it usually enters a rapid-growth stage. Sales volume and profits rise rapidly as new customers give the product a try and the early buyers go for repurchasing it. The product may gain reputation by word of mouth, advertising or acceptance by opinion leaders. Due to greater sales, the firm bothers less about promotion costs. Price remains high during growth stage to recoup heavy introduction losses. During later growth.phase, prices are lowered as other competitive firms introduce similar products to exploit the market opportunity. The rum should try to prolong the growth period as much as possible to take advantage of rising profits.

(4) Maturity. Growth rates remain stable during maturity period, but eventully decline as the backlog of potential buyers is exhausted.

Competition is tough and pressure to reduce price forces some firms to get out of the market. The maturity stage usually lasts longer than the introduction or growth phases. Customers develop loyalty to certain brands on the basis of their personal liking and sales for a particular product are mostly limited to the customers who are satisfied with that product. Prices are lower and comparatively stable among competitors. Attempts are made to increase sales by advertising with new phrases or slogans, developing new uses of the product, making slight improvements in the existing product and concentrating on those potential buyers which might have been left out earlier. For the first time the supply of available products exceeds their demand in the market.

(5) Decline. In the decline phase, the product starts fading and something else begins to shine the product gradually loses a sizable number of customers without replacing them. Both sales and profits go down steadily and films reduce promotional expenditure as they begin to accept the product's fate. Many firms leave the market and only few firms produce the product. Safety razor and electric shavers replace the straight razor, colour television supplants black and white and slode rules are exchanged for cheap pocket calculators. Ultimately the management of a firm may decide to drop the product from the market since there is no or very little demand for it

FACTOR TAKEN INTO ACCOUNT TO DECIDE THE LOCATION OF PLANT

One of the important problems of launching an industrial enterprise is the choice of suitable location which will help in minimisation of production cost and maximisation of profit. In order to select an optimum location, the promoters must carefully study the impact of the following factors:

(1) **Availability of Raw Materials.** The availability of the required quality and quantity of raw materials at a reasonable

cost is an important factor for determining the location of an industrial unit in most of the industries, the cost of raw materials forms more than 50% of the total cost of their products. The impact of raw materials on location depends upon their nature and the source of their deposits. Generally, ubiquities like wateclay, and sand which are found a all places have very little influence on location. That means the place of production would be fixed independently. But in some cases materials of ubiquitous nature may so very in quantity and quality that they are in fact regarded as fixed. For, example, paper manufacturing plants require a regular supply of a large quantity of pure water and they are, therefore, located near the banks of the rivers.

Localised raw materials may be further sub-divided into pure materials such as raw cotton and wool and gross materials such as sugarcane, iron ore and coal. The latter type of raw materials lost their eight in the process of production. If a large quantity of weight, losing material is to be used during production, it is better to locate the plant near the source of in at material because there will be greater savings of transportation costs.

(2) Proximity to the Market. Industrial units using non weight losing raw materials tend to locate near the markets because of so many advantages. A manufacturer can improve his customer relations and render rapid services to his customers. Industries producing perishable commodities and those producing for a local market are also drawn towards the market. Because it would reduce the cost of transport in distributing the finished products.

(3) Labour. Every plant requires an adequate supply of labour with appropriate skill. Weber deduced that an industrial unit will deviate from the point of minimum transportation cost to the cheaper labour centre if the additional cost of transportation at the new centreis more than compensated by the savings in labour cost. But this hypothesis has lost it significance in the recent years because of many reasons. Labour is easily mobile and there is a level of minimum wages fixed by law below which an industrial concern cannot go. Moreover, certain in industries are capital intensive and they require less labour.

(4) Transport and Communication Facilities. Transport services are required for assembling of material and distribution of products. While selecting the location it should be seen that transportation facilities are easily available at reasonable rates. The junction points of waterways, roadways and railways have the tendency to become industrial centres because of this reason only. If an industrial unit is directly linked with the means of transportation, its transportation costs are lower. Besides transportation, communication services also play an important role in the location of industrial units. Every business firm requires information as regards raw materials, finished goods and market price which can be made available only when there are communication facilities.

(5) Finance. Finance is the life-blood of any industrial venture. Availability of adequate funds at low rates of interests is an important factor influencing industrial location. But in these days capital has become a highly mobile factor of production. Despite this fact, availability of funds at cheaper price is an important consideration. For instance, there are State Financial Corporations in various states which offer loans at a very low rate of interest if the entrepreneurs start their projects in the specified areas.

(6) Power and Fuel. An adequate supply of power and fuel is an important factor for the un-interrupted operations of any enterprise. In the initial days of industrial revolution, industrial units were located near coal deposits because coal was the major source of power and fuel and was of weight losing nature and quite bulky. But with the introduction of other sources of power like electricity, gas, oil etc., the power factor has become more mobile. This has helped in dispersal of industries. The industrial units which mainly depend on electric power tend to shift from a place if they do not get its regular supply.

(7) **External Economics.** Sometimes industrial units are located in those centres where other industrial units are already located. It is because of the fact that transportation, warehousing, banking communication and other services are easily available. Secondly, the raw materials may be easily available at cheaper rates. For instance, by-product of one unit may be the raw material for another.

(8) **Climatic to Considerations.** Natural and climatic considerations like level of ground, topography (hilly and rocky surface) of a region, and drainage facilities influence the location of industries in certain cases. For example, cotton textile mills require a humid climate. The humid climate of Mumbai offered greater scope for the development of cotten textile industry. But the development of artificial humidification and air-conditioning has reduced the importance of climate to some extent. Entrepreneurs do not prefer to locate their units in hilly and rocky areas because of increase in transport cost.

(9) **Personal Factor.** Personal preference and prejudice of an entrepreneur may also play an important role in the choice of location. For instance, Mr. Ford started manufacturing motor cars in Detroit because it was his home town, and Lord Nuffield selected Cowley because the school in which his father was educated happened to be for sale. The success of the entrepreneur in such a location depends upon his extra personal efforts.

(10) **Government Policy.** In planned economies, the role of government policy with respect to location of industry is

crucial. In India, the Central Government follows the policy of balanced regional development of the country which is necessary from the point of view of defence and social problems like slum, disparity of income an wealth and optimum use of resources. In order to implement this policy, the Government encourages industrialists to invest their money in backward areas by giving various tax incentives in the form of remission of excise duty or sales tax. Government also offer certain non-tax incentives like loan at cheaper rates, factory sheds, etc. to attract the entrepreneurs.

(11) Miscellaneous factors like historical incidents and attitude of the community also influence location of industries. In Mughal days, cottage industries thrived near the courts of rulers due to the patronage of State. Industrial relations atmosphere also affects the location. Facilities like—housing, medical, recreation, banking and credit also attract the location of certain industrial units.

SELECTION OF THE SITE

The promoters of an industrial unit are confronted with the problem of choosing the exact site after deciding the area of location. While choosing the site, the following factors should be taken into consideration:

(a) Site is well connected with various modes of transport.

(b) Raw materials are available easily.

(c) There was facilities for disposal of polluted water and other waste material, if there is any.

(d) Municipality rules and regulations allow the construction of building suited to the plant.

(e) Labour is easily available.

(f) The site has good surroundings. There should be no congestion of traffic.

(g) Certain essential service organisations like post office, bank and warehouse exist near the site.

(h) The size of the plot has scope for expansion.

The guiding principle in the fixation of exact location for the plant is that it must result in the lowest unit cost in producing and distributing a product. For this purpose, industrialists will determine and compare the total cost per unit of product at various sites. The elements of total cost are transportation costs, costs of material and fuels, cost of power and water, cost of plant site and building, rates and taxes, and labour and administrative costs. Besides these economic factors, there are other considerations which are the matter of judgment rather than mathematical calculation. For instance, personal or historical factors may compel an industrialist to choose a particular site. Sometimes, a sub-optimum site may be chosen because no other site is available.

The total cost per unit of product varies according to the site chosen. Some industrialists are inclined towards cities while others towards the villages. The site in the city is associated with many benefits like availability of transport and communication, repair and maintenance facilities, facilities for disposal of effluent and water and presence of subsidiary services like education, health and recreation. But land is very costly and rents are high in cities or urban areas. Moreover, there is over-crowding congestion of traffic, noise and dust in these areas. That is why, some industrialists decide to move away from urban complexes. Rents, rates and taxes are very low in villages and semi-urban areas. Moreover, there is no congestion of traffic and over crowding.

It is the policy of the Government to have dispersal of industries so that there is balanced regional development in the country. Government provides many services and supplies raw materials at subsidised rates in these estates. The disadvantage caused by non urban siting are more than compensated by the facilities and subsidies provided by the Government. It is significant to point out that financial institutions also encourage the setting up of new plants in semiurban or rural areas. The licensing policy of the Central Government is also guided by the consideration of balanced regional development. In practice, an industrialist is not so free to choose the location and the site for his project.

Government Policy on Industrial Location. In a planned economy like India, location of industries is an important factor in the creation of a climate for the balanced economic growth of various regions. In the absence of regulation of industrial location by the Government, industrialists are generally attracted towards the places where the industries are already developed. They do so because they will get a large number of external economies from those places. The private entrepreneurs decide the location by keeping in view the economic considerations only. They do not think in terms of social cost-benefit.

Concentration of industries gives rise to problems of housing, transport, health and other social services. It gives rise to congestion of traffic, overcrowding and other problems also. Concentration of industries at particular places takes place at the cost of other areas. Thus, backward areas remain backward. Moreover, concentration of industries is not equitable because people living near the industrial places will enjoy many benefits of industrial development including employment opportunities. People living in other areas are deprived of these benefits.

The basic policy followed by the Indian Government after independence in regard to location of industries is the achievement of balanced regional growth of the country. Balanced regional development is a vital part of India economic planning. Different ways have been followed to achieve balanced regional development of different regions in the country during the Five Year Plans. The industrial policy statement made by the Government from time to time have also given due recognition to the fact that balanced growth of various regions has an important impact to generate employment, to remove poverty and to increase the standard of living of the people.

GOVERNMENT'S APPROACH TO LOCATION OF INDUSTRY

The Government can tackle the problem of concentration of industry by following two approaches:

(i) Positive approach—encouraging establishment of industrial units in the backward areas; and

(ii) Negative approach—restraining the establishment of industrial units in the concentrated areas.

Positive Approach. The adaptation of positive approach is likely to give more satisfactory results as compared to the negative approach. Under this approach, the State provides certain incentives for the establishment of industrial unit in the selected areas. These incentives may take the following forms:

(i) Provision of public utility services in selected areas. These services include electricity, water, gas, transport, etc.

(ii) Provision of social-economic amenities like recreation education, health, etc. In addition, the Government has also extended certain ancillary economic facilities in these areas like institutions for imparting technical knowledge to the workers and marketing organisations for the benefit of localised industries.

(iii) Giving assurance by the state to purchase the products of the industrial units established in backward areas.

(iv) Providing adequate and cheap financial facilities directly by the Government or through the financial institutions.

(v) Establishment of industrial estates in industrially backward regions. The main objectives of industrial estates is to enable a large number of small scale units to have the advantages of common services and other facilities. Being located near one another, they may also be able to use the goods and services of others.

(vi) Granting of direct and indirect subsidies. Direct subsidies may be in the form of price subsidisation, supply of raw materials and machinery at Low prices, etc. Indirect subsidies may be in the form of reducing the cost of certain services to offset the influence of unfavourable factors.

The negative approach includes certain deterrents which have not proved to be so effective in practice. To prevent excessive concentration of industries in certain areas, the State may introduce deterrents like enhanced local taxes. A levy may be imposed on the established industrial units for the benefit of new units in the backward areas. The State may also follow absolute prohibition to check excessive concentration of industries in particular areas. Licensing policy may be introduced to achieve balanced regional growth.

PRICING METHOD IN BUSINESS POLICY METHOD

The method or technique of price fixation depends upon the pricing objectives and policies of the final. The basic methods, based on costs, used by business concerns are:

(a) Cost plus Pricing

(b) Marginal Cost Pricing

(c) Break-even Analysis.

COST PLUS PRICING

Cost plus pricing is the most pervasive pricing method used by the business enterprises. Under this method, the cost estimate of the product is made and a margin for profit is added to it to determine the price. The basic philosophy behind this approach is that the sale pricing of a product must cover its cost and bring about a reasonable margin of profit. The margin is known as mark up and that is why, cost plus pricing is also known as 'mark up pricing'. The simple formula used in cost plus pricing is:

Selling Price = Unit Total Cost + Desired Unit Profit

Several different concepts of cost component may be used in cost plus pricing. In general cost means either actual, expected or standard cost. Actual cost usually means historical cost for the latest available period. It reflects recent wages and material prices and overhead charges at the current output rate. Expected cost is a forecast of actual cost for the pricing period on the basis of expected prices, output rates and efficiency. Standard cost is a conjecture as to what cost would be at some normal rate of output and with efficiency at some standard level. In practice, cost is determined on the basis of estimates and cost experience. Formulas for cost plus pricing differ widely among industries and even among firms within an industry. This variation is probably due to differences in accounting practices.

The size of the markup depends upon competition, distinctiveness of the product, habit of custom of the market and some vague notion of a reasonable profit. Some big organisations determine the average markup on cost necessary to obtain a required rate of return on their investments. Under this policy pricing starts with a planned rate of return on investment. To translate this rate of return into a per cent markup on cost, it is essential to estimate a normal rate of production and its standard cost. After this, the ratio of invested capital to a year's standard cost of normal production is computed. This is called capital turnover. Multiplication of capital turnover by target rate of return gives the markup percentage to be applied to the standard cost.

Merits of Cost Plus Pricing. Cost plus or full cost pricing helps in achieving reasonable return on the amount of capital invested. It discourages the manufacturers from cut-throat competition. It is the safest method of pricing. The manufacturer will sell those products which can give him sufficient return.

Inadequacies of Cost Plus Pricing. Cost plus pricing has been criticised by many authors on the following grounds:

(a) It ignores the level and nature of demand.

(b) It fails to reflect competition in the market.

(c) It presumes a fixed margin of profit. But in practice businessmen increase their margin of profit when they expect good demand.

(d) The firm using cost plus pricing never knows how much a customer is will ling to pay.

(e) In practice, businessmen use rules of thumb to determine the markup on the cost of the product.

(f) Cost plus pricing may not deliver goods particularly when there is idle plant capacity. In such a case, marginal costing may be useful.

MARGINAL COST PRICING

Marginal costing and break-even analysis are the important tools for determining the price of a product. They are very helpful techniques when a firm has full knowledge about the demand and revenue conditions in the market. Costs of production are divided into two parts, namely, fixed cost and variable cost. The fixed cost remains fixed up to a certain level of production and variable cost keeps on changing with the change in the number of units produced. Marginal cost is the amount of money at any given volume of output by which aggregate cost is changed if the volume of output is increased or decreased by one unit. It represents the variable cost per unit up to a certain stage of production. Marginal costing is quite helpful when a firm is confronted with the problem of quoting the price of its products.

BREAK-EVEN ANALYSIS

Break-even analysis uses market demand as a basis for price determination and also considers cost of production. It involves developing tables and/or charts which are useful to determine at what level of production the revenues will equal the costs assuming a certain setting price. It establishes relationship among cost of production, volume of production, profit or loss, and sale. It determines the break-even point which represents the volume of sale at which costs (fixed and variable) are fully covered. Sales at levels about the break-even point will result in a profit on each unit. Output at any stage below the break-even point will result in a loss to the seller.

Break-even analysis is the most sophisticated pricing technique which takes into consideration both fixed costs and variable costs. It uses market demand as the basis of price determination. Break even point (BEP) which represents the volume of production at which there is no profit and loss can be calculated by the following formula:

$$\text{BEP} = \frac{\text{Fixed Costs}}{\text{Selling Price per Unit} - \text{Variable Cost per Unit}}$$

$$= \frac{\text{Fixed Costs}}{\text{Contribution}}$$

Suppose, Fixed Costs = Rs. 1,60,000

Variable Cost = Rs. 6 per unit

Selling Price = Rs. 10 per unit

$$\text{BEP} = \frac{1,60,000}{10-6} = 40,000 \text{ units}$$

The vertical scale represents cost and revenue and the horizontal scale represents the sales. The fixed cost line is drawn horizontally through the fixed cost point and the total cost line is drawn from the inter-section of the fixed cost line at the left vertical scale. The sales line is drawn through the zero point on the left scale. The total cost line represents the total cost of production and the sales line shows the amount of revenues (rupees in lakh) at various volumes of sales. The point at which the total revenue line and the total cost line intersect is the break-even point.

Evaluation. Marginal costing and break-even analysis are not free from limitation. These techniques assume a single product which is not possible in practice. They also assume that all the costs can be divided into two categories only, *i.e.*, fixed and variable, but there are certain semi-variable costs also. Therefore, it is not easy to find the marginal cost of a product. Break-even analysis is a theoretical tool to know the volume of production at which profits could be maximised. In practice, the determination of the price is not so easy. Despite these limitations, marginal costing can prove very helpful. It can help in taking the decision whether to continue production or stop production. During depression, the management of a firm may decide to keep on marketing its products at the prevailing market price which is more than or equal to the variable cost because fixed costs have to be incurred whether there is any production or not.

In this way we conclude that full cost pricing is the most widely used pricing practice followed by the business enterprises. Under this method, the price represents the cost of the product plus a certain markup representing a reasonable profit. Deviation from full cost pricing takes place to clear old stocks, to get Government orders, to utilise idle capacity, and to meet depression. Many enlightened businessmen use marginal costing to determine the prices of their products when the demand is lower and there is idle plant capacity. In such a situation, it is advisable to maximise contribution towards variable cost and fixed cost rather than stop production.

PLACE OF ADVERTISING PUBLICITY AND SALES PROMOTION IN THE BUSINESS

It has already been observed how competition in the market makes it absolutely necessary for manufacturers to think of new and unfamiliar uses for their products or to find out new buyers for their products. Demand creation is, therefore, almost as important as meeting the existing demand. Both demand creation and catering to the existing demand require some means by which consumers—existing as well as potential—are informed about the availability of the product. Of the various means and devices employed to perform this essential function, advertising is easily the most outstanding and the most far-reaching approach.

To the layman, advertising is nothing more than the "use of bright ideas, stunts and slogans to popularise goods which appeal to the great body of ordinary consumers." But in believing so the layman is not merely missing the importance of advertising in the modern world, but is also confusing it with mere propaganda. Propaganda is employed to spread some ideology or doctrine.

Some firms would send their travelling salesmen round to canvass for their products from door to door. Shop windows were tastefully and attractively decorated so that the products could catch the eye (and the heart) of the customers who happened to pass by. A businessman would write to those consumers who are known to him or else would ring up to inform them that a certain product in which they would possibly by interested is available. All these efforts of the producers or sellers were directed towards informing the possible customers about their products or services. Underlying all of them was the desire to promote sales. But they could achieve their objectives within certain limitations. A travelling salesmen can call on a limited number of consumers or retail shops. Not many people may really care to notice the goods on display in show windows. The businessman may know a small number of persons whom he may contact personally to pass on information concerning his products. Thus sales may be promoted on a rather small scale by such means. It need hardly be pointed out that these techniques of sales promotion do not fully meet the requirements of the mass production industries of the modern times. When goods are produced on a mass scale, their sales can be effectively promoted only by those means which can be used to inform the largest possible number of possible consumers about certain goods which can meet certain requirements of theirs. In the modern sense, therefore, advertising has to be understood as a mass selling technique. The older devices of window-dressing, personal salesmanship and personal call can serve the purpose of small business only, though even there they may be used to supplement advertising rather than to supplant or replace it. The needs of the growing number of large-sized concerns established to cater to national and international markets can be met only by the technique of advertising through various media of mass appeal and mass communication.

Objects and Purposes. In the foregoing paragraph, the informative aspect of advertising has been stressed. Though the basic purpose of advertising is to bring the advertised product as well as its features and uses to the notice of consumers, has begun to be used for a number of other allied purposes now.

(i) The existence of intense competition has given rise to what may be described as competitive advertising. In other words, advertising is undertaken these days not only to inform people about a product, but is used to maintaing the demand for an existing product and to add to existing demand by weanin people away from rival products in the market. To take a concrete case, when the bottlers of Coca-Cola found a strong rival in Pepsi Cola, they changed the tone and emphasis of their advertisements and began to emphasize that only 'it is real'.

(ii) Advertising is used as a means to demand creation. Many needs of the people are the creations of advertising. Actually, advertising seeks to channelist the surplus incomes of the people towards those products which are not included among the basic necessities of life. In this process, it makes people conscious of the need for something without which they had been living so far. This consciousness is turned into a desire, and an ardent desire, when the advertisement continues to rub to the need for such a product.

(iii) It follows from the above that advertising may be used with a view to preparting ground for a new product that is proposed to be introduced in the market. Most of the cinema advertisements are designed to serve this purpose. But the time the film starts its run at a theatre the people are already prepared to receive it. That explained the gate-crashing and the heavy rush at the box-office right on the opening day of the picture.

(iv) Large-scale advertising is often undertaken with the objective of creating or enhancing the goodwill of advertising company. This, in turn, increased the market receptiveness of the company's product and helps the salesman to win customers easily.

In short, advertising aims at benefiting the producer, educating the consumer and supplementing the salesman. Above, all, it is a link between the producer and the consumer.

Advertising is non-personal communication. It is communication that is paid for. The sponsor is usually identified. He is conveying news or promoting ideas, goods or services to a specific group of people. He buys space or time in media which would reach them. He may resort to advertising with any or all of the following in mind: speed, economy, impact, convenience. Advertising is one channel of information for consumers. They get to know about new products, product improvements price changes, packaging innovations, special credit terms, new uses for the product and so on from the advertising columns.

"Publicity", in its restricted sense, is communication favourable to a company in the editorial part of media, be it press, radio, film or TV. Publicity is not paid for though the message that are printed or broadcast may have been inspired by the company concerned. This may be done through press conferences, which do cost money-invitation cards, telephone calls, tea or more elaborate fare for journalists, hire of hall where the conference is held, an information kit for the invites and so on. Sometimes transport is hired to take a party of journalists to a function or a plant. Special interviews and press releases (with or without supporting brochures) are other methods adopted. Often photographs are taken for pictorial coverage in media and these also cost money. Since the messages appear to emanate from the editor-who is regarded as an objective person unlike the sponsor of an advertisement—they command more credibility with the reader or the viewer or listener. But publicity messages are controlled by the editorial staff. These people-not the advertiser—will decide when themessages will appear, how much space or time will be devoted to them, and how they will be presented. Editors will seldom repeat the same story. Advertising, on the other hand, is controlled by the advertiser.

"Sales promotion" would cover three groups: salesmen, dealers and consumers. Training of salesman (in the case of technical salesmen—as in the case of pharmaceuticals or engineering goods-this can be expensive and time-consuming), conferences of salesmen, salesmen's kits, prizes for the best performers and so on are meant to cover the first group. Their morale, and enthusiasm are of immense value to a company. Some companies make the annual conference of safe men some thing of a gala affair, and often wives are invited. Sales promotion among dealers takes a variety of forms. Trade letters, house journals for the trade literature on products, displays and competitions, "mystery customer", schemes, painting of sign-boards, gifts like diaries, demonstrations, film shows, parties and conventions are some of these.

Value of Advertising. The importance of advertising is realised on all hands. In fact, advertising has already become such an integral part of our life that we never feel the need of pausing to consider its value and importance. There is no doubt about the fact that in the absence of advertising, our lives would have been lived very differently. Such being the place of advertising in our life, it will be worthwhile to consider some of the important advantages of advertising here.

1. Advantages to Manufacturers

There is justification in the adage, "it pays to advertise" because of the following advantages of advertising accruing to manufacturers:

(a) **Increased Sales.** The chief object of the manufacturer in advertising his products is to promote the sale of his products. Goods produced on a mass scale are marketed by the method of mass persuasion through advertising. By repeating advertisements, the manufactures are not only able to retain existing markets but are also able to expand the markets both by attracting more people to their products as also by suggesting new uses for them. Advertising acts as an aid to selling.

(b) **Steady Demand.** Advertising has led to the smoothening out of the seasonal fluctuations in demand for many products. The manufactures are generally trying to discover and advertise new possible uses of which a seasonal product may be put. The innovation of cold tea and cold coffee for the use during summer has helped in increasing the demand for these beverages even in that season. The same may be said for refrigeration.

(c) **Lower Costs.** Advertising provides a spure to the sale and increases the turnover tremendously. This is advantageous in two ways: on one side, the selling costs including the cost of advertising get spread over a large volume of salts, thus lowering the average cost of selling; while on the other side; higher turnover necessiates high volume of production, thus lowering the average cost of production per unit.

(d) **Greater Dealer Interest.** The retailers who deal in advertised goods are materially assisted by advertising in the performance of their functions. Advertising creates demand which every retailer gets an opportunity to share with others. The retailers have not to bother much about pushing up the sale of such products. So they evidence more interest in advertised products.

(e) **Quick Turnover and Smaller Inventories.** A well-organised advertisement campaign creates a highly responsive market thereby facilitating quick turnover of the goods, This, in turn, results in lower inventories in relation to sales being carried on by the manufactures.

(f) **Supplementing Salesmanship.** Advertising prepares the necessary ground for the efforts of the salesmen. When a salesmanship its a prospect, he has just to canvass for a product with which the consumer may already have been familiarised through advertisements. Thus, the salesman's efforts are supplemented and his task is made easier by advertising.

(g) **Encouragement to Better Performance.** Advertising gives the employees that feeling of pride in their jobs and the products they produce or help to produce, which is basic to high morale. It can, thus, inspire executives and workers to improved performance. Moreover, an advertiser may have built up a vast fund of goodwill which will serve as assurance of security to the employers. This will also serve to boost up the morale of the men working in the manufacturer's organisation.

(h) **Creation of Goodwill.** By constantly associating the name of the manufacture with certain standards of quality, advertising builds a fund of goodwill for him. Goodwill thus created is a valuable asset not merely because it enables him to get more and more of repeat orders for his existing products but also for the reason that the manufacture can introduce new products in the market with confidence. The Godrej concerns have been able to sell the whole range of products ranging from oils to-soap and from locks to typewriters mostly on the strength of their goodwill.

2. Benefits to Consumers

(a) **Facility of Purchasing.** Advertising makes purchasing easy for the consumers. Moreover, the resale prices (prices at which the goods are to be sold by the retailers) are generally fixed and advertised. Thus, advertising offers a definite and positive assurance to the consumer that he will not be overcharged for the advertised product. The consumer can make his purchases with utmost ease and confidence.

(b) Improvement in Quality. Goods are generally advertised under brand names. When a person is moved by the advertisement to use the product he proceeds on the hope that the articles of the particular brand will be better than the other brands of the same goods. If his experience confirms his expectation, a repeat order can be expected. Otherwise, the sales may rise very high once but may drop down very low subsequently when the consumer's confidence in the quality of the product is shaken.

(c) Elimination of Unnecessary Intermediaries. By advertising his goods, a manufacturer may seek to establish direct contacts with the consumers. In this process, the number of middlemen whose profits increase the price and reduce the manufacturer's margin of profits may be considerably reduced. This will mean large profits for the manufacturer and cheaper products for the consumers.

(d) Consumer's Surplus. Advertising increases the utility of given commodities for many people. It points out and emphasizes the qualities possessed by certain goods and leads consumers to appreciate more strongly the utility of such goods. As a result, the consumers may be willing to pay even more for certain products which appear to have higher utility to them. If these products are available at the original lower prices, there will naturally be a certain amount of consumer's surplus in terms of increased satisfaction or pleasure derived from these products.

(e) Education of Consumers. There is considerable truth in Sir William Leverhulm's remark that advertising is an educational and dynamic principle. Advertising aims at educating the buyers about new products and their diverse uses. In this process, it introduces new ways of life to the people at large and prompts them to give up their old habits and inertia. Advertising thus paves the way to better standards of living.

3. Benefits to Society

(a) **Encouragement to Research.** The manufacturers will undertake research and discover new products or new uses for existing products only when they are assured of sufficient profits. Advertising provides this assurance and thus encourages industrial research with all its advantages.

(b) **Substaining the Press.** When advertising made its beginning, advertisements generally occupied some odd nooks and corners in the newspapers. The present situation is just the reverse. The newspapers, periodicals, journals, may the whole press, look to advertisements for support and sustenance. In the absence of income from advertising, the newspapers have to be produced at a higher cost and may not be able to keep themselves free from party pulls and pressures from business lords.

(c) **Change in Motivation.** Advertising has radically changed the basis of human motivation. While people of earlier generations lived and worked mainly for bare necessities of life, the modern generation works harder to supply itself with the luxuries and semi-luxuries of life. Advertising has brought to the notice of the masses, numerous products which are more than mere necessities and has created in their minds a desire to possess them. Thus, the motive force of fear (or going without the bare essentials of life) has been replaced by desire (for more and newer products).

(d) **Encouragement to Artists.** Men of talent, including artists, story writers, announcers, etc., get an opportunity to do some creative work while earning their livelihood through the designing of advertisements and the use of ideas in advertising various products.

(d) **Glimpse of National Life.** Advertising does provide a glimpse of a country's way of life. It is, in fact, a running commentary on the way the people live and behave and is also an indicator of some of the future trends in this regard.

(f) **Higher Standards of Living.** Advertising leads to a rise in the standards of living, not only through the education of the buyers but also through greater consumption, increased production and a larger volume of employment.

Advertising in a Developing Economy. One sometimes comes across questions such as: Has advertising any role to play in a developing economy? Does its aim, *viz.*, promoting mass consumption and increased sales, not conflict with the aims of a developing economy? A developing economy aims at accelerating the rate of capital formation by means of encouraging savings and thrift. It has to make its production available for export to earn foreign exchange to be able to pay for its imports of capital goods and essential raw material. At first sight, advertising and a developing economy appear to be working at cross-purposes.

It is admitted that squandering is undesirable from the national point of view as savings are reduced. Nevertheless, one must always be chary of providing or implanting a hope and an expectation of better home, food or clothing if incentive to earn by hard work is to be retained. This incentive is crucial to successful implementation of any plan for economic development. It is here that advertising has a role to play. Advertising nourishes the consuming power of men. It creates wants for a better standard of living. Even otherwise, advertising is very well suited for selling the idea of saving. The advertising done by commercial banks and the Life Insurance Corporation of India is a case in point.

Advertising comes to the aid of a developing economy in promoting exports as well. 'Export or Perish' is the slogan of such economies. However, success in exports requires at least two things—first the prices must be competitive and second, the commodities must be of good quality. There are some who think that advertising expenditure raises the cost and price of the articles and thus regard advertising as "a mill-stone round the neck of a product" which checks its sales. But his notion is not well-founded. It has been the experience of all advanced nations like the U.K. the U.S.A., Germany, Japan, etc., that increased internal sales are necessary to lower the average costs or prices. It is also confinned by our own experience in the field of bicycles and sewing machines which we have been able to export because of low costs made possible by wider domestic market. Moreover, advertising sharpens competitive selling.

The last, but not the least, justification for advertising in a developing economy which, though poor, wants to spread literacy among its people, is that advertising makes it possible to drop the same thought into a thousand minds at the same time. In the absence of advertising, the hundreds of regional language publications would fold up for want of advertisements.

Objections Against Advertising. Advertising has also been subjected a number of objections mainly because it has been misused by some people to serve their own ends, overlooking the business interests. An examination of some of the forceful objections will be of interest.

(a) **Multiplication of Needs.** It is said that advertising compels people to buy things they do not need. Human instincts, like desire to possess, to be recognised in, the society, etc., are provoked in order to sell products. Sometimes, various types of appeals are advanced to arouse interest in the product. Sentiments and emotions are played with to gain customers.

(b) **Misrepresentation of Facts.** Through misrepresentation of the benefit a product will give, goods of no real value are sold. Tall claims are made by the advertisers to tempt people to take such actions as go purely to their advantage and cause tremendous loss to the consumer. Even adulterated food and medicines are marketed, which by no stretch of imagination can benefit anybody. By sheer exaggeration of facts, demand for the merchandise advertised is created without much difficulty even when the commodities carrying greater worth or satisfaction are already therein the market.

(c) **Consumers Deficit.** While advertising leads to increased satisfaction from commodities already in use, it also creates discontent in the minds of many people who are tempted to purchase/some commodities but are not able to do so because of insufficient purchasing power. Such discontent is obviously not very desirable from the point of view of society, particularly if it affects a large majority of people. But it is important if it acts as a spur to social change.

(d) **Increased Cost.** There is a great deal of controversy as to whether advertising leads to increase in the cost which the community has to pay for a product. In a sense it is true since expenses on it form a part of the total cost of the product. But at the same time it would be wrong to infer that if the advertising costs were cut down the goods would necessarily be cheaper. Advertising is, no doubt, one of the items of costs but it is a cost which brings savings in its wake on the distribution side. On manufacturing side, it is one of the factors that make large-scale production possible and anyone would agree that large-scale production leads to lower costs.

(e) **Wastage of National Resources.** A more serious objection against advertising is that it is used to destroy the utility of goods before the end of their normal period of usefulness. Now models of automobiles with nominal improvements are, for instance, advertised at such high pressure that the old models have to be discarded long before they become useless, Not that merely, the most-advertised products are delicate, fragile and brittle. In the U.S.A., there is evidence of a marked decline in the quality and durability of cars, furniture, rugs, television sets, refrigerators, etc. That appears to be the way in which the increased demand created through advertising can be sustained. The same is true of dresses, furniture and other products. From the points of view of the community it is a waste of resources.

STARTGIC PLANNING TO MEASURE THE SIZE OF THE BUSINESS

There has been a tendency of the business firms towards increase in their size in order to achieve economies in production, marketing, finance and management. In practice, different firms operate at different levels of operations. This is an important reason which explains that different firms are not able to operate with equal efficiency. Many economists have attempted to explain the size of a business firm which every business firm should try to achieve. These important concepts about the size of business unit which must be distinguished are: *(i)* Representative Firm, *(ii)* Equilibrium Firm, and *(iii)* Optimum Firm. These concepts are discussed below:

(i) Representative Firm. Alfred Marshall introduced the concept of representative firm. A representative firm is a model firm in an industry and it can be used as standard of reference, because it works under average conditions and at average efficiency. A representative firm is one which has had a fairey long life and fair success, which is managed with normal ability and which has normal access to the economies, external and internal, which belong to the aggregate volume of production, account being taken by the class of goods produced, the conditions of marketing them and economic environment generally.

Marshall meant a representative firm as one working under average condition and at average efficiency. It is an average firm with normal success. It is the size towards which every firm in an industry tends to grow. Such a firm can be found by undertaking a broad survey of the firm in an industry. The concept of representative firm is too abstract to be of much practical utility. There are many firms which started on a large scale from the very beginning and there are many firms which started on a small scale and do not find it profitable to expand even after a long period. Thus, a representative firm need not unnecessarily be an optimum firm. An optimum firm as the lowest average cost of production per unit of output in the given conditions of technique, knowledge and organising ability. A representative firm has a long period average concept and the optimum firm is the most efficient one.

(ii) Equilibrium Firm. The concept of equilibrium firm was developed by A.C. Pigou. Pigou was of the opinion that an equilibrium firm is one, which has reached a stage where there is no urge or incentive to expand further. In other words, the owners of the business firm are satisfied with its profitability and do not want any further expansion or contraction in its size. It may be pointed out that according to economics, a firm is in equilibrium when marginal revenue is equal to marginal cost and at this level of output.

The concept of equilibrium firm is imaginary and divorced from reality. Equilibrium firm can be achieved only under perfect competition. But in real life, perfect competition is not found. It is only under perfect competition that the size of equilibrium firm is equal to the optimum size. The idea of optimum firm is a relative concept and keeps on changing depending upon the techniques of production and organising ability. But equilibrium firm is to be found only under perfect competition which is a theoretical state of affairs.

(iii) Optimum Firm. A business unit may be launched on a small scale and then expanded gradually. With the increase in the scale of operations, it can enjoy various economies in regard to production, marketing, financing and management. But it must not be presumed that these economies will be available in increasing measure with every growth in the scale of operations. The law of diminishing return applies after a certain level of production.

In other words, a point will come beyond which further expansion of business operations may lead to inefficiency. This point indicates the optimum size of firm.

The optimum size denotes the size of a firm at which there is maximum efficiency in operations. Efficiency will be reduced whenever the size is reduced below the optimum level or expanded beyond the optimum level. The concept of optimum firm was developed by E.A.G. Robinson.

Implications of Robins on's Definition. An analysis of the concept of optimum firm shows that it has the following implications:

(a) Average cost per unit and not the total cost should be minimum.

(b) White calculating the average cost of production per unit, all long run costs must be included. Average cost means total cost divided by the aggregate output.. The total cost should include not only direct costs like those of materials and labour but also indirect costs like depreciation, administrative overheads, distribution overheads, etc.

(c) Lowest average cost of production is emphasised and not the maximum profits. We are concerned only with the relations of cost to size while ignoring the question of maximum profitability because when there is monopoly, the prices need not coincide with average cost and maximum profit may be earned by charging a higher price.

(d) There is fullest possible utilisation of the available technological potentials.

(e) Optimum size is a relative concept. It is not something absolute, static or fixed. It changes with the changes in the techniques of production, efficiency of management, mode of financing, and so on.

Assumptions. The concept of optimum size is based on the following assumptions:

(a) The market is sufficient to absorb the whole production of at least one firm of optimum size.

(b) There is perfect competition in the market.

(c) The establishment of the optimum firm will being part the result of conscious decisions by businessmen who are considering how they most profitably cap invest their resources; in part it will be the product of the forces of competition, which tend, as a rule, to eliminate the inefficient and encourage the efficient firm.

Criticism. The concept of optimum size has been criticised on the following grounds:

(a) The market may be limited and may not be able to absorb a large number of firms of optimum size.

(b) It is very difficult to determine the optimum point, because it keeps on changing with every change in production and techniques of organising ability.

(c) The assumption of perfect competition is not satisfied in practice. The price differs in different markets because of slight product differentiation, knowledge gap, etc.

Inspite of the above criticism, the concept of optimum size draws the attention of the businessman to reduce the average cost of production through the use of the available techniques of production and organising ability. It also induces the businessman to think consciously of achieving the optimum size by consider ngthe impact of various forces on the size of the firm.

PASSIMUM FIRM

When a firm expands towards the optimum size, the organisation and coordination of operations tend to become more complicated. Singular management is replaced by group management and local market is replaced by the national market. But the firm may not be able to reap the advantages of technical economies of large scale.

According to Robinson, it is a very critical period for art expanding firm and the problems involved can be overcome by expanding with speed and dynamism. He has used the word passimum firm to denote this temporary phase in the growth of the firm.

Factors Determining Optimum Size

E.A.G. Robinson has divided the factors or forces which determine the optimum size of a firm into the following five categories:

(a) Managerial forces leading to an optimum managerial unit;

(b) Financial forces leading to an optimum financial unit;

(c) Technical forces leading to an optimum technical unit;

(d) Forces of risk and fluctuation leading to a unit possessing the greatest power of survival in the face of industriar vicissitudes; and

(e) Marketing forces leading to an optimum sales unit.

The above listed five forces may lead to an approximately similar optimum size in certain cases and in other cases, there may be wide differences in the different optima. The optimum size will be determined at a point where these five forces are at equilibrium. The equilibrium point is a point where all the forces give the same optimum or where the diseconomies from further growth are offset by the economies. "The equilibrium may be similar either to that of tug-of-war rope which is motionless because no one is yet pulling in either direction, or to the tug of war which is motionless because the two terms are for the moment equally matched.

TECHNICAL FORCES

According to Robinson, technical forces fix a minimum scale of operations. They do not fix maximum scale beyond which growth will lead to progressively increasing average cost per unit. If other considerations require a scale larger than the technical optimum, the technical scale of production can be increased by the mere multiplications, until it coincide with that scale which those other considerations would demand. In other words, in every industry and for every method of production within each industry, there is more or less a fixed minimum size of plant below which production is technically impossible or economically unprofitable.

Technical optimum is attainable usually by a large sized business unit because technical forces operate mostly in favour of increasing the size of firms. The technical forces are the factors which influence the process of production. The important technical forces making for technical optimum unit are:

(i) Division of Labour. A large scale firm can reap great advantages of specialisation and division of labour. Through division of labour, the manufacturing process may be split into small operations which can be taken over by machInes specially designed for the purpose. Division of labour can be used only by a large sized firm which can afford to install machines. Adam Smith gave three reasons for the increase in the quantity of work which in consequence of division of labour, a given number of people are capable of performing:

(i) It increases dexterity in every workman.

(ii) It saves time which is commonly lost in passing from one piece of work to another.

(iii) It facilitates invention of a great number of machines which enable one man to do the work of many.

(ii) Integration of Processes. A large sized firm can achieve economies by the integration of processes. Integration of processes involves designing a large machine to take over what was previously done by a series of munual or less mechanical operations. That means the process of division of labour is reversed so that fewer rather than more processes of manufacture are required to do the job. The integration of processes may be horizontal to vertical. Vertical integration consists in the combination of one stage of production with the other previously by separate stages of production under control of a single firm. An increase in the size of the mechanical unit gives an increase of efficiency and if greatest technical efficiency is to be achieved. The size of the firm must be sufficient to use largest mechanical unit necessary to utilise its full capacity. A small firm can also operate efficiently by obtaining access to some of the technical economies of large scale production through vertical disintegration. Where some given process requires a scale of production considerable greater than the small firms in an industry can achieve, this process tends to be separated from the main industry, and all the small firms to get this particular process performed for them by an outside specialist firm.

The size of optimum technical unit will be larger in those industries in which the productive machinery is physically very large as in steel making, ship building, etc. and in those in which the final product is highly complex as in the case of manufacture of typewriters, watches, motor cars, etc. On the other hand, optimum technical unit will be smaller where the product is both small and simple and the productive process is routine and standardized, as in the case of baking of bread. The technical costs of production are likely to fall as more and more is produced upto a certain point as a result of economies, butthey are likely to remain constrained after a point, where the economies of further growth are compensated by the increased costs.

FINANCIAL FORCES

The stability and growth of the firms depend to a large extent on their ability to procure capital required for the conduct of their business. Firms having no assured access to financial facilities are unable to expand and may ever find it difficult to stay in business. They ability of the firm to raise the capital necessary for its activities is an important factor for the efficiency of business.

Financial forces favour the larger firms. A big firm can raise more funds easily on easy terms because of its reputation. It can expand its business easily. The financial cots per unit go on decreasing as more and more output is produced. However, the amount of capital required is largely influenced by the nature of the industry. Some firms have to start on a very large scale and so they need huge amount of capital. In these cases the joint stock company form of organisation with limited liability has become popular. The size of the company gives an impression of solidarity and security to an investor. Big companies are also favoured by the financial institutions and the commercial banks. There are certain limitations of big firms also. Greater investment involves increased risks, and there may be misuse of funds.

MARKETING FORCES

The optimum size in respect of marketing operations is attained by a firm through the conduct of its marketing operations on sufficiently large scale consistent with production capacity and sales potential. According to Robinson, marketing forces are concerned with both buying and selling. There are difinite economies in large scale buying and selling. The importance of efficient buying of materials can hardly be exaggerated. A large firm has more bargaining power as compared to the small firms. It can afford the services of purchase experts. Economies in the form of lower prices, higher discounts, lower transport charges, etc., are also obtained. On the selling side also, there are many economies. A large firm can afford elaborate and expensive sales organisation and can employ good sales persons. It can undertake marketing research and make use of advertising.

There are two points which go against a large firm and favour a small firm:

(a) Mistakes committed in buying or selling by a large firm may prove very costly and even difficult to rectify in some cases.

(b) If organised markets and distribution channels are available, a small firm would have no disadvantage as it can make use of these services.

CHANNEL OF DISTRIBUTION

Whether a firm will sell its product or service directly to the consumers or make use of intermediaries (middlemen) for the purpose constitutes a major policy issue. For certain service organisations, direct sale to consumers is invariably called for, like, for instance, civil airways, banks, consultancy firms, passenger and freight transport services. But for most manufactures of goods, selection of the channel of distribution involves a choice of great significance For one thing, on channel decisions depend the firm's pricing decisions, advertising decisions and sales force decisions. Pricing decisions depend upon whether it chooses wholesalers or retailers for distribution of its products; the firm's advertising decision depend upon the degree of co-operation from the agencies in the channel of distribution; the sales force decisions also depend upon whether the firm chooses to sell to retailers or uses its own representatives. Secondly, the significance of channel decisions lies in that they involve long-term commitments to and dependence on other firms.

Channel decisions refers to the managerial decision on the selection of the most suitable route for distribution of goods from the producers to the users. Following are the important reasons which place channels decision in policy decision areas:

(a) If the choice of channels is proper, fluctuations in production may be reduced. The manufacturer can obtain data regarding sales and stock of the middlemen and exercise control wherever he feels necessary. The stability of production will help to ensure steady employment and proper budgetary control.

(b) The channels chosen involve the firm in relatively long-term commitments to other firms or middlemen. The relations between the manufacturer and the middlemen depend mainly on the choice of appropriate channels of distribution. Therefore, it is necessary that channels decisions are taken with great care.

(c) The channels selected for the firm's product affect every other marketing decision like pricing, promotion, physical distribution and the cost involved in the use of trade channels enter the price of the product that the ultimate consumer has to pay. If the costs of trade channels are very high the firm may draw public criticism.

CHOICE OF CHANNELS OF DISTRIBUTION

The choice of a suitable channel of distribution is an important marketing decision. The importance of this decision arises from the following considerations:

(a) An appropriate selection of channels can reduce fluctuations in production. The stability of production is important both for reasons of stable employment and proper budgeting of costs and revenues.

(b) The costs involved in the use of a channel or channels enter the price that the ultimate consumer has to pay. A proper decision in this regard may enable the management to cut on these costs and reach a wider market.

(c) The decision regarding an appropriate channel or set of channels has a bearing on the other marketing decisions like pricing, product-line and promotion. This means that thoughtlessness on the part of the management in regard to the choice of suitable channels can affect adversely the whole marketing mix comprising various elements of the firm's offering to the consumers.

(d) The relations between the manufacturer and middlemen depend to a great extent on the choice of appropriate marketing channels. The manufacturer wishes the middleman to sell as much as possible at the lowest margin of profit while every middleman is interested in maximising his profit. A reconciliation of these conflicting interests can be brought out only through a rational decision regarding the choice of marketing channels.

Channel Decision. A rational decision regarding the choice of the appropriate channel (s) of distribution can be taken only after all the relevant factors are taken into consideration. The procedure for the purpose will depend upon the nature of the product. Specifically, the procedure for established products will be different from that followed for new products. Also the factors or criteria on which a decision is made may be quantitative and qualitative. Here we shall concern ourselves first with the criteria for the choice of channels for existing products. Of course, the goals underlying the criteria are; *(a)* maximum geographical coverage of the market, *(b)* maximum promotional efforts, and *(c)* minimum costs.

The choice of a suitable channel of distribution which can be utilised for canalising the flow of existing products from the producers to the ultimate consumers is generally governed by the following eight factors:

(1) The Type of Product. The peculiarities of the product influence and determine the number of middlemen through whose hands the products will pass before it gets into the hands of the consumers.

(a) ***Servicing Required.*** Products like automobiles and sewing machines which require servicing, expensive handling equipment, or instructions before use also pass through the hands of a few middlemen. Fashion goods generally require direct selling since their special features have to be explained to the consumers effectively. Retailers may not do this very well.

(b) ***Perishability.*** As arule, fewer middlemen are required for selling perishable goods and commodities. Most of the bakery products and food products, generally, pass through only one middleman—the retailer—and may in many cases be sold directly by the producer.

(c) ***Seasonal Character.*** If a commodity is in seasonal demand there may be no need for middlemen.

(d) ***Bulk or Weight.*** Where the movement of goods involves heavy freight and poses problems of transportation, limited channels may be employed. Selling may be mostly direct in such cases.

(e) ***Unit Value.*** Generally, producuts of lower unit value and high turnover are distributed extensively through indirect channels, *e.g.*, hosiery goods, cosmetics, etc.

(2) Consumers or Market Considerations. The consumers influence the choice of the distributive channels in the following ways:

(i) ***Geographical Location.*** If most of the consumers using a particular product (say, bread) live in the same city or locality as the producer, the producer can sell his products through his own salesmen. On the other hand, if the consumers are large in number and are scattered over a wide area, the producer will have to depend upon wholesale and retail channels for the sale of his products.

(ii) ***Consumer or Industrial Market.*** The purpose for which the product is purchased by consumers also influences the choice of channels of distribution. If a product is used for an industrial purpose, direct purchase from the manufacture will suit the consumer better and the manufacturer will adopt direct selling.

(iii) ***Number.*** If the number of consumers is small as in the case of bulky and expensive machinery, the manufacturer can employ his own sales force to sell directly to the consumers. If, however, there is a large number of consumer interested in a product, the producer has to make use of the services of wholesalers and cannot afford to employ sales staff for direct selling or even deal with the host of retailers. Cigarettes and other consumer goods belong to this category.

(iv) ***Order size.*** The size of orders received and the volume of goods supplied to individual firms will influence the channels used to reach them. A food products manufacturer will sell directly to large grocery chains because the total volume of business makes this channel economically feasible.

(v) ***Consumer Buying Habits.*** The channel policies are affected by the buying habits of consumers and industrial users, the amount of effort the consumer is willing to expend, the desire for credit, the desire for after-sales service etc.

(3) Size and Structure of Manufacturing. The larger the producer, the more profitable it may be for him to htablish direct contact with consumers through his own sales force. A small producer, on the other hand, finds it more profitable to rely on indirect channels making use of wholesalers and retailers. Also, if the manufacturing is widely dispersed geographically, in relation to the demand, the greater will be the necessity of using indirect channels, particularly wholesalers. This is so because the wholesalers will have to collect products from a wide area. Further the width or the range of the product-line also determines the broad pattern of distribution that a firm will adopt. If a manufacturer deals in a wide range of products, he will tend to serve the retailer directly eliminating the wholesaler because it is more convenient for the retailer to purchase from as few a sources as possible.

(4) Company Considerations. The character of the firm making the choice of channels of distribution will also affect the channel policies of firms. Some of the important factors in this regard are:

(i) ***Financial Resources.*** A financially strong firm will have a tendency to set up its own channels rather than depend upon middlemen.

(ii) ***Experience and Competence of Managemant.*** Where the management lacks marketing know-how, it may prefer to depend upon indirect selling through middlemen.

(iii) ***Reputation.*** Firms with established goodwill can usually make their own choice of middlemen and enter into advantageous agreements with them.

(iv) ***Desire for Control of Channel.*** A manufacturer may establish a short channel just because he wants to control the distribution. Moving closer to the final customer affords the manufacturer greater opportunity to gather current market information and control the freshness of the product and its retail price.

(5) Structure of Retailing. The structure of retail trade in a product has also an important bearing on the choice of channels. One important aspect of this factor is the number of stores selling mainly the product in question. Generally, if there are many such stores, the manufacturer will like to make use of the available retail channels instead of selling direct to the consumers. Also, retailers will be used for marketing a product if the retail stores provide convenience of shopping to the potential consumers.

In short, the important considerations relating to the structure of retailing are:

(a) Services provided by retailers.

(b) Availability of desired retailers.

(c) Attitude of middlemen toward manufacturer's policies.

(d) Sales volume possibilities.

(6) The Customary Channels. In cases where an established network of channels exists, the manufacturer may make use of such customary channels. For example, if washing soap is being marketed through grocers, a manufacturer may find that selling it through general merchants does not add substantially to the sales volume. However, the firm must be on the look out for new channels and should explore them and experiment with them.

(7) Selectivity of Distribution. An important decision in regard to the choice of channels is the one relating to the number of middlemen to be used. Three alternative policies are available to the manufacturer:

(a) Extensive distribution means that the manufacturer is willing to make use of any and all distributive outlets prepared to handle his product. A good example is provided by cigarettes. In following this policy, the manufacturer may use an independent wholesaler through whom he can reach all the retail outlets, or he may sell direct to the large retailers and reach the rest of the market through wholesalers.

(b) Selective distribution means that the manufacturer will select from among the available outlets rather than use all of the outlets. The purpose of this policy is to provide the channels chosen with large enough sales to keep them selling the manufacturer's product in satisfactory way. This may increase the sales at reduced distribution costs and bring forth better co-operation from the dealers. The manufacturer may be able to achieve a good measure of control overdistribution through this policy. On the other hand, it may happen that this market coverage is weak in that potential customers are not able to find his product because it is being marketed through selected channels.

(c) *Exclusive distribution.* This implies that grant of sole selling right for a product in a certain territory to a middleman under a contractual agreement. Generally, the middleman acting as the sole distributor for a territory does not handle competing products. The benefits and drawbacks of this policy are extension of those arising from selective distribution.

(8) The Profit Criterion. After the qualitative criteria indicated above have been applied and a broad choice regarding the type and number of channels made, the next step will be the use of the quantitative criterion in the form of estimates of profit. This means that estimates of demand, revenue and costs for each channel should be prepared and compared to make the final choice regarding the channels of distribution. The sales volume potential differs considerably channel by channel and the costs tend to move indirect relationship to the directness of the channel. As we move progresssively from a direct manufacturer-to-user channel to the most indirect channel through one or more independent wholesalers, the cost of distribution tend to become progressively lower. At the same time, the manufacturer's control over his products also gets reduced thus limiting the sales that might be achieved. The net gain from a comparison between these variables will be the criterion for the choice of a channel.

PRICE DECISION AND DIFFERENT TYPES OF PRICING POLICIES

Following are the factors to be considered in price making are:

(1) Public Policy. Sometimes, the Government may announce a general policy about pricing of goods (as these days in India, Government is averse to any rise in prices of necessities of life) or may specifically fix and control prices of goods as in the case of iron and steel cement, coal, sugar, etc. Under such circumstances the sales manager has little or no control over the prices, and he has to fall in line with the public policy.

(2) The Marketing Policies. Pursued by the Sales Organisation. The first important consideration here is of the channel of distribution selected to market the products. *Normally*, the longer the chain of distribution the higher is the margin added to cost in fixing the price. *Secondly*, warranties and after sale service facilities attached, to a sale will also have a bearing on the pricing of goods inasmuch as these cost the seller. *Finally*, proper adjustment should also be made for regular, or irregular rebates, concessions, cuts of other reductions in prices allowed to customers as an incentive to promote sales.

(3) The Competitors Prices for similar merchandise, and the effect of one's own price policy upon the price policies of the competitors, upon the sales of the merchandise in question and upon one's reputation in the community. No sales manager can afford to ignore the prices charged by other suppliers of identical products. A price higher than the one charged by others will wean customers away from him. But a very-much-lower price may create a suspicion in their minds about the quality of the product and may not increase sales. It is not suggested, however, that no margin should be provided for the firm's reputation, the product's superiority and the sales organisation's efficiency and efforts. Even in cases where competition is very keen, a higher price may be charged along with product differentiation.

ALTERNATIVE PRICING POLICIES

The pricing policies of a company should be coordinated with its policies regarding products, customers, sales appeals and sales promotion. If a company decides to sell quality products to a selective group of customers, the policy of the fatn will differ from that of a company which plans to sell products of ordinary quality to a wide range of customers. Besides this fundamental consideration in the formulation of a pricing policy some other factors also enter policy-making and influence and shape the price policies of a company. The more important among these are:

(a) The general relationship of company's price policy to prices of competing products.

(b) The relation of prices to cost of production and distribution.

(c) The relationship among prices of specific, items in the company's line of products.

(d) Price differentials among customers and the basis for these.

(e) Policy regarding change in prices.

Market-based Price Policy

The price policy of any form will in some measure, be influenced by the policy followed by the sellers of rival products. In case of highly standardised products or clearly graded commodities the price fixed by the company will conform to the market price. Deviation may be made only where the company product deviates from the standard quality or grade. This applies to wheat, iron, cotton, etc.

For most of the consumer products, however, quality does vary according to the personal taste of consumers. Differences in the quality of workmanship (as in case of a tailor), materials and services (*i.e.*, one month's credit and free delivery in case of a retail store) may justify the fixation of prices above (or below) the market level. Three alternative policies may be adopted where the company is able to differentiate its product and for services from those of others: *(a)* It may charge a higher price than that for competitive .products; *(b)* a comparable price may be set and the superior quality or service may be used to attract customers away from the competing products; or *(c)* the cream of the market may be skimmed off by setting a higher price in th beginning and the price may be lowered to competitive levels later on.

Cost-based Price Policy

Companies dealing in products whose prices are not controlled by the Government or a combination of firms generally adopt a broad policy regarding the relation of price to cost. One possible policy in this regard that is almost the most popular among managers is charging prices covering all costs of production and distribution plus normal profit. The problem with a large-scale manufacturer of several lines of products will be to determine the cost attributable to each product unit. Even if this can be done, the price may be fixed at such a high level that new competitors enter the market offering the product at compartively lower prices. Therefore, a firm must consider the possibilities of future competition before deciding upon this kind of price policy.

Another Policy in Relation to Costs will be to Sell Below Cost. When a firm is driven to sell below cost, it fixes the price level which enables it to recover the out-of pocket expenses or variable costs (materials and direct cost of labour) and as much of the fixed costs or overheads as possible. This policy may be followed when the company wishes to clear off its stock of finished goods due to urgent need for cash (say, to pay taxes) or because a fall in the price is anticipated or else when the goods in stock are likely to perish or become obsolete. Sometimes, the regular brand may be sold only at a price equal to the cost, but the brand name may be removed if it becomes neccessary to sell below cost. Another situation in which a company may offer some goods below cost is when the standard products are used as 'loss leaders'. This means that a standard product brand very much in demand may be offered at a price below cost with the object of attracting customers into the store. The loss on such brand may be made good by selling other brands at profit.

Policy Regarding Individual Products

Where a company deals in more than one product, it has to formulate a price policy establishing some relationship among the prices of different grades or guality of products. One possible policy will be to carry only one or two styles of a product at each price level. The prices have to be spread over the whole range from the highest to the lowest range to cater to the tastes, requirements, whims and fancies of different types of customers. This is particularly important in case of general merchandise stores or departmental stores. To tap several segments of the market, a manufacturer may have a deluxe brand and on ordinary brand and where the price competition is keen, an economy "fighting" brand without the fancy features of the other models. This is the kind of policy that electric fan manufacturers like the Jay engineering and the Orient Fans have been following. The All-Purpose or the Popular brand may be considered the fighting brand in their cases.

Price Differentials for Customers

A basic decision in price policy that every enterprise has to make whether the same price (one price as it is called) will be charged from all customers. Modern marketing practices seem to put—a premium on 'one price' policy but traditionally haggling has been a very common feature of marketing in countries like India. A decision in this regard will have to be made depending upon the nature of the product, the customers (women in India are particularly used to haggling), the location of the business, etc.

A sophisticated way of charging different price from different categories of customers is through the grant of discounts to a certain class of customers on the list prices. Discounts are neccessary when a company wishes to sell to wholesalers as well as retailers and may be sometimes to direct consumers. The wholesalers will naturally have to be allowed substantial discounts. The retailers may be given dealers discount and the customers may be given little or no discount. Discounts may also have to be allowed to bulk customers (like the Government) or the customers whose patronage is important for the company (Government officials, friends, etc.). Discounts in the form of price concessions may be offered also to build up volume in slack periods (a good example is the morning shows at cinema houses at reduced rates).

Another aspect of pricing policy is the regional differences in prices. In a country of long distances like ours, this may be a pertinent factor in pricing. The Vanaspati prices over different zones are a good case in point.

Policy Regarding Price Changes

An important decision in regard to price variations relates to 'mark downs'. While the prestige stores mark down their products only once in a while (say, annual, Diwali or X-mas clearance sales), general merchants, ready-made garment stores, speciality shops etc., find it useful to reduce the price as soon as it appears that the existing stock will not be cleared.

FINANCIAL PLANNING

Financial management is concerned with managerial activities related to procurement and utilisation of funds for business purposes. It deals with planning, organising, directing and controlling financial activities of the enterprise. Financial activities should not be merely restricted to raising of capital, but also to other aspects of financing like assessing the needs for capital, raising sufficient funds, cost of financing, budgeting, maintaining liquidity, lending and borrowing policies and distribution of profits.

In order to ensure the continuous availability of sufficient finance, financial management assesses the needs of the business in advance and then sets itself into motion to procure funds. Procurement of funds is complex problem as choice of sources of finance is based on complex factors like risk, period, control and cost. Various sources of finance like shares, debentures, banks and other financial institutions, public deposits, etc., have to be compared in the light of the factors. After the funds have been procured, their effective utilisation in another major task financial management. Funds should not be allowed to remain idle as they involve many costs. Funds should be put into those channels which generate an income higher than the costs of procuring them.

Objectives. Since financing is one of the functional areas of any business enterprise, the objectives of financial management must be in tune with the overall objectives of the enterprise. The main objective of a business enterprise is to earn sufficient profits so that a reasonable rate of return is paid on the capital employed and a part of the profit is ploughed back into the business to make it a stronger enterprise so that it may bear all the ups and downs in the business. The finance department can play an important role for the realisation of this objective. The objective of the finance department should be so devised that they contribute directly towards the achievement of the overall organisational objectives. Following is the list of the objectives of financial management of big enterprises:

(i) Ensuring better utilisation of capital by following the principles of liquidity, profitability and safety;

(ii) Co-ordinating the activities of the finance department with those of the other departments of the enterprise;

(iii) Ensuring regular and sufficient supply of capital to the business;

(iv) Ensuring a fair rate of return to the suppliers of capital.

Maximisation of profits is generally regarded as the objective of a business undertaking. Should this objective be followed in financial decision making? Modern authors on financial management have criticised the goal of profit maxim isolation and have advocated wealth maxim isolation as the goal of financial decision making. Any financial action which creates wealth or which has a net worth above zero is a desirable one and should he undertaken. The rationale in using wealth maximisation concept as an operating financial management goal is that it reflects the most efficient use of society's economic resources and thus leads to maxisation of society's economic wealth.

The objections raised against profit maximisation as an objective of financial management are listed below:

(a) It does not consider the risk or uncertainty or prospective earnings, stream. The prospective earnings stream would be more uncertain if the investment projects undertaken are more risky as compared to others.

(b) It does not specify the timing of expected returns. Few shareholders may like to invest in a project that promises its first return after 25 years or so. For most of the shareholders, the size of the total returns is not as important as the time patterns of returns.

(c) It does not take into consideration the interest of workers, consumers, government and other segments of the society. Thus, it is too narrowly centred. In practice, the goal of a business enterprise cannot be to maximise profits but to attain a certain level of profit, holding a certain share of the market or a certain volume of sales. The concept of social responsibility has also gained wide acceptance by the business houses these days.

(d) It does not allow for the effect of dividend policy on the market price of the share. The goal of profit maximisation prevents management to pay dividends so as to maximise earnings: To the extent payment of dividends can affect the market price of the stock (or share), the maximisation of earnings per share will not be a satisfactory objective by itself, said Ezra Solomon. It should also be noted that the objective of maximising earnings per share may not be the same as maximising market price per share.

The above mentioned reasons show that the objective of 'profit maximisation' or 'maximisation of earning per share' does not take care of the investment, financing and dividend decisions of the business. Ezra Solomon has made a good case for the adoption of the objective of wealth maximisation. He has pleaded for a distinction between profit and profitability. Maximisation of profits in the sense of maximising shareholders wealth is clearly an unreal objective. But profitability maximisation in the sense of using resources to yield economic values higher than the joint values of inputs required is a useful objective and it involves a different set of considerations. "In fact, achievement of wealth maximisation also maximises the achievement of the other objectives. To conclude, therefore, maximisation of wealth is the operating objective by which financial decisions should be guided."

SCOPE OF FINANCIAL MANAGEMENT

In order to realise the objective of financial management, the finance manager of a business enterprise has to manage various aspects of finance function which determine the scope of his duties. These aspects are explained below:

(a) **Determining the Structure of Capital.** By capital structure we mean the kind and proportion of different securities for raising finance for the business. Once the requirement of capital funds has been determined, a decision regarding the kind and proportion of various sources of capital has to be taken. For this, financial manager has to determine the proper mix of equity and debt and short-term and long-term debt ratio. These decisions have to be taken in the light of costs of raising finance from different sources, period for which fluids are required and several other factors.

(b) **Choice of Sources of Finance.** The management can raise finance from various sources like share holders, debentureholders, banks and other financial institutions, public deposits, etc. The choice of the source or sources of finance should be done very carefully as they involve different costs and conditions. For instance public deposits, though carry higher rates of interest than on debentures do not involve any security of the assets of the company. A company may like this source if it does not want to create a charge over its assets.

(c) **Estimating the Requirements of Capital.** The requirements of capital must be carefully estimated. A business requires funds both for long-term and for short-term. Estimating the requirements of funds involves the use of techniques of long-range planning. The financial management must also prepare budgets of various activities to estimate the financial requirements of the business. If proper thought is not given to the financial requirements of the business, there will be either deficiency or surplus of funds of the business has insufficiency of capital, it will not be able to meet its commitments in time. And if it has surplus funds, the management may become extravagant in spending.

(d) **Investment Decisions.** The funds procured from various sources are to be prudently invested in various assets so as to optimise the return on investment. The investment of long-term funds requires a careful assessment of various alternatives through capital budgeting and opportunity cost analysis. A part of the long-term funds has to be invested in the working capital of the company.

(e) **Disposal of Surplus.** The management has to decide how much to retain for ploughing back and how much to distribute as dividend to shareholders out of the surplus of the company. The factors which influence these decisions include the trend of earnings of the company, the trend of the market price of its shares the requirements of funds for self-financing, the future prospects and so on.

(f) **Management of Cash Flow.** Cash is required to payoff creditors purchase stock of materials pay to labour and to meet day-to-day expenses. There should not be shortage of cash any time as it will damage credit-worthiness of the enterprise. It is also to be seen that there is no excess cash. Excess cash may be invested in near-cash assets which may be converted into cash quickly when needed.

Role of Financial Management. Recent developments in business have placed the financial manager in a central position in the business enrerprise. Financial manager is incharge of the management of the funds of the enterprise. He is concerned with the determination of requirements of funds, selecting and tapping various sources of funds and allocation of funds to particular assets-fixed and current.

Financial management is concerned with three types of decisions: *(i)* investment decisions-financial plan capital budgeting, etc., *(ii)* financing decision-formulations of capital structure or financing mix; and *(iii)* dividend decision—dividend policy. Since most business activities involve the use of funds, financial management has come to occupy an important place in the modern business enterprises. Ezra Solomon has summed up the role of financial management in the following words: "Financial management is properly viewed as an integral part of overall management rather than as a staff speciality concerned with fund raising operations. In this broader view, the central issue of financial policy is the wise use of funds and the central process involved is a rational matching of the advantage of potential uses against the cost of alternative potential sources so as to achieve the broad financial goals which an enterprise sets for itself.

FINANCIAL PLANNING

Financial planning is an important part of the overall planning of any business enterprise. This task is done by the promoters at the time of floating the business and by the finance manager and the top management after that. A considerable thought has to be given to evolve a financial plan for any business venture. If a business is started with inadequate capital, it may not be able to function smoothly because of its inability to meet its commitments in time. Thus, survival of the business may be in danger. If on the other hand, it has more capital than is required, the earnings will have to be spread over an unnecessarily greater amount of capital and there may be a temptation of wasteful expenditure.

Financial planning involves three functions which are as follows:

(a) Determination of capital structure or form and proportion of different types of securities, namely, equity shares, preference shares and debentures.

(b) Laying down of financial policies in regard to cash control, borrowing and lending and other areas of financial management.

(c) Determination of amount of capital required. This depends upon many factors like promotional expenses, cost of fixed and current assets, cost of raising finance and future needs.

FACTORS IN FINANCIAL PLANNING

At the time of formulating the financial plans, the following points should be given due consideration:

(a) **Present and Future Requirements.** A good financial planning system should be based on imagination and foresightedness. It should take care of not only the present requirements of the business but also the future requirements of the business. It should also make a provision for various contingencies which may arise in future.

(b) Solvency and Liquidity. The financial plans should be so devised that they do not jeopardies the survival of the enterprise. The enterprise should be solvent and liquid both in the short and long-run. The funds should be invested in those ventures which are likely to give sufficient return on investment. At the same time, it is also essential that adequate cash is always available with the business to purchase the current assets and meet the current expenses.

(c) Objectives. The objectives of financial management should be consistent with the objectives of the enterprise. The main objectives of the financial department are raising of funds at the cheapest cost and utilisation of funds in the best possible manner.

(d) Flexibility. Many times, business conditions change drastically and financial readjustments become essential. The financial plans must be easily adjustable to such changes. Thus, financial planning should be flexible to allow the diversion of funds into more profitable channels. It should also make provision for raising more funds at a short notice.

(e) Independence. Financial planning should aim at sufficient return on investment so that the business enterprise may retain a part of earnings for ploughing back into the business every year. This will enable it to reduce dependence on outsiders which is necessary if the management does not want any interference by the outsiders with the internal working of the company.

CHARACTERISTICS OF A SOUND FINANCIAL PLAN

Sound financial planning is essential for the success of any business enterprise. It will provide policies and procedures to achieve closer coordination between the various functional areas of business.

This will lead to minimisation of waste of resources. Management can follow an integrated approach to financial policies, procedures and programme only if there is a sound financial plan. While preparing the plan of capitalisation in a company, the following factors should be given due consideration:

(a) ***Foresight.*** Financial planning should be based on vision and foresightedness of the management. There should be systematic forecasting of various contingencies. It should be decided well in advance the level of liquidity to be maintained in the enterprise.

(b) ***Flexibility.*** Financial re-adjustments become necessary quite often. The financial plan must be easily adjustable to them. A rigid capital structure will limit the scope of initiative by the management. The company should be in a position to finance its expansion programmes without much difficulty. This can be achieved only when the financial plan is dynamic in nature.

(c) ***Liquidity.*** The financial plan must provide sufficient financial liquidity. This will be possible only when there is adequate net working capital a major portion of which is represented usually by share capital, reserves and long-term loans. The degree of liquidity to be maintained is determined by the size of the company, its age, its credit standing, nature of its business, etc.

(d) ***Simplicity.*** A sound financial plan should provide simple financial structure which could be managed easily. It is not always necessary to include all type of securities in the capital structure.

(e) ***Anticipation of Contingencies.*** The finance department should anticipate various contingencies which it may have to face. This may lead to keeping the some idle capital for meeting some unforeseen events. It will be much better if these contingencies are anticipated in advance.

(f) ***Optimum use of Funds.*** It may prove very costly to keep idle funds. There should be optimum utilisation of available financial resources. If this is not done, the profitability will suffer. There should be a proper balance between the fixed capital and the working capital.

STEPS OF PRODUCTION PLANNING AND CONTROL

Following are the basics of production planning and control; *(i)* routing; *(ii)* loading; *(iii)* scheduling; *(iv)* dispatching; and *(v)* follow-up or expediting. These phases are discussed below:

(i) Routing. Routing deals with laying down of path which work will follow and the sequence in which various operations will be carried out. It determines the operations through which a product must pass and the arrangement of those operations in the sequence that will require a minimum of handling, transportation, storage and deterioration through exposure. A route for the movement of a manufacturing lot through the factory results from the determination of where each operation on a component part assembly or sub-assembly is to be performed.

The aim of routing is to determine the most feasible sequence of operations. Efficient routing permits the best utilisation of physical and human resources, employed in production. Routine is an essential element of production planning and control because its all other functions depend upon routing. The persons who draw a list of sequence of operations must be thoroughly familiar with all the operations and the machines and equipment in the plant so that they are able to establish routes which will ensure the maximum utilisation of the plant capacity.

(ii) Loading. After the route has been established, the work can be loaded against the concerned machines and equipment. Loading deals with the amount of work assigned to a machine or a worker. Persons concerned with loading keep all the records of the work load and capacity of different shops. The total time required to perform the work load is computed by multiplying the unit operation time given on the standard process sheet by the number of parts planned for the work station. This process results in a tabulated list or chart showing the planned utilisation of machines or work stations in the plant. The chart helps in assessing the spare capacity. If the loading charts indicate sufficient spare capacity, efforts should be directed through the sales department to obtain more orders for the utilisation of the spare capacity. Underload of certain departments may also arise from ineffective planning.

(iii) Scheduling. Scheduling is the last of the planning functions. It determines when various operations are to be performed. It consists of the assignment of starting and completion times for the various operations to be performed. Scheduling should be integrated with routing as it is difficult to route an item efficiently through a plant without cosulting previously designed schedules and it is equally difficult to prepare schedutes without determining the routing of sequence of operations. The other information required to draw production schedule include: *(a)* the date of delivery specified by the customer in his order; *(b)* past records; *(c)* production capacity; and *(d)* availability of equipment materials and specialised skills.

The aim in scheduling production is to schedule as great volume of work as the plant equipment can conveniently handle without adverse consequences. Scheduling usually starts with the preparation of a master schedule. The master schedule is usually a monthly breakup of the production requirements of each product for a year. The production requirements are based on sales forecasts. Forecasting is the first step towards planning of production. After this, the planning section makes detailed plans for the procurement of material and the best utilisation of the plant capacity. In order to implement the master schedule plant or shop schedules are prepared. Such schedules are usually used in industries following continuous manufacture of products. A plant schedule authorises the plant Superintendent concerned to manufacture the stipulated quantity of parts of products during a particular period of time.

(iv) Dispatching. Dispatching deals with setting the productive activities in motion through release of orders and instructions in accordance with previously planned timings as embodies in operation sheet, route card and loading schedules. Dispatching provides official authorisation an information for *(i)* movement of materials to different work places, *(ii)* movement of tools and fixtures necessary for each operation. *(iii)* beginning of work on each operation, *(iv)* recording of beginning and completion time, *(v)* movement of work in accordance with a routing schedule, *(vi)* control of progress of all operations, and *(vii)* making of necessary adjustments in the release of instructions.

Dispatching may be either centralised or decentralise. But most industries use both types of dispatching in verying degrees. Centralise dispatching means issuing of order from the central dispatch section directly to the machine shops. The section has the detailed information about the capacity and characteristics of each and every machine and so issues detailed instructions. The foremen are required merely to implement these instructions. But under decentralised dispatching, the dispatching instructions are issued by the foremen concerned.

Usually, work orders are issued to the foremen from the central office. The foremen are free to determine the sequence in which the orders will be carried out within their sections. The advantage of central-cum-decentral dispatching is that it minimises red-tapism, avoids delays and dispenses with elaborate reporting. This system is more flexible as it makes it possible to accommodate rush order by issuing the instructions from the central office and also gives sufficient discretion to the foremen to carry out the orders in the way they feel better.

(v) **Expediting/Follow-up.** Expediting or follow up help to ensure that the promise of delivery of the manufactured parts or items is kept by the workshops.

(1) It serves to coordinate the other functions of production planning and control.

(2) It ensure that the material and tools and equipments are received by the workers at right time for various operations.

(3) A good follow-up procedure helps to reveal the defects in routing and scheduling.

(4) It also detects where communication of instructions is not clear.

The responsibility for follow-up is given to a separate group of persons known as 'follow-up men'. Their function is one of obtaining information. They are essentially 'go betweens' who also attempt to achieve coordination among the various departments dependent upon one another.

Expediting can be organised either according to product or according to process. The former method is particularly suitable for continuous or line production. Here the task of follow-up is relatively simple because the manufacture of a particular product progresses automatically from one operation to the next. One man follows a particular assignment of a product through the various departments till it is completed.

Follow-up by process is used in intermittent production units under which the follow up men are assigned to various departments for checking the progress of work passing through the process in those department. Every follow-up man is acquainted with the processes and equipment on the department assigned to him and has responsibility for that particular department. The advantage of this method is that it avoids confusion which results when several follow-up men interested in different products are pressing the foremen or supervisors for information regarding their progress.

Follow-up involves human relations aspect also. Sometimes a follow-up man contacts a superivsor at a time when he is confronted with some problems. In such a situation the supervisor is most likely to be irritated and non-cooperative. For instance, if there is a breakdown of a machine, the supervisor is only interested in getting a repair man and pricing the machine back in operation as soon as possible. He may be impatient when the follow-up man comes around for asking questions.

Production, Planning and Control (PPC) under Various Types of Production. The nature of production planning and control system varies from firm to firm as it mainly depends upon the nature of operations carried on and the type of manufacturing process being used. There are certain firms which are mainly engaged in the assembling of the products, while other are engaged in both manufacturing as well as assembling.

In case of an assembly industry, a number of components or parts are brought together to make the finished product like bicycle, sewing machine, typewriter, motor car, etc. The components may be made from the same or different types of materials. On the other hand, a manufacturing industry is engaged in the conversion or transformation or raw materials into components, semi-finished products and finished products. Manufacturing industries follow three types of production systems, namely, *(i)* process production; *(ii)* job production; and *(iii)* intermittent production.

PPC in Assembly Industry. Production planning and control in assembly industries is simple as there is a uniform sequence of operations to be repeated. But the sequence of operations in the assembly is very important because it influences to a great extent the efficiency and effectiveness of the whole unit. After the sequence of operations is properly planned, it is important to ensure the regular supply of each component. If one single component fails to arrive at the proper time and in the required quantity, the whole production line will beheld, resulting in idle men and machinery: Therefore, it is essential to determine the quantity of various components needed at various stages of the assembly ora product. It will mainly depend upon the quantity of products to be assembled during a particular period of time. Schedules should be properly drawn up to achieve the targets. There should also be proper division of work among the personnel.

PPC in Process Industry. Since process industries follow standardized production techniques and use automatic equipment, routing is almost automatic and relatively simple, The raw materials enter the plants and move through the different processes until they come out at the end of the production line as the finished product Thus, there is no problem of follow up. It is also easier to chalk out the departmental schedules, because of standardised nature of the product. Departmental schedules are drawn, on the basis of the 'Master Schedule' which is usually a monthly break-up of the production requirements for each product for a definite period of time. The dispatching of repetitive orders can be pursued under process industries.

PPC in Job Production Industry. In job order plants, production planning and control is conditioned by the nature of the order as every order is different from the others. Routing and scheduling are very complicated. Each order requires a, different sequence of operations or route. Schedules are drawn up in the light of the imitations of equipment, personnel and materials. In some cases it may not be possible to schedule all operations relating to an order simultaneously. Dispatching and follow-up are also conditioned by the order.

PPC in Intermittent Production Industry. Under intermittent manufacturing components are made for inventory but are combined differently for different customers. The finished products are heterogeneous but within a range of standardised options assembled by the manufacturer. The products are generally manufactured in large batches. The system production planning and control to be followed in this type of manufacturing is a mixture of those used in continuous production and job order production. Routing and scheduling are simpler in case of manufacturer of standardised components than in case of manufacture of specialised components and assembly of products. The scheduling of intermediate operations is very important. If this is not planned, the material not schedule a is likely to be hopelessly delayed in process. Dispatching should also be done with great care as, it is often necessary to have new tools, to check equipment and to supply the material some machines may become overloaded with work while others may run out of work.

Follow up in intermittent production is a cumbersome task because products are diversified and a number of orders are running concurrently in different shops. The follow up may be organised either according to the product or the department. Usually a combination of both is to be employed. Quality control is necessary both at the stage of production of the components and after the assembly of the finished product.

❐

8

Corporate Policy in Personnel & Financial Management

Personnel management is primarily concerned with human resources with the organisation. Therefore, policy issues in the areas of personnel management should be concerned with:

(a) manpower planning, recruitment, selection and placement;

(b) training and developments of manpower;

(c) transfer, promotion, demotion, and separation;

(d) working conditions and employee service;

(e) communication consultative and negotiation;

(f) human and social implications of change in the internal organisation and methods of working of economic and social change in the community at large. The basic objective of personnel policies is to ensure adequate and effective manpower at the right to implement the strategy. Besides the organisation has to formulate policies in other areas which can support the implementation of basic strategy through the performance of main functions. Such areas may be research and development, legal, and public relations;

(g) terms of employment, methods and standard of remuneration.

The significance of personnel policy in strategy implementation hardly needs any elaboration. Both physical and human resources are crucial to the achievement of strategic goals. The basic objective of personnel policy in an organisation is to ensure consistency of action and equity in its relations with employees. These policies constitute the basis for sound personnel practices. They provide the yardstick by which implementation of strategic plans and programmes can be appraised. Besides, personnel policies are an integral part of the whole policy structure of an enterprise. Any weakness in personnel policy may thus weaken the other functional policies.

The close interrelation between the quality of personnel and strategic management requires the top executives to be concerned with the following policy issues.

RECRUITMENT POLICY

The appropriate match between strategic goals to be achieved and the kind of people employed require two different but related aspects of staffing to be examined.

On the one hand, there is the necessity of recruiting and maintaining the required number of work people and on the other it is retired, experienced persons available for employment and others employed in other organisation but seeking a change for better prospects. External recruitment obviously provides a wider choice from among personnel to select those with skill, training, education and experience required by the firm. For a firm which needs personnel for implementing growth strategy, the process of recruitment from external sources must be planned well in advance. The problems of external recruitment consist of the relatively higher turnover of new recruits and the demoralising effect of outside recruitment on the existing work organisation.

Sources of Recruitment

A. Internal sources Internal sources refer to the employees currently working in an enterprise. As and when a post falls vacant, someone already working in the enterprise is transferred or promoted to it.

While a promotion or transfer does not result in any increase or decrease in the number and kinds of persons working in the enterprise, it may leave a significant effect on this working of the departments effected by it.

B. **External Sources**

(i) Advertisements, Personnel Consultants, and Jobbers and Contractors.

(ii) Employment Exchange and Educational Institutions.

(iii) Field Trips, Miscellaneous.

CHARACTERISTICS OF A GOOD TRAINING AND DEVELOPMENT POLICY

A good training policy must be based on the following principles:

(1) Relevance to Job Requirements. To be effective, a training programme must be related to the requirements of the job for which it is intended. For this, a thorough analysis of each job is essential.

(2) Allowance for Individual Difference. A good training programme should take into account the difference in ability, learning capacity, interests and temperamental and emotional make-up of trainees.

(3) Management Support. Top managers should actively support all training programmes. It is in the nature of subordinates to look to their superiors for an indication on what to support and what to ignore. It is futile to expect subordinates to be serious about their training of their bosses themselves are indifferent about it.

(4) Determination of Training Needs. Training needs of employees should be determined carefully and the methods chosen for the purpose should be effective.

(5) Suitable Incentives. There should be provision for suitable monetary and non-monetary incentives to motivate trainee, so that they take training seriously.

Compensation and Supplementary Benefits. Policies with regard to wage and salary administration and policy on supplementary benefits are vital components of personnel policy because it is mainly on the basis of satisfactory compensation schemes that company is able to attract and retain capable personnel. In the absence of sound policy with respect to the compensation structure, wages and salaries are likely to be based on personalised arbitrary decisions and thus fall short of the essential elements of adequacy and equity in compensation plans. A satisfactory policy frame is invariably conducive to high morale and minimum frictions among individuals and groups of employees. For, apart from the adequacy of the level of compensation, inequities in the pay structure happen to be the most common causes of dissatisfaction and grievances among employees.

The basic issues to be resolved while formulating the compensation policy are those relating to:

(a) Incentive pay;

(b) Recognition of relative efficiency of performance;

(c) The internal structure of compensation or internal alignment of pay for different job so as to ensure that pay rates are equitable;

(d) The level of pay and its adequacy.

PROMOTION POLICY

Promotion refers to the advancement of an employee to a higher job involving greater responsibility, more pay and better status. It is the movement of an employee to a position of better remuneration, higher status and greater responsibility. A there in crease in pay or working conditions without an increase in status and responsibility is called upgrading or dry promotion. Demotion is the opposite of promotion.

The policy of filling vacancies at higher levels through promotion of lower level employees has several advantages:

(a) Employees have an opportunity for improving their status and earnings. Promotion, therefore, improves the motivation and morale of employees.

(b) It creates sense of royalty among employees. By satisfying the basic urge for advancement, it reduces industrial disputes, labour turnover and absenteeism.

(c) It improves the quality of performance. Reduction in waste and indiscipline results in lower costs. "The company that has no recognised promotion policy likely to have frustrated and restless employees as they have no opportunity for advancement."

However, all higher level vacancies need not necessarily be filled through promotion. Sometimes, lower level staff may not be fit for promotion. Moreover, recruitment from outside brings new blood and independent thinking. The basic aim should be to obtain the best possible personnel irrespective of where from they come.

Basis of Promotion—Merit *vs.* Seniority

There are two bases of promotion, *i.e.*, seniority and merit. Employers generally favour merit, while employees and their unions prefer seniority as the basis of promotion.

Seniority means length of recognised service. It is counted from the date of joining the organisation or from the date of confirmation. Seniority can be calculated in several ways. It is lost due to certain events. *e.g.*, frequent absence from duty.

Seniority is the oldest and most widely used basis of promotion. Promotion on the basis of seniority is justified of following grounds:

(a) It is an objective basis. It prevents favouritism and arbitrary action as there is no room for discretion or prejudices.

(b) It is very simple and practicable as seniority can be measured easily and accurately.

(c) It reduces labour turnover as employees try to remain in the firm to accumulate seniority.

(d) Every employee has a definite idea at all times of his place in the group. He feels secured and develops a sense of loyalty to the organisation. Promotion based of seniority is reward for loyalty.

(e) Length of service is an approximate measure of experience and ability.

(f) Seniority is acceptable to trade unions and gives a feeling of satisfaction to employees.

If a man has been in service for a long time he ought to be better than a newcomer, unless he has been dodging work. Seniority also fits with the cultural expectations for social customs of India.

Seniority as the sole basis of promotion has, however the following demerits:

(a) Rules for the accumulation of seniority have to be laid down with particular reference to the impact of suspension, lay-off, strike, discharge, etc.

(b) Rigid adherence to seniority makes it difficult to recruit and retain capable personnel.

(c) Employees with longer service are not necessarily more compete to Seniority overvalues experience and premium on merit.

(d) The quality and quantity of work suffers as employees try to stick around and do not make full use of their capabilities.

(e) It lowers the morale of ambitious and meritorious employees as they get no recognition. When less competent lose interest in efficiency.

(f) Seniority pro des performing and inefficiency, as no differentiation is made between efficient and inefficient employees.

Advantages refers to the efficiency and ability of an employee. Promotion on the basis of merit has following advantages:

(a) It provides a powerful incentive to work hard and make continuous improvement in efficiency;

(b) There is an overall improvement in operations and the profit of the enterprise.

(c) Ambitious and hard working employees are duty rewarded. They feel satisfied and contributed maximum to the success of the organisation.

Merit has been criticised due to following limitations:

(a) Employees feel insecure and become discontented.

(b) The morale of employees is low when they find that their juniors are promoted before them it causes frustration and loss of interest and loyalty for the organisation. Moreover, merit does not indicate an employee's promotability. An individual may be quite competent for the present job, but his overall personality may not be suitable for higher positions.

Thus, neither absolute seniority nor exclusive merit is a sound basis of promotion. A sound promotion policy should be based on a judicious balance between the two. In practice, seniority is given more weightage but merit should also be given due consideration. None of the two should be exclusive criterion for promotion. Seniority can be the wedding factor when two persons are equally meritorious. Similarly, out the two equally senior employees the more competent one should promoted first. If senior-most employee is incompetent to do the job well junior employees with merit should be promoted.

Essentials of a Sound Promotion Policy. A sound systematic promotion policy should consist of the following:

(1) The report of each employee should be prepared by his supervisor but subject to the approval of the departmental head.

(2) Accurate and uptodate records of seniority and merit should be kept. All employees should be kept informed of their record and opening for promotion.

(3) Promotion policy should be based on job analysis to define job requirements. Employees should know clearly what is expected of them in higher jobs, so that they can prepare themselves for advancement

(4) Objective and systematic plans of performance appraisal should be set up to identify promotable employees. This is necessary to avoid unfairness in promotions.

(5) The basis of promotion should be clearly defined. The relative weight to be given to merit and seniority should be specified.

(6) Lines of promotion should be clearly defined. For each job a schedule of jobs to which promotion can be made should be prepared.

(7) The policy management regarding filling of vacancies through promotion or from outside should be clearly stated.

Industrial Relations Policy

The personnel policies and practices of a rum in many ways are influenced by the state of union-management relations. To what extent the basic philosophy of top management *vis-a-vis* their human resources is subordinated to the bargaining power of employee union depends upon the company's policy with regard to:

The nature of relation with the union, recognition the support of the union organisation, the scope of collective bargaining and settlement of industrial disputes. Ideally, harmonious relation between management and employee union should develop on the basis of mutual co-operation. But company executive are often inclined to adopt a policy of belligerency toward union activities. This approach is born out of strong dislike and mistrust of the union by the executives, who refuse to recognise the union as a bargaining agent, of when forced to negotiate, do it grudgingly with a horse-trading approach. With a hostile attitude to management toward the union, the relationship is inevitably vitiated by mutual suspicion, and there is increasing militancy on the part of union leaders.

CHARACTERISTICS OF A GOOD TRANSFER POLICY

To be effective the transfer policy should possess the following characteristics:

(1) If a transfer is going to result in any change in the rate of remuneration this should be made sufficiently clear.

(2) It is quite likely that requests for transfer to the same job, or to the same shift are received from many employees. In such cases a decision should be taken in keeping with the predetermined policy.

(3) How a transfer is going to affect the seniority of the person concerned should be spelt out in clear terms.

(4) There should be accurate and complete job description of the jobs to which transfers are under consideration. Requirements as to training of the new jobs should be clearly laid down. Also the workers to be transferred should be clearly informed about the time during which they are supposed to adjust themselves to the requirements of their new jobs.

(5) If transfers become necessary because there is surplus of labour force in one department of unit and shortage in

another it should be ensured that workers in their new positions are not given completely new kinds of jobs.

(6) The departments or units within which transfers have to be made should be decided in advance.

(7) Responsibility for recommending and approving transfer should be clearly defined.

FEATURES OF A GOOD PERSONNEL POLICY

Every enterprise should relate its personnel policy to the economic, legal, social and technological factors present in the society in which it operates. This means it has to keep on adjusting and adapting personnel policy to suit and change in these factors.

A good personnel policy should possess the following features:

(1) Proper Communication. It should be properly communicated to those for whom it is intended.

(2) Acceptability. It should enjoy acceptability among the people for whom it has been formulated.

(3) Intergative. It must fully take into account the differing amenities, capabilities, interests, desires, aspirations, beliefs and tempramental make-up of the people for whom it is intended.

(4) Uniformity. It should be uniformly applicable to all members and units of the enterprise.

(5) Responsiveness to Prevailing Trends. Personnel policy should be adjusted to the prevailing norms and trends in ways. For example, if the current thinking is in favour of involving in the management process the policy should be against.

(6) Flexibility. It should not be so rigid and inflexible that it can not be adjusted and adapted to changes in economic, legal, social and technological factors.

(7) **Stability.** Even though personnel policy has to be consistently adjusted and adapted to suit any changes in economic, legal, and technological factor, it should be reasonably stable and permanent.

(8) **Precision and Certainty.** It should be clear to the point and complete in every respect. It should not lead to varying and conflicting interpretations.

(9) **Protection of the Interests of all Parties.** It should take into account the interests of all parties associated with the enterprise, *i.e.*, workers entrepreneurs, consumers, government and the community.

(10) **Promotion of Enterprise Policies.** It should fit into the basis of overall policies of the enterprise.

CONSIDERATIONS IN PROCURING LONG-TERM FINANCE

It has been observed that the management of a company can use different method for raising finance for different periods and purposes. The methods of financing can be classified, on the basis of the term for which the funds are required, into the following categories:

(i) **For Long-term Requirements.** Issue of shares, issues of debentures; Assistance from special industrial Finance Institutions; and ploughing back or reinvesting of retained earnings.

(ii) **For Medium-term Requirements.** Issue of preference shares; issues of debentures, assistance from Special Industrial Finance Institutions; receiving public deposits; and Borrowing from commercial banks.

(iii) **For Short-term Requirements.** Borrowing from commercial banks; trade credit; instalment credit; accounts receivable financing; and customer advance.

(A) Issue of Shares

A. Issue of ownership securities of shares is the most important method of raising long-term finance for permanent investment in the companies. Funds raised from issue of shares provide a financial floor to the capital structure of a company. A share may be defined as unit of measure of shareholder's interest in the company. The share capital of company is divided into a large number of equal parts and each part is individually known as share. According to Section 86 of the Companies Act, 1956, a public company limited by shares can issue two types of ownership securities *viz.*, equity shares and preference shares. An independent private company can issue deffered shares as well.

Perefence Shares. Section 85 (1) of the Companies Act defines preference shares as those which carry preferential rights as to the payment of dividend at a fixed rate either free of or subject to income tax, and as to the repayment of capital. Thus, preference shareholders enjoy two preferential rights over the other category of shares. *Firstly*, they are entitled to receive a fixed rate of dividend out of the net profits of the company prior to declaration of dividend on equity shares. *Secondly*, the assets remaining after the payment of debts of the company under liquidation are rust appropriated of returning the capital contributed by the preference shareholders.

Preference shares may be classified into following categories:

(i) ***Convertible and Non-convertible Preference Share.*** If the preference shareholder's are given a right to convert their shares into equity shares with a fixed period of time, such shares will be known as convertible preference shares. The preference shares which cannot be converted into equity shares are known as non-convertible preference shares.

(ii) ***Redeemable and Irredeemable Preference Shares.*** Redeemable preference shares are those which in accordance with the terms of their issue, will be repaid on

or after a certain date. The preference share which cannot be redeemed during the life time of the company are known as irredeemable preference shares.

(iii) ***Participating and Non-Participating Preference Shares.*** The holders of participating preference shares are entitled to a share in the surplus profits if they remain after paying dividend to preference shares and equity shares. Thus, participating shareholders obtain return on their investment in two forms: *(i)* fixed dividend; and *(ii)* share in surplus profits. The preference share which do not carry the right to share in the surplus profits are known non-participating, preference share.

(iv) ***Cumulative and Non-cumulative Preference Shares.*** The holders of cumulative preference shares are entitled to arrears of dividend on their shares to be paid out of the profits of subsequent years, if in any year the dividend on them cannot be paid. Thus, they are sure to receive dividend on the preference shares held by them for all the years out of the earnings of the company. If in a particular year they are not paid the dividend, they will be paid such arrear in the next year before any dividend can be distributed among equity shareholders. But the dividend on non-cumulative shares does not, accumulate if dividend is not paid in any year.

(B) Equity Shares

Under the Companies Act, shares which are not preference shares are called equity shares. They are also called ordinary shares. Equity shares provide intial capital on permanent basis to the company. Equity shareholders are the real owners of the company and they bear the risk of business. They get dividend only after the dividend on preference shares is paid out of the profits of the company. At the time of winding up, equity capital can be paid back only after every claim including that of preference shareholders has been settled.

Since equity shareholders bear higher risk, they also stand a chance of getting higher dividend if the company's earnings are higher.

Equity shareholders control the affairs of the companies as they have the voting right in the general body meeting of the company. They eject the board of directors of the company and frame policies of the company in general meeting.

(C) Issue of Debentures

Debentures are creditorship securities which provide funds to the company on loan basis rather than on capital basis. A debenture may be defined as an acknowledgment of a debt by a company. The debenture holders are entitled to periodical payment of interest as fixed rate and are also entitled to redemption of their debentures as per terms of debenture issue. The debentureholders are the creditors of the company. Their rights depend upon the type of debentures issued by the company A company may issue the following types of debentures:

(i) ***Convertible and Non-convertible Debentures.*** The convertible debentures can be converted into equity shares of the company after the expiry of specified period. But non-convertible debentures cannot be converted into equity shares. In the recent years, the practice of issuing debentures which are partially convertible into equity shares has gained momentum.

(ii) ***Redeemable and Irredeemable Debentures.*** In case of redeemable debentures, the companies reserve the right of paying off the principle on or after a particular date. In case of irredeemable or perpetual debentures, the company does not fix any date by which they should be redeemed and the holders of such securities cannot demand payment from the company so long as it is a going concern.

(iii) ***Registered and Bearer Debentures.*** In case of registerd debentures the name of the debenture holder is entered in the debenture certificates and books of the company. They

can be transferred by filling in the transfer deed. But bearer debentures can be transferred by mere delivery without any notice to the company. Debenture coupons are annexed with the such debenture certificates. The bearers of the debenture can fill in the coupons and claim interest after sending them to the company. But in case of registered debentures, the company pays interest to the registered debenture holders.

(iv) ***Secured and Unsecured Debentures.*** Secured debentures represent the fixed or floating charge on the assets of the company. When the particular assets are charged by way of security, it is known, as fixed change. Such debentures are also known as mortgage debentures. When the charge is created assets which are of general nature like stock, it is called a floating charge. Under floating change, the company is free to deal with the property forming the subject matter of the charge until, the said charge become fixes default of company in paying the interest of some other event stipulated in the deed of charge. Unsecured debentures, also known as simple or naked debentures, do not carry any charge or security on the assets of the company.

RETAINED EARNINGS

The use of retained earnings as a method of 'self financing' is commonly used by the established companies. It is also known as 'ploughing back of profits'. Under this method, the undistributed or retained profits of the company are used to finance the requirements of the company. The main feature of this method is that it is an internal source of finance. Every good company does not distribute its entire earnings in the form of dividend but rather retains a part of it every year. Such a policy helps the company to build up reserves which can be used for financing expansion programmes.

The practice of 'ploughing back of profits' is influenced by many factors. *Firstly*, it depends upon the net profits of the company.

If a company has earned huge profits in a particular year—its capacity to retain profits will be higher. *Secondly*, dividend policy of the company determines the extent to which profits can be retained for ploughing back. For instance, if a company follows a policy of declaring a consistent rate of dividend every year, it will not be able to retain much if in a particular year it earns less profits. *Lastly*, the age of the company affects the policy of ploughing back on profits. New companies generally do not retain much profits because of their desire to satisfy their shareholders. But an older company can declare less profits for distribution to shareholders and retain the major portion of its profit for reinvestment in the business.

Determinants of Retained Earnings. Once the importance of retained earnings is realised, it may interesting to know the extent to which a company can go or it. The amount of retained earnings is determined by a multiplicity of factors the most important among which are earnings of the company tax laws of the Government and dividend policy of the company.

(i) ***Earnings of the Company.*** The amount of profits earned by company is a basic factor determining the amount of retained earnings, greater the amount of profits, greater can be retained earnings. Clearly no retained earnings are possible if there are no profits. The amount of profits that a company would earn, is in turn, dependent on a numbers of factors including the demand and supply competition and price positions in the market, cost of production and distribution etc. Given the amount of profits, the size of a company's retained earnings should be decided in the light of purposes for which it is needed. The purposes may be to meet any known liability which may arise in future, to finance growth and expansion, to keep dividends at a uniform lever and to meet unknown contigencies or losses in future.

(ii) ***Dividend Policy.*** If a company adopts a generous dividend policy, it would have lesser amount of net earnings left for

retention of earnings. On the other hand, a conservative dividend policy is conducive to good accumulation of corporate savings. Although management is not legally bound to declare any dividend on company's share capital certain amount of dividend might become necessary due to naked conditions. A highly conservative policy of dividend can create feeling in the investor's mind that equity investment is not attractive. Besides, the prices of shares of a company following this policy may go down. On the other hand, a liberal dividend policy may not allow the company to carry out its expansion programme for want of sufficient funds, especially when external financing is difficult and costlier. The proper policy on retention of earnings would be one which strikes a balance between the two-fold objectives of enterprise growth, shareholder's satisfaction.

(iii) ***Tax Laws.*** The volume and rate of taxation on corporate income also influences the amount of retained earnings. In spite of huge profits that a company may earn its net earnings may be very little of the volume and the rate of taxation is very high. In our country the taxation policy of the Government hardly gives any encouragement for retention of earnings. A high rate of taxation has been preventing the business undertakings from ploughing back a desirable amount of profits for their growth and development. There is an urgent need to change the taxation policy of the Government and give positive incentive for corporate savings.

Utility of Retained Earnings

Retention of earnings is of great utility to a company primarily because it is a good source of finance. Besides, the retained earnings are useful for the shareholders and the society at large. We shall discuss the utility of retained earnings from these three angles:

(i) **Utility from Shareholder's Viewpoint.** If a company can benefit by the retention of earnings, the shareholder's can also gain by this practice in the long run since they are the owners of the company. In fact, retained earnings invested in profitable projects increase the value of company and ultimately the wealth of its shareholders. The market value of shares of such a company goes up. The shareholders can take advantage of high share prices by selling their holdings in the open market. Alternatively, they can retain their shares and benefit in the long run by the growth of the company.

(ii) **Utility from Company's Angle.** The retained earnings are of great importance to a company. The retained income or reserve acts as a shock-absorber A concern with large reserves is well armed to fight out depressions and seasonal changes in demand. Secondly, retained earnings enable a company to follow a stable dividend policy and add to its credit in the market. Thirdly, the company can finance the different types of projects for expansion and modernisation through retained earnings without having to borrow from outside. Internal financing is very economical method of financing. If the company were to issue debentures or raise a loan for this purpose, it will naturally have to pay a fixed rate of interest irrespective of profit, and return the amount after some time. Similarly, if more shares are issued, dividend will have to be paid on them. But if the reserves are used for this purpose, no such obligation is incurred. Fourthly, the undistributed income can be used for discharging such obligations as the redemption or retirement of debentures and others debts. Lastly, the reserves can also be utlised to maintain company's operating efficiency when the company is not able to make enough provision for depreciation and obsolescence due to which its efficiency is being adversely affected.

Dangers of Excessive Retained Earnings

Though a reasonable amount of retained earnings is useful for enterprise growth, excessive retained earnings may prove to be dangerous owing to various reasons:

(i) All over-enthusiastic policy of retained earnings may create dissatisfaction among the shareholders. They may be led to think that the directors are ignoring or even damaging their interest by paying a rate of dividend lower than that can be paid out of the available profits.

(ii) If the accumulated reserves are used for the issue of bonus shares, it may results in over-capitalisation later on.

(iii) The management may not always use the retained profits to the advantage of the shareholders *e.g.*, the funds may be invested in other concerns under the same management, bringing little gain to the shareholders.

(iv) By continuous ploughing back of profits over a long period of time, company may grow into a monopoly. This is more likely to happen when other companies find it difficult to raise funds from the market while an existing concern continues to grow on the strength of its internal resources.

(v) Prof. Pigou thinks that excessive ploughing back entails social waste, because money is not made available to those who can use it to the best advantage of the community, but is retained by those who have earned it.

(vi) It may give the management an opportunity to manipulate the share values. By withholding profits, lower dividends may be declared. When the share values fall in the market, the management. Play take them up at reduced prices. The rate of dividend may, then be increased out of the past profits and the management may dispose of the shares at a profit.

From the foregoing discussion, it is clear that the retention of earnings is a policy of undoubted merit for financing the long-term requirements of business enterprise. But it is necessary that the management follows a bold, though cautious, policy in this regard.

FACTORS AFFECTING CAPITAL GEARING

The following factors must be considered while determining the ratio of different securities or sources of capital:

(1) **Cost of Financing.** The cost of raising finance by tapping various, sources of finance should be estimated carefully to decide which of the alternatives is the cheapest. Prevailing rate of interest, rate of return expected by the prospective investors and administrative expenses are the various factors which affect the cost of financing. Generally, cost of financing by issuing debentures and preference shares is less particularly when the equity shareholders expect higher dividend and the other companies in the field are paying higher dividends.

(2) **Flexibility of Financial Structure.** A good financial structure should be flexible enough to have scope for expansion or contraction of capitalisation whenever the need arises. In order to bring flexibly , those securities should be issued which can be paid off after a certain number of years. Equity shares cannot be paid off during the life time of a company. But redeemable preference shares and debentures and public deposits can be paid off whenever the company feels necessary. They provide elasticity in the financial plans. They are generally not issued in the initial states of the company since they involve payment of fixed rate of dividend or interest every year. Fixed income securities are issued when the company is financially sound and it feels that it will be able to earn more than rate the interest or dividend to be given on such securities.

(3) **Exercise of Control.** The control of a company is entrusted to the board of directors elected by the equity shareholder. The equity shareholders have the voting right which can be exercised in the general body meeting to direct the board of directors of the company. But the preference shareholders possess veryfunited voting right and the debenture holders have no voting right. If the board of director and shareholders of a company wish to retain control over the company in their hands, they may allow to issue equity share to public. In such a case, more funds can be raised by issuing preference shares and debentures.

(4) **Trading on Equity.** The word 'equity' refers to the ownership of the company. Trading on equity means taking advantage of equity share capital to borrowed funds on reasonable basis. It refers to the additional profits that equity shares earn because of issuing other form of securities, *viz.*, preference share and debentures. It is based on the premise that if the rate of interest on borrowed capital and the rate of dividend on preference capital which are fixed, is lower than the general rate of the company's earning, the equity shareholders will get advantage in the form of additional profits. Thus, by adopting a judicious mix of debentures and preference shares with equity shares income on equity share can be maximised.

Trading on equity is an arrangement under which the financial management raises funds by issuing securities which carry a fixed rate of interest of dividend, which is less than the average earnings of the company, to increase the return on equity shares. If a company can earn much more than the rate of fixed dividend or interest, excess earnings will go to the equity shareholders and they would thereby earn a higher dividend per share than they would have without the use of gearing of capital structure.

Trading on equity has three limitations. Firstly when the earnings of the company are not sufficient to pay fixed return on all types of securities, the dividend rate is unduly depressed rather than accelerated. Secondly the company must have sufficient assets to offer them as security to lenders in order to borrow on a large scale. Lastly, trading on equity is profitable for company which is likely to have regular, stable and certain earnings.

(5) **Types of Investors.** The shape of capital structure is also influenced by the likings of the potential investors. Therefore, securities of different kinds and varying denominations are issued to meet the requirements of the prospective inverstors. Equity shares are issued to attract the people who have the desire to have a say in the management of the company. Debentures and preference shares are issued to attract those people who prefer security of investment and certainty of return on investment.

(6) **Capital Market Conditions.** The conditions prevailing in the capital market also influence the determination of the securities to be issued. For instance, during depression, people do not like to take risk and so are not interested in equity shares. But during boom, investors are ready to take risk and invest in equity shares. Therefore, debentures and preference shares, which carry fixed rates of return may be marketed more easily during depression.

(7) **Period of Financing.** When funds are required for permanent investment in a company, equity share capital is preferred. But when funds are required to finance expansion programme and the management of the company feels that it will be able to redeem the funds within the life time of the company, it may issue redeemable preference shares and debentures.

(8) **Statutory Requirements.** The structure of capital of a company is also influenced by the requirements of the

states applicable to it. For instance, banking companies have been prohibited by the Banking Regulation Act to issue any type of securities except equity shares.

FINANCIAL POLICY

Financial aspect of business activities deals primarily with raising, administering and distribution of funds by the organisation for the purpose of business operations. Thus financial policies have three major dimensions:

(i) determination of the total amount of funds to be used by the organisation;

(ii) determination of what specific assets the organisation should acquire, or allocation of funds among various assets in an efficient manner; and

(iii) determination of how the needed funds should be financed or obtaining the best mix of financing with relation to the overall valuation of the organisation. Accounting policies will be established to deal with questions as how to treat inventories, which accounts to capitalise, and how to treat expenses and cost. These policies affect the organisation's appearance of success or failure. Thus major policy decisions in the area of finance and accounting are as follows:

(a) ***Level of Dividend Payment.*** Dividend payment history the stability of earnings; rate of growth and profit levels, liquidity positions, ability to borrow, debt contract restrictions, legal constraints.

(b) ***Capital Structure.*** Nature of business operations, nature of capital market, cash generation capacity, tax savings.

(c) ***Level of Working Capital.*** Uncertainty of cash receipts and disbursements, borrowing capacity, efficiency

of cash management, volume of credit sales, reasonability of sales, credit policies.

The basic criterion in financial policies is that the funds needed are available at the right time and at the lowest possible costs.

DIVIDEND POLICY DECISIONS

Dividends represent that part of firm's earnings which is paid out to the shareholders. Dividend policy determines the division of earnings between payments to stockholders and reinvestment in the firm. Thus a proper dividend policy is tied up with the retained earnings policy. The dividend policies of companies are of great importance because they may affect thousand of shareholders just in one company. Dividend policy also influences the size of internal financing by a fifth The guiding principle in framing a company's dividend policy should be the maximisation of shareholder's wealth. The optimum dividend policy would be one which maximises the market value per share. However, some financial experts hold the view that dividend decision has the value of the firm. Therefore, we shall first examine the relationship between dividend decision and the value of the firm.

Relevance of Dividend Decision

There are two key theoretical view on whether or not the dividend decision is really significant influencing the value of the firm as measured by the, market price of its shares. According to one view, the dividends are irrelevant because the amount of dividends paid does not affect the value of the firm. The second viewpoint is that dividends are relevant and that the amount of dividend paid does have an impact on the value of the firm. The supporters of the first view argue that the value of a firm is determined by the earning power of the projects in which it has invested its money and not by the amount of dividends paid. Dividend decision only splits the firm's income between dividends and retained earnings. It is the investment policy of the firm which will determine its income level and, in turn, the net earnings available for dividend distribution. Given the investment decision therefore, the dividend decision has no effect on the value of the firm. If there are good investment opportunities, the firm will retain the earnings for financing them, resulting in long-term capital gains to shareholders. On the other hand, the firm will distribute its earnings to shareholders if it does not foresee adequate investment opportunities. Investors are indifferent to returns in the form of dividends or of capital gains.

Objectives of Dividend Policy

The firm's dividend policy represents a plan of action to be followed whenever the dividend decision must be made. Once the relevance of dividend decision is realised, the management should frame a dividend policy that best fulfils the find's overall objectives. The two major objectives possibly shaping the dividend policy of any rum are: maximisation of the shareholder's wealth the provision of sufficient financing. These objective are interrelated and not mutually exclusive Obviously, shareholder's wealth can not be maximised if there are insufficient funds to finance profitable projects; a provision of source of funds is meaningless if these funds are not used for shareholder's interest. These two objectives are explained below:

(a) ***Wealth Maximisation.*** The dividend policy of a rum should aim at the general objective of maximising the owner's wealth. It should be formulated not merely to increase the share price in the short run, but to maximise the owner's wealth in the long-run. Of course, the shareholders may not fully appreciate such a dividend policy and may prefer immediate dividends to future dividends and capital gains since they do not have a perfect knowledge of the implications of certain dividend policies in the light of market forces. As a result, the share prices may drop in the market. It is the responsibility of the firm management to make the owners aware of the objectives and implications of dividend policy, so that the market reaction is favourable.

(b) ***Providing for Sufficient Financing.*** Another important objective of dividend policy is the provision for sufficient funds without which profitable investment opportunities cannot be carried out. In the absence of adequate finance, wealth maximisation objective would remain a sheer dream. One of the important sources of long-term financing is retained earnings. But larger the amount of dividend, lesser would be the retained earnings. Therefore, the management has to decide what shall be the proper ratio between dividends and retained earnings so that the twin objective of short-term interest of the shareholders and long-term gain expansion are realised. The firm can also go for external financing. But the market forces may not be favourable for that and internal financing may be the easiest and the least costly choice. The ultimate decision in this regard is dependent on a multiplicity of factors which we shall now study.

FACTORS AFFECTING DIVIDEND POLICY

The dividend policy of rum should be formulated after taking into account the objective of wealth maximisation and provision for internal financing and a number of other relevant factors. Some of the determinants of dividend policy are as follows:

(a) **Legal Rules.** The various provisions of law imposed by the Government regulating corporate dividend provide the framework within which a company can formulate its dividend policy. Subject to certain statutory restrictions and the provisions of Article of Association, the directors are free to declare any amount of dividends. But there is a basic legal constraint that the dividend must not be paid out of capital, which in other words, means that it should only be paid out of profits. This rule is meant for protecting the interest of creditors and preference shareholders who may suffer because of reduced equity capital if the dividends are paid out of it. However, if the current year's profit are inadequate, the company can declare dividends out of accumulated profits (or retained earnings) in accordance with the rules framed by the Central Government. The dividends should be paid in cash, though a company is not prohibited from capitalising its profits or reserves (retained earnings) for the purpose of issuing fully paid bonus shares. A company is prohibited from paying dividends while it is insolvent, *i.e.*, when its liabilities exceed the assets or when it is unable to pay its bills. Within these legal boundaries, however, the dividend policy is primarily influenced by financial economic factors.

(b) **Liquidity Position.** Another restriction on the payment of dividends is the liquidity position of firm determined by the level of its liquid assets including cash and marketable securities. Quite possible, the firm may have a substantial amount of earnings to declare dividend, but may not have a substantial amount of earnings to declare dividend. This situation may exist, for example, when a firm declares dividends out of retained earnings which are not held as cash and have been invested in plant and equipment, inventories and other assets. A growing firm usually has a pressing need for funds. In such a situation, the firm may choose not to pay any cash dividends. Of course, it is possible for the firm to borrow funds to pay dividends, but this may be a costlier alternative.

(c) **Contractual Restrictions.** Often the firm's ability to pay cash dividend is restricted by certain specific conditions in loan when the finances are raised from external sources. Generally, conditions prohibit the firm from paying cash dividends until a certain level of earnings has been achieved or limit the amount of dividends paid to a certain amount of percentage of earnings. Such restrictions are imposed by creditors to protect themselves from possible insolvency of the firm in case its cash position is weakened by the payment of dividends. The financial manager must keep in mind various contractual requirements while formulating the dividends policy. If these requirements are violated, the creditors may withdraw their money from the firm.

(d) **Desires of Shareholders.** Directors of company are not legally bound to declare dividends. But shareholders are the real owners of the company and they appoint the directors to act as their true representatives. Moreover, the response of shareholders to the firm's dividend policy facts the market price of share which, in turn, determines the value of the firm. Therefore, the directors should give due weightage to the desires of shareholders. The shareholders may prefer dividends to Capital gains if they have tax advantage by such a decision or they want to use the dividend receipt in certain-personal investment channels-other than those offered by the Company.

(e) **Growth Prospects or Investment Opportunities.** Growth prospects or investment opportunities is another important determinant of the dividend policy. The management of successful enterprise would like to expand its scale of operations and try to ensure the growth of the firm. But a growing firm needs an increasing amount of financial resources to invest in the profitable ventures. Since external financing may be costlier, a growing firm may decide to depend heavily on internal financing through retained earnings. Such a firm is likely to payout a very small percentage of its earnings as dividends.

(f) **Access to Capital Markets.** A large, well-established firm with a fair record of profitability and stability of earnings will have easy access to capital market and will face little problem in raising finance through external sources. On the other hand, a small firm would attract less investors since they may consider that their investment in such a firm would be risky. As a result, a small firm may not be able to pay much dividend as it must retain more of its earnings to finance its operations, whereas well-established concern can afford to pay a higher rate of dividend since it can easily meet its financial requirements through external sources. Access to capital market, therefore, has a significant impact on the dividend policy.

(g) **Profit Rate and Stability of Earning.** Profit position of a firm is a very important factor that influences its dividend policy. A firm with a large rate of return on its investment will have larger profits and therefore, can pay more dividends to its shareholders as compared to a firm with lesser returns. Moreover, if the earnings are relatively stable and do not fluctuate time and again, a firm can predict what will be its future earnings. The unstable firm is not able to determine what will be its actual future earnings and, therefore, it is likely to plough back more profits to meet adverse future conditions.

(h) **Control.** The management may be interested that existing shareholders should continue to retain control over the company. In that case, it would not be wise to raise finances through issue of fresh shares lest the control is diluted into the hands of new shareholders. Besides, raising additional finances through the issue of debenture or other forms of borrowing can increase the financial risk of the firm. Under the circumstances, the firm may rely more on internal financing or retained earnings and is likely to have lesser dividend pay out ratio.

(i) **Inflation.** Inflation has an indirect impact on the dividend policy of a firm in the sense that it increases the replacement cost of assets which are being depreciated every year at the book value. Funds generated from providing depreciation may be insufficient to meet the rising cost of assets which might become obsolete and have to be replaced in future. Consequently, to maintain the earning power of the firm the management should decide to reduce the rate of dividend and increase the proportion of retained earnings during a period of inflation. In short, it is useful for every firm to establish a general policy with respect to the payment for dividends to its shareholders. An appropriate dividend policy must be shaped by multiplicity of considerations including legal and contractual constraints, growth requirements and financial position of the firm, the interest of owners, and market considerations. The aim of the financial manager should be to bring about a balance among various factors.

TYPES OF DIVIDEND POLICY

There are several patterns of dividend payments and therefore, there may be a number of possible dividend policies. Three of the more commonly used dividend policies are : Constant dividend per share, constant percentage of net earnings and small but regular dividend per share plus extra dividend.

(a) **Constant Dividend Per Share.** Many companies have attempted to establish a reputation for payment of annual dividends of a regular and fixed amount per share, irrespective of business conditions of profitable or unprofitable operations. Some companies that have a policy of constant dividend per share change it occasionally to a higher or lower depending on the changed conditions, but such shifts are infrequent and usually are followed for several years before another new rate is established. It is easy to maintain this policy when the earning of company .are stable. However, if these are side fluctuations in the earnings pattern, it is difficult to continue with such a policy.

(b) **Constant Percentage of Earnings.** Some companies follow the policy of declaring a certain percentage of earnings in the form of dividends and retaining the rest as a reinvestment of earnings. With this policy the amount of dividend per share will not be fixed but win fluctuate in direct proportion to earnings. For instance, the board of directors may decide that one-half of the earnings should be distributed each year and the remainder should be retained. Management would like this type of dividend policy because dividend are linked with the earning, power of the company more earning more dividend less earnings less divided. A company is automatically able to provide for certain amount of retained earnings in profitable years as per this dividend policy.

(c) **Small but Regular Dividend Per Share Plus Extra Dividend.** This dividend policy is a variation of the constant dividend per share policy. Under this policy, the regular fixed dividends per share are board of directors announces an extra dividend the share as special distribution in the periods when earnings are higher than normal. This policy is particularly suitable for those companies that experience cyclical shift in earnings. The policy has the credit of maintaining shareholders confidence in the company by regular dividend payment without giving them false hopes of increased dividends every year but giving them due share of the additional profits in the periods of prosperity.

MANAGEMENT OF FUNDS

The management of funds is an important area of financial plans and policies. It basically deals with decisions related to the systematic aspects of financial management. The major factor regarding which plans and policies related to the management of funds have to be made are the systems of finance accounting, and budgeting; management control system; cash, credit, and risk management; cost control and reduction and tax planning and advantages.

The management of funds can play a pivotal role in strategy implementation as to aims at the conservation and optimum utilisation of funds-objectives which are central to any strategic action. Organisations that implement strategies of a stability, growth or retrenchment cannot escape the rigours of proper management of funds. In fact, good management of funds often create the difference between a strategically successful and unsucessful company. For instance, Gujrat Ambuja Cements, currently the most profitable cement company in the country, has achieved tremendous financial success primarily on the basis of its policies of cost control. This company has been particularly successful in maintaining a low cost for power, which is a major input in cement manufacturing. Similarly, Tata Chemicals maintains a competitive edge, due to its policy of conservation of resources through internal power generation, over its competitors like DCW, GHCL, and Gujrat Alkalies. Another company, Asahi India Glass follows a policy of managing its cash flows strategically through conservation in the form of depreciation, which it does through the written-down value method. Finolex Cables has implemented its competitive growth strategies by following a policy of better management of project costs, which were less than half of what its competitor spent, and recovering these project costs much before its competitors could even break even. In this way, through a judicious management of funds, companies can implement their strategies in better manner.

ESSENTIALS OF SOUND CAPITAL STRUCTURE

Capital structure refers the make-up of the total debt and total equity. An effective capital structure involves the full use of financial leverage factor. (Leverage may be defined as the employment of funds which the company pays a fixed return). Financial leverage implies the use of funds carrying fixed commitment charge with the purpose of increasing return to the equity shareholders. If the proportion of debt is high in relation to the total funds employed, the company is said to be highly levered or geared. The use of leverage may be either favourable or unfavorable which has already been discussed. The capital stricture should be so devised that it achieves the favorable leverage, *i.e.*, return on investments exceeds the cost of debt.

The analysis of financial structure of company is very important to enable it—to make the best utilisation of its capital resources and to maximise its wealth producing capacity. It will help in adjusting the ratio between debt and equity. It is important to point out that there is no fixed optimum capital structure for a company. Capital structure varies from company to company depending upon the nature of its operations, efficiency of management, etc. It also varies for the same company from time to time. We have already discussed the factors influencing the capital structure of an enterprise. It may be pointed out that these factors they are intermixed and supplement the influence of one another. It is difficult to give objective weights to different factors. The experience and judgement of the finance manager are also used while planning the capital structure. Therefore, it can be concluded that there cannot be the optimum, ideal or perfect capital structure which should be adopted by all the firms for all times. However, a sound capital structure can be planned for every enterprise. It may be noted that sound capital structure is a relative concept. Every company has to devise its own capital structure and keep on reviving it from time to time in order to achieve efficiency and effectiveness in financial planning.

A sound capital structure should poses the following essential requisities:

(1) **Dynamic.** The nature of the financial structure of a company should be dynamic and not rigid. It should be revised periodically depending upon the changes in the business constitutions. If this is done, it will enable the company to achieve the lowest average cost on long-term funds and increase its profitability.

(2) **Economy.** The capital structure should ensure the minimum cost of capital which in turn would increase its ability to generate more wealth for the company.

(3) **Flexibility.** A sound capital structure should facilitate expansion and contraction of funds. It should be able to procure more capital in times of need and should be able to pay all its debts when it does not require funds.

(4) **Safety.** A sound capital structure should ensure safety of investment. It should be so determined that fluctuations in the earnings of the the company do not have heavy strain on its financial structure.

(5) **Balance.** The capital structure should represent a balance between different types of ownership and securities.

(6) **Clear-cut Objective.** The financial structure of company should be guided by clear-cut objectives. Its objectives can be minimisation of the value of the company and the minimisation of the company's cost of capital.

INVESTMENT POLICY

While formulating policies relating to the sources of finance and financial leverage, it is also necessary to keep in views the uses of capital for different activities including creation of additional facilities, acquisition of plants and equipments, sales promotion, and the like. For implementation of strategy involves estimating the funds requirements and deciding on the appropriate mix of debt and equity capital as well as setting limits on the allocation of capital for specific purposes. The main issues in capital allocation policy consist of *(a)* regulating investment in fixed assets, and *(b)* restraint on the holding of current assets.

Except in the case of retrenchment strategy, all other strategies leave a wide scope for managers to make proposals for deployment of capital either for increased production of higher efficiency in production or sales. Thus, for instance, executives concerned with production may propose investments in additional facilities or new equipments, while others may propose investment aiming at cost reduction through vertical integration, or investment in R & D, or management raining, and so on. Often, a basic policy on the minimum rate of return helps in the appraisal of investment proposals, so that proposals for the acquisition of additional fixed assets may be accepted or rejected using the acceptable minimum rate of return on investment as a 'hurdle rate'.

LEASING

In more recent years, long-term leasing of fixed assets has been found to an attractive proposition for different reasons. As an alternative to buying, long-term leasing may be preferred when the uncertainty of future outlook and the prospects of rapid expansion and relocation may suggest flexibility of asset commitments. It is also found advantageous in so far as the need for immediate outlay of capital is reduced. Long-term leasing is also termed 'off balance sheet' lease since neither the asset nor the source of funds appear on the firm's balance sheet. Where the asset for leasing needs to be constructed so as to serve special technical requirements, it may be built and equipped accordingly and then sold and leased back. The lease agreement may also provide for the lessee's option to buy the asset as depreciated value on the expiry of the lease period. However, long-term leasing involving a binding obligation to make annual rental payments just as periodical payment of interest and principal in the case on the debentures or loans. The operating cost of the asset and the tax implication of annual lease rentals must therefore be considered carefully before formulating any policy with regard to leasing.

DETERMINATION OF CAPITAL

Following determinants are kept in mind for capital.

1. Nature of Business

(a) Requirements of materials

(b) Period of Product life cycle

(c) Turnover of Capital

(d) Seasonal Fluctuations.

2. Plans of Business

(a) Product Planning

(b) Planning of the' Size of Production

(c) Marketing Planning

(d) Planning for Expansion.

3. Financial Policies

4. Managerial Policies

Optimum Size of Firm. There is always a tendency on the part of every businessman to expand his business unit in order to reap the economies of large-scale production and operation. However, there is limit beyond which an increase in size will not be advantageous earn to the businessman. The point from which further expansion of the unit will be disadvantageous to the businessman is called the optimum point and the firm that has reached this point is called optimum firm. Every businessman tries to expand his business up to optimum size so that he may obtain in the long run, the low to cost of production under existing conditions of financial, technical and entrepreneurial ability. Prof. Honey says, According to pretty definite conditions within and without the industry, there is a certain size of establishment which will give the maximum efficiency of production and towards this size all establishments tend." Prof. Robinson also gives a detailed analysis of an optimum firm. According to him, "By the optimum firm we must mean that firm which in existing conditions of technique and organising abili'y has the lowest average cost of production per unit, when all those costs which must be covered in the long run are included. Optimum, however, can never remain stationary. It changes along with the changes in the various factors such as technique, finance, market conditions and organising ability. These factors are dynamic and they change with the passage of time. Hence there is no fixed optimum and businessman must try to reach new optimum along with the changes in the factors. The force which determine the best size of the business unit are the technical forces, managerial forces, financial forces, marketing forces and the forces of risk and fluctuations.

Reconciliation. The various force discussed above may favour a different optimum size for the firm and hence the businessman has to reconcile the various optima. Some examples of reconciliation area: if the technical optimum is larger than the managerial optimum, an attempt may be made to reduce the optimum size of the technical unit by increasing its specialization, or steps may be taken to increase the efficient of management. On the other hand, if the managerial optimum is greater than the technical optimum the firm may duplicate: or triplicate its technical productive facilities. For example a cotton textile company may decide to have three or four mills. Another course is to expand the firm vertically. In case the technical optimum is smaller than the marketing optimum, the device is to sell goods manufactured by other firm in order to make marketing larger than production. On the other hand, if the technical optimum is larger than the marketing optimum, either the marketing may be entrusted to an outside firm or an attempt may be made to use the products to produce an article of a high order.

FINANCIAL SOURCES IN A BUSINESS

Every company requires funds for investment in the form of fixed capital and working capital. While estimating the need for funds, the period for which they are required is also to be ascertained. Funds may be required for long-term, for medium-term and for short-term period. It is the period of finance which determines the source or sources of finance to be tapped and the method of financing to be used. The term 'source' implies, the agencies from which funds are procured and the method of raising finance is linked with period for which funds are required and it deals with the mode of raising finance.

Sources. According to the length of the period for which funds are required, sources of raising finance may be classified as follows:

(a) ***Long-term Finance.*** It is required for investment fixed assets like land, building, plant and machinery, and for financing extension programmes. Long-term funds are raised for a minimum period of 10 years. The following are the sources of long-term financing: *(i)* shareholders; *(ii)* debenture holders; *(iii)* financial institutions; and *(iv)* retained earnings.

(b) ***Medium-term Finance.*** It is required for investment is working capital and for repayment of assets. It is raised for a period ranging from more than one year and less than ten years. The following are the sources of medium-term financing: *(i)* debentureholders; *(ii)* financial institutions; *(iii)* public deposits, and *(iv)* commercial banks.

(c) ***Short-term Finance.*** It is required for meeting the short-term needs of working capital. Its period is 12 months or less than 12 months and it can be raised from the following sources: *(i)*-public deposits; *(ii)* trade credits; and *(iii)* commercial banks.

Methods. It has been observed that the management of a company can use different methods for raising finance for different periods and purposes. The methods of financing can be classified, on the basis of the term for which the funds are required, into the following categories:

(i) For Long-term Requirements

(a) Issue of shares

(b) Issue of debentures

(c) Assistance from special industrial Finance Institutions

(d) Ploughing back-up reinvesting of retained earnings.

(ii) For Medium-term Requirements

(a) Issue of preference shares

(b) Issue of debentures

(c) Assistance from Special Industrial Finance Institution

(d) Receiving public deposits

(e) Borrowing from commercial banks.

(iii) For Short-term Requirements

(a) Borrowing from commercial banks

(b) Trade credit

(c) Instalment credit

(d) Accounts receivable financing

(e) Customer advance.

ISSUE OF SHARES

Issue of ownership securities of shares is the most important method of raising long-term finance for permanent investment in the companies. Funds raised from issue of shares provide a financial floor to the capital structure of a company. A share may be defined as a unit of measure of a shareholder's interest in the company. The share capital of a company is divided into a large number of equal parts and each part is individually known as a share. According to Section 86 of the Companies Act, 1956, a public company limited by shares can issue two types of ownership securities, *viz.*, equity shares and preference shares. An independent private company can issue deferred shares as well.

PREFERENCE SHARES

The Companies Act defines preference shares as those which carry preferential rights as to the payment of dividend at a fixed rate either free of or subject so income tax, and as to the repayment of capital. Thus, preference shareholders enjoy two preferential rights over the other category of shares. Firstly, they are entitled to receive a fixed rate of dividend out of the net profits of the company prior to declaration of dividend on equity shares. Secondly, the assets remaining after the payments of debts of the company under liquidation are first appropriated for returning the capital contributed by the preference shareholders.

Preference shares may be classified into following categories:

(a) **Cumulative and Non-cumulative Preference Shares.** The holders of cumulative preference shares are entitled to arrears of dividend on their shares to be paid out of the profits of subsequent years, if in any years the dividend on them cannot be paid. Thus, they are sure to receive dividend on the preference shares held by them for all the years out of the earnings of the company. If, in a particular year they are not paid the dividend, they will be paid such arrear in the next year before any dividend can be distributed among equity shareholders.

(b) **Participating and Non-Participating Preference Shares.** The holders of participating preference shares are entitled to a share in the surplus profits if they remain after paying dividend to preference shares and equity shares. Thus, participating shareholders obtain return on their investment in two forms: *(i)* fixed dividend; and *(ii)* share in surplus profits.

(c) **Redeemable and Irredeemable Preference Shares.** Redeemable preference shares are those which in accordance with the terms of their issue, will be repaid on or after a certain date. The preference shares which cannot be redeemed during the life time of the company are known as irredeemable preference shares.

(d) **Convertible and Non-convertible Preference Shares.** If the preference shareholders are given a right to convert their share into equity shares within a fixed period of time, such share will be known as convertible preference shares. The preference shares, which cannot, be converted into equity shares are known as non-convertible preference shares.

Evaluation. The issue of preference shares has the following benefits:

(a) The management can retain control over the company by issuing preference shares to outsiders because the preference shareholders have only restricted voting rights.

(b) Preference shareholders are entitled to a fixed rate of dividend which enable the equity shareholders to get higher dividend.

(c) The preference shares attract funds from those investors who prefer safety of their investments and a fixed rate of return on their investment.

(d) Preference shares do not impose heavy burden on the company because they carry a fixed rate of dividend.

(e) A company can raise finance for a long-term without creating any charge over its assets.

(f) Redeemable preference shares may be issued to bring flexibility in the financial structure of the company as they can be redeemed whenever it is desired.

There are certain limitations of raising funds by issuing preference shares. The investors may not like these shares because preference shareholders have restrictedly noting rights only. The issue of preference shares is costlier than the issue of debentures because these shares have to be given a rate of dividend which is higher than the prevailing rate of interest on debentures.

EQUITY SHARES

Under the Companies Act; shares which are not preference shares are called equity shares. They are also called ordinary shares.

Equity shares provide initial capital on permanent basis to the company. Equity shareholders are the real owners of the company and they bear the risk of business. They get dividend only after the devidend on preference shares is paid out of the profits of winding up, equity capital can be paid back only after every claim including that of preference shareholders has been settled.

Equity share capital has certain drawbacks also. If the equity shares are issued excessively, it may result in over-capitalisation which may be difficult to cure. In such a case, the company will also lose the benefit of trading on equity. Since the control of the company is with the equity shareholders.

ISSUE OF DEBENTURES

Debentures are creditorship securities which provide funds to the company on loan basis rather than on capital basis. A debenture may be defined as an acknowledgement of a debt by a company. The debentureholders are entitled to periodical payment of interest at a fixed rate and are also entitled to redemption of their debentures as per terms of debenture issue. The debentureholders are the creditors of the company. Their rights depend upon the type of debentures issued by the company. A company may issue the following types of debentures:

(a) **Secured and Unsecured Debentures.** Secured debentures represent the fixed or floating charge on the assets of the company. When the particular assets are charged by way of security; it is known as fixed charge. Such debentures are also known, as mortgage debentures. When the charge is created assets which are of general nature like stock, it is called a floating charge. Under floating charge, the company is free to deal with the property forming the subject-matter of the charge until the said charge becomes fixed by default of company in paying the interest or some other event stipulated in the deed of charge.

(b) **Redeemable and Irredeemable Debentures.** In case of redeemable debentures, the companies reserve the right of paying off the principal on or after a particular date. In case of ill irredeemable or perpetual debentures, the company does not fix any date by which they should be redeemed and the holders of such securities cannot demand payment from the company so long as it is a going concern.

(c) **Convertible and Non-convertible Debentures.** The convertible debentures can be converted into equity shares of the company after the expiry of a specified period. But non-convertible debentures cannot be converted into equity shares.

(d) **Registered and Bearer Debentures.** In case of registered debentures, the name of the debenture holder is entered in the debenture certificates and books of the company. They can be transferred by filling in the transfer deed. But bearer debentures cash be transferred by mere delivery without any notice to the company. Debenture coupons are annexed with such debenture certificates. The bearers of the debentures can fill in the coupons and claim interest after sending them to the company.

❐

9

Foreign Trade Policies

IMPORT-EXPORT ACT, 1947

Economic development is characterised by the growth of the foreign trade sector and the structural changes in the economy are usually reflected in the changes in the direction and composition of foreign trade. Government of India earlier imposed many types of restrictions has relaxed its export and import policy recently. The objective of commercial policy of India is to transform the business sector according to the Objectives of national development.

In India, the trade is required because of following reasons:

1. To have favourable balance of payments and increase in foreign exchange reserves.
2. To protect domestic industries from the competition from rest of the world.
3. To encourage import substitution.
4. The encourage exports and for export promotion.
5. To keep foreign exchange reserves upto a reasonable extent.
6. To develop economy of India.

The role of foreign trade has become very important in India. The value of foreign trade has been increased many folds since the introduction of first five year plan. The value of foreign trade Rs. 1972 crores in 1950-51 increased to Rs. 75,698 crores in 1990-91. If we look at data of foreign trade, then we find that the gap between export and import value is continuously increasing like Import and Export control Act. 1947 etc. steps to reduce the gap between export value took many steps like import and export control Act, 1947 etc. to reduce the gap between export value and import value. Now we shall discuss import and Export act, 1947 in detail.

IMPORTS AND EXPORTS (CONTROL) ACT

The Imports and Exports (control) Act 1947, amended from time to time empowers the central government to prohibit or control certain imports and exports in the public interest.

The act enables the Central Government to make provisions for prohibiting, restricting or otherwise controlling:

(a) The import, export, carriage, stores of goods of any specified desription; and

(b) The bringing into any part or place in India of goods of specified description intended to be taken out of India without being removed from ship or conveyance in which they are being carried.

The Government can also prohibit, restrict or impose conditions on the clearance, whether for homes consumption or for shipment abroad, of any goods or class of goods imported into India.

There are provision in the Act according to which imported goods or materials can be confiscated in certain cases. An authorised person, as specified in the Act, may enter, at any reasonable time, any premises in which any imported goods or materials which are liable to confiscation under this Act are suspected to have been kept or concealed, and inspect such imported goods or materials as he may think fit. Such kinds of inspections may be made by the authorised person of any books of account or other documents of things which, in his opinion, will be useful for, or relevant to, any proceeding under this Act. If the authorised person has any reason to believe that any such imported goods or materials or documents are secreted in any place, he may enter into the search such place or premises for them.

If the authorised person has any reason to believe that any imported goods or materials are liable to confiscation under this Act, he may seize them. Where it is not practicable to seize andy such goods or materials, the authorised person any serve on the owner of the goods or materials an order that he shall not remove, part with or otherwise deal with, the goods or materials, except with the previous permission of such authorised person.

Any imported goods or materials in respect of which:

(a) any condition of the licence of letter of authority, under which they were imported, relating to the utilisation or distribution of such goods or materials, or

(b) any condition relating to the utilisation or distribution of such goods or materials subject to which they were received from, or through, a recognised agency, or

(c) any direction given under the control order with regard to the sale of such goods or materials, has been, is being or is attempted to be, contravened shall, together with any package, covering or receptacle in which such goods are found, be liable to confiscation and, where such goods or materials are so mixed with any other goods or materials that they cannot be readily separated, such other goods or materials shall also be liable to confiscation.

It has been laid down in the act that any authorised person may stop, or compel to land, as the case may be, any conveyance or animal which is suspected to be used or is about to be used for the transport of any imported goods of materials liable to confiscation under this Act, and search/examine the conveyance and the goods or materials in the conveyance or on the animal.

Any means of transport which has been is being or is attempted to be, used for the transport of any imported goods or materials which are liable to confiscation under this act, shall be liable to confiscation unless the owner of the means of transport proves that it was, is being or is about to be, so used without the knowledge or connivance of the owner himself, his agent, if any, and the person in change of the conveyance or animal, and that each of them has taken all reasonable precautions against such use.

IMPORTS (CONTROL) ORDER

In exercise of the powers conferred by the impors and exports control Act 1947, the central government made on 7th December, 1955, an order namely, the Imports (Control) Order, 1955. This Order has been amended from time to time.

This Imports (Control) order prohibits the import of any goods of the description specified on schedule I of the order except under, and in accordance with, a licence or a customs permit granted by the central government or by any officer specified in schedule II of the order.

The order lays down that it, in any case, it is found that the goods imported under licence do not conform in every respect *(i)* to the description or value of the goods as contained in the licence, or *(ii)* to the other conditions relating to such goods, contained in, or applicable to the licence, the Import of Such Goods shall be deemed to be Prohibited.

The order states that the licensing authority issuing a Licence under this order may issue the same subject to one or more of the conditions stated below:

(i) That the goods converted by the licence shall not be disposed of except in the manner prescribed the licensing authority or otherwise dealt with without the written permission of the licensing authority or any peron duly authorised by it;

(ii) That the goods coverd by the licence on importation shall not be sold or distributed at a price exceeding that which may be specified in any direction attached to the licence;

(iii) That the applicant for a licence shall excute a bond for complying with the terms subject to which a licence may be granted.

A licence granted under the order shall also be subject to the conditions contained in schedule *V*, which deals with certain payment conditions, "Actual user" conditions applicable to import licences issued to "Actual User", and conditions applicable to licences issued for the import of capital goods.

It has also been laid down that it shall be deemed to be a condition of every such licence that:

(i) No person shall transfer and so person shall acquire by transfer any licence issued by the licensing authority except under, and in accordance with, the written permission of the authority which ranted the licence or any person empowered in this behalf by such authority;

(ii) The goods for the import of which a licence is granted shall be the property of the licences at the time of import and thereafter up to the time of clearance through the customs. (There two conditions, however, shall not apply to licences issued to the State Trading Corporation of India, the Minerals and Metals Trading Corporation of India and other similar institutions or agencies owned or controlled by the central overnment and which are entrusted with the canalisation of imports. The above two conditions shall also not apply to the licences issued to eligible Export Houses for the import of goods meant for disposal to actual users under the import policy for registered exporters);

(iii) The goods for the import of which a licence has been granted shall be new goods, other than disposal goods, unless otherwise stated in the licence.

A licence granted under this order may contain such other conditions, not inconsistent with the Act or this order, as the licensing authority may deem fit.

A licence shall comply with all the conditions imposed or deemed to be imposed under the order.

The Order also deals with the details of matters like refusal of licence; amendement of licence; power to debar from importing goods or from receiving licences or allotment of imported goods; power to suspend importation of goods; grant of licences or allotments of imported goods power to keep in abeyance applications for licences or allotments or imported goods. Cancellation of licences; declaration as to the value, sort, quality etc. of imported goods; uilistion of imported goods; power to make directions for the sale of imported goods in certain cases; exceptions from this order, etc.

EXPORT CONTROL ORDER

In exercise of the powers conferred by the imports and exports (control) Act, 1947, the central government on 24th March, 1977, made an order called the Exports (control) order, 1977.

The exports control order restricts the export of certain goods. Accordingly, no person shall accordingly, no person shall export any goods of the description specified granted by the central government or by an officer specified in schedule II of the order {clause 3(1)}. The same rule is applicable to exports to Pakistan {Clause 3(2)}.

Notwithstanding anything contained in sub-clauses (1) and (2) mentioned above, goods specified in schedule III of the order may be exported on fulfilment of the terms and conditions specified therein.

The order states that if, in any case, it is found that the value, sort, specification, quality and description of the goods to the exported are not in conformity with the declaration of exporter in those respects, or if the quality and specification of such goods are not in accordance with terms of the export contract, the export of such goods shall be deemed to be prohibited.

It has been laid down in the exports (control) order that a licence granted under this order may contain such condition, not inconsistent with the Imports and Exports (Control) Act, 1947, or this order, as the licensing authority may deem fit.

It shall be deemed to be a condition of every licence that:

(i) No person shall transfer and no person shall acquire by transfer any licence issued by the licensing authority except under, and in accordance with, the written permission of the authority which granted the licence or of any other person empowered in this helf by such authority,

(ii) The goods for the export of which the licences has been granted shall be the property of the licence at the time of the export.

The licence shall comply with all the conditions imposed or deemed to be imposed under the relevant clause of the order.

The order also deals with the details of matters like refusal of licences amendment of licences, power to debar from receiving licences of exporting goods, power to suspend grant of licences or permission to export goods, cancellation of licences, declaration as to value, sort, quality, etc., of exported goods, prohibition regarding making, signing, etc., of any documentation, statement of document, exemptions from the order, etc.

FOREIGN TRADE ACT, 1992

Foreign Trade (Development and Regulation) Act, 1992 replaced the Imports and Exports (Control) Act, 1947. The objective of the Act is to provide for the development and regulation of foreign trade by facilitating imports into and augmenting exports from, India and for matters connected therewith or incidental thereto.

The main provision of the Act are as follows:

1. Power to Make Provisions Relating to Imports and Exports. Section 3 of the Act deals with the powers to make provisions relating to imports and exports. According to this Section, the Central Government may by order published in the official gazette, make provision for *(i)* the development and regulation of foreign trade by facilitating imports and increasing exports, and *(ii)* prohibiting, restricting or otherwise regulating the import or export of goods. Section 5 authorises the Central Government to formulate and announce, by notification in the Official Gazette, the export and import policy and also, in like maner, to amend that policy.

2. Importer-Exporter Code Number. According to Section 7, no person shall make any import or export except under an Importer-Exporter Code Number granted by the Director General or the officer authorised by the Director General in this behalf , in accordance with the procedure specified in this behalf by the Director General. Section 8 states that if any person has contravened by law relating the Central Excise or Customs of Foreign Exchange or has committed any economic offence under any other law in force at that time, or the Director General has reason to believe that person has made any export or import in a manner gravely prejudicial to the trade relations with other countries, the Importer-Exporter Code Number given to him can be cancelled. In such circumstances, the person whose code number has been cancelled or suspended will not be entitled to import or export goods except under a special licence granted.

3. Issue, Suspension and Cancellation of Licence. According to Section 9, the Director General or an officer authorised by him may, after making an enquiry, grant or renew or refuse to grant or renew a licence to import or export goods. In the event of suspension or cancellation of the licence of any person to import or export goods. he shall be provided a reasonable opportunity of being heard.

4. Director General of Foreign Trade. Section 6 provides for the appointment of Director General of Foreign Trade by the Central Government for the purposes of this Act. The Director General replaces the Chief Controller of Imports and Exports under the Imports and Exports (Control) Act, 1947. His job is to advise the Central Government in the formulation of the export and import policy and he shall be responsible for carrying out that policy.

5. Power Relating to Search and Seizure. According to Section 10, the Central Government may authorise any person for the purpose of exercising such powers with respect to entering such premises and searching. inspecting and seizing of such goods, documents, things and conveyance, subject to such requirements and conditions, as may be prescribed.

6. Penalty for Contravention. According to Section 11, no export or import shall be made by any person except in accordance with the provisions of this Act, the rules that orders made thereunder and the export and import policy for the time being in force. Any contravention to this provision will invite a penalty not exceeding one thousand rupees or five time the value of the goods in respect of which any contravention is made or attempted to be made, whichever is more. Failure to pay the penalty could lead to the suspension of the Importer-Exporter Code Number of the person. Section 11 further state that where any contravention of any provision of this Act or any rules or orders made thereunder or the export and import policy has been is being, or is attempted to be made, the goods shall be liable to confiscation by the Adjudicating Authority. Section 14 provides that before imposing any penalty or confiscating goods. the person concerned would be given a proper notice in writing and would also be given an opportunity of being heard.

7. Appeal and Revision. Section 15 lays down that any person aggrieved by any decision or order made by the Adjudicating Authority may appeal against any such decision or order within a period of fortyfive days from the date on which the decision or order was served on him. The Appellate Authority can, if it so wishes, futher extend the period by thirty days, and can, at its discretion, dispense with the penalty to be deposited by the appellant either unconditionally or subject to such conditions as it may impose. The Appellant Authority may, after giving to the appellant a reasonable opportunity of being heard, confirm, modify or reverse the decision or order appealed against. The order made in appeal by the Appellant Authority shall be final. Section 16 confers the power on the Central Government to examine the records of any proceeding in which a decision or an order imposing a penalty or redemption charge or adjudicating confiscation has been made and against which no appeal has been preferred, for the purpose of satisfying itself as to the correctness, legality or propriety of such decision or order and make such orders thereon as may be deemed fit.

COMPOSITION OF FOREIGN TRADE

In order to study the composition or structure of India's foreign trade, it is necessary to analyse the changing pattern of imports and exports.

Pattern of Imports. Inputs have been classified into Bulk imports and non-bulk imports. Bulk imports are further subdivided into petroleum, oil and lubricants (PoL) and non-PoL items such as consumptions goods, fertilizers and iron and steel. Non-bulk items such as consumption goods (which include electrical and non-electrical machinery), pearls, precious and semi precious strong and other items.

The structural changes in imports since 1951 show:

(a) rapid growth of industrialisation necessitating imports of capital goods and raw materials.

(b) growing imports of raw materials on the basis of liberalisation of imports for export promotion; and

(c) declining imports of foodgrains and consumer goods due to the country becoming selfsufficient in food gains and other consumer goods through agricultural and Industrial growth.

TREND OF PRINCIPAL IMPORTS

Foodgrains. The imports of food grains were necessitated by the partition of the country and the growing demand for food for the rising population. The average annual imports of food grains which were about Rs. 200 crores during the first plan rose to Rs. 161 crores during the second plan, further increased to an average rate of Rs. 241crores during the third plan. The drought of 1965-66 further worsened the situation and consequently, foodgrains imports worth

Rs. 1,201 crores were made during the three years *i.e.* 1966-67 to 1968-69. During the 5-years period (1980-81-1984-85) food grains worth Rs. 66 crores were imported a negligible figure indeed. But during 1991-1992, they again rose to Rs. 395 crores. In later years the share of foodgrains fill almost to zero. The import of foodgrains during the year 1999-2000 was of Rs. 222 crore and it declaimed sharply to Rs. 20 crore in 2000-2001. This has happened mainly because of continuance rise in the production of food grains in the country.

Mineral Oils. Imports of mineral oils are also on the increase. India is short in the supply of mineral oils, especially petroleum. Annual import of mineral oil during 1969-70 to 1973-74 averaged Rs. 226 crores. On account of the sharp increase in the prices of crude announced by the organisation of petroleum exporting countries, during 1973-74 alone, petroleum imports were of the order of Rs. 569 crores. Their annual average during 1974-75 to 1979-80 was of the order of Rs. 2,063 crores. Though the share of mineral oils in imports has declimed from 45.1 per cent in 1990-91 to 39.6 per cent in 1999-2000 but it has increased from Rs. 10,816 crore to Rs. 54,649 crore during the period in abosolute terms.

Machinery. This item includes electrical and non-electrical equipment. In a country which is rapidly industrialising her economy imports of machinery are bound to increase. Compared to the average annual import of machinery which was about Rs. 1991 crores during the 1951-61, the annual average during the third plan rose to Rs. 472 crore. During the fourth plan, they were of order to Rs. 484 crore. Machinery imports during Seventh Plan jumped to Rs. 6,415 crore annually and further to Rs. 11,895 crore during the year 1999-2000.

Metals. India imports iron and steel and also some non-ferrous metals. The annual average imports of ferrous and non-ferrous metals which were about Rs. 54 crores during the first plan have gone up steadily with every plan and are about Rs. 2,450 croes during 1985-86 and 1989-90 Import of metals on such a large scale is necessitated by the vast programmes of industrial expansion, development of railways and hydro-electric projects. With improvement in capacity utilisation of our steel plants, imports of iron and steel should be cut down. During 1990-91 metals worth Rs. 1,528 crore were imported which futher increased to Rs. 3,789 crore in 1999-2000.

Chemicals Drugs and Medicines. There has been an increase in the imports of chemicals, drugs and medicines. The anual average of these items was about Rs. 55 crores during the third plan. Imports of chemicals, drugs and medicines rose to Rs. 113 crores per annum on the average during the Fourth plan. During 1980-81 and 1984-85 annual average imports of this item rose to Rs. 660 crores. They further rose to Rs. Rs. 2,289 crore in 1990-91 and to Rs. 12,420 crore in 1999-2000.

Pearls and Precious Stones. The imports of pearls and precious stones averaged Rs. 223 crores during 1974-79 and they have further increased to Rs. 2,405 crores per annum for the period 1985-86 to 1989-90. Part of these imports is meant to satisfy the demand of the afluent sections and part of these imports serve as raw material for the handicrafts export industry. It may be noted that the India imported pearls and precious stones worth of Rs. 3,738 crore in 1990-91 and it further increased to 23,556 crore in 1999-2000.

Fertilisers. Following the adoption of the new strategy in Indian agriculture, the imports of fertilizers were stepped up. The average annual imports of fertilizers which stood at Rs. 28 crores during 1966-67 to 1968-69. During 1980-81 to 1984-85 the annual imports of fertilizers were of the order of Rs. 698 crores. As a consequence of liberalisation, fertilizer imports jumped to Rs. 1,436 crores in 1985-86 and were of the Rs. 1,114 crores per annum on an average during 1985-86 to 1989-90. Imports of fertilizers touched a level of Rs. 1,765 crore in 1990-91 and Rs. 6,063 crore in 1999-2000.

The data related to average annual principal imports is shown in the following table.

AVERAGE ANNUAL IMPORTS OF PRINCIPAL COMMODITIES

Items	*1951-52 to 1960-61*	*1980-81 to 1984-85*	*1985-86 to 1989-90*	*1990-91 to 1999-2000*
1. Foodgrains	141	374	516	624
2. Machinery	191	2,515	6,415	14,976
3. Mineral Oils	77	5,264	4,498	27,469
4. Metals	93	1,448	2,450	7,003
5. Chemicals	44	660	1,868	1,921
6. Fertilisers	–	698	1,114	4,707
7. Pearls and Precious Stones	–	730	2,405	9,993

PATTERN OF EXPORT

Exports of India are broadly classified into four categories:

(i) Agriculture and allied products which include coffee, tea, oil cakes, tobacco, cashew kernels, spices, sugar, raw cotton, rise fish and fish preparations, meat and meat preparations, vegetable oils, fruits, vegatables and pulses;

(ii) ores and minerals include manganese ore, mica and iron ore;

(iii) Manufactured goods include textiles and ready-made garments, jute manufactures, leather and footwear handicrafts including pearls and precious stones, chemicals, engineering goods and iron steel; and

(iv) mineral fuels and lubricants.

Table : Classification Indian Exports

(Rs. crore)

	1970-71	*1980-81*	*1991-92*	*1999-2000*
1. Agriculture and Allied Products	487 (31.7)	2,057 (30.6)	7,638 (17.3)	24,301 (15.2)
2. Ores and Mineral 164	413 (10.7)	2,281 (6.2)	2,643 (5.2)	3,970 (2.5)
3. Manufactured Goods	772 (50.3)	3,747 (55.8)	32,384 (73.5)	1,28,761 (80.6)
4. Petoleum Products	13.28 (0.8)	102.2 (0.4)	905.2 (.23)	168 (0.1)
5. Others	99.0 (6.5)	465 (6.9)	717 (1.6)	2,361 (1.5)
Total	1,535 (100.0)	6,710 (100.0)	44,042 (100.0)	1,59,561 (100.0)

Data given in table reveal that traditional exports dependent upon agriculture and mineral wealth accounted for 42 per cent of total exports in 1970-71, their share has, however, declined to about 18 per cent in 1999-2000 in 1970-71 to about 80.6 per cent in 1999-2000. An interesting feature of the changing pattern of exports is the sharp increase in the share of manufactured products. Obviously, the structure of Indian exports is changing in favour of manfactured goods and petroleum products whose combined share has gone up from about 51 per cent in 1970-71 to about 81 per cent in 1999-2000.

Exports of Principal Commodities

Tea. Tea is one of the most important items of Indian exports. It had the first position in our exports in certain years. The average annual exports of tea were Rs. 106 crores during the first plan period. Tea exports further picked up to touch Rs. 195 crores in

1960-61. But later they declined. Tea exports earned Rs. 1,985 crores during 1999-2000.

Cotton Yarn and Manufactures. During the first plan period, the average annual exports of cotton yarn and manufactures touched Rs. 81 crores, but they declained to a small figure of Rs. 55 crores during the Third plan. On account of relatively high cost in Indian textile industry, Indian found it diffcult to capture the international market. In fact high costs were due to rising labour cost and use of old and worn-out machiner. In the post-devaluation period exports of cotton textiles have increased on account of their competitiveness in the international market. During 1970-71 and 1991-2000 exports of cotton (yarn and manufactures) improved from Rs. 75 crores to Rs. 18,151 crores.

Engineering Goods. In 1970-71 exports of engineering goods were of the order of Rs. 130 crores, During the 1970's engineering exports surged forward. In 1976-77, they exceded Rs. 500 crores and in 1999-2000 they were of the order of Rs. 22,325 crores, this is really creditworthy.

Readymade Garments. In recent years, the exports of cotton apparel or ready-made garments have shown significant improvement. These exports were just Rs. 9 crores in 1970-71. They jumped to Rs. 196 crores in 1974-75. During 1999-2000 cotton apparel exports touched a record of Rs. 20,649 crores. This indicates the increasing importance of this item in our exports.

Leather and Leather Manufacturers. One of the traditional items of Indian exports is raw hides and skins. But recently, in the exports of this item, the proportion for leather and leather manufactures to raw hides and skins is on the increase. This is really a healthy development. India earned about Rs. 39 crores in 1960-61 from this item. It touched Rs. 486 crores in 1979-80 and rose further to Rs. 6,891 crores during 1999-2000.

Handicrafts. The exports of Indian handicrafts assumed great importance in the 1970s. From a low level of Rs. 70 crores in 1970-71 they increased to Rs. 120 crores in 1972-73 and stood at Rs.

6,285 crores in 1989-90. The most important item among the handicrafts was pearls and precious stones which averaged Rs. 3,177 crores during 1985-86 to 1989-90. At present, the single largest item of export in handicrafts. During 1999-2000 handicrafts exported were of the order or Rs. 37,568 crores.

Iron ore. Indian exports iron ore. India earned about Rs. 30 crores per year from iron ore during the first first plan. During 1970-71 exports of iron ore rose to Rs. 117 crores and touched Rs. 1,175 crores during 1999-2000. This is an unhealthy development. India should increase the share of steel in exports by utilising iron ore in her own steel plants.

Changing Structure of Exports

The structure of Indian exports is typical of a developing economy. India has traditionally been an exporter of agricultural raw materials and manufactures based on agricultural raw materials. There has been a continuous decline in the share of agricultural raw materials and allied products. One reason for the relative decline of food, beverages and tabacco in the total exports is the increase in population and consequent increase in domestic consumption of these goods, Accordingly, the export surplus in many traditional commodities like tea has not been increasing as much as the Government would have wished. In this connection, the growing importance of certain products in this category should be noted, *i.e.*, fish and fish products, cashew kernels and coffee.

We should not, however, conclude that only non-traditional items are to the fore and the traditional items have suffered are treat. Exports of traditional items are also expanding, though probably not to the extent desired. Examples are the respectable growth in cotton fabrics, tea, leather and leather manufactures etc.

Thus the pattern of India's exports indicates that:

(a) The Indian economy is being diversified and both traditional and non-traditional items of exports are growing in importance.

(b) India is now in a position to take advantage of both favourable demand situation and attractive price assituation in international markets and this explains the expansion in the exports of many traditional and non-traditional items.

(c) The large expansion of engineering goods is partly the result of pick-up in demand in industrial countries and also from the Middle east countries which have undertaken infra-structural projects like roads, ports and rail construction, tele-communication and civil construction.

(d) While some commodities have tremendous exports poetential (*e.g.* handicrafts, engineering goods and readymades), others (like sugar, jute, yarn and manufactures, iron and steel) have fluctuated hopelessy.

DIRECTION OF INDIA'S FOREIGN TRADE

Our trade with East European socialist countries *viz.*, U.S.S.R. Poland, Romania, Bulgaria, Hungary, East Germany, Czechosolovakia and Yugoslavia has developed in recent years. The main items of imports from these countries are iron and steel, non-ferrous metals, chemicals, capital equipment, railway stores, paper, medicines and pharmaceuticals and petrolium products. The imports of most of these commodities are of crucial help for our core projects and several industries of strategic kernels, tobacco, oil seeds, leather, metallic ores, jute manufactures etc.—the traditional items of Indian exports. The composition of imports from these countries suggests the significance of the trade from the viewpoint of economic development. In 1960-61 India imported 4 per cent of her total imports from this region and exported about 8 per cent of her total exports to this region. But soon after the Indo Chinese conflict in 1962 and Indo-Pak war in 1965 our trade relations with the East European Socialist countries improved remarakably. In 1969-79 this group of countries accounted for 18 per cent of total imports and about 22 per cent of our exports. U.S.S.R. the chief contributor and accounted for nearly 84 per cent of trade with this region. By 2000-

2001 India's imports from East European countries declined to about 1 per cent and our exports to these countries which declined to 14 per cent in 1979-80 further fell to about 2 per cent in 2000-2001 with the disintegration of the soviet Union into common wealth of independent states (CIS) Trade relations with these countries are undergoing a change.

Our trade with the countries in Asia and oceania has been of great significance. Our exports of these countries which were about 28 per cent of total import in 1951-52 increased to 32 per cent in 1969-70. As against it, imports from these countries declined from about 23 per cent in 1951-52 to 19 per cent in 1969-70 (Refer table 13) the ECAFE* region was of great significance and four countries, viz, Japan, Austalia, Iran and iraq were very important.

Table—Direction of India's Foreign Trade

Region/Country	*1980-81*		*2000-2001*	
	Exports	*Imports*	*Exports*	*Imports*
(1)	*(2)*		*(3)*	
1. OECD of which	3,126 (46.6)	5,747 (45.8)	1,07,238 (52.6)	92,090 (39.9)
(a) European Union	1,447 (21.6)	2,639 (21.0)	47,561 (23.4)	48,015 (20.8)
(i) Belgium	144 (2.2)	296 (2.4)	6,718 (3.3)	13,112 (5.7)
(ii) U.K.	395 (5.9)	731 (5.8)	10,512 (5.2)	14,472 (6.3)
(b) North America	806 (12.0)	1,851 (14.8)	45,509 (22.4)	15,588 (6.7)
(i) Canada	62 (0.9)	332 (2.6)	2,999 (1.5)	1,814 (0.8)
(ii) U.S.A.	744 (11.1)	1,519 (12.1)	42,570 (20.9)	13,774 (6.0)
(c) Other OECD	708 (10.5)	932 (7.4)	14,168 (6.9)	28,487 (12.3)
(i) Japan	598 (8.9)	749 (6.0)	8,198 (4.0)	8,416 (3.6)
2. OPEC	745 (11.1)	3,490 (27.8)	22,223 (10.9)	12,358 (5.4)

Contd.

(1)	(2)		(3)	
3. Eastern Europe	1,486 (22.2)	1,296 (10.3)	6,020 (2.9)	3,884 (1.7)
USSR/CIS	1,226 (18.3)	1,014 (8.1)	4,061 (2.0)	2,365 (1.0)
4. Developing Countries	1,266 (18.9)	1,971 (15.7)	59,381 (29.2)	50,865 (22.0)
(i) Asia	880 (13.1)	1,428 (11.4)	45,858 (22.5)	38,647 (16.7)
5. Others	65 (0.9)	45 (0.4)	350 (0.2)	8 –
Total 1 to 5	6,711 (100.0)	12,549 (100.0)	2,03,571 (100.0)	2,30,873 (100.0)

However, due to increasing importance acquired by the import of Crude oil, OPEC countries have assumed very great significance in our import. These countries acounted for barely 8 per cent in our total imports in 1970-71 but as against it their share in 1980-81 has jamped upto about 27.8 per cent. Much of the increase is due to the sharp hike in the price of oil and does not indicate a corresponding increase in the quanitity index, of imports. On the export front also our exports to OPEC countries have also increased from 6.4 per cent in 1971-72 to about 11 per cent in 2000-2001 with a fall in the international price of oil, the share of OPEC countries in our imports declined to 5.4 per cent in 2000-2001.

The share of Japan in our export which was about 8.9 per cent in 1980-81 has come down to 4.0 per cent in 2000-2001. As against it, the share in our imports from these two countries has also declined from 6.0 per cent to about 3.6 per cent during the same period.

India has a great potential for increasing her foreign trade with Asian countries, because the Indian manufactures can be readily acceptable in these countries. Similarly, India can import raw materials for her growing industries from these relatively more under-developed regions. This is evidenced by the fact that during 2000-2001, imports from this region accounted for 16.7 per cent of our total imports whereas they were in the range of 11.4 per cent in 1970-71 to. On the export side, there has been a gradual and steady improvement and exports to this region increased from 13.1 per cent during 1980-81 to a level of nearly 22.5 per cent in 2000-2001.

It would be of interest to examine the direction of trade with reference to some important countries. U.S.A. U.K. west Germany U.S.S.R. Japan, Saudi Arabia, Australia and Canada were the 8 countries of significance in our trade. The share of these 8 countries in our exports has ranged between 54.7 and 41.6 per cent during 1980-81 to 2000-2001. As against it, their share in our imports has ranged between 46 and 24.5 per cent during this period.

Although U.K. was of prime importance in our foreign trade before independence, U.S.A. was growing in importance up to 1970. During the Seventies, especially after the Indo-Pak war of 1971, U.S.S.R. has grown in significance in our foreign trade. On the import side, the share of U.K. was the highest in 2000-2001 followed by USA, Belgium, Germany, Japan, Saudi Arabia and Switzerland. On the export side, Indian exports to U.K. were always higher than the exports to U.K. and subsequently exports to U.S.A. but during the Third Plan, the exports of U.S.A. levelled off with exports of U.K. and subsequently exports to U.K. fell futher to an abnormally low level of about 5 per cent. Our imports from West Germany were on the increase till 1965-66, but have declined since then. As against it, our exports to this country have been of the order of 2-3 per cent of total exports in the past but have risen to about 2 per cent in 2000-2001. Japan and U.S.S.R. are both growing in importance in our foreign trade. We had trade relations with Japan in the pre-war period, but trade was cut off during the war. It has been revived again. With U.S.S.R. Although our foreign trade is of recent origin, the share of imports was 1.0 per cent in 2000-2001 as against 8.1 per cent in 1980-81. Similarly the share of exports of USSR has risen from 1.0 per cent in 1951-52 to 18 per cent in 1980-81 but declined to 2.0 per cent in 2000-2001. Iraq and Iran also became important especially for oil imports, but due to continued Iran-Iraq was imports from these two countries became negligible but imports from Saudi Arabia rose to 1.3 per cent and from Indonesia to 1.8 per cent in

2000-2001. With the distintegration of Soviet Union our trade with this retio has suffered a serious setback.

Some salient features of the changes in the direction of trade in the post-independence period may be noted here.

(i) **New Trading Partners.** Before Independence, U.K. was the principal trading partner for India, accounting for 34 per cent of India's exports and 30 per cent India's imports. After Independence, even though India has continued to be a member of the British commonwealth, she has succeeded in getting new trading partners. Besides U.K. other countries of importance are U.S.A. U.S.S.R. West Germany, Japan and members of OPEC. Thus an important future of the new direction of trade since 1951 is the increasing in the number of trading partners for India. This spatial or geographical diversification has helped India to go for diversification of industries along with specialisation in certain goods, and secure new markets for her products.

(ii) **Larger and More Attractive Outlets for Exports.** India has been diversifying her exports to match her imports. Naturally, she has to search for new countries to sell her goods. Even though U.K. continues to buy a larger volume of goods from India, it has been relegated to second and even third place. U.S.A. has become the biggest buyer of Indian goods. Likewise, UAR, Honkong and Japan along with U.S.A. and UK constitute the first five leading countries absorbing 42 per cent of India's exports. These are rich countries with high national and per capita income and they manufactures, specially carpet backing, leather manufacturers and non-traditional items such as marine products, pearls and precius stones, etc. Middle East countries offer a good market for Indian exports.

(iii) **Larger Sources of Imports.** The increase in the number of countries from whom we by has been necessitated by many factors peculiar to the post-World War II. For one thing, the planned economic development and the tremendous increase in the requirements for machinery, equipment, industrial raw material, etc. could not be met by U.K. alone, or even by USA. For another reason, grant of aid and other assistance by international institutions like the World Bank allowed India to by from the cheapest sources (through global tenders). Thirdly, tied aid and grants from some countries willing to help India in per planning effort necessitated India to import from particular countries. Fourthly, foreign exchange shortage with reference to some capitalist countries induced India to make bilateral rupee arrangements with U.S.S.R. and other socialist countries. Finally, since the hike in the price of oil in 1973 India's imports from Iran, Iraq, Kuwait, Saudi Arbia and other members of the OPEC have gone up.

Scope for Direction. The share of Africa and South America is only marginal. These are rich continents with very bright future. India should cultivate trade relations with these countries-they could offer huge markets for India's exports. Likewise, the scope of India's exports to the development countries of the Middle East Asia is vast and in recent years, India is increasingly cultivating these markets. The Composition of imports by source reveals that OECD countries as a group accounted for the largest share in India's imports accounting for 40 per cent in 2000-2001. This was followed by the developing countries (excluding members of the OPEC) whose share was about 22 per cent. OPEC and East European countries accounted for 5.4 per cent and 1.7 per cent respectively in India's imports in 1991-92.

The destination-wise share of India's exports shows sufficient diversification. In 2000-2001, the share of exports going to industrial market economies as represented by OECD group was 52.6 per cent, while developing countries accounted for 29.2 per cent. The countries of OPEC accounted for 10.9 per cent of our total exports. During recent years, the share of countries of Asia and Pacific region in particular has been increasing in our exports. The economic survey reviewing the position mentions: "There has been a high growth in exports/imports to/from India to developing countries of Asia (excluding members of the OPEC). Some of these economic (Korea, Singapore, Malaysia, Hong Kong and Taiwan) have withnessed continued economic growth along with significant trade liberalisation and economic deregulation. Therefore, these economies provide excellent opportunities for export thrust. On the other hand, India's exports may have to contend with uncertainty in East European market arising out of proposed economic reforms underway. Exports from India will now have to face increasing competition in view of switch over by these economies to trading based on world prices and convertible currencies."

INDIA'S TRADE POLICY

The trade policy played an important role in the development of advanced countries like U.S.A., U.K., Germany, France, Japan etc. It restricted their imports and provided a sheltered market for their own industries so that could develop rapidly and promoted their exports so that expanding industries could secure foreign markets. India, however, did not have a clear trade policy before independence, though some type of import restrictions-known as discriminating protection was adopted since 1923 to protect a few domestic industries against foreign competition. It was only after independence that a trade policy as a part of the general economic policy of development was formulated by India. The time period of India's Trade Policy can be divided into five different phases:

1. First Phase (1947-48 to 1951-52)
2. Second Phase (1952-53 to 1956-57)
3. Third Phase (1956-57 to June 1966)
4. Fourth Phase (1966-67 to 1977-78)

5. Fifth Phase (1978-79 to 1990-91)

6. Sixth Phase (1991-92 and onwords)

First Phase. During the first phase up to 1951-52. India could have liberalised imports but on account of the restrictions placed by the U.K. on the utilisation of the sterling balances, she had to continue wartime controls. Since our balance of payments with the dollar area was heavily adverse, an effort was made to screen imports from hard currency areas and boost up exports to this area so as to bridge the gap. This also necessitated India to devalue her currency in 1949. By and large, the Import policy continued to be restrictive during this period. Besides this, restrictions were also placed on exports in view of the domestic shortages.

Second Phase. During the second phase (1952-53 to 1956-57) liberalisation of foreign trade policy. Import licences were granted in a liberal manner. An effort was also made to encourage export by relaxing export controls, reducing export duties, abolishing export-quotas and providing incentives to exports. Liberalisation led to a tremendous increase in our imports but exports did not rise appreciably. Consequently, here was fast deterioration in our foreign exchange reserves.

Third Phase. During the third phase which began in 1956-57; the trade policy was re-oriented to meet the requirements of planned economic development. A very restrictive import policy was adopted and the import controls further screened the list of imported goods. On the other hand, a vigorous export promotion drive was launched. The trade policy assumed that a lasting solution to be balance of payments problem lies in the promotion and diversification of our export trade. Not only should the export of traditional items be expanded, but export of newer items should also be encouraged. Similarly, import substitution industries should also be encouraged so that dependence of foreign countries should also be encouraged so that dependence on foreign countries be lessened. It was in this period that India's trade policy was thoroughly reviewed by the Mudaliar Committee (1962).

Fourth Phase. The fourth phase stated after the devaluation of the rupee in June, 1966. During this period trade policy attempted to expand exports and strangely liberalised imports too. Actually, export promotion was given a big boost through the acceptance and implementation of the recommendations of the Mudaliar committee (1962). The major recommendations included increased allocation of raw materials to export-oriented industries, income tax relief on export earnings, export promotion through import entitlement, removal of disincentives, and setting up of Export Promotion Advisory Council, a ministry of International trade, etc. When these export promotion measures did not succeed and adverse balance of payments persisted, the government of India undertook devaluation on the rupees in 1966 as a major step to check imports and boost exports. Initially devaluation was not successful and the adverse balance of payments worsened during the annual plans. But during the Fourth plan, the trade policy was quite successful in restricting imports and promoting exports. This period continued till 1977-78.

Fifth Phase. During the last phase (1978-79 onwards), the Government adopted a policy of import liberalisation, with a view to encourage export promotion. During Janata rule import liberalisation was also adopted to augment domestic supply of essential goods and to check rise in price level. Import-export policy of the Indian government attempted to achieve such objectives as: *(i)* to provide further impetus to exports; *(ii)* to provide support to the growth of indigenous industry; *(iii)* to provide for optimum utilisation of the country's resource endowments, especially in man power and agriculture; *(iv)* to facilitate technology up-gradation with special emphasis on export promotion and energy conservation; *(v)* to provide a stimulus to those engaged in exports and in particular, to manufacturing units contributing substantially to the export efforts; and *(vi)* to effect all possible savings in imports. Thus it is clear that the present trade policy has been to stimulate economic growth and export promotion via import liberalisation.

Import liberalisation along with export promotion at a time when *(a)* prices of imported goods were rising such faster, and *(b)* foreign markets for Indian goods were depressed, resulting in huge adverse balance of trade and payments from 1979-80 onwards. Instead of curtailing imports, the Tandon Committee (1981) recommended a policy of vigorous export promotion and further import liberalisation as a means of export promotion. The IMF loan (1981) had also stipulated that India should use export promotion and not import restriction as the strategy for controlling adverse balance of payments. Such a trade policy has forced India almost into a debt trap and the Indian bureaucrats are knocking at the doors of Aid India consortium and other advanced countries to bail India out.

While framing the export-import policy (1985) the Government was guided by the recommendations of Abid Hussain Committee. Whereas the committee emphasized the need for striking a balance between export promotion and import substitution, the Government in its wave of import liberalisation permitted a much greater quantum of imports in the name of export promotion and capital goods imports for technological upgradation. Thus, grave distortions have appeared in the process of implementation of the recommendations of the committee's report which need to be rectified.

Sixth Phase (New Trade Policy and Trade Liberalisation). The massive trade liberalisation measure adopted since 1991-92 to mark a major departure from the relatively protectionistic trade policies pursed in earlier years. The main features of the new trade policy since 1991 are as follows:

1. ***Free Imports and Exports.*** In the pre-reform period, India's trade policy regime was complex and combersome. There were different categories of importers, different types of import licences, alternate ways of importing etc. Substantial simplication and liberalisation in all these respects has been carried out in the reform period. Under its commitment to the World Trade Organisation (WTO) India, in November 1997, agreed to phase out all curbs on 2,714 tariff lines over a six year phase out period starting April 1, 1997. However, USA did not agree to this schedule and appealed

to the WTO which ruled against India. As a result, India has to remove all quantitative restrictions by April 1, 2001. After the announcement of Exim Policy, 2000-2001 the number of items on which quantitative restrictions remain in 715 and exim policy 2001-02 removed quantitative restrictions on the balance 715 items. Thus in line with India's commitment to the WTO quantitative restrictions on all import items have been withdrawn.

2. ***More Facilities to EOUs and EPZs.*** The 1992-97 policy conferred higher benefit to 100 per cent export oriented units (EOUs) and units in export processing zones (EPZs) over those exporting from the domestic tariff area (DTA). The EOU and the EPZ schemes have now been extended to newer activities and services. By a separate notification, such units dealing with broad agro-based products can sell 50 per cent (twice the normal) output in the DTA. This can prove to be a powerful initiative for boosting exports.

3. ***Decanalisation.*** A large number of export and imports used to be canalised through the public sector agencies in India. The supplementary trade policy announced on August 13, 1991 reviewed these canalised items and decanalised 16 export items and 20 import items. The 1992-97 policy decanalised imports of a number of items including newsprint, non-ferrous metals, natural rubber, intermediates and raw materials for fertilisers. However, 8 items (petroleum products, fertilisers, edible oils, cereals, etc.) were to remain canalised. Large scale decanalisation is an important step towards opening up more areas of the economy to the private sector. The Exim policy 2001-02 put 6 items under special list. These itmes would be allowed though state trading agencies.

4. ***Trading Houses.*** The 1991 policy allowed export houses and trading houses to import a wide range of items. The government also permitted the setting up of trading houses

with 51 per cent foreign equity for the purposes of promoting exports. Under the 1992-97 trade policy, export houses and trading houses were provided the benefit of self certification under the advance licence system, which permits duty free imports for exports.

The 1994-95 policy introduced a new category of trading houses to be called Super Star Trading Houses. To attain the status of a Super Star Trading House, an exporter must have registered an average FOB value of exports of Rs. 925 crore during the preceding three years or Rs. 1,387.50 crore during the preceeding year. On the basis of NFE criterion, an exporter must have registered an average net foreign exchange (NFE) value of exports of Rs. 740 crore during the preceding three years or Rs. 1,100 crore during the preceding year. These houses will be entitled to membership of apex consultative bodies concerned with trade policy and promotion, representation in important business delegations, special permission for overseas trading and special import licences at enhanced rate.

5. ***Export Scheme for the Services Sector.*** Since trade in services is becoming increasingly important for our country a new scheme called the "Export Scheme for the Services Sector" has been introduced. Under the scheme, person who render professional services have been allowed to import capital equipment at a concessional rate of duty of 15 per cent. The export obligation to be achieved by them will be in the form of the foreign exchange earned by them, regardless of whether the services are rendered in India or abroad.

6. ***Export Promotion Capital Goods Scheme.*** The Export Promotion Capital Goods (EPCG) scheme has been revamped by having only one window with a concessional customs duty rate of 15 per cent with export obligation (earlier there were two windows—15 per cent and 25 per

cent). The 1994-95 policy simplified the EPCG scheme and third party exports were permitted for purposes of fulfilment of export obligations. The 1995-96 policy placed the services sector at par with the supply of goods under the Export Promotion Capital Goods (EPCG) scheme. This ensures rich dividends for several companies in wide ranging sectors like financial services, banking, hotels and airlines, advertising, software and legal firms. In March 1996, the EPCG scheme was enhanced by inclusion of 'mining' in the definition of manufacture for the purpose of export-import policy.

7. ***Export Promotion Industrial Parks.*** A centrally sponsored Export Promotion Industrial Parks scheme was introduced in Aug. 1994 with a view to involving the State governments in the creation of infrastructural facilities for export-oriented production. It provides for 75 per cent of capital expenditure towards creation of infrastructural facilities limited to Rs. 10 crore of grant to the State government. So far 11 parks have been completed.

8. ***Duty Exemption Scheme Enlarged.*** The duty exemption scheme has been strengthened under which imports are provided at two concessional rates of 15 per cent and 25 per cent subject to appropriate export obligations. The exporters have been given a choice to opt for advance import licences under the duty exemption scheme either under quantity based or (for the first time introduced) value based norms. This will given greater flexibility to the exporter to import and export goods within the overall value limits and without any quantitative restrictions except in the case of sensitive goods.

9. ***Rationalisation of Tariff Structure.*** In its Final Report published in January 1993, Chelliah Committee had advocated drastic reductions in import duties. The committee expressed the opinion that the rupee had depreciated

considerably in the eighties and the early nineties, pushing up the level of protection to Indian industries considerably. For instance, the committee pointed out that in the seven year period 1985-86 to 1992-93, the real exchange rate of the rupee has depreciated by 57.45 per cent. This had pushed up the cost of the imports considerably leading to very high levels of protection to the Indian industry. The Committee, therefore, recommended that the prevailing import duties be rationalised and drastically lowered by 1997-98 so that parity in prices of goods produced domestically and internationally can be established. Action on the recommendations of the Committee, the Finance Minister announced substantial cuts in import duties in the 1993-94, the 1994-95 and the 1995-96 Budgets. The 1993-94 Budget reduced the maximum rate of duty on all goods from 110 per cent to 85 per cent except for a few items including passenger luggage and alcoholic beverages. The 1994-95 Budget further brought down the maximum rate of duty from 85 per cent to 65 per cent. This was brought down to 50 per cent in the 1995-96 Budget, to 40 per cent in the 1997-98 Budget and further to 35 per cent in the 2000-2001 Budget. In the budget 2002-03, the Finance Minister announced that by the year 2004-05, there would be only two basic rates of custom duties, namely 10 per cent and 20 per cent. For the year 2002-03, the peak custom duty rate has been reduced from 35 per cent to 30 per cent.

Rupee Depreciation and Convertibility. Prior to the devaluation of 1966, one US dollar was equal to Rs. 4.76. After the devaluation in 1966, one U.S. dollar became equal to Rs. 7.50. The system of fixed exchange rates was abandoned by most countries in 1973. The Government of India also abandoned it and pegged Indian rupee to a basket of currencies of the countries which are her major trading partners. This floating exchange rate system has been in operation since September 1975. Under the new system, the rupee started to slide against the dollar and other major currencies of the OECD countries. By the end of 1990, one US dollar had become equal to Rs. 18.07. The rate, Rs. per SDR, was 7.58 in 1970 and reached Rs. 25.71 by the end of 1990. The Government devalued the rupee in early July 1991 which led to a depreciation in the value of the rupee against the five major international currencies by roughly 22 per cent.

(i) ***Partial Convertibility of Rupee.*** The Finance Minister announced the liberalised exchange rate mechanism system (LERMS) in the Budget for 1992-93. Under this system a dual exchange rate was fixed under which 40 per cent of foreign exchange earnings were to be surrendered at the official exchange rate while the remaining 60 per cent were to be converted at a market determined rate. The foreign exchange surrendered at official rate was to be used for the import of essential items (like crude oil, petroleum products, fertilisers, life saving drugs, etc.) and the foreign exchange converted at the market rate was to be used to finance all other imports. Since the official exchange rate was lower than the market rate, this system meant taxing the exporters to subsidize the government's bulk imports. The implicit export tax was between 8-12 per cent and was highly resented by exporters.

(ii) ***Full Convertibility on Trade Account.*** The 1993-94 Budget introduced full convertibility of the rupee on trade account. Side by side, the official RBI rate also stayed on for the conversion of items not permitted under the unified markets rate, *i.e.*, more than half a dozen of invisible items of current account as well as capital account. In addition, various exchange control norms of the Reserve Bank remained in operation all along, albeit with some relaxation of provisions.

(iii) ***Full Convertibility on Current Account.*** In February 1994, the Reserve Bank undertook several steps towards achieving current account convertibility when it announced relaxation in payment restrictions for a number of invisible transactions and liberalisation of exchange control regulations upto a specified limit relating to *(a)* Exchange Earners' Foreign Currency (EEFC) Account; *(b)* basic travel quota; *(c)* studies abroad; *(d)* gift remittances; *(e)* donations; and *(f)* payments of certain services rendered by foreign parties. India achieved full convertibility on current account on August 19, 1994 when the Reserve Bank further liberalised invisible payments and accepted obligations under Article VIII of the IMF, under which India is committed to foresake the use of exchange restrictions on current international transactions as an instrument in managing the balance of payments. Many other relaxations of restrictions on current transactions were announced in later years.

After the country moved to a single market-determined exchange rate system in March 1993, the rupee exhibited goods stability and for over two years after March 1993, the rupee-dollar exchange rate remained steady at about Rs. 31.6. After reasonable stability the Indian rupee, in August 1997, experienced a mild attack on contagion emanating from currency turmoil in East Asia. Beginning in the second week of November, 1997, the exchange rate of the rupee against the dollar came under renewed downward pressure. The rupee depreciated to a low of Rs. 40.36 per dollar by January 16, 1998. and fell further to Rs. 48.58 per dollar at the end of January 2002.

The Government of India has introduced convatibility on capital account in stages. For this the Union Budget, 2002-03, announced following measures:

1. There will be full convertibility of deposit scheme for Non-Resident Indians.

2. The schemes which do not offer full convertibility to NRIs will be discontinued from April 1, 2002.

3. NRIs will be free to repatriate in foreign currency their current earnings in India such as rent dividend, pension, interest and the like based on appropriate certification.

4. Indian mutual funds will now be allwed to invest in rated securities in countries with fully convertible currencies, within the existing limits.

5. With a view to liberalising the capital account transactions it is proposed to put foreign currency Convertible Bond (FCCB) scheme under the automatic route upto $ 50 million.

6. Indian companies wishing to invest abroad may now invest upto US $ 100 million on an annual basis through the automatic route, up from the existing limit of US $ 50 million.

7. Corporates with proven records can set up educational chairs in educational institutions abroad from their foreign exchange earnings.

The Government of India announced the new Exim policy for the 5 year period (2002-07) on March 31, 2002. The highlights of this new policy are the following:

1. Indian banks have been allowed to set up offshore banking units in special Economic Zones to attract foreign direct investment.

2. The promote the export Hardware and Software industry, the government modified Electronic Hardware Technology Park (EHTP) scheme. Now this sector will face zero duty regime under information Technology Agreement. The government has allowed free import of equipment and other goods used aborad for more than one year.

3. Exim policy has initiated a member of measures in the field of agriculture, cottage sector and handicrafts, small scale sector etc. Exim policy has removed all quantitative restrictions on all agricultural products excepts jute and onion. The Govt. has earmarked Rs. 5 crores for the promotion of exports of cottage sector and handicrafts. Three towns namely Tirpur, Panipat and Ludhiana have been granted special status for their export excellence. The Government has allowed the import of rough diamonds on zero custom duty basis.

4. Like focus LAC (Latin Amercican Countries) launched in 1977, the government had been launching focus Africa since April 2002. In the first phase 7 countries will be focus. Links with CIS (Commonwealth of Independent States) to be revived. To encourage relocation of industries in India plant and machineries would be permitted to be imported without a licence, where the depreciated value of such relocated plants exceeds Rs. 50 crore.

5. With a view to reducing transaction cost, govt. has introduced various procedural simplifications. For example a new 8 digit commodity classification for inputs has been introduced. It will help to eliminate the classification disputs and hence transaction costs and time.

6. To make the system, trust based, the following measures have been taken:

   (i) Penal interest rate for bonafide defaults to be brought down from 24 per cent to 15 per cent.

   (ii) No seizure of stocks in trade so as to disrupt the manufactuing process affecting delivery schedule of exports.

7. The Government has decided to abolish Duty Exmption Entitlement Certificate (DEEC) book. The govt has withdrawn annual advance licence requriement. Now the

exporters can avail of advance licence for any value. The government granted to continue value cap exemption on 429 items.

The Government hopes that as result of the Exim Policy (2002-07) India will be able to capture 1 per cent of global share of trade by 2007, up from the present level of 0.67.

Critical Evaluation of the New Trade Policy. The trade policy reforms initiated in 1991 have shifted its eruphasis from inward-oriented to an outward-oriented policy. Due to liberalisation, the level of protection of Indian industry has declined significantly. Many people view the foreign trade sectors as the leading sector of the economy—a sector will change the face of the economy. But economists have raised serious doubts against it because of the relative importance of home market, the nature or the degree of State intervention, and the acquisition or development of the technology. Hence it will be very difficult to capture 1 per cent of global share of trade by 2007.

DEVALUATION OF RUPEE

Devaluation of a currency means lowering of the value of a currency in terms of gold or in terms of other currencies. The difference between devaluation and depreciation is that while develuation is the reduction of the value of a currency by the government, depreciation stands for automatic in the value of a currency by market forces. But in substance, both mean the same thing-lower value for a currency in terms of foreign currencies and both have similar effects. When the local currency depreciates in value and the foreign currency appreciates in value, the foreign commodities are made costly and hence imports are checked while the local commodities are made cheap and hence exports are promoted. Thus, a tendency towards a favourable balance of payments is created.

Conditions for the Success of Devaluation. The immediate effect of devaluation of a currency will be reflected in the increase in exports and decrease in imports. This is to be expected since, by devaluation the domestic currency will become cheap and, therefore, the domestic goods will also become cheap to foreigners, while the foreign currency will become costly and, therefore, foreign goods will become costly to consumers of the devalued currency. But curtailing imports and by expanding exports, devaluation creates favourable balance of payments and removes the chronic adverse balance of payments which had existed earlier. It will, however, the successful only under the following favourable circumstances:

(a) ***Cost-price Structure.*** There should be no change in the cost price structure in the devaluaing country. Only the external value of the currency unit has been reduced through devaluation. But it is possible for costs and prices within a country to change for two reasons : First, the merchants and speculators may raise the prices of those goods whose imports have been cut off or reduced owing to devaluation. Seconldy, imports which have now become costly because of devaluation may form a significant part of the consumption of the working and middle classes, in which case, the cost of living will rise, necessitating higher wages and higher prices. As a result of these reasons, the cost-price structure in the devaluing country may change and thus may prevent the favourable effects of devaluation to come into existence.

(b) ***Elasticity of Demand.*** The demand for imports and exports should be elastic. If Indian demand for foreign goods is inelastic, that is, whatever be the price of the foreign commodities, India will buy more or less the same amount; the total value of imports will increase as a result of devaluation. At the same time, if foreign demand for Indian goods is inelastic, India will not gain anything by lowering its price level through devaluation, for the same amount will be sold whatever be the price and, therefore, as a result of devaluation the total value of exports will fall. Thus, if the demand for imports and exports is inelastic, devaluation

will worsen the balance of payments situation by increasing the total value of exports. It can be successful only if demand is elastic on both sides—that is, demand for imports is elastic, and as a result when the prices of foreign goods are high due to devaluation, imports will be curtailed; likewise, demand for exports by the foreigners is also elastic and as a result, when the local goods are cheap, exports will be stimulated.

(c) ***Co-operation of Other Countries.*** The efficacy of devalution of a currency by a country will depend upon the co-operation of foreign country or countries whose currencies have appreciated as a result of devaluation. Foreign countries will experience contraction of demand for their exports from the devaluing country, while their own demand for the goods of the devaluing country will expand due to lower exchange rate of the latter's currency. The natural tendency under the circumstances is to retaliate. This may take the form of high tariffs to prevent imports from the devaluing country or grant of subsidies to push up exports of devaluation of their currencies too.

India devalued its currency for the first time in 1966. Prior to the devaluation of 1966, one US dollar was equal to Rs. 4.76. After the devaluation in 1966, one U.S. dollar became equal to Rs. 7.50. The system of fixed exchange rates was abandoned by most countries including India and government pegged Indian rupee to a basket of currencies of major trading partner countries. Now government adopted floating exchange rate system, which resulted into the depreciation of the rupee against dollar and major currencies of the OECD countries. The government again devalued rupee in July 1991 which led to a depreciation in the value of the rupee against the five major international currencies by roughly 22 per cent. The purpose of this devaluatin was to boost the exports of goods and contain imports by making them cheaper and costlier respectively.

After the devaluation of currency the exports and imports both have gone in absolute terms. The value for exports gone up from U.S. $ 17,865 million in 1991-92 to U.S. $ 44,560 million in 2000-2001. Similar by the imports have also gone up from $ 19,411 million to $ 5,05,036 million during the same period. Hence the trade balance has increased from $ 1,546 million to $ 5,976 million during 1991-92 to 2000-2001. This shows that devaluation did not help in narrowing the trade deficit.

If we compare the growth rate of foreign trade pre-devaluation period with post-devaluation period, we find that devaluation has not made any significant impact on foreign trade.

During 1980-81 to 1989-90 the Growth Rate of Exports was 8.1 and Imports was 7.2. During 1990-91 to 1999-2000 it was 8.6 (Exports) and 9.6 (Imports).

This trade reveals that growth rates of exports has increased marginally and growth rates of imports has increased significantly. The main cause for high increase in imports is their inelastic demand trade liberalisation policies the Govt. Near stable export growth rate and higher import growth rate has widen the deficit in trade balance. Thus devaluation has not affected foreign trade sector significantly and India is still facing deficit it its trade balance.

10

Industrial Growth and Policy in Business

INDUSTRIAL GROWTH

At the time of independence, India was industrially and economically backward. In 1951-52, the share of agriculture was 56.5 per cent of GDP while the share of industry was just 13.3 per cent. Due to the programme of industrialisation, the share of industrial sector has gone up to 25.0 per cent in 2000-01. The industrial sector has become well diversified. The structure of industrial growth in India during the five decades of planning can be more easily examined and analysed under two broad heads *viz.*, *(I)* Industrial growth and *(II)* Pattern of industrialisation.

I. INDUSTRIAL GROWTH

India's industrial growth can be looked from three different aspects:

(i) Growth rate in industrial output.

(ii) Industry's contribution in national income, and

(iii) Industry's contribution to employment.

(i) Growth Rate in Industrial Output. The compound rate of growth was quite impressive during the first three plans. The industrial growth rate in first plan was 5.7 per cent and it rose to 7.2 per cent in second plan and further to 9.0 per cent in third plan. During the eleven year period (1996 to

1976) growth rate declined to 4.1 per cent per annum. The position did not improve even after.

Industrial Growth Rate

Period	*Annual growth Rate (per cent)*	*Period*	*Annual Growth Rate (per cent)*
1951-1956	5.7	1985-90	8.5
1956-1961	7.2	1990-91	9.0
1961-1966	9.0	1991-92	0.8
1966-1976	4.1	1992-94	0
1976-1980	3.8	1994-97	8.6
1980-1985	6.4	1997-2002	4.9

1975-76 as the annual rate of industrial growth during the four period (1976-80) remained very low *i.e.* 3.3 per cent per annum. During sixth plan *i.e.* 1980-85 the industrial activities picked up and achieved the growth rate of 6.4 per cent per annum. The industrial growth rate during 1985-90 (Seventh plan) was satisfactory *i.e.* 8.5 per cent per annum. Industrial sector requested a robust growth of 9.0 per cent in 1990-91. However, industries suffered a serious set-back in 1991-92 and production declined by 0.8 per cent. In the following year there was near stagnation. The industrial recovery started in 1993-94 and in two four period from 1993-94 to 1996-97 the industrial production increased at the annual rate of 8.6 per cent which is quite encouraging. But the indstrial growth declined again during the Ninth Five Year Plan (1997-2002) and it has been 4.9 per cent per annum. In the terminal year of this plan the rate of industrial growth registered a further decline and was low as 2.7 per cent.

(ii) **Industry's Contribution to National Income.** During the first three plans, similar trends relating to the distribution of NDP by different sectors were aslo observed in India. The share of the secondary sector to the NDP went up from a meager 13.3 per cent in 1950-51 to about 17.0 per cent in 1960-61; correspondingly, the share of the primary sector declined from 59.2 per cent in 1950-51 to 50.1 per cent in 1960-61. The fact that during this period, the national income has recorded a sizable increase would prove the fact that industrial production was increasing at a faster rate than agricultural production. In the subsequent decade, however, this trend could not be maintined but the share of the scondary sector, was still rising and it reached at 19.7 per cent in 1970-71. Over the seventies no change worth mentioning occurred in the structure of national output, except during 1967-77 when industrial production had shown a remarkable recovery. Eighties, however, brought a welcome change, as borne out by the recent CSO data. Based on the 1980-81 prices (the new base year now being used by the CSO), industry share in NDP which is reported as 23.3 per cent in 1981-82 went up to 25.9 per cent in 1991-92. However during the 1990s the share of industrial sector declined and it was just 21.7 per cent in 1999-2000. But during the year 2000-01, it has increased to 23.0 per cent.

(iii) **Industry's Contribution to Employment.** The contribution of industrial sector in providing employment is not encouraging. During 1951 to 1969, factory production rose at an annual compound rate of 7 per cent per annum, while employment rose at less than 3 per cent per annum. Recent estimates of employment elasticity with reference to the growth of manufacturing sectors shows that employment elasticity India is falling. The employment elasticity in manufacturing sector during 1972-73 to 1977-

78 was 1.0 and it declined to 0.67 in 1977-78 to 1983 and further to 0.33 during 1983 to 1993-94.

If we look at the absolute number of workers employed in manufacturing sector, we find that it has increased from 34.03 million in 1983 to 42.50 million in 1933-94 and further to 48.01 million in 1999-2000. In absolute terms it looks quite impressive however in per centage terms, the importance of manufacturing as a provider of employment has not changed significantly. The per centage of workers employed in manufacturing sector has marginally increased from 11.3 per cent during 1983 to 1993-94 to 12.1 per cent in 1999-2000.

II. PATTERN OF INDUSTRIALISATION

The second important aspect of industrial growth relates to the pattern of industrialisation that has been followed since Independence. The pattern of industrialisation can be studied under two heads: *(a)* Functional Pattern of Industries, and *(b)* Ownership Pattern of Industries.

A. Functional Pattern of Industries

The pattern of industrialisation can be studies with the help of the following three criteria.

(i) compound rates of growth in different industries;

(ii) change in weights assigned to different industries;

(iii) contribution to the value-added.

(i) Compound Rate of Growth in Different Industries. Four distinct phases relating to the compond rates of growth in different industries can be observed, *viz. (a)* the first phase till mid-sixties, *(b)* the second phase of 1965-80, *(c)* the third phase of 1981-91, and *(d)* the fourth phase since 1991-92 onwards. In the earlier phase, the rate of growth of industries, in general, had picked up very fast. A major contribution in this direction was made by the basic and capital goods industries. The annual rate of growth in basic industries had gone up from 4.7% during 1051-55, to 10% during 1955-60: similarly, the annual rate of growth in capital goods industries had gone up from 9.8% during 1951-55 to 13.3% during 1955-60, and further to 19.6 during 1960-65. On the contrary, consumer goods industries recorded only a marginal growth. The annual rate of growth in these industries was only 4.8 during 1955-55 which came down to 4.4% during 1955-60, and recorded a little improvement to go up 4.9% during 1960-65. In short, the pattern of industrilisation that evolved during the first fifteen years had shown two features: one, a rapid growth of basic and capital goods industries, and two, a slow growth of consumer good industries. This pattern was in consonance with the strategy of growth evoloved during the Second Plan and followed during the subsequent Plan.

In the next phase, beginning with the mid-sixties the rate of industrial growth, as already seen, began to trigger off. The growth of basic and capital goods industries has been slower than in the past and also slower than even the meagre average growth in industrial output; where growth has been moderately high, a majority of the industries belonged either directly or indirectly to elite-oriented consumption goods' sector, like consumer durables. In the third phase, as would be seen from table below, basic goods industries picked up fast and their rate of growth accelarated between the Fifth and Sixth Plan periods, intermediate goods industries and consumer goods industries slowed down. In the first half of the Seveth Plan it was the capital goods industries sector that recorded the stupendous growth as also the basic goods industries. Intermediate goods and consumer goods industries picked up well during the First year of the Plan, but subsequently lost momentum. Over all, the growth momentum in the industrial sector during these two plans, as also during the first three years of the Seventh Plan, was maintained largely by growth in basic goods industries.

Table : Annual Average Growth Rates (Per cent)

Industry	*1974-79*	*1980-81 to 1991-92*	*1992-93 to 2000-01*
Basic Goods Ind.	8.4	7.4	5.9
Capital Goods Ind.	5.7	9.4	5.4
Intermediate Goods Ind.	4.3	4.9	8.6
Consumer Goods Ind.	5.50	6.0	6.5
All Industries	6.10	7.8	6.6

The table reveals that the industrial growth rate during 1980-81 to 1991-92 (Sixth and Seventh Plan) was 7.8 per cent and it reduced to 6.6 per cent during 1992-93 to 2000-01 (post-reform decade). This poor performance is basically due to a steep fall in the rate of growth of capital goods sector. On the other hand, the intermediate goods sector and consumers goods sector put up a better performance during 1992-93 to 2000-01. The main causes for poor performance of industrial sector are exposure to external competition, slowdown in investment, the infrastuctual constraints, lack of funds for expansion, sluggish growth in exports, anomalies in tariff structure and contraction in consumer demand.

(ii) Changes in Weighs Assigned to Different Industries. The pattern of industrialisation can also be studied with the help of changes in weight assigned to different industries. These weights are generally expressed in proportion to their share in value added in the organised manufacturing sector. The weight of capital goods industries expanded from 4.21 per centages points in 1956 to 11.76 per centage points in 1960 and further to 18.66% in 1965; subsequently, the weight of consumer goods industries declined from 48.37 in 1956 to 37.25 in 1960, and further to 30.89 in 1965. It, however, increased to 31.03 in 1970. During the seventies, the weight of basic and capital goods industries kept on falling down, while that of consumer goods industries moved up. The following table revals the weights in index of industrial production.

Weights in Index of Industrial Production

	1951	*1960*	*1970*	*1980*	*1990*
Basic Goods	19.8	25.1	32.3	39.4	38.4
Capital Goods	3.5	11.8	15.3	16.4	23.7
Intermediate Goods	29.0	25.9	21.0	20.5	17.5
Consumer Goods	47.6	37.3	31.5	23.7	20.4
Denable Goods	–	5.7	3.4	2.6	–
Non-durable Goods	–	31.6	28.1	21.1	–

(iii) Contribution to the Value Added. The industrial sector growth rate in post-reform decade has declined in comparison to the pre-reform decade. Similarly the compound annual rate of growth of manufacturing sector during the 1990-91 to 1998-99 has also fell in comparison to pre-reform decade.

Table : Compound Annual Rate of Growth of Manufacturing

(Per cent)

Year	*Combined Rate of Growth of Gross value added of Registered Manufacturing Sector at Constant Prices*
1950-51 to 1965-66	7.03
1955-56 to 1965-66	7.47
1980-81 to 1990-91	7.66
1990-91 to 1998-99	5.91

This table reveals that the rate of growth of growth value added in industry during pre-reform period was highest *i.e.* more than 7.0 per cent per annum. But the gross value added in industry during the eight year period of 1990s (1990-91 to 1998-99) was just 5.91 per cent per annum. It was lowest. This shows that economic reforms and 'opening up' of the inudstrial economy in 1990s did not accelerate industrial growth as expected but slowed it down. Moreover, as the above table shows the growth record during the reforms of 1990s has been worse than the during 1980s.

B. Ownership Pattern of Industries

On the basis of the type of ownership, the industrial units can be divided into the following categories:

(i) public sector,

(ii) joint sector and

(iii) private sector.

Table presents information on the structure of Indian industrial sector by type of ownership for the year 1996-97.

This table reveals the following factors regarding the structure of Indian industries by type of ownership:

1. The total number of factories in 1996-97 was 1,34,556 of which as many as 1,22,772 (*i.e.* 91.2 per cent) were in the private sector. Only 8,825 units (6.6 per cent) were in the public sector.

2. Of the total fixed capital of Rs. 3,84,560 crore in the industrial sector in 1996-97, as much as Rs. 1,42,156 crore (*i.e.* 36.9 per cent) was in the public sector. The share of the private sector was Rs. 2,12,920 crore (*i.e.* 55.4 per cent). Thus with only 6.6 per cent of the factories, the public sector had 36.9 per cent of fixed capital. This shows that the public sector units are much more capital intensive as compared with the private sector units.

Table : Structure of Indian Industry of Ownership 1996-97

	Factories Number	*Employment '000s*	*Fixed capital*	*Gross output*	*Value added*
				Rs. crore	
Public Sector	8,825	2,285	1,42,156	1,51,174	36,915
	(6.6)	(23.5)	(36.9)	(21.8)	(25.8)
Joint Sector	2,899	524	29,416	59,882	11,458
	(2.2)	(5.5)	(7.6)	(8.7)	(8.0)
Private Sector	1,22,772	6,891	2,12,920	4,81,218	94,664
	(91.2)	(71.0)	(55.4)	(69.5)	(66.2)
Unspecified	60	7	68	246	39
	(...)	(...)	(...)	(...)	(...)
Total	1,34,556	9,707	3,84,560	6,92,520	1,43,076
	(100.0)	(100.0)	(100.0)	(100.0)	(100.0)

3. Out of the gross output of Rs. 6,92,520 crore, the private sector units contributed Rs. 4,81,218 crore (or 69.5 per cent). As against this, the public sector units contributed Rs. 1,51,174 crore of gross output which is 21.8 per cent of the total.

4. Total employment in the industrial sector was 9,707 thousand in 1996-97. Of this, 71.0 per cent were employed in the private sector and 23.5 per cent in the public sector.

5. The Industrial Policy Enquiry Committee which was constituted by the Government of India in July 1967 under the chairmanship of Dr. Subimal Dutt had strongly recommended the setting up of the joint sector. However, the concept proved to be a still born child. As is clear from table only 2.2 per cent indusrial units were in the joint sector in 1996-97 and they possessed only 7.6 per cent of fixed capital and provided employment to only 5.5 per cent

industrial labour. Their share in gross output was 8.7 per cent and in value added, 8.0 per cent in 1996-97.

6. The total value added in the industrial sector in 1996-97 was Rs. 1,43,076 crore. Of this, private sector contributed Rs. 94,664 crore (66.2 per cent) and the public sector contributed Rs. 36,915 crore (25.8 per cent).

FEATURES OF INDUSTRIAL GROWTH

Some distinguishing, but disturbing, features of the industrial development process in India can be indentified as follows:

Firstly, along with external financial assistance, technological dependence on MNCs increased. The old private foreign capital, which had operated in the colonial period, worked mainly through branches in India or through managing agency house. It was organised in pools which were small by the standard of metropolitan countries and operated in areas like trade, finance and export oriented activites. A goods part of this capital either left the country in the wake of independence or clung on in a stagnant or precarious state. The new private foreign capital which entered particularly during the Second and Third Plans went into technologically intensive areas and produced mainly for the domestic market which was cordoned off by high protective barriers.

Secondly, industrial growth was accompanied by a considerable increase in the country's indebtedness. The share of foreign aid, as a proportion of gross investment, of Plan outlay and of national income increased dramatically during the decade 1955-65. The entire industrialisation drive, however, impressive, was indeed far from being financially self-reliant.

Thirdly, industrialisation in India had virtually a negligible impact on either unemployment or the sectoral distribution of the work-force. The employment-creating capacity of industrialisation was not enough either to make a dent in the backlog of urban unemployment which also experienced a natural growth over time or to absorb immigrants from rural areas. The economic stagnation since the mid-sixties worsened the unemployment situation.

Fourthly, inudstrial growth in India has been accompanied by a virtual stagnation in real wages. This is not to say that with changing industrial composition and the creation of many more skilled job, opportunities have not been opened up or utilised but the picture of stagnation remains roughly valid for any particular category of workers, especially unskilled workers.

Fifthly, although the share of agro-based industries has dclined over the years the impact of agricultural growth on industrial growth does not seem to have weakened. This is borne out by the fact that as Prof. K.N. Raj has noted the fluctuations in indusrial production are preceded by fluctuation in agricultural production.

Finally, few of the industrial groups appear to have been interested in providing for systematic reasearch. In this respect, the Indian experience has been contrary to the Japanese and this lacuna, to be traced historically perhaps to the dominance of trading and money lending communities in industrial entrepreneurship in India and an explicit state policy for import-substitution in an attentuated from through the planning period for different reasons arising primarily from the operation of industrial and trade policies.

PROBLEMS OF INDUSTRIAL GROWTH

(i) Growth of Big Industrial Houses. Despite the various policy measures taken by the Government such as the MRTP Act and the licensing policy, the share of the large industrial house in the total assests of the private corporate sector has increased. According to Prof. S.K. Goyal, "during the period 1964 and 1976, the number of

Big Houses in India rose from 33 to 75; and the number of large independent undertakings increased from 8 to 26. The combined assets of the big houses and the large independent undertakings expanding from Rs. 2,412.04 crore to Rs. 8,955.70 crore in 1979, *i.e.*, an increase of 271.3% in 13 years". And, similarly, a recent study by the Economics Times Research Bureau has brought out that as on March 31, 1990, the 20 large industrial houses had assets worth Rs. 33, 919 crore constituting 68.9 per cent of the assets of 78 large industrial houses. The top 10 houses, have total assets worth Rs. 1,53,091 crore in the year 1998-99. The largest house in terms of assets and not sales in Tata. This industrial house had assets worth Rs. 47,446 were in 1998-99. This shows that large indusrial houses worth most in the post liberalisation phase.

(ii) Increase in Regional Imbalances. Another unfavourable aspect of the industrial science is the imbalance that exists in the industrial development of different regions. Massive investment in the Central sector projects in the expectation that this would have a wide ranging 'ripple effect' in stimulating small and ancillary industries have not succeed in many states such as Bihar, Orissa and Madhya Pradesh. The natural tendency of enterpreneurs to go where the infrastructure is strong, markets are close and various services are readily available cannot be ignored.

(iii) Higher Cost of Industrial Product. Another weakness of the industrial scene is the high cost of some of its products as compared to international prices. *(a)* This has partly arisen out of the absence of healthy competition, a situation which industrial licensing tends to foster. High tarriff barriers and tight controls on imports have tended to shield these units from international competition and projected them from the consequences of the relatively low rate of inflation in India as compared to other countries. Non-competitiveness, in general, has resulted in the slowing down of growth through a pervasive waste in the utilisation of scarce capital resources or a parts of the economy. Dealing with it is, therefore, important not only for the export effort but more fundamentally to bring about an acceleration in the rate of economic growth in the country. *(b)* High costs have sometimes been a direct outcome of the Government's licensing policy. Where the demand was large enough to sustain only one plant of an economic size, several plants with suboptimal capacity were licensed in the name of diffusing ownership and preventing monopolies. *(c)* In the policy of import substitution also insufficient attention has been paid to costs and a few industries have been set up whose cost of production is not low according to international standards. While this may be necessary in certain strategic areas, it was not essential in many other.

(iv) Industry's Dependence on the Government. A consequences of a regime of government-imposed constraints has been that the industry has become heavily dependent upon the government. Hence the contradictory demands that the government should reduce this tax or duty (to protect an importer), raise that duty (to protect a local manufacturer), make imports easier or more difficult, allow the expansion of capacity (to achieve economies of scale) or prevent new capacity from coming up (to protect existing producers), etc. If an individual unit or an industry faces a problem and a simple, adaptive answer is elusive, the tendency is to run to the government for help without making a thorough search for self-relient solution. This habit has become widespread and even those without fewer controls often fall a prey to the soft option of appealing to the government for an instant solution usually with a penalty to offers or to the economy as a whole.

(v) Lack of Proper Employment Planning. Perhaps the most serious lacuna in our industrial planning has been the lack of attention paid to the employment implications in choosing technologies. The main victim of this policy has been the cottage sector where the growth of industries like textiles, oil crushing, shop making, matches, leather and leather goods has been stifled. Another area in which industrial development could have been directed better both from the point of view of cost reduction and employment generation is the development of ancillaries particularly by way of off-loading existing low technology activities to the small-scale and ancillary industry. While there have been areas and industries which have done well in this field, the rate of growth of ancillaries suggests that inadequate attention has been paid to this problem.

(vi) Sickness in Industry. The incidence of sickness in large and medium-scale industries has increased in recent year; and in the case of some of the traditional industries like cotton textiles, jute textiles and sugar, the economic viability of a large number of units has been seriously eroded. The phenomenon of industrial sickness not only tends to aggravate the problem of unemployment, but also renders infructuous capital investment any generally creates an adverse climate for further industrial growth. While in advanced countries, where there are adequate social security benefits, this is accepted as a normal features of the industrial scene, such sickness has much more serious economic consequences in a country where unemployment is a major problem and resources are scarce.

(vii) Growing Dependence of the Organised Private Sector on Financial Institutions. The growing capital-intensive nature of industry and relatively high corporate tax rates have increased the dependence of the organised private sector on financial institutions. This has meant that the role of financial institutions in financing new ventures has grown substantially. Increasingly, therefore, the agencies which determine the pattern and structure of industrial growth are the term lending institutions rather than the Industrial Licensing Committee which at best can play a negative role. Since this is not the purpose for which these institutions were set up, some new mechanism would have to be devised to ensure that the flow of funds from financial institutions is in accordance with national priorities.

(viii) Poor Productivity Performance. Dr. Hollis Chenery in a recent study covering 40 countries has found India at the bottom of the list in terms of productivity growth. Productivity growth has been a major contributing factor, in the economic growth of many industrial countries. Productivity can be measured either in the form of a partial productivity like labour productivity, capital productivity and material productivity, or as total factor productivity (TFP). Labour productivity can be defined as the output per unit of labour.

Other partial productivities are also similarly defined. TFP is defined as the ratio between real product or output and real factor input (a weighted sum of the different inputs). TFP is a better measure of productivity as it relates output to all the conventional inputs simultaneously.

(ix) Underutilisation of Industrial Capacity. Another major problem of industrial development in India has been the underutilisation of industrial capacity. Some of the important industries have been reporting utilisation rates of only 50 to 60 per cent. Underutilisation poses serious problems to the process of growth. All out efforts have to be made to create conditions conductive to optimm utilisation of capacity.

INDUSTRIAL POLICY

At the time of independence, there was no well coordinated industrial policy of India. The Government of India along with investors and entrepreneurs felt the need of a well coordinated industrial policy because rapid growth of industries was almost impossible in the absence of such an industrial policy. Consequently within less than one year after independent the Government of India announced the Industrial policy Resolution on 6th April 1948.

INDUSTRIAL POLICY RESOLUTION 1948

The Government of India evolved its first new Industrial policy after independence which envisaged a mixed economy with overall responsibility of the government to secure planned development of industries and their regulation. The government also acknowledged the valuable role of the private entreprise properly directed and regulated. The main features of this industrial are the following:

(i) Acceptance of the importance of both private and public sectors.

(ii) **Division of the Industrial Sector.** The Resolution divided industries in four categories namely—*(a)* industries where state has the monopoly (3 industries); *(b)* mixed sector

(6 industries); (c) the field of government control (18 industries); and (d) the field of private enterprise (all other industries not included in the above three categories.

(iii) Role of small and cottage industries.

(iv) Other important features (less importance to foreign investment, harmonious relations between management and labour force).

Indian capitalists were satisfied with the Industiral Policy Resolution of 1948 since the role assigned to the public sector in that policy was, on the whole, acceptable to them. However, there were certain weakness and gaps in the 1948 policy and it was subjected to a number of criticisms.

INDUSTRIAL POLICY RESOLUTION OF 1956

In 1956 came the second Industrial policy Resolution of the Government of India which sought to start an era of stabilisation against the background of the declared goal of a socialist pattern of society.

The 1956 Resolution laid down the following objectives for the industrial policy: *(i)* to accelerate the rate of growth and to speed up industrialization; *(ii)* to develop heavy industries and machine making industries; *(iii)* to expand public sector; *(iv)* to reduce disparities in income and wealth; *(v)* to build up a large and growing cooperative sector; and *(vi)* to prevent monopolies and the concentration of wealth and income in the hands of a small number of individuals. The main features of this Resolutions are the following:

1. **Division of the Industrial Sector.** As against four categories in the 1948 Resolution, the 1956 Resolution divided industries into the following three categories:

   (a) Monopoly of the State. In the first category, those industries were included whose future development would be the exclusive responsibility of the State. Seventeen industries were included in this category and were listed in Schedule A. Of these, four industries—arms and amunition, atomic energy, railways and air transport, were to be governement monopolies. In the remaining 13 industries, all new units were to be established by the State. However, existing units in the private sector were allowed to subsist and expand.

(b) ***Mixed Sector of Public and Private Enterprise.*** In this section 12 industries listed in Schedule B (appended to the Resolution) were included. In these industries, State would increasingly establish new units and increase its participation but would not deny the private sector opportunities to set up units or expand existing units.

(c) ***Industries Left for Private Sector.*** All industries not listed in schedules 'A' or 'B' were included in the third category. The main role of the state in this category was to provide facilities to the private sector to develop itself.

2. **Assistance and Control of Private Sector.** According to the 1956 Resolution, the government could assist expansion and development of private sector through participation in its risk capital and share capital and by providing other types of services, fiscal incentive etc. However, the private sector was also to fit into the "framework of the economic and social policy of the State". Thus, the private sector was to remain subject to various government regulations and controls. Such regulation and control was to be exercised by the government through the Industries (Development and Regulation) Act, 1951, and other related legislations.

3. **Mutual Dependence of Public and Private Sectors.** The only four industries in which private sector was not allowed to function were arms and ammunition, atomic energy, railway and air transport. In all other industries either to private sector was allowed to operate freely or its help

could be obtained if the government deemed fit. Accordingly, the 1956 Resolution emphasized not only the mutual coexistence of private and public sectors but also provided for their mutual cooperation and help.

4. **Importance of Small-scale and Cottage Industries.** The 1956 Resolution recognized the importance of small-scale and cottage industries just as the 1948 Resolution had done. Such industries could create large scale employment opportunities, ensure a more equitable distribution of income and wealth, and help in effective mobilization of human and physical capital. Assistance to this sector was to be provided either through direct means or through indirect means.

5. **Technical and Managerial Personnel.** Shortage of technical and managerial personnel to carry out the programmes of industrial development in the economy has been accepted and emphasized by the government right from the beginning of the planning era. According, the 1956 Resolution advocated the establishment of proper technical and managerial cadres through the organisation of apprenticeship schemes of training on a large scale, establishment of technical institutions, etc.

6. **Reduction of Regional Inequalities.** The 1956 Resolution called for reduction in regional imbalances and inequalities. For this purpose it was advocated that transport facilities, power and other facilities should be provided in the backward regions. Stress on balanced development of agriculture and industry in each region was also laid.

An Appraisal of the Industrial Policy of 1956. The industrial policy of 1956 contemplated a mixed or controlled economy in which public and private enterprises work hand in hand so as to make the development plan a success. The industrial policy of 1956 has been appreciated for bringing about an excellent synchronisation between government's industrial policy and industrial development programmes included in the plan. The 1956 industrial Policy was a positive Policy improvement over the 1948 industrial policy since it was broader and more liberal. The 1956 industrial policy has held good till today even though some changes have been made in it in the last few years.

Cooperative Sector. In respect of agro-industries specially industries processing sugarcane, jute and other agricultural commodities, preference in licensing will be given to applicants from cooperative sector.

INDUSTRIAL POLICY RESOLUTION OF 1980

The 1980 industrial policy is based on 1956 Industrial policy. As a matter of fact it is a supplement to it. The new Industrial production through optimum utilisation of the installed capacity and expansion of industries. The policy emphasises on rapid and Balanced industrialisation of the country with a view to benefitting the common man by increasing availability of goods at reasonable prices, larger employment and higher per capita income. The new policy aims at the revival of the economy by solving the problems of shortages of major industrial inputs like energy, transport and coal. This industrial policy has been formulated to achieve these objectives-modernisation, expansion and development to backward areas or regions.

The 1980 industrial policy also emphasise the need to make available the benefits of industrialisation to all the sectors of the society by extending preferential treatment to agro-based industries, by promoting the development of small, medium, and large enterprises, by promoting the dispersal of industries in backward rural and urban areas and protecting consumers against high prices and bad quality of goods.

Chief Objectives and Features. The 1980 industrial policy envisages the following objectives:

(i) Maximum use of the existing production capacity;

(ii) to obtain the highest level of production;

(iii) to give priority to agro based industries and there by strengthen the agricultural base;

(iv) to remove regional imbalance by giving priority to development of industrially backward areas;

(v) to create more employment opportunities;

(vi) to accelerate the development of export oriented and import substitution industries;

(vii) to protect consumers against high prices and bad quality goods;

(viii) to encourage economic federation through coordinate development of small medium and large enterprises.

Growth of Cottage, Village and Small Industries. The limits of Industries were enhanced as follows:

(i) tiny units-from one lakh rupees to two lakh rupees.

(ii) small scale units-from ten lakh rupees to twenty lakh rupees.

(iii) ancillary units-from fifteen lakh rupees to 25 lakh rupees.

Sectors where efficient production can be secured on a small scale would continue to be reserved for future expansion only by the small scale units.

3. Public Sector. The policy statement reiterates that public confidence in the public sector would be restored and the public sector would continue to occupy a vital position in the country's economic structure.

4. Private Sector. The private sector industries would also be allowed to develop in accordance with the objectives and targets of national plans and policies. However, the government would not allow monopolistic tendencies to grow in the private sector units.

5. Removal of Regional Imbalances. To achieve this end the policy encourages the establishment of new industrial units in industrially backward areas. Further, for securing greater regional balance the policy emphasises the dispersal of those industries in which economics of scale are not important. This would be economically and socially desirable. Special concession and government aids would be made available in industrially backward areas.

6. Export Production. This industrial policy statement also emphasises on increasing export production. To achieve this end 100 per cent export oriented units would be set up the existing units would be expanded exclusively for purpose of export.

7. Technological Self Reliance. The industrial policy statement lay adequate stress on keeping the technology in use up to date. To achieve this end import of technology particularly for export oriented and key industries may be liberalised.

8. Sick Units. The industrial policy statement reiterates that strict action would be taken against those industrial units which are sick by their own mismanagement and financial misappropriation. Government would determine such sick units which are found in critical condition. The government would make effort to revive such sick units by encouraging them to merge into healthy units who are in a position to revive them.

NEW INDUSTRIAL POLICY 1991

The Congress (I) Government led by Mr. Narasimha Rao has announced the new industrial policy on July 24, 1991. The main aim of the new industrial policy is to unshackle the Indian industrial economy from the cobwebs of unnecessary bureaucratic control, to introduce liberalisation with a view of integrate the Indian economy with the world economy, to remove restrictions on direct foreign investment as also to free the domestic entrepreneur from the restrictions of MRTP Act. All these reforms of industrial policy have led the government to take a series of initiatives in respect of policies in the following areas:

1. Industrial Licensing. In the sphere of industrial licensing, the role of the government was to be changed from that of only exercising control to one of providing help and guidance by making essential procedures fully transparent and by eliminating delays. This calls for bold and imaginative decisions designed to remove restraints on capacity creation, which at the same time, ensure that over-riding national interests are not jeopardised. The industrial licensing will henceforth be abolished for all industries, except those specified, irrespective of levels of investment. These specified industries will continue to be subject to compulsory licensing for reasons related to security and strategic concerns, social reasons, problems related to safety and overriding environmental issues, manufacture of products of hazardous nature and arcticles of elitist consumption.

2. Foreign Investment. In order to invite foreign investment in high priority industries, requiring large investment and advanced technology, it has been decided to provide approval for direct foreign investment upto 51 per cent foreign equity in such industries. For the promotion of exports of Indian products in world markets, the government will encourage foreign trading companies to assist Indian exporters in export activities. Besides this, the government will appoint a special board to negotiate with such firms so that purposive negotiations can be carried out with such large firms which provide the avenues for large investment in the development of industries and technology in the national interest.

3. Public Sector Policy. Public enterprises have shown a very low rate to return on the capital invested. This has inhibited their ability to regenerate themselves in terms of new investments as well as in technology development. The result is that many of the public enterprises have become a burden rather than being an asset to the Government. The original concept of the public sector has also undergone considerable dilution. The most striking example is the take over of sick units from the private sector. The category of public sector units accounts for almost one-third of the total losses of central public enterprises. Another category of public enterprises, which does not fit into the original idea of the public sector being at the commanding heights of the economy, is the plethora of public enterprises which are in the consumer goods and services sectors.

It is time therefore that the Government adopt a new approach to public enterprises. Units which may be faltering at present but are potentially viable must be restructured and given a new lease of life. The priority areas for growth of public enterprises in the future will be the following:

(a) Essential infrastructure goods and services.

(b) Exploration and exploitation of oil and mineral resources.

(c) Technology development and building of manufacturing capabilities in areas which are crucial in the long term development of the economy and where private sector invesment is inadequate.

(d) Manufacture of products where strategic considerations predominate such as defence equipment.

Government will strengthen those public enterprises which fall in the reserved areas of operation or are in high priority areas or are generating good or reasonable profits. Such enterprises will be provided a much greater degree of management autonomy through the system of memoranda of understanding. Competition will also be induced in these areas by inviting private sector participation. In the case of selected enterprises, part of Government holdings in the equity share capital of these enterprises will be disinvested in order to provide further market discipline to the performance of public enterprises. There are a large number of chronically sick public enterprises incurring heavy losses, operating a competitive market and serve little or not public purpose. These need to be attended to.

4. Foreign Technology. With a view to injecting the desired level of technological dynamism in Indian industry, government will provide automatic approval for technology agreements related to high priority industries within specified parameters.

Similar facilities will be available for other industries as well if such agreements do not require the expenditure of free foriegn exchange. Indian companies will be free to negotiate the terms of technology transfer with their foreign conterparts according to their own commerical judgement.

5. Industrial Location Policy Liberalilsed. In a departure from the earlier locational policy for industries, the new industrial policy stated that in locations other than cities of more than 1 million population, there will be no requirement of obtaining industrial approvals from the Centre, except for industries subject to compulsory licensing. In cities with a population of more than 1 million, industries other than those of a non-polluting nautre, were required to be located outside 25 kms of the priphery. Major amendments in the industrial location policy were effected during 1997-98. Now notified industries of a non-polluting nature such as electronics, computer softwer and printing, may be located within 25 kms of the periphery of cities with more than 1 million population. Other industries are permitted only if they are located in designated industrial areas set up prior to July 25, 1991. Zoning and Land Use Regulation as well as Environment Legislation continue to regulate industrial locations.

6. Monoplies and Restrictive Trade Practices Act (MRTP) Act. With the growing complexity of industrial structure and the need for achieving economies of scale for ensuring higher productivity and competitive advantage in the international market, the interference of the Government through the MRTP Act in investment decision of large companies has become deleterious in its effects on Indian industrial growth. The pre-entry scrutiny of investment decisions by so-called MRTP companies will no longer be required. Instead, emphasis will be on controlling and regulating monopolistic, restrictive and unfair trade practices rather than making it necessary for the monopoly houses to obtain prior approval of Central Government for expansion, establishment of new undertakings, mergers, amalgamation and takeover and appointment of certain directors. The trust policy will be more on controlling unfair or restrictive business practices.

7. Removal of Mandatory Convertibility Clause. A lare part of industrial investment in India is financed by loans from banks and financial institutions. These institutions have followed a mandatory practice of including a convertibility clause in their loans into equity if felt necessary by their management. Although this option has not generally been exercised, it has often been interpreted as an unwarranted threat to private firms of takeover by financial institutions. The new industrial policy has provided that henceforth financial institutions will not impose this mandatory convertibility clause.

8. Abolition of Phased Manufacturing Programmes for New Projects. To force the pace of indigenisation in manufacturing, Phased Manufacturing Programmes have been in force in a number of engineering and electronic industries. The new industrial policy has abolished such programmes in future as the government feels that due to substantial reforms made in the trade policy and the devaluation of the rupee, there is no longer any need for enforcing the local content requirements on a case-by-case, administrative basis. Various incentives that are currently available to manufacturing units with existing Phased Manufacturing Programmes will continue.

According to J.C. Sandesara, the new indutrial policy seeks to raise efficiency and accelerate industrial production in five different ways.

(1) The changes in repsect of foreign investment and foreign technology agreements are also designed to attract capital, technology and managerial expertise from abroad. This will raise the availability of such scarce resources in the country on the one hand, and will improve the level of efficiency of production on the other hand.

(2) Some changes as regards public sector may enhance the 'allocative efficiency'. Opening up to eleven areas (so far reserved for the public sector) to the private sector implies an opening for the sector which has, by the large, given a better account of itself. Closure, liquidation or rehabilitation etc. of sick/weak public sector units will free resources for more productive use. Similarly, privatisation may make for improved efficiency of the public sector, through its being subjected to the stock market discipline.

(3) A number of changes in industrial licensing policy, foreign investment, foreign technology agreements and MRTP Act are such as to do away with the prior clearance of the government. In such cases, project time and 'getting things done' will be reduced. Material and human resources engaged in cultivating contacts and 'getting things done' will be released for more productive uses. Thus efficiency will improve.

(4) Greater emphasis in controlling and regulating monopolistic, restrictive and unfair trade practices and the strengthening of powers of the MRTP Commission will curb anti-competitive behaviour of firms in the monopolistic, oligopolistic and ineffectively competitive markets and thus promote competition and efficiency.

(5) Other measure in this area such as purposeful formulation and implementation of Memorandum of Understanding and its monitoring, professionalisation and greater autonomy may be expected to improve the performance of the enterprises that will remain in the public sector.

Critics of the new industrial policy, however, point to the dangers of 'opening up' the economy to too much foreign influence. For instance, H.K. Paranjape argues that the list of high priority industries (in which direct foreign investment up to 51 per cent will now be freely permitted) includes industries which have been well established in the country for long and where technological development with indigenous R and D should not prove difficult. Invitation to foreign investors in these industries "would make it possible for large transnationals to dominate certain growing areas of our economy and push to the wall any Indian concerns which attempt to stand out on their own. Indigenous R and D will be doomed." Moreover, as correctly pointed out by Parajape, the past record of the multinationals operating in the country does not warrant much enthusiasm. None of the multinationals operating in this country has attempted to develop India as an important base for a significant part of its world-wide research and development work. Despite various tax concessions and incentives none of the multinationals tried to expand export markets. They undertook export activities only to the extent they were compelled to do so under export obligations, or when it was found necessary to do so in order to be able to earn foreign exchange for importing some of their essential requirements. In fact, instead of developing India as a major production and export base, many multinationals have only attempted to use their international trade capacities and contacts mainly for exporting goods manufactured by other—usually small scale—units. Thus they have operated more as trading than as manufacturing and exporting concerns.

Moreover, despite talks of globalisation, many rich countries are reluctant to permit unrestricted export of technologies as, in many areas, technologies are common for civilian and defence-related items. Multinationals which make a technological breakthrough are also usually reluctant to permit the use of their up-to-date technologies even by their subsidiaries unless these are located in politically 'safe' countries. India obviously does not satisfy this criterion from the viewpoint of these multinational companies, or the defence authorities of the USA and other rich countries. Coming to the import of foreign technology, Paranjape again expresses some reservations. According to him, in the whole eagerness to import foreign technology, little attention seems to have been paid to the possibility that production and managerial technologies found more suitable in other countries may not necessarily prove to be the best in our circumstances. As correctly pointed out by him, one of the very purposes of India's industrialisation is to ensure that our very large manpower resources are effectively utilised. This implies the adoption of labour-intensive and capital saving technologies in whichever areas it is feasible to do so. This may imply major readjustments in technologies that have developed in the labour scarce and capital abundant rich countries. This will not be an easy task.

❐

11

Business Environment

Generally Business refers to those activities which are related to the buying and selling of goods. Modern business covers activities related to both production and distribution. A firm or company normally carries a number of activities connected with production, trade, transport, finance, banking, insurance, advertising and certain other activities related to industry and commerce. All these activities are normally motivated by profits. In case, any of these activities is carried out by some organisation for purpose other than profit seeking, it cannot be justifiably considered as business. Further, business includes only those efforts on the part of manufactures, traders and other agencies which comply with legal requirements. This implies that any activity connected with production, trading, financing, advertising etc. must be excluded from business if it is violative of the laws of the country. Thus any activity carried out by an organisation for seeking profit can be called business if it does not violate the laws of the country.

Over the years business has undergone radical changes and thus modern business is quite different in comparison to yesteryears business. The main characteristics of the modern business are the following:

1. The size of modern business is very large in most of the developed countries. In India, its size is low. Indian companies in terms of market capitalisation, sales etc. are not impressive in comparison to developed countries. For example, there is only one Indian company in world's 500 largest companies *i.e.* Indian Oil, a public sector undertaking.

2. Another feature of modern business is its oligopolistic nature. In this type of market, any change in the price, sales or in the quality of the product by one firm evoke retaliation from other firms in the same line of business. In oligopolistic markets, usually the same firm produces different qualities to sell them to different groups at different prices.

3. Now a days modern business firms do not confine their production activities to a single commodity. These firms go for diversification of the production.

4. Till recently, even big companies had confined their business to domestic markets. Now companies which matter have expanded their revenue and assets base across countries and engage in cross-border flow of capital, goods and know-how.

5. In modern business life, modern technology and its upgradation play an important role. If business houses ignore technological changes for whatever reasons, they may lose in competitiveness and be pushed out of the market.

6. 'Change' is the basic mantra of modern business. The business follows the strategy of making changes in product quality, design or packaging speedily so that the demand for the product can be increased over a period of time.

7. Since the beginning of1991-92, the role of the government has dimnished with the dismantling controls over modern business in India. It is widely accepted that controls affects modern business adversely.

Internal Environment. Internal environment may be defined as the set of value system, goals and objectives, management structure, relationship among the various constituents, physical assets, technological capabilities and human, financial and marketing resources.

Business is normally undertaken for profit maximisation. In the traditional theory of business firm, profit maximisation has been assumed to be the sole objective of the firm. Since short run profit maximisation does not necessarily result in profit maximisation in the long run, some experts assert that rational firms attempt to maximise longrun profit. Managerial theories of firm, however state that sales revenue maximisation and the balanced rate of growth maximisation rather than profit maximisation are the real goals of modern business firms. In the behavioural theory of the firm, it is asserted that a firm seek to satisfied, that is to affair a satisfactory overall performance in terms of set aspiration goals, rather than maximise profits, production, sales or some other magnitude.

These divergent approaches with regard to goals of a modern firm are based on empirical evidences. From the one things that clearly averages is that in modern times all firms do not pursue a single goal. There are often major differences in the goals and objectives of the various firms which, in turn leads to differences in their overall interval environment and also in priorities, policies and direction of development.

Apart from differences in goals and objectives, other factors like availability of physical resources, management of the firm, production technology, R & D work, distribution logistics also influence the companys internal environment. For example the nature of management also influence the internal environment significantly. A corporate enterprise may be professionally managed or family controlled. On its board of Directors there may be dynamic entrepreneurs capable of taking quick decisions or the Board of Directors may be dominated by persons with conservative or bureaucratic outlook. Nominess of financial institutions having large holdings in companies may or may not have decisive say in decision making. Thus this factor also influence the company's internal environment.

External Environment. External environment of business consists of institutions, organisations and forces operating outside the company. In other words, any institution or institutions and forces individually or collectively influence the company, is called external environment. The external environment of business may be classified into micro environment and macro environment. The micro environment refers to such players whose decisions and actions have a direct bearing on the company. Since modern business has two aspects namely production and selling of goods, therefore micro environment affects both aspects of the business. Workers unions, customers, market intermediaries, competitors and public influence production and or salling of goods, constitutes micro environment. Macro environment, on the other hand, comprise larger societal and physical forces which affect the company and also the players in the company's micro environment.

Micro Environment. The micro environment consists of the factors, having direct bearing on the performance of the company. It includes such players like suppliers, markeing intermediaries, competitors, customers and the public whose decisions and actions affect the working of the firm of company. These players are more intimately linked with the company than the macro factors. The micro factors need not necessarily affect all the firms in a particular industry in the same way. Some of the micro factors may be particular to a firm and may affect significantly than their micro factors.

Macro Environment. Macro environment of a company refers to all those economic and non-economic factors which exercise their influence on the business activity in general and thus determine opportunities that a company may have to promote its business. Macro environment can be classified into economic environment and non-economic environment. Since business in basically an economic activity, economic environment of business national and global is of strategic importance. In the economic environment of the country, country's economic system, macroeconomic scenario, phase of businesscycle through which the economy is passing, organisation of the financial system and economic policies of the government are most important elements.

Business is also get influenced non-economic environment. Political system, ideology of the government, legal framework, social system, cultural values, demographic factors, level of technological development and natural and physical environment of the country constitution non-economic environment of business. In fact, all these non-economic elements are of great relevance to present day business.

The role of macro environment which includes economic and non-economic environment both, from the point of view of the business may be both positive and negative. This implies that the larger forces in the company's environment do not always provide wider space for business operations. They often put restraints on the business activities of the firm.

Factors Influencing Micro Environment

From the point of view of a company's business operations micro environment has great relevance usually the factors of micro environment do not affect all the companies in an industry in the same way. Their decisions and actions *vis-a-vis* individual company differ in accordance with the size, capability and stateges of each company. For example, a competitor does not mind starting price on if the rival company is small but he will be reluctant to do so if the rival firm is large and capable of retaliating. Sometimes micro environment of the various firms in an industry is almost the same but their response may be different. The main factors constituting micro environment are the following.

Customers. A business exists only because of its customers. The major task of a business is to create and sustain customers. A company may have different categories of consumers. For example, the customers of tyre company may include of individual automobile owners, automobile manufactors, public sector transport undertakings and other transport operators.

Depending on a single customer is often too riscky because it may place the company in a poor bargaining position, apart from the risks of losing business consequent to the winding up of business by the customers or due to the customer's switching over to the competitors of the company. The choice of the customer segments should be made by considering a number of factors including the relative profitability, dependability, stability of demand, growth prospects and twe extent of the competition.

2. Suppliers. An important force in the micro environment of a company is the suppliers, *i.e.*, those who supply the inpus like raw materials and components to the company. The importance of reliable source of supply to the smooth functioning of the bsuiness is obvious. Uncertainty regarding the supply or other supply constraints often compel companies to maintain high inventories causing cost increases. It has been pointed out that factories in India maintain indigenous stocks of 3-4 months and imported stocks of 9 months as against an average of a few hours to two weeks in Japan.

It is very risky to depend on a single supplier because a strike, lock out or any other production problem with that supplier may seriously affect the company. Similarly, a change in the attitude or behaviour of the supplier may also affect the company. Hence, multiple sources of supply often help reduce such risk.

Because of the sensitivity of the supply, many companies give high importance to vendor development. Vertical integration, where feasible, helps to solve the supply problems.

3. Marketing Intermediaries. The immediate environment of a company may consist of a number of marketing intermediaries which are "firms that aid the company in promoting, selling and distribution its goods to final buyers".

Marketing intermediaries are vital links between the company and the final consumers. A dislocation or disturbance of this link, or a wrong choice of the link, may cost the company very heavily, retail chemists and druggists in India once decided to boycott products of a leading company on some issue such as poor retail margin. This move for collective boycott was, however, objected to by the MRTP

Commission; but for this the company would, perhaps, have been in trouble.

The marketing intermediaries include middlemen such as agents and merchants who "help the company find customers or close sales with them", physical distribution firms which "assist the company in stocking and moving goods from their origin to their destination" such as warehouses and transportation firms; marketing service agencies which "assist the company in targeting and promoting its prodcuts to the right markets" such as advertising agencies, marketing research firms, media firms and consulting firms; and financial intermediaries which finance marketing activities and insure business risks.

4. Competitors. A firm's competitors include not only the other firms which market the same or similar products but also all those who compete for the discretionary income of the consumers. For example, the competition for a company's washing machine may come not only from other washing machines manufactures but also from cooking ranges, two-wheelers, refrigerators, stereo sets and so on and from firms offering savings and investment schemes like banks, Unit Trust of India, companies accepting public deposits or issuing shares or debentures etc. This competition among these products may be described as *desire competition* as the primary task here is to influence the basic desire of the consumer. Such desire competition is generally very high in countries characterised by limited disposable incomes and many unsatisfied desires.

If the consumer decides to spend his discretionary income on recreation (or recreation cum education) he will still be confronted with a number of alternatives to choose form like washing machine, stereo, two-in-one, three-in- one etc. The competition among such alternatives which satisfy a particular category of desire is called *generic competition*.

If the consumer decides to go in for a washing machine, the next question is which form of the washing machine - semi automatic or fully automatic etc. In other words, there is a *product form competition*. Finally the consumer encounters the *brand competition i.e.*, the competition between the different brands of the same product form.

An implication of these different demands is that a marketer should strive to create primary and selective demand for his products.

5. Public. "A public is any group that has an actual or potential interest in or impact on an organisation's ability to achieve its interests". Media public, citizens action publics and local publics are some examples. Growth of consumer publics is as important development affecting business.

Some companies are seriously affected by such publics. For example, one of the leading companies in India was frequently under attack by the media public, particularly by a leading daily which was allegedly bent on bringing down the share prices of the company by tranishing its image. Many companies are also affected by local publics. Environmental pollution is an isssue often taken up by a number of local publics.

It is wrong to think that all publics are threats to business. Some publics, are an opportunity for the business. For example, the media public may be used to disseminate useful information.

Factors Affecting Macro Environment

The macro environment consits of the larger societal forces that affect all the sectors in the Company's macro environment—namely, the demographic, economic, natural, technological, political and cultural forces. These environmental factors are beyond the control of a firm, its success will depend to a very large extent on its adaptability to the environment, *i.e.* its ability to properly design and adjust the internal variables to take advantage of the opportunities and to combat the threats in the environment.

From the point of view of analysis macro environment is broadly classified between economic and non-economic environment. There we shall analyse both economic and non-economic macro environment of business.

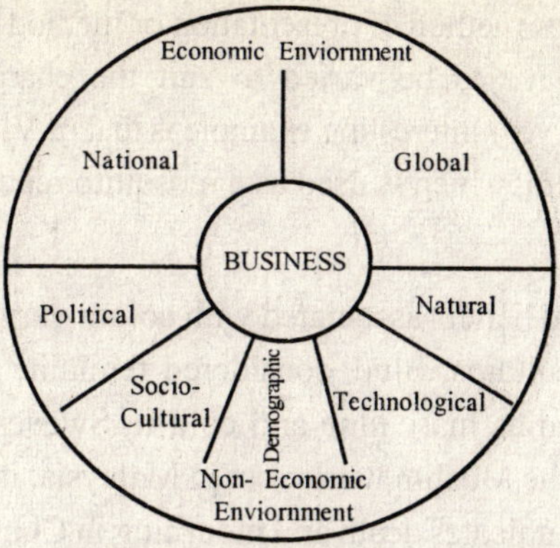

Fig. Macro Environment of Business

(A) Non-Economic Environment of Business. Business is an economic activity. It is nonetheless influenced by its non-economic environment. The non-economic environment of business can be broadly classified as socio-cultural, natural, demographic, physical and technological, political and government.

1. Socio-cultural Environment. The buying and consumption habits of the people, their language, beliefs and values, customs and traditions, tastes and preferences, education etc. are the constituents of socio-economic environment.

The socio-cultural fabric is an important environmental factor that should be analysed while formulating business strategies. The cost of ignoring the customs, traditions, taboos, tastes and preferences, etc., of a people could be very high.

For a business to be successful, its strategy should be the one that is appropriate in the socio-cultural environment. The marketing mix will have to be so designed as best to suit the environmental characteristics of the market. Nestle, a Swiss multinational company, today brews more than forty varieties of instant coffee different national tasts.

Even when people of different cultures use the same basic product, the mode of consumption, conditions of use, purpose of use or the perceptions of the product attributes may vary so much so that the product attributes, method of presentation or method of promoting the product may have to be varied to suit the characteristics of different markets. A very interesting example is that of Vicks Vaporub, the popular pain balm, which is used as a mosquito repellant in some of the tropical areas.

The values and beliefs associated with colour vary significantly between different cultures. Blue, considered feminine and warm in Holland, is regarded as masculine and cold in Sweden. Green is a favourite colour in the Muslim world; but in Malaysia, it is associated with illness. White indicates death and mourning in China and Korea; but in some countries, it expresses happiness and is the colour of the wedding dress of the bride. Red is a popular colour in the communist countries; but many African countries have a national distaste for red colour. There are also a number of demographic factors, such as the age and sex composition of population, family size, habitat, religion, etc., which influence the business. While dealing with the social environment, we must also consider the social environment of the business which encompasses its social responsibility and the alertness or vigilance of the consumers and of society at large.

2. Natural Environment. Geographical and ecological factors, such as natural resource endowments, weather and climate conditions, topographical factors, locational aspects in the global context, port facilities, etc., are all relevant to business.

Differences in geographical conditions between markets may sometimes call for changes in the marketing mix. Geographical and ecological factors also influence the location of certain industries. Climatic and weather conditions affect the location of certain industries like the cotton textile industry. Topographical factors may affect the demand pattern. For example, in hilly areas with a difficult terrain, jeeps may be in greater demand than cars.

3. Demographic Environment. Demographic factors like the size, growth rate, age composition, sex composition, etc. of the population, family size, economic stratification of the population, educational levels, language, caste, religion etc. are all factors which are relevant to business.

Demographic factors such as size of the population, population growth rate, age composition, life expectancy, family size, spatial dispersal, occupational status, employment pattern etc. affect the demand for goods and services. Markets with growing population and income are growth markets. But the decline in the birth rates in countries like the United States have affected the demand for baby products. *Johnsons and Johnson* have overcome this problem by repositioning their products like baby shampoo and baby soap, promoting them also to the adult segment, particularly to the females. A rapidly increasing population also indicates a growing demand for many products. The population growth rate, is an important environment factor which affects business. Cheap labour and a growing market have encouraged many multinational corporations to invest in developing countries.

The occupational and spatial mobilities of population have implications for business if labour is easily mobile between different occupations and regions, its supply will be relatively smooth, and this will affect the wage rate.

If labour is highly heterogeneous in respect of language, caste and religion, ethnicity, etc., personnel management is likely to become a more complex task. The heterogeneous population with its varied tastes, preferences, beliefs, temperaments, etc. gives rise to differing demand patterns and calls for different marketing strategies.

4. Physical and Technological Environment. Physical Factors, such as geographical factors, weather and climatic conditions may call for modification in the product, etc., to suit the environment because these environment factors are uncontrolable. For example, Esso adapted its gasoline formulations to suit the weather conditions prevailing in different markets.

Business prospects depend also on the availability of certain physical facilities. Some products, like many consumer durables, have certain use facility characteristics. The demand for refrigerators and other electrical appliances is affected by the extent of electrification and the reliability of power supply.

Technological developments may increase the demand for some existing products. For example, voltage stabilisers help increase the sale of electrical appliances in markets characterised by frequent voltage fluctuations in power supply. However, the introduction of T.*Vs.* Fridges etc. with in-built voltage stabiliser adversely affects the demand for voltage stabiliers.

The television has added a new dimension to product promotion. The advent of TV and VCP/VCR has, however, adversely affected the cinema theatres.

5. Political and Government Environment. Political and government environment has close relationship with the economic system and economic policy. For example, the communist countries had a centrally planned economic system. In most countries, apart from those laws that control investment and related matters, there are a number of laws that regulate the conduct of the business. These laws cover such matters as standards of product, packaging, promotion etc.

In many countries, with a view to protecting consumer interests, regulations have become stronger. Regulations to protect the purity of the environment and preserve the ecological balance have assumed great important in many countries.

Certain changes in government policies such as the industrial policy, fiscal policy, tariff policy etc. may have profound impact on business. Some policy developments create opportunities as well as threats, in other words, a development which brightens the prospects of some enterprises may pose a threat to some others. For example, the industrial policy liberalisations in India, particularly around the mid-eighties have opened up new opportunties and threats. They have provided a log of opportunties to a large number of enterprises to diversify and to make their product mix better. But they have also given rise to serious threat to many existing products by way of increased competition; many seller's markets have given way to buyer's markets. Even products which were seldom advertised have come to be promoted very heavily. This battle for the market have provided a splended opportunity for the advertising industry. Advertising billing have been increasing substantially.

Many countries today have laws to regulate competition in the public interest. Elimination of unfair competition and dilution of monopoly power are the important objectives of these regulations. In India, the monopolistic undertakings, dominant undertakings and large industrial houses are subject to a number of regulations which prevent the concentration of economic power to the common detriment. The MRTP Act also controls monopolistic, restrictive and unfair trade practices which are prejudicial to public interest. Such regulations brighten the prospects of small and new firms. They also increase the scope of some of existing firms to venture into new areas of business. The special privileges available to the small scale sector have also contributed to the phenomenal success of the Nirma.

(B) Economic Environment. Economic environment of business is of strategic importance. In economic environment global and national environments are included.

1. Global or International Environment. The global or international environment is very important from the point of view of certian categories of business. It is particularly important for industries directly depending on import competing industries. For example, a recession in foreign markets, or the adoption of protectionist policies by foreign nations, may create difficulties for industries depending on exports. On the other hand, a boom in the export market or a relaxation of the protectionist policies may help the export-oriented industries. A liberalisation of imports may help some industries which use imported items, but may adversely affect import-competing industries.

In has been observed that major international developments have their spread effects on domestic business. Oil price hikes have seriously affected a number of economies. These hikes have increased the cost of production and the prices of certain products, such as fertilisers, synthetic fibres, etc. The high oil price has led to an increase in the demand for automobile models that economise energy consumption, the demand for natural fibers increased because of the oil crisis. The oil crisis led to a reorientation of the Government of India's energy policy. Such developments affect the demand, consumption and investment pattern.

A good export market enables a firm to develop a more profitable product mix and to consolidate its position in the domestic market. Many companies now plan production capacities and investment taking into account also the foreign markets. Export marketing facilitates the attainment of optimum capacity utilisation; a company may be able to mitigate the effects of domestic recession by exporting. This will lead to adverse developments in foreign exchange recession by exporting. However, a company which depends on the export market to a considerable extent has also to face the impact of adverse developments in foreign markets.

Economic conditions, economic policies and the economic systems are the important external factors that constitute the national environment of business in a country.

2. National Environment. The economic conditions of a country—for example, the nature of the economy, the stage of development of the economy, economic resources, the level of income, the distribution of income and assets, etc.—are among the very important determinants of business strategies.

In countries where is investment and income are steadily and rapidly rising, business prospects are generally bright, and further investments are encouraged. There are a number of economists and businessmen who feel that the developed countries are no longer worthwhile propositions for investment because these economies have reached more or less saturation levels in certain respects.

In a development country, the low income may be the reason for the very low demand for a product. The sale of a product for

2. **Educational-Cultural Environment and Economic Environment.** These are also interrelated. The stage of economic development is a decisive factor for the available system of education; only a relatively high income country can afford to impart costly higher education in science and technology. The sysem of education on the other hand, may be responsible for a given economic environment; the emphasis on liberal arts, education and the lack of vocational training courses may be held responsible for the economic problem of unemployment in many countries. At the corporate level, the interdependence between educational and economic environmental factors may at time work out to be a vicious circle. For example, a low profit-making business concern may not find resurces to finance training or executive development programme. As a result, there may be skill deformation among its staff-managerial inefficiency may cause low business efficiency as measured in terms of profitability of the business.

3. **Historical Environment and Social Environment.** These are also interdependent. The present environment of business can be treated as a legacy of past environment. Every business has a history, every history has a lesson. As such, the present is a reflection to the past, and the present can also be handled in terms of the experience of the past. A number of examples may be quoted. The economic environment of a country today is partly constitued in terms of the available structure of industry in that country. The past history is a record of events—storehouse of lessons which can provide guidelines for present economic policy decisions. The achievements of the Five-Year Plans of Reforms Programme in the past may provide direction to the formulation and implementation of the present Five-Year Planned programmes of an economy. And the present performance of a plan will make the course of history of

planning. This suggests that the environments factors are interrelated on the the time scale.

4. **Political-Legal Environment and Economic Environment.** These too affect each other. In a situation of political stability business enterprises happened to grow better, businessmen venture to shoulder more economic risks. But if there is political instability, business uncertainties multiply and, therefore, individuals may not like to step in business ventures. In the same way, the ideology of the ruling party influences the economic system. The government which believes in socialism (Swadeshi) as a strategy and nationalisation of enterprises (closed door to Videshi multinationals) as a tactic may remove the private business sector and kill the business incentives to expand its scale of operations. On the other hand, sometimes a series of political legislations may be necessary to cope with the economic environment. To fight economic crisis and industrial recession, streamlining of administration and simplification of procedural matters may be evoked.

5. **Physical Environment and Economic Environment.** These are inter-related too. The environment considerations limit the expansion activities of a business firm. On the other hand the size of plant, the scale of output, the organisation or firms, the structure and location or industries may lie at the root of either environmental improvement or environmental decay. Thus, the social responsibility of business to-day is to take care of the environmental impact of its economic and technological activities. To the extent this social responsibility is not discharged, laws relating to the business and industry will increasingly turn out to be laws relating to the physical environment of business. The point remains that the physical environment as a factor is assuming so much significance day to day that it may be trated as critical element within the economic environment of business, rather than outside.

ENVIRONMENTAL SCANNING

It is the process by which managers and promoters of firms and companies tries to monitor the economic changes, governmental change, suppliers attitude and changes in the market to decide about new options, opportunities and threats if any. In very simple words environmental analysis relates of identification and analysing environmental influences individually and collectively to face the future effects upon the society and business. In environmental scanning, the main emphasis is on finding out the sources of new opportunities or threats. Environmental scanning or analysis is useful for evaluating the present strategy, new norms for future strategic decisions.

Every business fortune is influenced by non-economic change apart from economic changes. Among non-economic changes, social changes and political changes influence business strategy and planning significantly. If a firm or company does not keep an eye on economic, political and social changes occurring in the country then it will affect the business fortunes adversely. Here we can give the example of textile industry. In textile industry, except Reliance, no other industry is making remarkable progress and profitability. The reason is that Reliance took advantage of market needs and formulated strategies so that products are related to market needs. On the other hand, the management philosophy, practice, procedures, products and technology of other textile mills were out of line with change in environment. Hence, these textile mills suffered from sickness and lesser profitability.

Thus the management must be altert to new opportunities arising out of new product so that it can expand the business and earn high profits.

Requirement for Environment Scanning

The objective of most of the business managements is to earn more profit. Environment scanning helps every management in attaining more profits and growth and at the same time helps in minimisation of future threats. The future of an organisation is related with the environment in which the business is running. The growth and innovations and philosophy of change should be viewed with environmental effects. A fast changing business needs close study of facts: What are the probable threats to company. Some of the future events can be predicted by systematic scanning and follow up of environmental effects. The environmental scanning comprises information processing of social, economical, political, technological, product and changed market conditions.

The Research work on desirability of environmental analysis has revealed that there is high degree positive correlation between environmental analysis and success of corporates. The related areas which are needed for growth due to environmental analysis needs the following considerations:

(A) Firms growing by mergers and thus increasing the complexity of environment.

(B) Firms which had to face competition, Government regulations and healthy environment.

(C) Firms which are facing environment problems and headed by risk and uncertainty.

The study revealed that corporations succeeded with little or no extra efforts at environment appraisal. The following are such firms:

(i) Firms with slow effect of Environment changes and having risk prone management.

(ii) Firms with a desire of Innovation of new product.

(iii) Dominant firms with moderate risk-prone management.

It is a considered opinion that increasing knowledge of the strategists in environment scanning there is a positive gain to the firm.

FEATURES OF ENVIRONMENTAL ANALYSIS

Changing environment, the process of environmental analysis is very well comparable with the functions of radar. If a boat is sailing on a "sea of uncertainty", there are two essential requirements for a successful voyage. There has to be a star to steer the ship. Secondly, there must be radar to signal the existence of rocks, reefs and clear water in the uncharted sea. Thus in a business firm operating in an uncertain environment must have a vision (a giding star) and a system of environmental analysis (the radar). From this analogy, it is possible to derive three important characteristics of the process of environmental analysis.

1. The analysis of environment must be a continuous process rather than being an intermittent scanning system. Like the radar, it must operate continuously in order to keep the speed of development.

2. Environmental analysis is an exploratory process. While the monitoring aspect of the system is concerned with present developments, a large part of the process seeks to explore the unknown terrain, the dimensions of possible futures, what-could happen, not necessarily what will happen.

3. Environmental analysis is an exercise that it must comprise a total view of the environment rather than viewing trends piecemeal. A radar covers 360 degrees of the horizon, not just a segment, although it can focus on a particular segment if need be. The corporate radar must scan the whole circumference of its environment in order to minimise the change of surprises and maximise its utility as an early warning system.

Which aspect of the environment should be management of any Organisation be concerned with? The factors that can influence future events and the sheer weight and volume or primary data be studied covering all major aspects.

Each company to set for itself the boundaries of the relevant environment and examine those variables which are critical to its own activities. This does not mean that firm engaged in manufacturing and selling products for the domestic market should monitor only the national environment, or an export firm should ignore the demestic product market conditions. For example, Reliance Textile Industries Ltd. initially focused on importing nylon yarn and polyster filaments for manufacturing fabrics primarily for the export market. The company deliberately chose not to expand its activities in the domestic market at that stage as it had identified that the market which was dominated by established leaders was not ripe for high-priced-quality products. It was in 1977 that the management realised potentiality of the internal market and decided to expand their operations on a large scale having the benefit of accumulated experience of supplying high-quality fabrics in the more competitive markets abroad.

Environmental factors are economic, political, social, legal/ regulatory and technological—may be of general specific relevance to enterprises. Further, each enterprise may perceive the relevant environment in the light of its own interest and set of circumstances which affect its functioning. Distinction may be made three orders of environment indicators to decide upon the question of relevance. Thus, depending on the nature of environment factors to be considered, management may distinguish between:

(i) Indicators relevant to individual enterprises, *e.g.*, for a company manufacturing agricultural pumpsets for irrigation—the progress of rural electrification; for a transport company—planned investment in the expansion of railway tracks and haulage capacity road construction, costs fuel and user needs for additional freight capacity.

(ii) Indicators which affect all business enterprises at the national level. These indicators may be easy to identify but difficult to measure, *e.g.*, attitude of political parties towards private enterprise as reflected in election manifestos, foreign economic relations, possibilities of armed conflicts, encounters, cold war and hostilities with neighbouring countries. etc.

(iii) Indicators relating to particular industry sectors, *e.g.*, for garment industry in India—the import-export policy of the Government of India, import restrictions in the United States and Western European countries, reservation of industries for the small-scale sector, delicensing of specific industries, and the like. These indicators may be relatively easier to measure though not so easy to identify.

Thus business environment may be defined as the set of external factors such as; economic factors, Geo-physical factors Government and Legal factors which are uncontrollable in nature and affects the business decisions.

Process of Environment Scanning

The study or scanning process is not difficult but not so easy as to which areas be covered and which should be left out.

Researches conducted in the late 60s and 70s being revealed that the process of environmental analysis has been far from being systematic except with regard to information relating to current developments. Oral information from personal sources dominated the total input of information. Written and documentary information was much less frequently used by strategists. When written information were used they tended to be general information sources. Formal forecasting, if at all used, was viewed with great scepticism. Very little use was made of written studies, research reports, and meetings for environment search. Notwithstanding the above findings of research studies in the sixties and seventies and, perhaps because of these findings combined with the research findings on the beneficial effects of systematic analysis and diagnosis of external conditions the critical importance of developing as effective system of information gathering and information evaluation has been increasingly recognised over time by large enterprises.

Essentially, environmental scanning requires information inputs which can be derived from different sources:

1. **Industrial Informations.** Industrial espionage (spying) could also be a source of information about actual and potential competitors based on contacts with the employees, suppliers or customers of the competitors. Judging by survey data and expenses incurred on systems to protect trade secrets and industrial processes, it has been observed that industrial espionage and spying have been increasing in the United States. There is very little evidence in this respect about Indian industries.

2. **Verbal Informations.** Verbal information from such sources as the audio-visual media (radio and television); conversation among employees, managers, supervisors and subordinates; customer; distributors of the company's products (wholesalers, dealers, retailers); suppliers; competitors and their employees, financial executives in banks; stock brokers; consultants; government employees.

3. **Written Informations.** Written and documentary information from news papers, trade journals, industry newsletters, reports, documented clipping services;

4. **Management Informations.** Information made available through the management information system which is specially designated to served the needs of strategic planners.

Forecasting and reports based on forecasts regarding changes in economic, social and financial conditions available from governmental agencies and other specified consultancy service organisations.

Important Publications. A number of publications in India provide valuable information and forecasts relating to environmental conditions:

1. *The State of the Nation Report* (Annual) *Quarterly Survey of Industries*; and *Economic Scene* (monthly) published by the Tata Economic Consultancy Services.

2. *Business Intelligence and Data* published by the Centre for Monitoring Indian Economy.

3. *Indian Trade* Journal (Weekiy) published by the Directorate General of Commercial Intelligence and Statistics, Calcutta.

4. *Economic Trends* (fortnightly) published by the Federation of Indian Chamber of Commerce and Industry, New Delhi.

5. *Economic Survey* published annually by the Ministry of Finance (Economic Division), Govt. of India.

6. Decennial Census Reports, Govt. of India.

7. Reserve Bank of India Bulletins (monthly) and annual Reports on Currency and Finance.

8. *Guidelines to Industries* in two volumes published by the Union Ministry of Industries.

9. *Five year* plans and mid-term survey reports on planned development published by the Planning Commission.

10. ICCI Portfolio Studies (Annual).

11. *Economic Times* (Bombay, New Delhi), *Financial Express* (New Delhi), and Business Standard (Calcutta, New Delhi)—dailies.

12. *Business Indian* (fortnightly), Bombay.

    Business World (fortnightly), Calcutta.

    Capital (fortnightly), Calcutta

    Commerce (Weekly), Bombay.

13. *Yojana trends* (fortnightly) published by the Planning Commission.

14. *Foreign Trade* (monthly) published by the Indian Institute of Foreign Trade, New Delhi.

The following publications relating to international business provide economic, trade and financial data;

15. Bombay Stock Exchange Directory.

1. **United Nations Publications**

   World Economic Survey (Annual)

   Economic Survey of Latin America (Annual)

   Commodity Trade Statistics (Quarterly and Annual)

   Statistical Year Book (Annual)

   International Financial Statistics (Monthly)

   Economic Survey of Asia and the Far East (Annual)

   Year Book of International Trade Statistics

   Economic Bulletins for Europe, Latin America and Africa (Biannuals)

2. Annual Report on Exchange Restrictions published by the International Monetary Fund.

3. Indian Export serivce Bulletins (Weekly) published by the Trade Fair Authority of India.

4. Overseas Business published by United States Department of Commerce.

5. Monthly Statistics of the Foreign Trade of India in two volumes published by the Department of Commercial Intelligence and Statistics.

6. Fortnightly, monthly and quarterly Bulletins/Newsletters/ Journals published by the Export Promotion Councils for different products.

❐

12

Economic Reforms

THE ORIGIN OF ECONOMIC CRISIS

In early 1991, a major economic crisis surfaced in India. It was the worst crisis that India had experienced since Independence. Increasing fiscal deficit adverse balance of payments position, high rate of inflation and Gulf crisis in late 1990 led to the economic crisis. Let discuss these factor in detail.

1. The Fiscal Imbalance. When a country faces budgeting deficit, revenue deficit, monetised deficit and/or gross difical deficit for a long period of time, is called fiscal imbalance. The steep rise in non-development expenditure was the main cause for rise in governmental expenditure. If the government revenue does not match with the increased expenditure, government fill this gap through, market borrwings, small savings, provident funds, external borrowings etc. The conventional measures of fiscal imbalance do not reflect this. In contrast, the concept of gross fiscal deficit is a complete measure of fiscal inbalance. It equals the excess of total government expenditure over revenue and grants. The gross fiscal deficit rose from 4.1 percent in 1975 to 8.4 percent in 1990-91. Since the fiscal deficit had to be met by recourse to borrowings, the internal debt of the government increased rapidly. This naturally made burden of servicing the debt overones. Interest payments which were 10 percent of total Central Government expenditure in 1980-81, rose to 20 percent total Central Government Expenditure in 1990-91. It was equivalent to 36.4 percent of the total revenue collections of the Central Government. This was an unsustainable situation. The danger of the government falling into debt-trap was real.

2. Adverse Balance of Payments Situation. The balance of payment situation was very serious. The deficit in current account was continuously rising. It increased from $2.1 billion in 1980-81 to $9.7 billion in 1990-91. As a consequence of this govt. had to resort to external borrowings. The continuance increase in external borrowing led to an increase in debt service burdern from 15 percent of export earnings in 1980-81 to 30 percent of expert earnings in 1990-91. This put strains to the breaking point in 1991 due to Gulf crisis. The balance of payments position was on the brink of disaster and the level of foreign exchange reserves dropped to levels which were not sufficient to finance imports of even ten days in the month of June, 1991. The country's balance of payments position was extremely vulnerable and to avert the default, of the Government used stocks of gold to obtain foreign exchange, took emergency bilateral assistance from donor countries and borrowed under special facilities from the IMF. All these pushed the country into a recessionary situation.

3. Increasing Inflationary Pressures. The price situation was not alarming in the later half of the 1980s as the average rate of inflation was 6.7 percent annum. However, the rate of inflation rose to 10.3 percent perannum in 1990-91. During this inflationary situations, the prices of food rose sharply in spite of three good monsoons in a row. The abnormal increase in food prices was mainly due to the excessive growth of money supply. This liquidity overchange, in conjunction with real disproportionalities and underlying supply demand inbalances was bound to fuel inflation.

The counter the economic crisis government introduced economic reforms to deal with demand side and supply side management.

ECONOMIC REFORMS

In response to the crisis situation the government introduced economic policy reforms which consisted to two distinct strands-macro-economic stabilisation and structural reforms. While stabilisation deals with demand management, structural reforms deal with sectoral adjustments designed to tackle the problems on the supply side of the economy.

Under macroeconomic stabilisation (*i.e.,* demand management) government tried:

(i) to control inflation;

(ii) to adjust fiscal inbalance and

(iii) to adjust balance of payment situation.

On the other hand, under structural reforms (*i.e.,* supply side management) the govenrment introduced:

(i) trade and capital flows reforms

(ii) industrial deregulation

(iii) disinvestment and public enterprise reforms

(iv) financial sector reforms

(v) reforms in agriculture sector, human resource sector etc.

A. MACROECONOMIC STABILISATION

Macroeconomic stabilisation or stabilisation involves returning to low and stable inflation and a sustainable fiscal and balance of payments position. Stabilisation in necessary to overcome a crisis but it assumes a special importance if structural reforms are also introduced together with stabilisation. This is because structural reforms often add to macroeconomic pressures. Under the stabilisation programme, government took the following steps:

1. Control of Inflation. The rate of inflation in 1990-91 was well above 10 per cent annum. This could be brought down on the one hand by introducing fiscal and monetary discipline in the economy and on the other by improving output and supply position. It seems that the government's achievements are modest on both the fronts.

During the period from 1990 to 2000, government followed liberal monetary policy in one and strict monetary policy in another year. In the year 1991-92 money supply and wholesale price index increased by 20.6 percent and 13.7 percent respectively. In 1992-93, satisfactory growth in agriculture and industrial production along with control money supply it increased by 7.6 percent) brought down the rate of inflation to 7.6 percent and further came down to around 1.5 percent in 2000-01. This was mainly the result of slower monetary growth.

A low trend rate of inflation in Indian context requires firm control of the rate of monetary expansion. Joshi and Little argued that if the controlled expansion of money supply is accompanied by a high rate of fiscal deficit, real interest rates are driven up and private investment is squeezed. If high rates of private investment are necessary for rapid growth, this in effect means that low inflation becomes incompatible with high growth.

2. Fiscal Adjustment. Fiscal adjustment is necessary for dealing with the twin problems of high domestic inflation and large deficits in the balance of payments. Fiscal deficit of the government (Centre, State and Union Territories together) was less than 7 per cent of GDP at the beginning of the 1970s. It, however, rose to about 11 per cent of GDP in 1990-91. The factor which contributed most to the growing fiscal deficit was sharp deterioration of the balance on revenue account. The government having recognised that such high levels of fiscal deficits, both overall and on revenue account were not sustainable, committed itself to a policy of fiscal adjustment. The Central government initiated a programme of fiscal adjustment under which its fiscal deficit which was around 8.3 per cent of GDP in 1990-91, was reduced to 5.9 per cent in 1991-92 and further to 5.7 per cent in 1992-93. The fiscal deficit once again rose to a higher level because. States never committed themselves to any fiscal adjustment programme. Indulging in populism they are neither inclined to curtail nonplan revenue expenditure, nor willing to optimise resources mobilisation through tax and non-tax sources.

In India, the fiscal imbalance has been caused mainly by imprudent increase in public expenditure. The government expenditure which was about 19 per cent of GDP in 1970-71 rose sharply to 37 per cent of GDP in 1990-91. Therefore, if fiscal imbalance is to be corrected, it is necessary to reduce the government expenditure to aroud 25 per cent of GDP. However, in 1997-98, the government expenditure constituted about 28.8 per cent of GDP. To curtail if further, the government should reduce particularly the consumption expenditure mainly of defence expenditure and administrative expenditure, subsidy payments and interest payments. Although for the purpose of fiscal adjustments containment of the government expenditure should receive overriding priority, some efforts at additional resource mobilisation through tax and non-tax sources may also be necessary in the short-run. In India, since built-in revenue elasticity with respect to GDP is around unity, almost all the increase in revenue has to be obtained from additional revenue mobilisation efforts. The Planning Commission has stated, "The required additional revenues may have to be generated by a judicious mixture of broadening the tax base, rationalising the tax rates and through non-tax sources." An area where there is considerable scope for revenue mobilisation is public services. User-charges on publicly provided utilities such as irrigation, electricity, water, road transport and higher education are much below their cost of provision. The government can justifiably raise user charges on public utilities like electricity, irrigation, transportation and water. The government, however, does not seem to be serious about additional resource mobilisation through raising the recovery rates on public utility services. It has also failed to cut down its consmption expenditures and subsidy payments. Its interest payments continue to increase as there is no serious attempt to liquidate substantial part of the existing stock of internal debt. Having failed in adopting hard corrective measures, the government has opted for some soft options such as reduction in capital expenditure and social services in real terms. A fall in capital expenditure by government is generally expected to cause an overall decline in the rate of capital formation, while the containment of expenditure on social services adversely affect the human well-being.

3. Balance of Payments Adjustment. At present balance of payments situation is not as precarious as it was in 1990-91. The level of foreign exchange reserves has risen from a meagre $ 2.2 billion in March 1991 to $ 60.0 billion on Aug. 10, 2002. This accumulation of foreign exchange reserves suggests that the Indian economy has moved to a somewhat stable and sustainable balance of payments position in the last eight years. The current account deficit was 3.3 per cent of GDP in 1990-91 but fell to 0.4 per cent in 1991-92 mainly due to import compression which in trun adversely affected the overall performance of the economy. The government adopted a policy of import liberalisation considering a relatively comfortable foreign exchange reserves position. An impressive growth of export reduced the trade deficit bringing down the current account deficit to 0.4 per cent of GDP.

In later years a higher import growth and lower export growth widned the trade deficit. The current account deficit was 1.0 per cent of GDP in 1989-99 and 1999-2000.

Policies relevant to the balance of payments which were adopted during the past seven years were guided but both stabilisation and structural reform considerations. In India's case, the balance of payments problems arose largely from inadequate coverage of import by export earnings. In the beginning of the 1980s, this coverage ratio was only 52.4 per and led to a massive trade deficit. There was some improvement in it during the 1980s and in 1990-91 export earnings accounted for about 66.2 per cent of the value of imports. Hence there is need to boost the export growth rate.

According to experts, export will have to grow at around 14 per cent in value (9 per cent in volume) to achieve a sustainable balance of payments position. However, for rapid export growth the real exchange rate is critically important because export competitiveness largely depends on it. According to Joshi and Little, "The correct policy assignment in India is to target the exchange rate on export competitiveness." Joshi and Little further argue that an appropriate exhcange rate policy is necessary but not sufficient to promote exports. It will have to be accompanied by fiscal consolidation, trade reform, infrastructure development and incentives for private investment in export capacity.

B. STRUCTURAL REFORMS

The major structural reforms and the following:

1. Trade and Capital Flows Reforms. Since July 1991, the government has introduced a series of reforms in the trade sector which will help integration of the Indian economy better with the rest of the world. Among these reform measures, devaluation of rupee in July 1991 and subsequently its depreciation against the currencies of the leading industrialised countries, introduction of the convertibility of the rupee first on trade account and then for the entire current account transactions, liberalistion of import regime, substantial reduction in customs tariff rates, decanalisation of many items of trade and wide ranging measures to give a thrust to exports are important. The details of the steps taken are following:

(i) The system of fixed exchange rates was abandoned by India in September 1975 and since then the system of managed exchange rate float has been in operation. However, due to higher rate of inflation in India as compared to that in the developed countries, the real effective exchange rate of rupee did not fall as much as the nominal effective exchange rate of rupee. Hence, as already written earlier, the government formally devalued rupee by around 22 per cent in July 1991 to restore India's international competitiveness. This was followed by a liberalisation of the foreign trade through dismantling of some physical controls. Not only the import procedures were simplified but a significant number of items were shifted outside the purview of import licensing. The partial convertibility of rupee was also introduced. The 1993-94 Budget introduced full convertibility of rupee on trade account and thus the dual exchange rate system was replaced by a unified exchange rate system. Since the rupee exhibited good strength after the announcement of full convertibility of the rupee for the entire current account transactions was introduced in August 1994 alongwith some relaxation of exchange control.

(ii) As a first step towards a gradual reduction in the tarrif, the 1991-92 Budget had reduced the peak rate of import duty from more than 300 per cent to 150 per cent. The process of lowering the customs tariff rate was carried further in subsequent Budgets. The Budget reduced the peak rate of import duty to 30 per cent in 2002-03.

(iii) Earlier a large number of export and imports used to be canalised throgh public sector agencies. During the past six years a large number of export and import items have been decanalised. However, 8 items including petroleum products, fertilisers, foodgrains and edible oils remain canalised. Decanalisation of imports and exports as it has been done in recent years is an important step towards opening of more area of the external sector to the private sector.

(iv) Over the past few years not only substantial import duty cuts have been made in the case of machine tools, steel ores and concentrates, leather industry, electronics and telecommunications sectors, but the prevailing system of imports duties has also been considerably rationalised with the purpose of establishing a party in prices of goods produced domestically and internationally.

(v) As a part of structural reforms the government has taken various export promotion measures. A part from the systems of Eximscrips and liberalised exchange rate mechanism which were short lived, the government adopted a variety of export promotion measures under the Exim Policies (1922-97 and 2002-07). The important measures introduced were–establishment of Export Oriented Units for promoting exports from the agricultural and allied sectors, simplification of Export Promotion Capital Goods Scheme, introduction of Export Promotion Capital Goods scheme for the services sector, adoption of a more rational and convenient criterion for recognition of export houses/traditing houses/star trading houses, broadening of areas of activity in Export Processing Zones, duty free import for exports under advance licensing scheme, and creation of an exporters' grievance cell in the Ministry of Commerce to facilitate action on problems being faced by exporters.

(vi) The government has also liberalised capital flows in the form of foreign direct investment as a part of the package of external sector reforms. Important measures in this direction are *(i)* automatic approval of foreign equity participation upto 51 per cent in 48 industries and automatic approval upto 50 per cent foreign equity in 3 industries related to mining; *(ii)* approval of foreign equity participation upto 51 percent in service areas; *(iii)* delinking technology transfer from equity investment to import flexibility in the choice of technology; *(iv)* automatic clearance for import of capital goods in cases where foreign exchange flows through foreign equity; and *(v)* amending Foreign Exchange and Regulation Act (FERA) to place FERA companies on par with Indian companies for all operational pruposes. Now FERA has been replaced by Foreign Exchange Management Act (FEMA). These liberalisation measures in respect of foreign investment though highly acclaimed in the official circles, have exposed the industrial activity to extensive control of multinational corporations (MNCs). According to Dalip Swamy, the possible onslaught of MNCs in coming years will lead to increasing use of capital intensive technology and the consequent displacement of labour.

2. Industrial Deregulation. Historically, India's dometic economic activities have been subject to a wide array of physical controls. In the industrial sector, such controls took various forms: industrial licensing which regulated entry and expansion; reservation of a large number of industries for the public sector as well as small scale sector; time consuming procedures required for the exit of industrial units; and price and distribution controls on various industrial products. Isher J. Ahluwalia blamed the industrial licensing system and bureaucratic controls for the industrial stagnation during the second half of the sixties and the seventies. L.K. Jha recognised the positive role of regulatory appratus in a planned economy, but nonetheless argued that the industrial licensing machinery over the years had become a major obstacle to industrial development. The long time taken by the industrial licensing authorities to give clearance to the various proposals made it impossible for any project of importance to be completed within the scheduled time period. The industrial licensing authorities often took exception to the attempts of the industrial units to produce more than licensed capacity. Thus the objective of maximisation of ouput from a given licensed capacity got undermined.

Limit on the size of the companies which was earlier enforced under the monopoly and Restrictive Trade Practices Act has now been scrapped. This will allow industrial units to grow to optimum size and enjoy the benefits of economies of scale. The anti-monopoly legislation until this relaxation was made, had prevented many firms from growing to optimum size and thus achieve higher efficiency levels. The industrial location policy has been both simplified and liberalised. The phased manufacturing programme under which domestic manufactures were required to increase the domestic input-content of their products in a specified period has also been abolished under the new indsutrial policy.

In recent years, it has been increasingly realised that the regulatory device has led to widespread inefficiency in the industrial sector. The government had, therefore, been relaxing some of these controls even before it committed itself to structural reforms in 1991. The thrust of the new industrial policy announced in July 1991 is on deregulation of the industrial economy in a substantial manner and opening up a large number of industries to the private sector. The requirement of industrial licensing has been abolished for all but 6 product categories. These are alcohol, cigarettes, hazardous chemicals, industrial explosives, durgs and pharmaceuticals (excepting bulk drugs), electronics aerospace and defence equipment. In another significant step the number of industries reserved for the public sector has been reduced from 17 to 4.

3. Public Sector Reforms and Disinvestment. The public sector has failed to generate sufficient internal resources for its further expansion and, as a result, has now become a major constraint on economic growth. Under structural reforms the government has decided to give greater managerial autonomy to public enterprises to enable them to work efficiently. In addition to this, two other key elements of the government's strategy for public enterprises reforms are the promotion of increased private sector competition in areas where social considerations are not paramount and partial disinvestment of equity in selected enterprises. The government has taken concrete steps for encouraging private entry into sectors previously dominated by the public sector. Disinvestment in the form of transfer of a part of the ownership of State owned enterprises to the public is another form of privatisation undertaken by the government.

It is often argued that there are strong reasons for disinvestment in public sector undertakings. R.K. Mishra *et al* point out that disinvestment of shareholdings enables public sector undertakings in acquiring their corporate identity whereby they can "keep pace with the market dynamism flowing from quick business reflexex resulting from their being distanced away from the government." Further, disinvestment permits public enterprises to develop their own financing plans reducing thereby their dependence on the government. In any case, the government has undertaken disinvestment of shareholdings on a modest scale during the past seven years.

4. Financial Sector Reforms. The government, set up a Committee on Financial System (CFS) under the chairmanship of M.

Narasimham, to examine the country's financial system and its various components and to make recommendations in respect of the following:

1. For improving the efficiency and effectiveness of the financial system, with special reference to economy of operations, accountability and profitability.
2. For infusing greater competition into the financial system so as to enable the banks and other financial institutions to respond more effectively to the credit needs of the economy.
3. For ensuring appropriate and effective supervision over the various entities in the financial sector, in particlar the commercial banks and term lending institutions.

The Committee was also required to review the existing legislative framework and to suggest necessary amendments for implementing the recommendations.

The report of the Narasimham Committee on Financial System (submitted in December 1991) has now become the basis for financial sector reforms in this country.

The CFS has among other things, recommended *(a)* establishment of a four tier hierarchy of the banking structure with 3 or 4 large banks including State Bank of India at the top and rural banks at the bottom mainly engaged in financing agriculture and related activities; *(b)* assigning supervisory functions over banks and financial institutions to a separate quasi autonomous body sponsored by the Reserve Bank of India; *(c)* phased achievement of 8 per capital adequacy ratio as recommended by the Basle Committee; *(d)* abolition of branch licencing policy; *(e)* phased reduction in statutory liquidity ratio starting from 1991-92; *(f)* deregulation of interest rates which are related to the bank rate on the basis of guidelines provided by the Chakravarty Committee; *(g)* competition among financial institutions which will adopt a syndicating or participating approach rather than a consortium approach; *(h)* retention by the Industrial Development

Bank of India of only its refinancing role and delegation of its direct lending activity to a separate corporate body; *(i)* prudential guidelines should govern the functioning of financial institutions; *(j)* proper classification of assets and full disclosure and transparency of accounts of banks and other financial institutions; and *(k)* setting up of a separate institution by the Government of India to be known as Asset Reconstruction Fund with the pupose of taking over a portion of the loan portfolio of banks which has become bad and doubtful and whose recovery is not easy due to slow legal process.

The report of the CFS was placed before the Parliament in December 1991, and since then it has become the basis for introducing reform in the banking sector. The major reform measures undertaken during the past few years are as follows:

1. The government has over the past eight years brought down both statutory liquidity ratio and cash reserve ratio in a phased manner. The effective statutory liquidity ratio has been lowered down to 25 per cent. The cash reserve ratio which is the only effective instrument of monetary control in India is being no longer depended upon to combat inflation. It has thus been brought down to 10 per cent.

2. The earlier formats of the balance sheet and profit and loss account did not reflect the true financial position of the banks. Hence, they have been revised and made effective from the bank accounting year 1991-92.

3. The RBI has introduced new prudential norms in respect of income recognition, classification of assets, provisioning of bad debts and capital adequacy. The minimum capital standards have been prescribed in accordance with the Basle Committee norms under which banks are required to maintain unimpaired capital funds equivalent to 8 per cent of the aggregated of the risk weighted assets.

4. Commercial banks attaining capital adequacy norms and prudential accounting standards have been given freedom to set up new branches without the approval of the Reserve

Bank of India. Banks can now also rationalise their existing branch network by relocating branches, opening of specialised branches, setting up controlling offices etc.

5. The Central Government provided budgetary support of Rs. 17,346 crore for recapitalisation of public sector banks till 1996-97. This, however, was not sufficient for achievement of norms by all banks. Hence banks had to raise had to raise debt and equity resources from the public. By the end of March 1997, only two public sector banks could not achieve the prescribed 8 per cent capital to risk weighted assets ratio.

6. The RBI has announced guidelines for setting up banks in the private sector. These banks should be financially viable and should avoid concentration of credit and crossholdings with industrial groups. Further, they will have to observe priority sector lending targets as applicable to other banks. Ten banks have already started functioning and, "in principle approvals" have also been given to three other proposals for setting up new local area private sector banks one each in Andhra Pradesh, Karnataka and Maharastra.

7. Number of interest rates slabs on banks advances were reduced from about 20 in 1989-90 to 2 in the financial year 1994-95. This attempt to unify interest rate structure aims at reducing the degree of cross-subsidy in the banking system.

8. The supervisory system of the RBI is being strengthened with the establishment of a new Board for Financial Supervision under the chairmanship of Deputy Governor of the RBI. The Board will ensure implementation of the regulations with respect to credit management, asset classification, income recognition, provisioning, capital adequacy and treasury operations.

9. Agreements between the RBI and public sector banks have been made to improve the management and the quality of

the performance of the latter. This includes management information system and the internal audit and control mechanisms.

10. Recovery of debts due to banks and other financial institutions in the past has been unsatisfactory. Hence, an Act was passed in 1993 under which Special Recovery Tribunals have been set up to facilitate quicker recover of loan arrears.

11. The guidelines for determning the maximum permissible bank finance have been made more flexible. Banks will now have greater freedom in determining the working capital needs of the borrowers and responding to local requirements in an appropriate manner.

Following the recommendations of the Narasimhan Committee on Financial System (CFS) the above reform measures were undertaken. The government appointed the Committee on Banking Sector Reforms (CBSR) under the chairmanship of M. Narasimham. The Committee (CBSR) submitted its report in April 1998. Its major recommendations are as follows:

1. Strong banks should be merged and relatively weak and unviable ones should be closed.
2. The Committee recommended new and higher norms for capital adequacy. It suggested that the minimum capital to risk assets ratio be increased to 10 per cent from its earlier level of 8 per cent.
3. Legal framework is not adeqaute for credit recovery. It should be strengthened.
4. The country should have two or three banks with international orientation, eight to ten national banks and a large number of local banks. The third-tier banks should remain confined to smaller geographical regions.

The first and the second tier banks shall take care of the needs of the corporate sector.

5. There should be rationalisation of branches and staff.

6. Bank board should be depoliticised under the RBI supervision.

7. Budgetary support for recapitalisation is not viable and should thus be abandoned.

8. Net non-performing assets for all banks be brought down to below 5 per cent by the year 2000 and to 3 per cent by 2002.

9. The polcy of licensing new private banks may be continued.

10. Foreign banks may be allowed to set up subsidiaries or joint ventures in India. Such subsidiaries or joint ventures should be treated on par with other private baks and subject to the same conditions with regard to branches and directed credit as these banks.

11. There has to be an integrated system of regulation and supervision to regulate and supervise the activities of banks, financial institutions and non-bank finance companies. The agency for this purpose be renamed as the Board for Financial Regulation and Supervision (BFRS).

AN APPRAISAL OF ECONOMIC REFORMS

Since July 1991 the government has undertaken both stabilisation programmes and structural reforms as two components of the economic reforms package.

In the real sectors, the structural reforms have started showing some results. In 1991-92 there was near stagnation. However, during the period of the Eighth Plan, the industrial production rose at the rate of 8.4 per cent per annum. Since 1990-91 there was a steep fall in both savings and investment rates for three years. However, both savings and investment rates showed an upturn in 1994-95 which could not be sustained in later years. These gains from structural reforms notwithstanding, the economic reforms have been subjected to various criticism which are following:

1. Absence of a Broader Development Strategy. The focus of both macroeconomic stabilisation and structural reforms is to create a competitive environment in industry in which entrepreneurial decision-making will depend entirely on the market forces. The government's new industrial policy therefore lacks a well defined strategy. The case of industrialisation in South Korea is quite revealing. The government in this country steadfastly pursued a policy of heavy and chemical industrialisation despite the still opposition from the IMF and the World Bank. Judged against the experiences of these countries, the interventionist strategy of the government in this country can be criticised only for lack of dynamism. On the basis of our experience in the past it is patently wrong to conclude that a well articulated industrial strategy and heavy State intervention have no positive role to play in accelerating industrial growth.

2. Hasty Pace of Reforms. The rapid pace of reforms has been determined by the controversial goal to globalise the Indian economy quickly. This has led to rapid deterioration in the quality of industrial structure. *EPW* Research Foundation points out, "A sharp reduction in industrial growth, reduction in the growth of capital goods' industries, a relative shift of exports away from manufactures, and arresting of the growth of industrial employment, have been some of the glaring effects of rapid reforms without providing for some breathing time and appropriate checks and balances for the Indian industry."

3. Wrong Sequencing of Reforms. As a result of wrong sequencing of reforms, serious distortions have surfaced in economic management. There are at least three examples of wrong sequencing of reforms. First, while for drastic reduction in fiscal deficit, revenue deficit and even budget deficit the prerequisites are decisive reduction of non-development expenditure and widening the tax base, the government has initiated fiscal correction programme with surrendering of revenue through substantial reductions in tax rates and compression of capital expenditure. Second, a more obvious case of inappropriate sequencing relates to compression of government's capital expenditure and contraction of public investment before ensuring that the private sector and the foreign investors will fill the gap. The third case of flawed sequencing is of liberalising imports of capital goods before adopting a strategy for technology advancement of the domestic capital goods sector. The latter was necessary for adopting outward oriented stratgy of economic growth.

4. Absence of Human Development Goals as an Integral Part of the Strategy. The stabilisation and structural reform programme in India is implemented against a background of incomplete structural transformation, widespread poverty, low level of human development and distorted pattern of expenditure on health and education oriented towards the relatively well off sections of the society. Given these dismal conditions and a low rate of economic growth, structural reforms must be undertaken with a human face. This requires that human development goals should be an integral part of the strategy of structual adjustment. Unfortunately in India no such attempt has been made.

5. Prerequisites of Reforms Ignored. The literature on stabilisation and structural reforms is full of evidence that the shocks of these policies are better absorbed and their consequences for the well-being of the masses are very much reduced if the society has already reached a certain minimal level of human development. South Korea, Malaysia, Thailand and Indonesia are the recent successful cases but in all these countries not only the socio-economic structure was far more egalitarian due to land reforms and such other measures but the human development indices like expectancy and literacy rates were at higher levels, while infant mortality was at a lower level before they embarked on significant structural reform programme. In contrast, the Indian situation is not at all encouraging from the point of view of human development and socio-economic structures.

Because of these reasons the economic reforms lack sustainbility led to low growth rate and recession in the economy.

ECONOMIC CRISIS : CONTEXT OF REFORMS

Indian economy faced a major economic crisis in 1990 which is known as macro economic imbalances. To start with, the Gulf war led to a sharp increase in oil prices. Foreign exchange reserves began to decline since September 1990; it declined from Rs. 5480 crore (31 Aug., 90) to R. 1,666 crore (10th Jan., 1991). During this period our Government took recources to the IMF for Credit Tranche (CT) Arrangement and also Compensatory and Contingency Financing Facility (CCFF). But the decline in foreign exchange reserves continued unabated.

The payments crisis (1990-91) was due not only to a decline in trade account, it was accompanied by other adverse developments on the capital account reflecting the loss of confidence in the Government's ability to manage the economic environment. Short-term credits began to dry up, as India's credit-rating started deteriorating to a low level. This imposed a severe strain on our balance of payments position. The drying up of commercial loans in 1990-91 was accompanied by a net ouflow of NRI deposits at the monthly average rate of $ 190 million during April-October 1991. The then payments crisis had become overwhelmingly a crisis of confidence of confidence in the Government's ability to manage the situation. A default on payments had become a serious possibility in June 1991, and this was for the first time in our history.

A default is essentially a failure to repay debt. Our public debt, both internal and external, had assumed such a massive proportion by then that it was but natural for everyone to think that Indian economy would collapse *under debt service burden*. This confidence reaction led to a breakdown in credit availability and in normal payments arrangements. Suppliers became reluctant to sell goods and services and insisted on advance payments through banks of their own country. This led to *trade disruption*, which in turn forced severe and prolonged import compression, and resulted in shortage, *industrial dislocation, severe/unemployment and higher inflation*-a series of crises in the Indian economy.

The new Government which assumed office in June 1991 had to act swiftly to deal with that deteriorating economic environment and bring our economy back from the brink of default. Therefore, an emergency action was taken in organising the *sale of gold* by our Government. The Government immediately leased 20 tonnes of gold out of its stock to the State Bank of India to enable it to sell gold abroad with an option to repurchase it at the end of six months. In addition, the Government allowed the Reserve Bank of India to ship 47 tonnes of gold to the Bank of England in July 1991 when the exchange rate of the rupee was also adjusted to bring it to a creditable level which could be defended. A massive *devaluation* of the rupee in successive bouts by a sum-total of about 20% against major currencies was aimed at improving the trade-and payments situation. It was expected that devaluation would make our exports cheaper and imports dearer, and thereby reverse the trend of growing trade deficits.

In the wake, of devaluatution, came the inflation. An *inflationary spriral* began in October 1990. The wholesale price index, on a point-to-point basis, showed a rapid increase in our annual inflation rate from 70% to about 17% during, October and August 1991. A number of demand-pull and cost-push factors together with a set of long-run structural factors and short-run shock factors-all factors together triggered the then inflation rate. The rate and structure of inflation adversely affected the terms of trade between agriculture and industry. In particular, the then prevailing inflation brought out clearly the damage done by fiscal imbalances.

Fiscal imbalances were reflected in growing budget deficits mainly because of escalating non-Plan expenditure in the face of sluggish revenue growth. Increasing budget deficit on the revenue account indicated danger signal. In fact, budget deficits, trade deficits and payments deficits-all became organisationaly linked to damage the state of our national economic. As the deficits in the budget were financed by money creation, the demand-pull inflation got engineered.

And some of the cost-push factors like hike in administered price, poor performance of public sector, alarming size of subsidy got together to throw our fiscal economy totally out of gear.

It was evident that the Indian economy needed substantial reform if those crises were to be fully overcome. The new Government moved urgently to implement a programme of *macro-economic stabilization* through a number of structural reforms of trade, industry and public sector. The objective was to initiate a series of fiscal and financial reforms to ensure both efficiency and equity norms in managing our economy. Structural reforms were necessary to reverse various unhealthy economic trends and tendencies. Without engineering, initiating and then accelerating the pace of such reforms, our economy could not have been brought back on the rail and thereby signalled its engine-of-growth which came to a temporary halt, to proceed further and forward.

The major economic reforms undertaken are the following:

1. **Fiscal Policy Reforms.** When the volume of fiscal deficits assumed a huge proportion of Rs. 43,331 cr. in 1990-91, it was decided to bring down the fiscal deficits from 8.4% of the GDP in 1990-91 to 6.5% in 1991-92 and further to 5% in 1992-93. To this end, a number of tax reforms were introduced in the Budget Proposals since 1991-92 in line with the Chelliah Committee Report. Also, some improvements in fiscal performance were made possible by the decision to abolish export subsidies of CCS, to increase fertilizer prices and to keep non-Plan expenditures (including defence expenditure) in check.

2. **Trade Policy Reforms.** New initiatives were taken in trade policy to create an environment to seize the opportunities of globalisation. Devaluation of our currency facilitated 18% exchange rate adjustment towards promoting exports and restricting imports. A few other measures were taken in 1991-92: import entitlement (introduction of Eximscrips), advance licensing system for exports, permission to import

capital goods. Export and Trading Houses, 51% foreign equity in Trading Houses. Subsequently by way of new EXIM policy, a few more progressive steps have been taken, such as abolition of Eximscrips, partial and finally full convertibility of the rupee, abolition of foreign exchange travel tax, introduction of liberalised exchange rate management system (LERMS), pruning of negative list of imports etc.

3. **Industrial Policy Reforms.** Industrial policy reforms announced in July 1991 should be seen complementary to those undertaken in trade, financial and fiscal policies. The central elements of these reforms were: abolition of industrial licensing for all but 18 industries amendment of MRTP Act defining the asset limit to allow Indian firms to grow in size to compete globally, discontinuance of the phased manufacturing programme (PMP), privatisation except for 8 industries of strategic and security concerns, reservation of items for small units, public sector disinvestment, new guidelines for joint venutres, amendement of FERA to facilitates the inflow of foreign capital, foreign technology and foreign enterprises; enhancement of the limit of foreign equity holding to 51% and more; deregulation, open sky policy, liberalised industrial location and mineral policy, dispersion of industries, decentralisation, debureacratisation etc. These measures have been instrumental in assisting the trend towards economic liberalism and market-friendly approach.

4. **Public Sector Reforms.** The performance of public sector units deteriorated so sharp in 1990-91 that is was immediately felt that these units must work towards improvement in its profitability and productivity. These units must earn an adequate return on its own investment. The Public sector has become a public burden, they are to be subsidized such that they yield a higher net social return than before. The Government undertook a limited public disinvestment of a

part of public sector equity to the public through public financial institutions and mutual funds in order to raise non-inflationary finance for development. It is argued that such policies of disinvestment will bring in greater public accountability. The Government specially amended the Sick Industrial Companies Act, in view of growing sickness and took ameliorative measures like BIFR. A National Renewal Fund has been set up to facilitate modernisation of industry and to provide a safety net to its workers. Our Government is also involved in the process of finalising a draft on the exit policy. All these measure taken together are expected to tone up the level of operational efficiency of our public enterprises.

5. **Financial Reforms.** The operation of both banking and non-banking sector has come in for criticism time and again since the days of nationalisation of banks. From time to time, a number of Committees have been set up, and some of their recommendations have also been accepted. Of late attention has been drawn towards specific structural reforms of the financial sectors. For example, Late Prof. Sukhomoy Chakravarty, while commenting on the need for monetary reforms obseved that the RBI "has tremendous responsibility but not enough authority", as a result of which the non-banking organised sector as well as unorganised sector often remain outside the effective control of the RBI and, therefore, the instruments of monetary policy fail to perform their functions. Also, the Report of Narasimham Committee (1991 Dec.) has been considered. The Government initiated a set of measures, in line with the theme of liberalisation, to introduce structural reforms in the financial sector. It has been accepted that the financial markets should work on laissez faire principles applicable within a regulatory framework. The office of Controller of Capital Isses has been abolished. Among other measures introduced in 1991-92, we may note:

(a) enhancement of bank rate from 10% to 12%;

(b) additional CRR of 10% on incremental deposits of the scheduled commercial banks;

(c) withdrawal of finance facility;

(d) ceilings imposed on drawing power of big borrowers;

(e) easier terms for export credit,

(f) liberalised guidelines for commercial paper (CP) and certificates of deposits (CD);

(g) concessional housing loans etc. Also, a number of institutional developments has been ushered in the establishment of National Housing Bank (NH B), Money Market Mutual Funds (MMMFs), Discount & Finance House of India (DFHI), Credit Rationing Information Services in India Ltd. (CRISIL), Security & Exchange Board of India (SEBI).

Despite all these development in the capital market and the money market, the recent *security scam* has brought the banking and financial reforms to a grinding halt. The extent of corruption and incompetence right acros the financial sector has come as a shock. The Government has now enacted special legislation and has brought in the CBI to prosecute the guilty. The Joint Parliamentary Committee (JPC) is also on the job. Legal process will take its own time, but the agenda of financial reforms should not be suspended.

The critics have stated that the security scam, on the whole, is a price that the economy must pay for hectic liberalisation. It is the process of uncontrolled liberalisation, without any checks and balances, that allowed the scam to happen. This does not mean that the economic reforms must stop; rather, based on the lesson we have learnt, the reforms must continue within the framework of care and caution, rules and regulations. Economic reforms do stand at a critical stage now.

The Government is currently reviewing the pre-and post-reforms gains and pains so as to work out future strategy with regard to the size, structure and speed of these reforms. There is no two opinions that the reforms must continue, that the recommendations of various committees must be re-examined and adopted with or without modifications, wherever desirable and feasible. To understand the future course of economic reforms, a reference to the Reports of several Committees which stand as solid background, is, therefore, in order.

Consequences of Economic Reforms

The consequences of economic reforms can be of two types, short range and long range. The short term purpose of economic reforms was to set the economy at the right track. This objective has been achieved at a great extent. The foreign exchange reserves have increased manifold, the deficit in balance of payment has brought down to the lower level, foreign investment is picking up and moreover the reforms have increased the confidence of domestic, non-resident India and foreign investors. The short run impact of economic reforms is excellent.

The long run impact of these economic reforms is to increase the pace of development so that social welfare can be increase and India can be placed in the category of developed nations. Due to the scarcity of capital and non-availability of superior known how, the rate of growth has been quite low during the four decade of planned development. Indian has a big potential market. Natural resources, skill labourers and other key inputs are also available in plenty. By bringing foreign capital and techinical known how in India, growth rate can be increased. The economic reforms undertaken recently by government will encourage the growth rate in long run.

❐

13

Socio-Cultural Environment

CONCEPT OF BUSINESS

The term business is used in different senses. In a functional sense, it is used to refer to the functions or activities of an organisation or individual. Sometimes it is used to refer to the enterprise or units rendering the business. Traditionally, the term business commonly refers to commercial activities aimed at making a profit or to organisations formed to make a profit. Indeed, in the past economic theory made a fundamental assumption that profit maximisation was the basic objective of every firm. The modern outlook, however, is different. For many organisations, profit maximisation in the short run is not the primary objective. For them, profit is only secondary. There are, moreover, many organisation, both private and public, which do not aim at profit from their business.

The old concepts of business, confining it to commerce and private profit, has undergone a radical change. Today, business is regarded as a social institution forming an integral part of the social system. As Davis and Blomstorm observe, business is "a social institution, performing a social mission and having a broad influence on the way people live and work together."

Thus, "viewed in a broad way, the term business typically refers to the development and processing of economic values in society. Normally, we used the term to apply to the private (non-government) portion of the economy whose primary purpose is to provide goods and services to customers at a price, but the lines of distinction are getting hazy as business and government overlap their functions in organisation such as the Communications, Satellite Corporation and the Tennessee Valley Authority. In addition, business is a term applied to economic and commercial activities of institutions having other purposes, such as the business office of an opera association."

The modern concept of business is thus, a very broad one. Business is viewed as a subsystem of the total social system. According to Davis and Blomstorm, "our modern view of society is an ecological one. Ecology is concerned with the mutual relations of human populations or systems with their environment. It is necessary to take this board view because the influence and involvement of business are extensive. Business cannot isolate itself from the rest of society. Today the whole society is a business' environment."

According to modern thinking, business is an integral part of the social system. It is a social organ to help accomplish the social goals. Its activities and attitudes are therefore, subject to public judgement, which may have far reaching implications. A business enterprise shall make profit only by accomplishing the socially accepted goals and by satisfying society.

CONCEPT OF CULTURE

There are very varying definitions of culture, "Culture in its broadest definition, refers to that part of total repertoire of human action which is socically as opposed to genetially transmitted." A very popular definitions is that of E.B. Tylor, "Culture or civilization is that complex whole which includes knowledge, belief, art, morals, law, customs and other capabilities and habits acquired by man as a member of society."

On the basis of various definition of culture, Francis Merill formulates the concept of culture as follows : culture he says:

(a) is the characteristically human product of soical interaction.

(b) provides socially acceptable patterns for meeting biological and social needs;

(c) is meaningful to human beings because of its symbolic quality;

(d) is learned by each person in the course of his development in a particular society;

(e) is cumulative, for it is handed down from generation to generation in a given society;

(f) is, therefore, a basic determinant of personality; and

(g) depends for its existence upon the continued functioning of society but is independent of any individual or group.

Culture consists of both material culture and non-material culture. Material culture involves man-made things (*e.g.*, automobiles, television, telephone, etc.) and man-made alterations in the environment. Non-material culture includes such factors as language, ideals, beliefs, values, music etc.

ELEMENTS OF CULTURE

Culture, the sum total of social behaviour, includes at least three elements, namely knowledge and beliefs, ideas and preferences.

Ideals. Ideals refer to the societal norms which define what is expected, customary, right or proper in a given situation. Norms are enforced by sanctions, *i.e.*, by rewarding the right behaviour and punishing the wrong behaviour.

Folkways and mores are important aspects of every culture. Folkways are norms of proper behaviour (like the proper way to greet a friend) that are informally enforced. But mores are norms of obligatory behaviour considered vital to the welfare of the group.

Knowledge and Beliefs. The knowledge and beliefs refere to a people's prevailing notions of reality. They include myths and metaphysical beliefs as well as scientific realities. As Rose remarks : "One of the features of culture in general that is of special sociological interest is the shared quality of a belief system. People who share a given culture tend to take a hostile attitude towards those within their midst who cannot, or will not, accept conventional definitions of fact."

Preferences. Preferenes refer to society's definition of those things in life which are attractive or unattractive as objects of desire. Preferences may differ between cultures. Interestingly enough, the judgement of the ideal or the proper do not always correspond to our judgements of the pleasant or enjoyable. An example in point is the temptations (not proper but desirable). All the things I really like to do are immoral, illegal, or fattening," said Alexander Woolcott.

Cultural characteristics are very important in the formulation of pragmatic business strategies. The cost of ignoring customs, traditions, taboos, tastes and preferences, etc., can be very high. For example, in Italy, a US company that set up a corn-processing of corn as "pig food". Similarly, Compbell Soup tried to sell its US tomato formulation to the British; but it discovered, after considerable losses, that the English prefer a more bitter taste. Is it, than, any wonder that the Nestle company should brew more than 40 varieties of instant coffee to satisfy different national tastes? The culture therefore helps in deciding about preferences.

ORGANISATION OF CULTURE

The term organisation of culture refers to the social structure and the integration of traits, complexes and patterns that make up the cultural system. That cultures are organised or integrated "does not mean that every single item of each culture is neatly and precisely integrated with everything else. It means rather that it is normal for the parts to be somewhat organised, and that culture traits receive their significance and meaning out of their relation to the rest of the culture."

The social structure—"the web of organised relationship among individuals and groups that defines their mutual rights and liabilities"—together with traits, complexes and patterns, reflects the organisation of a culture.

The economic system; the political administrative system; the educational system; religion; family; expressionistic, aesthetic and recreational institutions, etc. Such institutions have been established to meet society's common needs of a biological, sociological, psychological, economic, and political nature-the type and nature of institutions reflect the common goals, aspirations and the ways of achieving them, definition and regulation of roles, positions, inter-relationships, etc., of the individuals and sub-groups and groups and the overall organisation of the culture. Culture traits, complexes and patterns also help us to understand the organisation of a culture. A trait is a unit of observation.

Sometimes it is necessary to know the process and nature of the cultural environment for a successful formulation of business strategies. For example, while introducing new ideas, techniques, products; while segmenting the market; while formulating the product and promotion mix strategies; one should consider the extent to which different categories of consumers adapt to the new things or environment and the factors favouring and disfavouring adaptations (and also the general attitude of society to the new ideas and environment and their impact on different categories of consumers).

Transmission of Culture

A very important character of culture is its transmissive quality. The elements of culture are transmitted among the members of the culture, from one generation to the next and to the new members admitted into the culture. Some of the aspects of a culture may be transmitted to other cultures also. The transmissive quality of cultures makes its cumulative. Every generation inherits a stock of cultural elements, many of which have been accumulated over a long period of time. As time goes on, cultures accumulate more techniques, ideas, products and skills. It is also quite obvious that certain old elements are dropped as new ideas and traits are acquired.

Many cultural behaviours are handed down by one's parents teachers and other elders. The reference groups play an important role in handing down new traits and ideas. Some cultural behaviours are, however, "handed up" to the elders. It is not uncommon to come across elders imitating or adopting some of the new traits of the youngsters who are the trend-setters. Cultural transmission is not only downward and upward; a lot of transmission takes place among contemporaries, too *e.g.*, styles of dress; recreational fads; reading and learning habits; political, social and economic views. These are often transmitted among contemporaries. Cultural transmission, thus, takes place horizontally as well as vertically. One rather learns it. However, as cuber points out, "much of the learning process, both for the teacher and the learner, is quite unconscious, unintentional, or accidental; but it is learning and teaching nevertheless."

Transmission also facilitates cultural diffusion, *i.e.*, the spread of cultural elements from one areas to another. Cultural transmission and diffusion are easy in a culture with high educational levels and a well-organised communication system. An effective communication system and high educational levels facilitate socio-economic change through better cultural transmission and diffusion, for new ideas and innovations are easily and quickly transmitted, diffused and absorbed in such a culture. In the context of the generally low literacy rates in India, the government has realised the importance of the media, such as film, television and radio, in transmitting useful information, such as better agricultural practices and techniques, market information, the concept and importance of family planning, and so on.

Relationship Between Business and Culture. The nature and process of cultural transmission and diffusion in a society is important to business-making. For example, to formulate a promotional policy for a product, a service or an idea, it is important to identify the relevant element of transmission, to evaluate the relative effectiveness of alternative communication media, to identify the reference groups and the extent of their influence, to identify the channel of influence on the reference groups, and so on. People of different cultures use the same product, the mode of consumption, conditions of use, purpose of use or the perceptions of the product attributes may very so much so that the product attributtes, method of presentation or method of promoting the product may have to be varied to suit the characteristics of different consumers. An example of Vicks Vaporub, the popular pain balm, is used as a mosquito repellant in some parts of the world.

SOCIAL STRUCTURE

The social structure of Indian society is characterised by diversities but unity. India has been a country where numerous groups migrated from Asia and Europe during different time in past. But over the centuries, the culture of each groups had undergone enough changes and become the part of Indian society and culture.

The population of India is racially diverse, containing elements from six main racial types—the Negrito, the Proto-Australoid, the Mongoloid, the Mediterranean, the Western Brachycephals and the Nordic. The population of India is not only divided racially, the study of Indian society will prove that it is divided both horizontially and vertically. The caste system in Indian society is an important institution which constituted different layers of the society. Linguistically too Indian society is divided in many groups. Diversity is also seen in the patterns of rural as well urban settlements, community life, forms of land tenure and agricultural operations. All the great religions of the world are represented in this country. In kinship, marriage rites and customs, inheritance, and the general mode of living, there are striking differences between groups. Moreover, except the urban and rural population, there are many tribal groups, with different religions and rituals. Thus the study of Indian society, at a first glance, shows the mutual differences among different groups. Therefore, a thorough study is required to understand the binding forces in society and their origin.

India is a geo-political entity under one constitution. In fact the British rule of India helped it in beoming a single political entity in modern times. After independence, the Indian Government tried to maintain the unity and enforced a common law. Constitutional supremacy was established. India was declared a secular state. The Process of economic development ushered in by the Five Years Plans and the spread of egalitarian ideals have brought about, revolutionary changes in the Indian pattern of social life. Now we will discuss role of caste, kinship and religion in Indian society

Caste System. The first literary traces of caste system are to be found in Rig Veda. The Purusasukta hymn speaks of four classes—Brahmana. Rajanya, Vaisya and Sudra. These are referred as Chaturvarna. In the earlier literature Verna was applied to differentiate between Arya and Dasa—fair and dark respectively only. Later it developed in three and then in four varnas. The occupations of the first two varnas—Brahmana and Rajanya or Kshatriya are clearly stated to be priesthood and administrative and military duties respectively. But the duties of the Vaisya an Sudra are not very clear. The village headman was usually a Vaisya and Sudras were servants.

The post-vedic period sow the growth and consolidation of the power of Brahmins. This defined the duties and rights of each caste and its place in the hierarchy. In the Bhagavad Gita for instance, the caste system is sought to be justified on the basis of the ideas of Guba, Karma, and Dharma. Thus the institution of caste has existed in India for thousands of years. The essence of caste is the arrangement of hereditary groups in hierarchy. Brahmins are at the top and Harijans are at the bottom of the hierarchy.

In the Indian society caste system prevails not only among Hindus but also among Muslims, Sikhs and Christains, though all these religions preach equality of all. In Utter Pradesh, Muslims, who have a tradition of foreign ancestry (Iran, Arbia) are called Shurafa or Ashaf and are considered to be the highest. After them come converts from high caste Hindus and at the bottom are occupational castes such as weaver, Barber, Potter etc.

Among the Sikhs, there are broadly two groups—Sardara and Mazhabis, the former consisting of high castes and the latter of Sweepers. Sansi (Shepherd) converts to Sikhism rank even lower than Mazhabis.

Jews and Christians are not exception to this caste division. The Beni-Israel Jews, found principally in Bombay and considered higher in rank. They are divided into groups Gora and Kala. Gora are in higher rank than Kala. Caste division occur among Indian Christians—both Catholic and Protestant. The Syrian Christians of Kerala, the earliest converts of Christianity in India claim to have been recruited from Nambudri Brahmins and Nayars, hence they think themselves higher in the rank. Caste restrictions are rigidly observed among the Christians of the West Coast. A Catholic Brahmin from Maharashtra would marry only a Catholic Brahmin.

The caste conflict in Indian society is very common. It had given birth to the concept of untouchability. The higher caste groups refused to accept cooked food and water from the lower castes. Inter caste marriages were also forbidden and punishable. The Brahminical writers continued their attempts to systemize and codify inter-caste relations in among Hindus.

The hereditary association of a caste with an occupation was a striking characteristic of Indian society till recent past. The cast was associated with an occupation and had a limited kind of monopoly over it. Generally the Kumhars were potters and Nais were barbers. But most castes also practised agriculture in the monsoon months in addition to their traditional occupation. Often the artisan and servicing castes had not an adequate income from their traditional occupations and they therefore work on land either as tenants or as casual labourers. Indeed, in the context of growing population and changes in tools and apparatus, the occupation aspect of the caste system have broken down.

In the Hindu society, occupations are classified into high and low, those practised by the high castes being regarded as high Manual labour is looked upon as low, and certain occupations like Swine-herding and butchery are considered to be polluting.

Among Muslims, only artisans castes such as the Teli, Darzi and Julaha are associated with traditional occupations. Priests tend to come more from the Syed and Shaikh castes. Among Sikhs, the traditional occupation is often practised along with agriculture. Jats were generally landowners, while the Mazhabis were agriculture labourers.

An individual in a caste society lives in a hierarchical world. It is not only the people, who are divided into higher and lower groups, but even the food, dress and ornaments, customs and manners are also divided. Elaborate rules govern the acceptance of cooked food and water from another caste. Pakka food, cooked with Ghee, butter may be accepted from the inferior castes, but not Kaccha food, which is cooked with water. It may be accepted normally only from equivalent or superior castes. In North India, hukka smoking offers an index of caste-status. Castes which may share, on occasions, a single hukka are equals.

The culture of each caste is to some extent peculiar to itself. There are differences in dress, speech, manners ritual and ways of life. The lower castes are barred, at least in theory, from taking over the customs and rituals of the higher castes. The concepts of pollution plays a crucial part in maintaining the required distance between different castes. There is a broad line between caste Hindus and Harijans in the matter of pollution. The village barber and washerman do not serve Harijans. They had to take water from a lower end of a river or canal than the high castes and they could not use the caste Hindu well. The breaking of pollution rules resulted in the higher castes becoming "impure", and the latter had to perform certain purificatory rites to regain normal status. Sometimes, the person breaking the rules used to be even thrown out of caste irrevocably.

The idea of pollution is present among the Sikhs, The Mazhabis had a well of their own everywhere. Their wedding parties were not accommodated in gurudwaras as they were regarded as "impure".

In the Indian society, which was very much based on village, the relationship between different caste groups was of a particular form. Most Indian villager do not have more than a few of the essential castes and hence people depend on neighbouring villages for certain services skills and goods. In rural India, with its largely subsistance and not fully monetized economy till recently, the relationship between the difference groups in a village takes a particular form. The essential artisans and service castes are paid annually in grain at harvest. In some parts of India they are provided with fine food, clothing fodder and some times residential site. Primarily and economic or ritual tie has tendency to spread to other fields and become a patron-client relationship. This relationship is generally stable and mostly inherited.

Caste was related to the exercise of differential rights in land. At the top were the castes who were either absentee or non-cultivating owner. Next come the cultivating tenants, and at the bottom of the hierarchy came the landless agriculture, meant that the stratification rase deep. This enabled the landowners to exploit the tenants as much as they could.

Indeed, the caste system in India has such a deep root in the society that it covers all the aspects of social life of an Indian. The Indian Government, after independence has introduced many socio-econmic and cultural reforms to erase the system. Provisions were envisaged in an constitution of India and laws were also made to wipe of out the caste division and its negative affects on the society, but it is still a burning issue. It is to be noted that its intensity is lesser in the urban areas and particularly in the metropolitan cities. But in the rural area, it is still a crucial problem which often disturbs peace and law and order conditions. Inspite of increasing literacy and social consciousness, caste differences and caste-hatred and the major social issues even today.

Kinship. The social institution of marriage ensures the children both of it a recognised and legally sanctioned position in society. A domestic group consisting of a man and his wife and unmarried children is called an elementary or nuclear family. Domestic groups which are bigger than the elementary family, and often include two or more elementary families, are termed joint or extended families. They may be patrilineal as in most parts of India, or matrilineal as among the Nayars of Kerala or the Khasis of Assam. Several joint families descended from the same ancestor and acting together on certain occasions form a lineage.

In several parts of the country people live in lineage groups. The members of the lineage lived under the same roof on in a group of neighbouring houses, held property together and ate together. Such a lineage formed a coparcenary, every member (male in the case of partrilineage and famale in the case of a matrilineage) have a share in the ancestral property. Among the poorer and uneducated folk in rural areas, the residential groups generally tend to be small, being confined to members, of the elementary family and one or two relatives. In this section of the population, the family group holds together during the father's lifetime, partition being usually after his death. Joint family system is mostly in practice among richer. Every joint family has a manager who takes decisions on behalf of all. Every male member has a vested interest in the ancestral property. A joint family splits up into constituent elementary families when partition occurs. Indeed joint and elementary families are parts of a single cyclical process.

The composition of a joint family depends upon the mode of descent and the pattern of residence general to a group. Decent may to partrilineal or matrilineal or cognatic, and residence may be virilocal (staying with husband) or uxorilocal (staying with wife) or neolocal (both moving to a new house). Virilocality is the general rule in India and this is not confined to Hindus only but extends to Muslims, Christians, Sikhs and Jains. The wife joins her husband soon after marriage and the latter generally lives with his own parents and brothers. It is only after, the death of the parents that the brothers separate from each other. Even this may not happen and the brothers may decide to stay together. Among the poorest groups and the lowest castes, the family breaks up soon after parents death. Among the westernized and urban sections, neolocality is most common. But the establishment of a new home does not mean the severance of ties with kin-groups of the husband and wife. Kinship connections are recognised on both the sides and a close relative of either side may live with the couple. In recent years spatial mobality has increased considerably and young men have jobs away from their natal towns. This means, in the urban areas, there are many families which are seemingly elementary.

While the composition of a household is usually determined by the particular principles of descent and the type of post-martial residence obtaining in a caste, the bilateral principal finds greater recognition than is commonly thought. A household may include not only patrilineal relatives such as two full brothers, their wives, their children and unmarried sisters, but also the brother or sister of a wife of one of them. In a matrilineal household, on the other hand, increasing recognition of the bilateral principle may result in the parents of either the husband or wife residing with the couple. Among the urban and educated sections of the population, the household consists of the husband, wife, their children and a relative of the husband or less frequently a relative of the wife. These households are justifiably considered as part of wider kinship groups elsewhere. In metropolitan cities, high rent act as a limiting factor on the size of the household.

In the traditional Hindus joint family the senior male is usually the head of the household. It is his duty to look after the property meet the expenses out of the income of the ancestral estate and clear the debts. The head of the house hold the manager of the joint familycorporation and as such he wielded much power and authority. Mostly power and privilege being concentrated in the hands of elders. The younger members in the family are required to show respect to the elder. Ideally, the children in a joint family are the children of all the male members of two parental generation, and discrimination by a parent in favour of his own children in rejected as reprehensible.

The relation between women members in a joint family in frequently one of conflict. The mother-in-law and daughter-in-law relationship is celebrated in folklone for its intensity of conflict. Relations between a woman and her husband's sisters and between here and her husband's brothers, wives are also conflict-ridden. The relation between a man and his parents-in-law is a formal one.

With the changing socio-economic conditions, the relationship is also changing, large traditions pattern of kin-groups, in rural at any rate had been confined to a few landowning higher castes. The new economic opportunities which came through the link-up the local economy with a much wider one, increased monetization, greater opportunities for trade and increased spatial mobility due to the building of roads and railways led to the emergence of smaller in groups. The present economic conditions and political developments operated against living in big joint families. Spread of education has developed a sense of individuality which is against the norms of joint family system, Residence away from the natal kin-group removed the stresses and strains to day-to-day living, while increased communications kept the links alive.

All Hindus are patrilineal, with the expected of the Nayars and Bants, and other castes on the West Coast and Khasis and Garos of Assam. Muslims, excepting the Moplahs of North Malabar and Christians excepting Khasi converts, are patrilineal. All Jain Buddhist and Sikhs are patrilineal, Among the patrilineal groups some movable property is given to daughters, women did not inherit the immovable property In the matrilineal system of inheritance, a person inherits from his maternal uncle and not from his father. The Hindu succession Act and the Hindu Adoption and Maintenance Act, 1956, has made the husband legally responsible for the maintenance of his wife and children.

All Muslims excepting matrilineal Moplahs, are governed by the Shariat Act of 1937. Under Islamic Law, the mother, wife and daughter are the three famale heirs. The maximum share of the mother is one-third and the minimum one-sixth, depending on the existence or otherwise of other heirs. The share of the wife is one-fourth or one-eighth. The wife is also the owner of the Meher given to her at wedding. She is also entitled to be maintained by her husband, The daughter is a primary heir like the son. Her share fluctuates, depending upon the member of surviving children.

The Hindu succession Act of 1956, governs the inheritance of Hindus, Buddhists, Sikhs and Jains. It applies to both matrilineal as well as patrilieal groups. According to this Act, the property of a Hindu dying in state devolves on his sons, daughters, widow and mother. This Act included mother in the same category of heirs as the widow and children of the deadman. Thus the Act had introduced some changes in the traditional system and gave them legal sanction.

Religion. India has all the important religion of the world—Hinduism, Islam, Christianity, Zionism, Bhuddhism, etc. The census reports have revealed that Hindus are in majority. Among the minority religions groups, a few have fared better in the economic field and specially commerce. Some of the minority religious groups are well educated and well employed such as Christians and Parsis.

We shall now consider the role of religious groups in the social and political structure of India.

(i) Religion and Society. Though villages embracing multi-religious groups are not as common as multi-caste villages, they are not infrequent, such villages are not confined to any one part of India, but are found everywhere. There are villages with Hindu tenants and Muslim land lords and Hindu landlords and Muslim tenants. A few Hindu landowners had Muslim tenants and servants, while Muslim tenants. A few Hindu landowners had Muslim tenants and servants, while Muslim landowner had Hindu servants. The bulk of the Muslims were engaged in a variety of actvities—trading in several articles, including paddy and mangoes, tailoring, carpentary, smithy and butchery. Ownership of land, seemed to prevent a majority of the Hindus from becoming traders. In some regions Hindu and Muslim families are liked together by friendship and patron-client ties, Muslims often provide the goods needed in Hindu festivals. Muslims are invited to Hindu weddings when the members of a religion or sect dominate trade or commerce, the customers are drawn from serval religious groups. At the local level, economic-social ties are mained by different religious groups.

Some religious groups have played an important role in the economic department of the country. The small community of Parsis in Bombay is an example. Jains have also played important role in economic development of Bombay, Gujrat and Rajasthan as they are mostly traders and businessmen. The Syrian Charistians of Kerala played a pioneering role in banking and in growing plantation crops, such as tea, coffee and rubber.

(ii) Religion and Politics. The role played by religion in the political life of the country is similar to that the caste. In the thirties, the Muslim League first began to press its demand for an independent Muslim state to be called Pakistan. This led to the antagonizm between Hindus the Muslims. Even after creation of Pakistan. This led to the antagonizm between Hindus and Muslims. Even after creation of Pakistan, Muslim Leage remain active in Sourth as a political party.

The Akhil Bharat Hindu Mahasabha is another religious party, which aimed at promotion of Hindu Rastra. Vishwa Hindus Parisad and Janasanga were also very much guided by religious motives. Later, Janasangha was renamed as Bhartia Janta Party. This party is today the major opposition party which is guided by staurich Hindu nationalism.

Rastriya Swayam Sevak Sangha (R.S.S.) is another Hindu Organization which though claim to be an organization interested only in reviving Hindu religion and culture, it exhibited a para-military character with uniform, drill and training in the art of self-defence.

Sikh politics is closely connected with the control of the gurudwaras, which are in charge of the Siromani Gurudwara Prabhandhak Committee (S.G.P.C.). The Akali Dal, led by Master Tara Singh was long in control of SGPC. But the party is now divided in factions, and some of them are agitating for a separate Sikh dominated state.

The Christians have not formed any prominent political party. Their role is like caste role in politics. But the Anglo-Indians enjoy some concessions including reservation of seats in Parliament and in some of the states.

From the social viewpoint most of the religious groups belong to the minorities and they create problems in socio-political life of the country. The present environment of the Indian society is very much dominated by the caste and religious differences. It has dominated all the aspects of socio-political life of people. Inspite of the constitutional legal and political efforts of the Indian Government, the caste and religious differences among the Indian citizens could not be sorted out. The Indian Government could not enact any law which effects institutions of Muslims and Christians. Therefore, the difference continued and those were exploited by the politicians for the benefit of their own political organization.

In recent years, this problem has become very intense. The caste conflicts have become very common in rural areas. They control people's socio-political and economic activities particularly in rural areas and small towns. Metropolitan cities are least affected by it. Again, religious difference, has recently became an alarming problems, particularly after the fall of Babri structure in December 1992. Hindu-Muslim amnity has more or less vanished from society. Communal riots has become a common phenomenon in all parts of India.

Caste and religious difference are not the only problems of the society today. The problem of the minority—representation and the benefits granted to them has also became an acute problem to be solved by the authorities. The stratified and multi-religious society is suffering from instability and feeling of insecurity among minorities. All these problems posed a challenge to the government and cause, in turn a political instability within the country.

SOCIAL AND POLITICAL ISSUES

As a political system of a country affects the socio-economic environment of the country, it is also affected by the socio-economic environment of the country. It does not work in isolation, rather there is a causal relationship between the political system and the socio-economic process-each affecting the other and in turn be affected by it.

Usually, the political system and the socio-economic process of a political not only complement and supplement each other; rather they work simultaneously and harmoniously. But in India this did not happened. After the 200 years of colonial rule, dawn of independence in 1947 and sudden introduction of democracy raised peoples' hopes and aspirations from the newly formed political system. Thus, the democratic political system was looked upon the change the static socio-political process in the country and ameliorate the lot of the common man. With no previous experience in the working of democracy in India, the newly imposed democratic set-up was a mixed blessing in dealing with the socio-economic process.

The contemporary social and political Issues Indian Society has been a traditional society—ridden with archaic considerations *e.g.*, caste, community race, language, region and with the deepest stress possible-religion. These characteristic features of the Indian society made specific demands from the new democratic polity and in turn influenced its course in the following years. Also, the policy of new policy vis-a-vis these traditional features was to modify or modernize them and not to completely and these.

1. Casteism. One of the specific feature of the traditional Indian society has been Casteism, which has existed in India for thousands of years. Caste system in Indian politics has come in for severe condemnation only in recent years due to its increasing politicisation and consequent parochial outlook of politics. The modern politics is certainly caste-ridden politics—candidates are chosen on caste considerations, caste issues are fanned to the extent of leading to violent conclusions in the society; the national interests get receded to the background; each political party vies with one another in seeking the reservations of advantages of some castes; political parties are constituted on caste-considerations; and the political patronage in distributed on caste-considerations. There is increasing domination of higher caste on the lower ones. However, the casteism in Indian politics over the years, has been suitably modernised not to stress upon the hereditary factor. The importance of a man in the new set-up has come in be determined by his socio-economic status and not heredity alone. The introduction of universal adult franchise in India, devoid of its caste, colour and creed nature, has politicised the lower castes and increased their political importance. The lower castes have taken the advantages offered to them in the Indian Constitution for their political, social and economic uplift. Many of them have come to hold important positions in the administrative set-up of the country.

2. Communalism. Another important feature of the traditional Indian society is its multi-religious character with due place to each religious community. The religions in India have generally not worked at cross-purposes and hence the multiplicity of religions has not posed a serious problem in the smooth functioning of the Indian polity. Religions, have generally taught us to be tolerant towards one another. But conditions have particularly changed in 1990s, when the religion became the tool of power-Carving by the political parties. One needs to distinguish between religion and communalism; while religion binds the people communalism is divisive in character. The problem of communalism was in fact the legacy of the British colonial rule which fanned antagonism between various religious communities in order to reap political advantages for itself. The problem of communalism whether in colonial days or in free India has assumed proportions only when the political power has tended to use religions for sectarian political interests. Thus, it is not religious but the political use of the religions which needs to be decried and condemned.

Political parties such as Hindus Mahasabha, Muslim League, Jamait-e-Islami, Akali Dal and Vishwa Hindu Parisad etc. have come to be formed on religious basis to work and fight for narrow religious demands. These religious groups and leaders have at times tasted the fruit of political power and hence when out of it, they fail to reconcile with the situation and adopt the extra-constitutional methods to acquire power. It would however be wrong to blame these religious groups alone since many national parties, at times, have joined hands with these religious groups of remain in political power. This unholy alliance of religion with politics, has created distortions in the polity.

The problem of communalism, a serious canker eating into the vitals of India; can only be solved when the national political parties rise above their parochial vote-catching devices and are able to see directly into the fact of the communal monster with a purpose to quell its head.

3. Language Problem. India is a unique polity with people of difference languages inhabitating it. Besides 15 fully developed languages found in the Eighth Schedule, there are various dialects being spoken in the country. Also, English has continued to enjoy a special status in the country. After independence, since the ruling class was deeply entrenched in English should remain the official language alongwith Hindi. This posed many problems. It led to the rivalry between Hindi and English—It led to antagonism between the advocates of two different education-systems owing to increasing disparties. Also, the antagonism between Hindi and the other Indian languages grew. Many states in the southern part of India were against what they called the imposition of Hindi. The language problem has acquired new dimensions with the state reorganisation having been accepted on lingual basis with the creation of Andhra Pradesh in 1953, Gujarat and Maharashtra carved out of the erstwhile Bombay state in 1960, and Haryana in 1966 etc. The language-based organisation of the states has also led to many secessionist movements in the country thus complicating the problem.

4. Illiteracy. Another important feature of Indian social system has been widespread illiteracy in the country. Despite government effects, the situation has remained stagnant over the years. A large part of the male and female population of rural India still remains illiterate. Despite provisions in Part IV of the Constitution *viz.* Directive Principles of State Policy, the free and compulsory education for children upto the age of 14 to a far cry. Thre is a constant problem of dropouts from the schools are the primary level. There are no equal opportunities for seeking education due to sharp class-differences in the country. Hence, there is a lop-sided development of education in the country. Only a few convent educated elites rule over the multitudes of people who could not afford public school education due to economic constraints.

The Government has taken up major steps recently and helping economically the adult education centres. The literacy drive of the Government and the Non-Government Organisation (NGOs) is gradually helping the people at least be become literate.

5. Economic Disparity and Poverty. In additional to socio-cultural problems of the Indian society, one cannot affort to ignore the appalling economic disparities in the Indian society, largely as the legacy of the colonial rule besides the colonial exploitation, even the policies of the rulers of independent India have not improved conditions considerably for the common man. Poverty even today continues to be an untackled problem despite tall claims by the ruling governments. It has grilled the common man of India over the years and even today almost half of the population in the country lives below the poverty line. Poverty is a universal phenomenon in India—it is present both in the rural and the urban parts of the country; and amongst the educated and the uneducated sections of the Indian population. Even a change in the ideology of the Indian State—from a mixed economy to socialist and then liberalization policy—has no helped in providing benefits to the poorer section of the society. However, on the whole, these economic measures by the Indian State has widened the gulf between the rich and the poor. These policies have led to concentration of wealth in fewer hands. There has been enormous increase in black money in the Indian economy by way of tax-evasion and unlimited appropriation of unaccounted money by some vested interests. There is an unholy alliance between the political and the economic elites-while the economic elites provide tons and tons of black money to the politicians to contest and win elections, the political elites in turn benefit their accomplice, the economic elites, through legislation of class policies. The hold of the economic-elites on the Indian political sytem has increased.

The populist measure of the Indian State cannot really solve the problem. There is need for real commitment on the part of the government and the bureaucracy to really benefit the poor and the downtrodden. There is need to check all kinds of corruption and nepotism including political corruption, to restore the confidence of he common man in the democratic institution.

The poverty in rural parts of Indian society need to be tacked with greater vigour and strength. One finds greater economic disparities and tensions amongst the rural folk. Consequently, the lower castes especially the Harijans are the targets of violent attack by the upper castes and are no better than bonded labourers. The democratic process in the country has increased the political consciousness of the rural masses who no longer feel shy to take recourse to forced violence in a bid to fight their exploitation by the rural haves.

It is not to deny that any social or political change in a polity without corresponding economic change is partial and lopsided. Nehru and the other leaders of independent India were hence keen to seek the corresponding economic freedom—freedom from want—through constitutional means, using the Constitution of India as an instrument of economic change besides social and political upliftment. It was with this aim in view that the policy of Mixed Economy was announced. The three main planks of the policies of Nehru era were: Democracy, Socialism and Secularism. Socialism was sought to be achieved within democratic framwork. It is not that only democratic socialism of Nehru era failed to benefit the common man, event he subsequent changes in the ideology of the state in the post-Nehru years failed to satisfy the aspersions of the common man.

6. Regionalism. There is growing regionalism in the country. Regionalism is as much an economic problem as social. At the root of the growth of regionalism lies the discriminatory policies of the British colonial rule and also of the rulers of new independent India. Consequently, some regions have enormously developed as compared to some others, due to the political patronage of the new set of rulers. The economic development of a region has been closely linked with the position of a political leader at the helm of national affairs. Hence, one finds enormous regional disparities even today. The Eastern and the Southern regions in India have remained comparatively less developed than the Western and the Northern regions.

It is not shocking to find the growth of regional parties in these less developed regions. The economic discontent of the people of the region is suitably exploited by these regional parties to capture political power; and once in power these regional parties fan the regional and communal instincts of their people to remain in the saddle of power. These regions generally complain of step-motherly treatment by the Central Government, raise parochial issue *e.g.* language, boundary and water disputes in order to enlarge the gulf with people of the neighbouring states, raise communal and regional issues at the time of elections.

It is undeniable that the Central Government does discriminate between "loyal" and "unloyal" states at the time of distributing the economic resources. The Central Government should become magnanimous in its approach by not economically punishing the non-Congress regional governments; through it alone the evil of regionalism would be checked.

7. Political Unstability and Corruption. Political unstability has become a major issue in Indian policy today. The Government in the Centre is now-a-days, mostly a minority government which is influenced by the many vested interest groups. Therefore, such a government could not take strong decisions and even if the decision are taken, such Government cannot implement those decisions. The frequent change of Government at the centre or the State has created a fluid situation.

The political instability has led to the corruption among the political leader and the bureaucrats. realising their short term in the power, mostly they try to accumulate more and more money and power. Under such a condition, masses also loose the moral strength. All these recent developments are posing new problem to the Indian society and polity.

8. Lack of United and Strong Opposition. In a democratic policy, opposition plays a very important role. It is called a "Shadow Government" as it influences the Governmental policies, and compel them to the moulded according to the need of masses. But since last few year, Indian polity lacked a strong opposition. Opposition is divided in multiple parties with their differences of opinion on different issues.

This is a major political problem for a democratic system. The party in power mostly is benefited due to this characteristics of Indian democracy.

The foregoing discussion would enable to understand the social and political issues in contemporary India. There is an unmistakable relation between the social and political issues and they cannot be separated in water-Light compartments. The nature of the polities is verymuch determined by the policies. The present issues like casteism, communalism, regionalism etc., are the off-springs of political decision, and only a political solution could check increasing intensity of the problems. The populist slogan are not enough to solve the problem.

The policy of the Government is not proving advamtageous to the common people. Consequently, the disgruntled common man at times is forced by the circumstances to keep the democratic means in abeyance and take his battle to the street. Hence, the phenomenon of violence is gaining momentum with the years passing because the common poor is being pushed to the position of his back with the wall. The socio-economic constent of the Indian polity would have to change drastically in favour of the poor if the democratic system in India is to survive. There can be no hope for the survival of Indian polity as a strong and vibrant system if the mass of its population remains alienated with it due to its anti-people policies and practices.

❐

14

Legal Environment

The Government of India uses a number of economic legislation to regulate various aspects of private business. Some 'of the main instruments of economic legislation are Industries (Development and Regulation) Act, the Monopolies and Restrictive Trade Practices (MRTP) Act, the Foreign Exchange Regulation Act (FERA) and the Imports and Exports (Controls). Now we shall discuss a few of them.

1. Industries (Development and Regulation) Act, 1995. To control and regulate the process of industrial development in the country, an Act was passed by the Parliament in October 1951 and came into force on May 8,1952. The objectives of this Act were: *(i)* the regulation of industrial investment and production according to plan priorities and targets; *(ii)* protection of small entrepreneures; *(iii)* prevention of monopoly and concentration of economic power; and *(iv)* balanced regional development.

In the initial stage 37 industries were brought under the purview of the Act which was later extended to include 70 inudstries. The Government made a number of changes in this Act from time to time. An important change came in 1960 when all enterprises with fixed capital of Rs. 10 lakh or less were exempted from licensing produce. The exemption limit was raised to Rs. 25 lakh in 1963 and to Rs. 1 crore in 1970. Later on the limit was raised from Rs. 1 crore to Rs. 3 crore and then to Rs. 5 crore. A major change came in 1988-89. Now there was no need to take licensing for installing a unit involing investment in fixed assets of Rs. 50 crore in backward areas and Rs. 15 crores in non-backward areas. The year 1991 saw a major change in industrial policy which abolished licensing policy for all but 18 industries. With the passage of time, most of these industries have also been delicensed. Licensing is compulsory only in case of 6 industries. These are alcohol, cigarettes, hazardous chemicals, electronics, aerospace and defence equipment, drugs and pharmaceuticals (excepting bulk drug industry which has been delicensed and industrial explosives. In respect of delicensed industry, no approval is required from the government. An Industrial Entrepreneum Momorandum (IEM) to the Secretariat for Industrial Approval (SIA) which acknoweledges receipt. Thus inudstrial licensing has been abolished for all except a few industries.

2. The Monopolies and Restrictive Trade Practices (MRTP) Act. Under the MRTP Act, all firms with assets above Rs. 100 crore since 1985 were classified as MRTP firms. Such firms were permitted to enter selected industries only and this also on a case-by-case approval basis. In addition to control through industrial licencing, separate approvals were required by such large forms for any investment proposals. The government felt that this was having a deleterious effect on many large firms in their plans for growth and diversification. The new industrial policy scrapped the threshold limit of assets in respect of MRTP and dominant undertakings. The MRTP Act has been accordingly amended. The new amended Act gives more emphasis to the prevention and control of monopolistic, restrictive and unfair trade practices so that consumer are adequately protected from such practices.

3. The Foreign Exchange Regulation Act (FERA). FERA was promulgated in 1973 and came into force on Jan 1,1974. According to the Section 29 of this Act, all non-banking foreign branches and subsidiaries with foreign equity exceeding 40 per cent had to obtain permission to establish new undertakings, to purchase shares in existing companies, or to acquire wholly or partly any other company. Guidelines for administering this section of FERA were announced in 1973 and later amended in 1976.

In line with the liberalisation measures, the government announced major concessions to FERA companies in November

1991 and Jan 1992. On Jan 8, 1993, the government promulgated an ordinance to amend FERA with immediate effect. The ordinance removed a large number of restrictions on companies with more than 40 per cent non-resident equity, removed FERA controls on Indian forms setting up joint ventures abroad and allowed Indians to hold immovable property abroad, subject to certain conditions. The removal of restrictions made FERA redundant and FERA companies were at per with Indian companies. The Union Budget, 1998-99 advocated repealing FERA and replacing it with FEMA. The Government adopted FEMA in 1999. Under FEMA, the emphasis is on 'management' rather than 'regulation.'

MRTP ACT

The Monopolies Inquiry commission had submitted its report and recommendations in the form of a draft bill in 1965. With this draft as the basis, the Monopolies and Restrictive Trader Practices Bill was presented to Rajya Sabha in August 1967. It was passed by Parliament in December 1969. The objectives of the legislation are:

(i) to ensure than the functioning of the economic system does not result in concentration of economic power to the common detriment; and

(ii) to control such monopolies and rsestrictive trade practices as are injurious to the public welfare. For counteracting the adverse effects of concentration of economic power, the Act seeks to invest the Central Government with wide powers, *inter alia*, to investigation and control mergers as well as expansion.

A regards monopolies and restrictive trade pratices, the Act seeks to establish a permanent statutory commission to be called as the Monopolies and restrictive trade practices commission. (MRTPC) which will consist of not less than two and not more than nine members including the Chairman. It will perform two main functions; investigation and control of monopolies and all restrictive trade practice. It will also be available for advice on matter relating to concentration of economic power. In relation to monopolistic pratice, the Commission will have only advisory status with no powers of enforcement. In relation to restrictive trade practices its status will be that of judicial court with powers of enforcement. In matters pertaining to concentration of economic power (expansion of existing undertakings, setting up of new undertakings, and mergers), powers of investigation and enforcement shall vest with Government which will decide whether or not to refer a particular case to MRTPC for advice which, again, will not be binding on Government.

The Monopolies and Restrictive Trade Practices Act provides for the appointment of two officials, the Director of Investigation and the Registrar of Restrictive Trade Practices who will assist the Commission in its work. The function of the Director of Investigation is to carry out preliminary investigations into the complaints of restrictive practice with a view to etablishing their veracity and importance. The Registrar will mainly look after the registration of restrictive trade agreements.

On August 2, 1970, Government set up a three-man, Monopolies Commission to prevent concentration of economic power, for the control of monopolies and for prohibiting monopolistic and restrictive trade practices by controlling the activities of dominant or large undertakings as defined under the Act. The Act defines a dominant undertaking as one which, either by itself or along with inter-connected undertakings, controls not less than one-third of items of production, supply or distribution of a commodity or provides or otherwise controls not less than one-third of any services rendered in India. The Act also defines a monopolistic undertaking as any dominant undertaking which by itself, or together with not more than two other independent undertakings, supplies or distributes or otherwise controls not less than one-half of total goods or services.

APPRAISAL OF LEGISLATION

Both within Parliament and outside, the provisions of this 'verbose piece of legislation' have been subject to criticism and doubts have been raised as to whether the Act may not become the fifth wheel of India's industrial cart. We have today a plethora of controls which regulate corporate sector. The number of such controls is almost infinite. They cover evey segment of corporate activity from the very point of conception of a project. The Monopolies and Restrictive Trade Practices Act is the latest in the armoury of the State to regulate the corporate sector. Main criticism against this legislation are discussed below.

1. The serious lacuna in the Act is that it mixes up considerations about concentration of economic power and monopoly. The provisions of the Act dealing with concentration of economic power seek to regulate expansions, mergers, amalgamations and take overs, and appointment of directors in respect of *(a)* dominant undertakings have assets of Rs 1 crore and more; and *(b)* undertakings which by themselves or together with inter-connected undertakings have assets of not less than Rs. 20 crores in value. It also seeks to regulate starting of new undertakings which would become inter-connected undertakings of such existing undertakings, the total assets of which exceed Rs. 20 crores.

The restrictions are merely in the form of securing approval of the Union, Government. In actual practice, the delay they will involve if past experience is any guide, will seriously handicap the growth of the so-called dominant undertakings or industrial groups. This would postpone and delay development and the bais objective of the Act will not be attained.

2. Monopoly in economic terms implies an industrial unit which can so control production in the industry as to restrict competitive forces in the market and have a price structure based on various non-competitive considerations and devices like manipulation of production. In India, there does not seem to be a place for monopoly of this kinds because our industrial development is expected to take palce on planned lines. Merely because some individuals or companies are able to do better than this, there should be no room for us to condemn them as monopolists or monopolies. Already industry has to contend with a variety of controls such as industrial licensing, import control, clearance for capital issues and so on.

3. If we take cognizance of the international trends we may find ourselves going in the reverse direction. The world trend is towards larger companies, amalgamations, and mergers of units. They are aimed at improving competitive strength and technical efficiency.

4. The provisions of MRTP Act relating to diversification and expansion of large undertakings are difficult to harmonise with anti-monopoly legislation are world over. Nowehere else has monopoly legislation taken assets into account for the purpose of restriction and control on companies regarding their expansion or diversification. This is so, because assets *per se* are not considered a sound criterion for determining monopoly power. The only valid consideration is the functioning of big companies against the interest of the consumers.

5. All public undertakings controlled, managed or sponsored by Government and the trade practices in which they participate as parties are exempt from the provisions of the Act. It is undersirable to exempt all public undertakings not only from the control against concentration of economic power but also from the provisions on restrictive trade practices and on the behaviour of dominant firms. Many public undertakings compete with private firms in the same product and many of them enjoy dominant positions in their respective markets. The profit motive is very much a part of their operation. It cannot be assmed that just because they are owned by Government they will not take advantage of their dominant market position to adopt discriminatory and restrictive pratices unfair to customers and/ or competitors. They are subject to the same danger of losing the urge for improving efficiency and productivity that private enterprises in monopolistic situations are subject to. In fact, all public industrial and commercial undertakings should be on part with private undertakings and they should been brought within the scope of a least the provisions regarding the investigation and control of monopolistic and restrictive trade practices.

6. Sufficient thought has been given by the Government to the need to reconcile the provision of this legislation with Governments

other economic policies. It will not be surprising, therefore, if enforcement of this law lands Government in embarrasing situations. For instance, how will it reconcile the provisions of this legislation with the policy of enforced voluntary price fixing through producers' associations (in case of vanaspati) or with the working of Joint Plants Committee in steel? Or, for that matter, how will it reconcile the provision for curbing concentration with, the need for achieving investment targets particularly in industries which may call for allowing big business house to expand existing units or set up new units? For this very reason Government has been considering the amendment of Section 27 of the Act to delink some of the units belonging to larger house with a view to allowing the expansion of such concerns.

7. The fundamenal difficulty of administering this Act is that we have hardly any knowledge of economics of business concentration. As the intention behind the Act is not to control concentration *per se* but to control it only to the extent that its effects are detrimental to the public interest, some rudimentary information and analysis of the economic effects of concentration of economic power are absolutely essential. The debate on concentration has been extremely vague on the basic economic issues involved. No attempt has been made to answer the question; assuming that a sbstantial portion of private industry and trade is concentrated is increasing, what is wrong with such concentration? In what way does this tendency harm or help the economic interests of the community? Hazari's "Structure of the Corporate Private Sector" also did not analyse the economies of concentration. No information is available regarding the effects of concentration on the incentive from growth of enterpreneurial talent and specialised managerial known-how on the rate of incentive for technological development on the growth and pattern of private industrial investment, on the productivity of such investment on the market performance of industries in which such groups have predominant interest, on the development of bank credit. There are no hypotheses on the basis of which workable critieria can be set up for judging whether any development that has the effect of

increasing concentration of economic power is or is not against the public interest.

8. The policy envisaged in the Act is fashioned on British model and has very little in common with American anti-trust laws. It goes by the abuse principle', *i.e.* it strikes not at the position of acquisition of monopoly power but at the abuse of such power. The American approach, generally described as the *per se* approach, identifies public interest with the maintenance of free or unrestricted competition. Its primary emphasis is more on market structure than on market performance. Broadly speaking, under United States anti-trust laws, any action (individual or collective) that results or is likey to results in diminution of competition is considered *per se* detrimental to the public interest and is, therefore, un-lawful. The British (or abuse) approach is by contrast neutral between the intrinsic superiority of free competition or monopoly. This type of anti-monopoly policy requires individual investigation of each situation of monopoly or restricted competition in order to assess its effects on the public interest. The public interest is broadly defined in terms of performance variables like the reasonableness of prices, costs and profits, output and investment growth, quality of products, innovation and technical efficiency, exports, etc., Under the abuse principle, therefore, the law requires not only proof of the fact of monopoly or restriction of competition, but also proof of pubic deteriment resulting therefrom.

9. The references made to the Monopolies Commission so far show that the Commission is going to be tied down to investigation proposals for expansion, mergers, and new undertaking from the stand point of concentration of economic power. The Government is inclined to refer almost every proposal which technically comes within the purview of the Act. Given the number of applications for industrial licences for exampsion or new units pending. Licensing Committee will have to clear them at the rate of more than 100 applications a month. Of these, if 50 per cent are sponsored by large houses or dominant companies and if Government refers even 120 per cent of these to the Commission, it seems the Commission will have its hands more than full with just concentration enquiry. It

appears from the cases which have been referred to the Commission that the Government finds the Commission as a useful device for shrugging its responsibility to take decisions. A cursory reading of the public notices issued in connection with these references suggests that many of the proposals are really insignificant from the point of view of concentration of economic power to the common deteriment.

10. Examining licence applications from the concentration angle is, however, something which can be done better at licensing stage. As the cases referred to the Commission so far illustrate, all that the Commission will do is to duplicate the work done by the Licensing Committee or in the case of margers, by the Company Law Board. The Commission's investigations and recommendations can be useful only if it is called upon to investigate proposals before the Licensing Committee has taken its decisions on them. Only then the commission can examine a particular proposal in relation to the rival claims for licence. Otherwise, the Commission might be put in a awkward position of having to suggest reversal of a Government decision already taken. Surely it cannot be the Government's intention to keep the Commission busy but not ineffective.

11. The present activity of the Commissions gives an impression that it is going to be bogged down in concentration enquiries and may never find time to work on the other two and no less important objectives of the Act-control of the working of existing monopolies and of restrictive trade practices. Actually, for the point of view of safeguarding the interest of the public as consmers and as small traders and producers, these on two objectives are far more important.

WORKING AND ADMINISTRATION OF THE MRTP ACT

In the four years from 1970 to 1973 a total of 12,086 applications for industrial licences were received by the Government. Of these, those falling within the purview of Sections 21 (substantial expansion) and 22 (establishment of new undertaking) of the MRTP Act numbered on more than about 400, from the enforcement of the Act in June 1970 to November 1973. These 400 applications pertained to 917 undertakings registered with the Government 803 as inter-connected undertaking having assets worth Rs. 20 crores or more and 114 as dominant undertakings having singly or jointly assets of the value of not less than Rs 1 crore. The figure of 400 applications from large house and dominant undertaking out of total of 12,000 applications is small. The reason for this is obvious. The provisions of the MRTP Act with regard to registration have been applied legalistically and restrictively that a large number of inter-connected undertakings have evaded registration. For instance Birlas as a large industrial house had a total of 276 concerns under them according to the Dutt Committee Report in 1966. Against this, as revealed in the Government's reply to a question in Parliament, only 45 undertakings belonging to Birlas have been registered as inter-connected undertakings. With so many undertakings belonging to the large house registered with the Government it is not surprising that the number of applications for industrial licences falling within the MRTP should bear little relationship to the actual number of a applications made by the large houses.

Out of these 400 applications, only 32 were referred to the Monopolies Commission for detailed inquiry. The rest have been disposed of by the government without reference to the Commission. There is no apparent logic behind the government's decision to refer to not to refer to the Monopolies Commission particular cases pertaining to the large houses. The Commission itself complains in its annual report for the year 1972. That as against 72 references received in 1971 only 10 references were received in 1972. A number of cases of large magnitude and importance to the economy were decided by the Central Government without reference of the Commission. The Commission is not able to understand the policy which is being pursued in this respect. The Commission cannot help feeling that there is some incongruity in that sometimes cases not involving any major issues are referred to the Commission while other, which would *prima facie* involve important considerations, are not referred. The present chairman of the Commission Justice J.L. Nain confirmed the general compression about the irrelevance of the Commission when he was rebutting the criticism that the MRTP

Act had impeded industrial growth. He stated that "the Commission plays even a less important role than what the act envisages." One of the members of the Commission has observed that people give us too much credit. We are not that effective because the number of cases covered by the MRTP constitutes a very small part of total industrial growth."

The position at present seems that only 4 per cent of the industrial licence applications come under the provisions of the MRTP Act as restrictively interpreted by the Government. Of these 4 per cent, less than 10 per cent are referred to the Monopolies Commission. Of the number of proposals referred to the commission, those rejected from less than 10 per cent. In the circumstances, even a cursory cost-benefit study of the Monopolies Commission and the attendant paraphernalia can lead to only one conclusion; disband the Commission and Scrap the Act. As things are, the existence of the Act and the Commission only serve to create a false impression that the government is concerned about checking the growth of the large business houses and the concentration of economic power.

Proposed Reorganisation. In March 1973, it was reported in the Press that a major decision had been taken by the Government to break up monopoly industrial houses. Section 27 of the MRTP Act was proposed to be amended to provide for the dilution of control of business groups on companies and to break up big conglomerates into functional units. This decision had been taken as part of the new industrial policy aimed at the twin objectives of preventing concentration of economic power and at the same time allowing the expansion of industrial units in priority sectors. These twin objectives were proposed to be harmonised by assuming powers to break inter-connections where necessary and promote mergers and amalgamations where needed so that these unit were allowed to expand without inhibition to achieve economies of scale.

An official committee set up by the Ministery of Industrial Development also endorsed the above suggestion after gaining experience in clearing applications of larger industrial houses, particularly the difficulties faced in reconciling the conflicting aims of prevention of conentration of economic power and increasing the production capacity.

It was in March 1973 that the Union Law Minister has announced that he would soon introduce a bill to amend the MRTP Act. The amendment bill, again an indication was given in March 1975, would be introduced in the budget session. But it had not been introduced. This delay is being attributed to the failure to come to an agreed draft to amend the MRTP Act to empower the Union Government to de-link such undertaking having regard to the primary object of increasing industrial porduction.

The Monopolies Commission is being restructured and broken up into two wings. There will be a tribunal for restrictive trade practices and a monopolies commission to check concetration of economic power. The tribunal will be basically a judicial body which will deal with all problems relating to monopolistic and restrictive trade practices. At present more than 9,000 restrictive trade agreements have already been registered with the Registrar Trade Agreements. Even a small proportion thereof would burden the work of the Commission to an extent that would leave no time for it to handle the work visualised under the proposed break-up of conglomerates. The MRTP Commission combines economics power and monopolistic trade practices as also independent disposal of cases concerning restrictive trade practices. This combination of functions owes itself to the recommendations of the Monopolies Inquiry Commission which had in mind very limited role for the MRTP Commission.

The Government wants to break up the conglomeretes because it has come to the conclusion that the fundamental source of concentration of economic power is the existing conglomerate which operates either as a single unit with several activities or in the shape of family control over the entire business. There has been a feeling that some of the industrial houses are unwilling to effect expansion because they do not want any diluation of their control. It has been felt that some of these houses try to prevent the entry of professional management so that they may retain their family control. There have been cases where larger business houses have tried to enter fields reserved for small and medium entrepreneurs.

The Monopolies Commission, as now envisage, will be expected to go into the entire question of inter-connection between various undertakings and also adivse the Government on product classification. It is officially agrued that this has become all the more necessary as substantial number of large undertakings have not got themselves registered under Section 26 of the MRTP Act and thus avoided the regulatory provision of the Act Secondly, the Ministry has received more than 120 applications for deregistration of the ground that the undertakings are inter-connected with such undertakings whose assets when added to their own assets amount to not less than Rs. 20 crores. Thirdly, some undertakings have advanced the argument that according to the product classification prescribed by the Government, they are not dominant.

REVERSAL OF POLICIES TOWARDS MRTP

As a first step towards reversal of policy the Government has announced that large industrial houses will be allowed to set up industries in 90" zero indusry" districts in the country—districts rich in reasources but without any industry whatsoever big business houses will not attract the provisions of MRTP Act. To help the big business houses to set up units in backward districts, infrastructual facilities are being provided on a top priority basis. The Government is also considering an increase in transport subsidy to make the scheme more cost compenstory and to mitigate the logistical handicaps in the far flung areas.

Further, under the proposed amendments of the Industrial (Development and Regulation) Act, the Government plans to remove restrictions on MRTP companies to bring them into key sector areas to boost production. The Government also intends to encourage MRTP companies in core sector where high capital and sophisticated technology are involved. It also intends to facilitate investment by such companies in areas where small-scale entrepreneurs are not in a position to meet the growing needs of the economy for specific items, which sometimes are in short supply. For instance, it has been suggested that the areas where private investment could flow into area two-wheeler scooter, heavy automobile sector and manufacture of trucks.

A major decision announced by the then Union Finance Minister Mr. Vishwanth Pratap Singh while presenting the 1985-86 budget related to raising the limit of assets for MRTP companies from Rs. 20 crores to Rs. 100 crores. Even the monopolies did not expect that the Government will, in one single jump raise the ceiling of assets for MRTP companies to five time the existing limit. The immediate impact of raising the assets limit was the delinking of almost 49 out of 101 large industrial houses from the provision of the (Section 26) MRTP Act. Obviously the aim is not have a pattern of growth in which investment is judiciously allocated between large, medium and small sectors. but to have excessive dependence on large, corporate sector.

MRTP Amendment Act, 1984. The MRTP (Amendment) Act 1984 introduced certain changes in the MRTP Act on the basis of the experience gained and the recommendations made by Sanchar Committee. The main thrust of the amendment was to clarify certain definitions so as to include certain categories which were hitherto left uncovered. Some of the important definitional changes were:

> ***Definition of Goods.*** Goods have now the same definition as in the sale of Goods Act 1930 and include shares and stocks. Thus a major deficiency in the existing provision of the MRTP Act has been removed and investment companies have been brought within its ambit.
>
> ***Group and Inter-connected Undertakings.*** Another important change introduced is the concept of Group to include enterprises under the same management, Sachar Committee recognised the existence of the concept in the Companies Act of 1974 and recommended its transference

to MRTP Act since it had a special importance in this context. The MRTP (Amendment) Act 1984 has incorporated it.

The (Amendment) Act 1984 has redefined interconnected undertakings. Under the existing provision in the MRTP Act, not less than 1/3rd control over voting power or positions of the Board is required for establishing inter-connection. The (Amendment) Act 1984 has reduced this proportion to 25 per cent.

Definition of Undertaking. The (Amendment) Act of 1984 has made the definition of 'undertaking' exhaustive so as to widen the scope of the MRTP Act. The earlier definition of undertaking covered enterprises engaged in production, sale distribution or control of goods etc. The Supreme Court criticising the lacunae in this regard pointed "out the word undertaking is a coat of many colours as it has been used in different sections of the act to convey different ideas. In some of these sections it has been used to denote enterprise itself while in many other section it has been used to denote a person who owns it "There was therefore, an urgent need to bring about consistency in the various sections of the act so as to make its coverage wide so that mergers which went unchecked could be controlled. The revised definition of 'undertaking' covers enterprises engaged or proposed to be engaged in the production, storage, supply, distribution, acquisition or control of articles or goods or the provisions of any services either directly or through one or more of its units or divisions whether located at the same place or at different places. Thus any branch or office established for the provision of any service is also coverd. Besides this a body corporate which is, or has been, enaged only in the business of acquiring, underwriting or dealing with shares, debentures or other securities of any other body corporate shall be deemed to be an undertaking. Thus the definition of undertaking becomes comprehensive to include companies dealing in goods and services, stoks and shares as well as investment companies. This is a welcome rationalisation.

Limits to Capacity Expansion. The (Amendment) Act of 1984 has tried to limit the misuse of the provision by taking recourse to expansion of capacity to an unlimited extent under the garb of modernisation. As rcommended by the Sachar Committee, the Amendment provides that exemption of these lines would be permitted only to the extent of 25 per cent of the licensed capacity. However, it has been clarified that this is in addition to the normal expansion upto 25 per cent of licensed capacity which does not require approval under the Act.

The Amendment Act has removed the concept of monopolistic undertaking since it served no useful purpose because monopolistic practices can exist even without "monopolistic undertaking" and what is relevant in this context is the dominant undertaking. This has been incorporated in the Amendment Act.

Severance of Interconnection. A very important provision introduced in the Amendment Act 1984 is the power given to the Central Government regarding severance of interconnection, if the Government forms an opinion that such interconnection "is deterimental to the interests of the principal undertaking, or the steady growth of the industry to which the principal undertaking pertains or the public interest." The Central government can refer the matter for inquiry by the MRTP Commission. The merit of this new provision 27-A of the Amendment Act lies in the fact that it binds the Government to the scheme suggested by the MRTP Commission once the Central Government has decided to act on the report of the Commission on the lines recommended by it. However, it is left open to the Central Government to reject the report as a whole.

Unfair Trade Practices. On the lines suggested by Sachar Committee, the MRTP (Amendment) Act 1984 has brought within the purview of the Act certain unfair trade practices like mis-leading advertisements, bargain selling etc. Although the Commission held the view that such unfair practices were automatically covered under the Act, the Supreme Court held in the case of TELCO *vs.* RRTA in 1977 that the practices enumerated in section 33 do not provide statutory illustrations of restrictive trade practices, but merely of trade practices, which required registration. In order to get over this difficulty created as a result of the judgement, the Amendment Act 1984 provides that every agreement falling within one or more of the categories specified there in shall be deemed to be an agreement relating to restrictive trade practices.

But under Section 38, The Government has justified the provision of certain restrictions to meet the requirements of the defence of India or the Security of the State, or where the restrictions are necessary to ensure the maintenance of supply of goods and services essential to the community. Criticising this provision, MR. H. K. Parnjape writes "Section 38 of the original Act provided what has been called gateways" through which restrictive trade practices can pass so as not to be deemed prejudicial to public interest. The Amendment Bill proposes more gateways namely in cases where the restrictions have been expressly authorised and approved by the Central Government."

CHANGES IN MRTP ACT IN 1990

In response to the demands of big business the government in its Industrial policy of 1991 decided to abolish MRTP asset limit altogether. The industrial policy (1991) states the following with regard to MRTP Act." The interference of the government through the MRTP Act in investment decisions of large companies has become deleterious in its effects on Indian industrial growth. The pre-entry secruity of investment decision by so-called MRTP companies will no longer be required. Instead emphasis will be on controlling and regulating monopolistic, restrictive and unfair trade practices rather than making it necessary for the monopoly houses to obtain prior approval of central government for expansion, establishment of new undertakings, merger, amalgamation and takeover and appointment of certain directors. The thrust of policy will be more on controlling unfair or resrictive business practices.

The new Industrial Policy announced in July 1991 scrapped the assets limit for MRTP companies altogether. The MRTP Act was amended and Chapter III on monopolies dropped so that now a company no longer need prior permission of the Commission for investment decisions (pertaining either to establishment of new undertakings, capacity expansion or diversification.) The government hopes that this will enable Indian firms to become large enough to compete effectively in global markets. The MRTP Act as amended now will give more emphasis to the prevention and control of monopolistic, restrictive and unfair trade practices so that consumers are adequately protected from such practices.

NEW LICENSING POLICY AND PROCEDURES 1970

In February, 1970 the Government announced its new industrial licensing policy. It accepted the recommendation of the Industrial Licensing Policy Inquiry Committee that there should be a list of core industries in the economy. The core sector would consist of:

A. Agricultural inputs. *(a)* fertilisers: *(i)* Nitrogenous, *(ii)* Phosphatic, *(b)* Pesiticides; *(c)* Tractors and power tillers; *(d)* Rock-phosphate and pyrit;

B. Iron and Steep : *(a)* Iron Ore; *(b)* Pig iron and steel; *(c)* Alloy and special steel;

C. Non-terrous metals;

D. Petroleum *(a)* Oil exploration and production; *(b)* Petroleum refining; *(c)* Selected petro-chemical such as integrated petro-chemical complexes, D.M.T. Caprolactum Acryonitrile and Synthetic rubber;

E. Coking Coal;

F. Heavy Industrial mechinery;

G. Ship-building;

H. News-print an Electronics.

Such of the industries in the 'core' list as are included in Schedule 'A' of the Industrial Policy Resolution, 1956 (as amended from time to time) are reserved for the public sector.

Apart from this, all new investment propositions of over Rs. 5 crores were deemed to be in the 'heavy investment' sector. Except for industries reserved for the public sector under the Industrial Policy Resolution (1956), larger industrial houses, foreign companies, subsidiaries or branches of foreign companies, were allowed to participate in the core and heavy investment sector, leaving the opportunities in the remaining sectors primarily to other class of entrepreneurs.

In the joint sector, involving investment ranging from Rs. 1 crore to Rs. 5 crores, licence applications of parties other than undertakings belonging to the larger industrial houses were to be given special consideration. Licence applications from undertakings belonging to or controlled by the larger industrial groups and foreign branches/subsidiaries, were to be considered for normal expansion where such expansion was necessary to develop to a minimum economic level or which would ensure greater cost efficiency.

The existing policy of reservation for the small-scale sector was to be continued and the area of such reservation was to be extended in the future.

The exemption limit from licensing provisions including licensing of new undertakings and substantial expansion of existing units was to be raise from Rs. 25 lakhs to Rs. 1 crore (by way of fixed assets in land, of building and machinery) in the cases of undertakings which had existing assets of less than Rs. 5 crores and which *(i)* did not belong to the larger indsutrial houses, as classified by the Industrial Licensing Policy Inquiry Committee; *(ii)* did not require more than Rs. 10 lakh or more than 10 per cent by way of foreign exchange for import of machinery and equipment and did not also require foreign exchange, except marginally, for import of raw materials, components and the like, and *(iii)* were not included in the category of 'dominant undertakings' as defined in the Monopolies Act.

The Industrial Policy Statement of Feburary, 1973 modified the licensing policy and procedures further. Import modifications were:

(a) In the list of core industries, such Industries as were included in schedule A of the industrial policy were reserved for the public sector. Larger houses (with assets of not less than Rs. 20 crores) were made eligible to participate in the contribute to the establishment of such industries along with other applicants, provided that the item was not one that was reserved for production in the public sector or in the small sector.

(b) The Government (both Centre and state) would develop joint sector as a promotional instrument in priority areas.

(c) Foreign concerns and subsidiaries and branches of foreign companies were also made eligible to participate in these industries.

(d) Cooperatives and small and medium enterpreneur were to be encouraged to participate in the production of mass consumption goods with the public sector also taking an increasing role.

In October 1975, the Government announced major changes liberalising industrial licensing policy. It delicensed 21 industries and permitted unlimited expansion, beyond the licensed capacities to foreign companies and monopoly houses in 30 other important industries.

Subsequently, on November 5, 1975, the Government announced that 25 per cent of excess unauthorised capacity was declared legal on the basis of normal expansion, another 25 per cent was sought to be covered in five years by automatic licensing. Although in the large-scale sector, industrial licensing has not been formally withdrawn, but in actual practice the industrial houses create unauthorised capacities which have later ractified by the government. The principal objective of the Government was to raise production and the objective of checking concentration of economic power was relegated to the background.

LIBERALISATION MEASURES 1985

Soon after resumption of power in 1984, the then Prime Minister Rajiv Gandhi's Government brought about a sea-change in terms of liberalisation of licensing policy in favour of large business houses, particularly in terms of making them free from the provisions of MRTP Act and FERA. The major changes introduced were as under:

1. Liberalisation of Licensed Capacity in the Name of Economies of Scale and Modernisation. The policy changes of 1985 envisaged the need for the industry to grow at a rapid pace, achieve economies of scale and undertake modernisation which signified the introduction of latest technology. With this end in view, the scheme for re-endorsement of capacity was liberalised automatic increase was granted to units wanting to achieve economies of scale and a 49 per cent rise in capacity due to modernisation was allowed. The Government decided to delicense 23 industries for MRTP and FERA companies provided the industrial undertaking is located in any of the Centrally-declared backward areas in 1986.

2. Concept of Broad-banding Introduced. To encourage production and to provide flexibility to the manufacturers to adjust their product-mix depending on the market demand, the concpet of broad-banding was introduced in a large number of items. Some of these are machine tools, motorised two wheelers, motorised four wheeler, paper and paper pulp, chemical, pharmaceutical, petro-chemical and fertilizer machinery industry and entertainment electronics.

3. Raising the Asset Limit of MRTP Companies. The threshold asset limit for companies under MRTP Act was raised from Rs. 20 crores to Rs. 100 croes. As a consequence, 112 companies came out of the purview of the MRTP Act leaving 379 units still under MRTP Act. Besides, the Government announced in May 1985, its decision to exempt 27 industries from the Section 22A of the MRTP Act and in December 1984 again, 22 of these industries were delicensed for MRTP and FERA Companies. These two measures together virutally abolished all controls on MRTP and FERA companies in respect of the 22 industries.

4. Attitude Towards Small-scale Sector Units. Some scopes were provided for the small-sector. The limit on investment by small-scale units and ancillaries was enhanced from Rs. 20 lakh and Rs. 25 lakh to Rs. 35 lakh and Rs. 45 lakh respoectively. However nearly 200 times which were on the reservation list were de-reserved and made open for the medium and lrge-scale sector.

INDUSTRIAL LICENSING POLICY, 1988

The Union Government announced on June 3, 1988 further liberalisation of the industrial licensing system and also provide incentives to give a stimulus to industrialisation of backward areas.

Non-MRTP and Non-FERA companies will not be required to obtain industrial licences under IDRA for project involving investment in fixed assets upto Rs. 50 crores if they are located in Centrally declared backward areas and upto Rs. 15 crores if they are located in non-backward areas. The number of industries requiring compulsory licensing has been reduced from 56 to 26. The delicensed sector under the new dispensation has been extended to units importing upto

30 per cent of their input needs against 15 per cent in the past. This is a case where import liberalisation has been combined with industrial liberalisation to good effect.

For the development of backward areas, the Government intends to establish 100 growth centres throughout the country over the next five years. Each growth centre will be provided with funds of the order of Rs. 25 crores to Rs. 30 crores for creating infrastructural facilities particularly in respect of power, water, telecommunications and banking.

To promote industrialisation in backward areas new industrial undertakings established in declared backward areas, are entitled to the income tax relief under Section 80 HH of the Income Tax Act by way of deduction of 20% of the profits available for a period of 10 years. Furthermore, under section 80-I of the I.T. Act, all new undertakings are entitled to an income tax relief by way of deduction of 25% of the profits for the period of 8 years. The benefits of both these sections are available cumulatively to industrial undertakings established in notified backward districts.

There is no doubt that there was justification for revision of asset limits of large business houses in view of the sharp escalation of prices that had taken place earlier, but it was no expected that the Government would take a quantum jump and raise it 5 times. Considerations of liberalising investment with the objective of raising production have been paramount with the Government. Moreover, the Government is dead set to promote computerisation and electronics along with expansion of communications. Any obstacles in this regard in the form of MRTP and FERA regulations are sought to be removed. But in this process, the Government is making the small-scale industry a victim of its programme of modernisation. The de-reservation of about 200 items will hit small-scale sector. The abnormal benefits provided to the large corporate sector to compete with the small-scale sector will hit it further. As a consequence, the objective of promoting full employment via encouragement to small sector will be jeopardized.

NEW INDUSTRIAL POLICY (1990)

The Janata Dal Government announced its new Indsutrial Policy on May 31, 1990. The salient features of third policy are the following:

The Pormotion of Small-scale and Agro-based Industries. In pursuance of our policy to reorient industrial growth to serve the objective of employment generation, dispersal of industry in the rural areas, and to enhance the contribution of small-scale industries to exports it has been decided to take the measures enumerated below.

1. The investment ceilling in plant and machinery for small-scale industries (fixed in 1985) was raised from the present Rs. 35 lakhs to Rs. 60 lakhs and correspondingly, for ancillary units from Rs. 45 lakhs, to 75 lakhs. In order to enable small-scale industries to play an important role in the total export, such of the small-scale units which undertake to export at least 30 per cent of the anual production by the third year would be permitted to step up their investment in plant and machinery to Rs. 75 lakhs.

2. Investment ceilling in respect of tiny units would also be increased from the present Rs. 2 lakhs to Rs. 5 lakhs.

3. (i) Presently, 836 items have been reserved for exclusive manufactures in the small-scale sector. Efforts would be made to identify more items amenable to similar reservation.

   (ii) A new Scheme of Central Investment Subsidy exclusively for the small-scale sector in rural and backward areas capable of generating higher level of employment at lower capital cost would be implemented.

   (iii) With a view to improving the competitiveness of the products manufactures in the small-scale sector, programmes for modernisation and upgradation of technology would be implemented. A number of technology centres, tool rooms, process and product development centres, testing centres, etc. will be setup under the umbrella of an apex Technology Development Centre in Small Industries Development Organisation.

(iv) The existing regime of fiscal concessions would be reviewed both to provide sustained support to the units in the small-scale sector and to remove the disincentives for their graduation and further growth.

(v) An exercise will be undertaken to identify locations in rural areas endowed with adequate power supply and intensive compaigns would be launched to attract suitable entrepreneurs, provide all other inputs foster small-scale and tiny industries. Similary, industries which are not energy intensive will be identified for proliferation in rural areas where power supply is presently a constraint.

(vi) To ensure adequate and timely flow of credit for the small-scale industries, a new apex bank known as SIDBI and other commercial bank/financial institutions would be to channelise need based, higher flow of credit, both by way of term loan and working capital, to the tiny and rural industries.

(vii) One of the persistent complaints of the small-scale units is their being subjected to a large number of Acts/ Laws, being required to maintain a number of registers, submit plethora of returns and face an army of inspectors, particularly in the field of labour legislations. These bureaucratic conrols will be reduced so that unnecessary interference is eliminated.

4. In order to assist the large number of aritsans engaged in the rural and cottage industries, the activities of the KVIC and KVI boards would be expanded, and these organisation, would be strengthened to discharge the responsibility more

effectively. Special marketing their products and also in supply of raw materials. Besides, providing concessional credit, training facilities and free consultancy to group of artisans will also be provided.

5. Agro processing industry would receive high priority in credit allocation from the financial institutions.

6. In sector where units require licensing, the policy would also encourage location of processing units in rural areas where growers are concentrated. Apart from economic benefits of proximity to raw materials it would help in dispersal of industry and increasing employment in rural areas.

7. In agro-processing indsutries greater success has been achieved where growers and processors have been integrted, as in the case of sugar. For the successs of other agro based industries also, close links must be forged between the growers and processor units. Industrial Policy would therefore, specially promote projects which are organised in close co-operation on the basis of joint ownership. Growers will be encouraged to set up processing units within the framework of co-operative societies or similar institutional framework. This will also ensure the transmission of better technology for enhanced agricultural production.

8. Import of Raw Materials and Components. From imports of raw materials and components imports would be permissible upto a landed value of 30 per cent of the ex-factory value of annual production. The ex-factory value of production will exclude the excise duty on the item of production. Raw materials and components on OGL will not be included within this 30 per cent limits.

9. **Import of Capital Goods.** For the import of capital goods, the entrepreneur would have entitlement to import upto a

landed value of 230 per cent of the total value of plant and machinery required for the unit.

10. **Delicensing.** All units up to an investment of Rs. crores on fixed assets in non-backward area and Rs. 75 crores in Centrally notified backward areas would be exempted from requirement of obtaining licence/registration.

11. **Foreign Collaboration.** In respct of transfer of technology, if import of tecnology is considered by the entrepreneur, he can conclude an agreement with the collaborator, without obtaining any clearance from the Governments, provided that royalty payment does not exceed five per cent on domestic sales and eight per cent on exports.

12. **Foreign Investment.** It may be clarified that in the application of the proposals listed above, 836 items which are reserved for production in the small scale sector will continue to be excluded.

13. **Export-oriented Units.** 100 per cent export oriented units (EOUs) and units to be set up in export processing zones (EPZs) are also being delicensed under the scheme up to a investment limit of Rs 75 crores.

Units set up by MRTP/FERA companies will be covered by the procedures set out above, but they will continue to need clearances under the provision and regulations of these two Acts.

Abolition on Industrial Licensing

The Government of India announced a New Industrial Policy on July 24, 1991. This policy aimed at liberalising the industrial economy considrably and, with this end in view, announced a series of initiatives in respect of industrial licensing, foreign investment and technology agreements, public sector, and MRTP Act. As far as industrial licensing is concerned, the new industrial policy abolished all industrial licensing, irrespective of the level of investment, except for certain industries related to security and strategy concerns, social reasons, concerns related to safety and overriding environmental issues, manufacture of product of hazardous nature and articles of elitist consumption. The 1991 industrial policy listed 18 industries for which industrial licensing would remain compulsory. These industries were as under—coal and lignite; petroleum (other than crude) and its distillation products; distillation and brewing of alcoholic drinks; sugar; animal fats and oils; cigars and cigarettes; asbestos and asbestos-based products; plywood and other wood based products; raw hides and skins, and leather; tanned or dressed furskin; motor cars; paper and newsprint; electronic aeroscape and defence equiment; industrial explosives; hazardous chemicals; drugs and pharmaceuticals; entertainment electronics; and white goods (domestic refrigerators, washing machines, air conditioners, etc.). However, of these 18 industries, three industries were delicensed in April 1993. In later years more industries were delicensed. Thus at present only 6 items of health, strategic and secuirity considerations remains under the purview of industrial licensing. These are alcohol, cigarettes, hazardous chemicals, electronic aerospace and defence equipment, industrial explosives and dogs and pharmaceuticals (excepting bulk dry industry which has been delicensed.

FOREIGN EXCHANGE REGULATION ACT, 1973

The Foreign Exchange Regulation Act, 1973, serves as tool for implementing the national policy investment in India. Sections 28, 29, 30 and 31 of the Act empower the Reserve Bank of Inida to regulate or exercise direct control over the activities of foreign companies and foreign nationals in India.

In this section the term *foreign companies* means companies (other than banking companies) which are not incorporated in India or in which the non-resident interest is more than 40 per cent, or any branch of such company.

Under Section 28 of the FERA non-residents (including Indian citizens), foreign citizens resident in India and foreign companies require the permission of the Reserve Bank to accept appointment as agents or technical management advisers in India of any person or company, or permit the use of their trademarks by any person or company, for direct or indirect consideration.

The trading, commercial and indsutrial activites in India of persons resident abroad, foreign citizens resident abroad, foreign companies are sought to be regulated under section 29 of the Act. They have to obtain the prior permission of the RBI for:

(i) Carrying on in India any activity of a trading, commercial or industrial nature:

(ii) Opening branches/offices or other places of business in India;

(iii) Acquiring any business undertaking in India; and

(iv) Purchasing share of Indian companies.

Correspondingly, under Section 19, the transfer or issue of any security, including shares, to a non-resident requires the prior permission of the RBI.

Those persons and companies already functioning on the date of coming into force of the Act, had to seek the RBI's permission to continue their activities in the country or to hold the share already acquired. Repatriation of investments made in India with the approval of the Central Government or the Reserve Bank is permissible, provided that the disinvestment has also been made with the approval of the RBI.

Section 30 of the Act prohibits foreign nationals from taking up any profesion, etc., without the permission of the Reserve Bank, if they wish to have remittance facilities for transfer of their earnings outside India. Section 31 regulation the acquisition, holding, transfer and disposal of immovable property in India by foreign citizens and foreign companies. General permission has been granted by the RBI to foreign companies (other than those established purely as liasion offices) to acquire or hold any immovable property in India which is necessary for, or incidental to any activity undertaken by them with the permission of the Reserve Bank under Section 28 or Section 29 of the Act.

Foreign Exchange Regulation Act (FERA) was promulgated in 1973 and it came into force on January 1,1974. Section 20 of this Act referred directly to the operations of MNCs in India. According to the Section, all non-banking foreign branches and subsidiaries with foreign equity exceeding 40 per cent had to obtain permission to establish new undertakings to purchase shares in existing companies, or to acquire wholly or partly any other company. Guidelines for administering this Section FERA were announced in 1973 and later amended in 1976.

According to these guidelines, the principal rule was that all branches of foreign companies operating in India should convert themsevles in India companies with at least 60 per cent local equity participator Furthermore, all subsidiaries of foreign companies should bring down the foreign equity share to 40 per cent or less. The 1976 guidelines provide for three levels of foreign equity: 74 per cent, 51 per cent, and 40 per cent Companies were allowed to retain foreign equity holdings above 40 per cent and upto 74 per cent, on condition that they were enagaged in *(i)* core industries; *(ii)* predominantly export oriented production; *(iii)* activities requiring sophisticated technology or specialised skills; or *(iv)* the plantation activities.

If the turnover from any or all of these activities combined exceed 75 per cent of the total turnover of the company, it was entitled to retain up to 74 per cent foreign equity. The same level applied to companies exporting more than 40 per cent of their own production or the equivalent of at least 60 per cent of their total turnover.

Implementation of FERA. There were substantial delays in implementing FERA. A large number of companies which were issues directions for dilution, did not carry out the directions. Some did not even initiate the process of dilution. The Government itself exempted a number of units. Martinussen's study shows that of the 895 companies 249 companies were exempted from the general rule stipulating a maximum of 40 per cent non resident interest 132 companies were allowed to continue with more than 40 per cent foreign equity, 116 with more than 51 per cent or upto 74 per cent foreign equity and one company was given permission to hold 100 per cent foreign equity.

In regard to the companies that did not comply with FERA regulations Martinussen observe a certain pattern. For instance, he found that almost all these companies belonged to only three groups. They were either engaged in tea plantation activites or in the manufacture of drugs and pharmaceuticals or they were affiliated with particularly large TNCs. The special treatment to tea companies was due to the importance of tea in India's foreign trade. As far as the drugs and pharmaceutical industry is concerned, India's heavy dependence on MNCs for bulk durgs came in the way of compliance of FERA regulations. As far as the third category of powerful MNCs is concerned, Martinussen gives in detail the experience with regard to Hindustan Lever Ltd. This company managed to secure concessions from the government on flimsy grounds. For instance, it succeeded in getting 60 per cent of its toiletries manufacturing classified by government as high technology activity as it helped in 'import substitutions'.

❐

15

Technology Environment

Technology plays important role in the economic development of accounting. It is an essential tool to get rid of socio-political and economic backwardness. It is mainly essential for the developing and less developed countries. The fate of nation and of civilization has often been determined by a different in the technology of production and warfare for which the inferior side was unable to compensate in other ways. Power of a nation dependence very much on the modern technology it possess. The quality and productive capacity of the industrial plant, the know-how of the working man, the skill of the engineer, the inventive ganius of the scientists, the managerial organization—all these are the factors upon which the industrial capacity of a nation depends. Therefore, a technological prerequisite is needed which could lead a country to establish itself in international community.

PATTERN OF SOCIO-ECONOMIC CONDITIONS IN THE DEVELOPING COUNTRIES

Most of the underdeveloped countries in Latin America, Asia and Africa have already set in motion a process of growth along the classical path of capitalist development. Their growth exercise is very much similar to the process of industrialisation in the West particularly in terms of output and mechanical technology and human skills used. The developing countries force the socio-economic backwardness and could not fulfil their pressing social and public needs. The masses in these countries are below poverty line. They are illiterate and uneducated. Unemployment is the common phenomenon in these countries which gives birth of disgrumble elements. The society is divided due to caste, creed or colour differences.

This type of social set up, when adopts a capitalist system of economy, there are less chances of solution of any socio-economic problems. These countries became independent from colonial rule in forties fifties or early sixties. But till today, they are not able to over come these socio-economic problems. They still remain backward group of countries.

Need of Technology. The developing countries need modern technologyto get rid of their backwardness. They need new industrial ventures and managerial experience. The adoption of modern means and new technology can only help them in getting rid of illiteracy and poverty. It could improve the agriculture sector to make them self-sufficient in food. The establishment of new industries may provide job opportunities to the unemployed youths. The technology could innovate new systems of education which can be job oriented. The people in the developing countries are very much influenced by the development of the west and inspired by its economic success. Therefore, they felt a need to import technology of the West.

The modern technology of today the monopoly of the Multi-national Corporations. They have the know-how and capability to run new projects in the developing countries. But there are a few countries which suspected the aims and objectives of MNCs in their land. It is true that the MNCs generally transfer an inappropriate technology to the developing countries. Their technologies were developed according to the needs of west which is capital intensive technology, while the developing countries are labour surplus countries and they need a technology which could fulfil the local aspirations. Moreover the high technology of west creates many socio-economic problems in the developing countries. It leads to destruction of capital goods industry of the developing countries and produce over-sophisticated items which could not fulfil the needs of masses.

The Governments in the developing countries is also fearful of the MNCs as those may encroach their sovereignty and independence by imposing terms and conditions. But inspite of the fear and doubts, the developing countries are dependent on the developed countries and multinational corporations for the import of technology which in turn would bring socio-economic development in their country.

Technology According to Local Needs. Technology must suit local needs and fulfil the aspirations of the people. The absolute technology is of no use, rather it creates problems in society. The highly westernize technology is unless for the developing countries as the later is a labour-surplus country and need employment for them. But the imported technology would need only a small groups of skilled labour. Moreover, the products of the MNCs and their venture should also be according to the needs of the larger part of the backward society of developing countries.

The above discussion shows that, in fact, the developing countries do not need highly westernize technology for their own socio-economic development.

Need to Develop Indigenous Technology. It has been already admitted that technology is essential for the economic development of a country and as the economy is very much related with the society, technology is essential for socio-economic development, Therefore the policy makers of the developing countries put stress on the development of the indigenous technology. The attempt should be made to modernise and upgrade the indigenous methods which could remilalise economic growth. The leadership of the country should not be ignorant of the new technology and carefully judge and decide the need of the nation and its people. The economic and the industrial policies of the country should be carefully formulated to promote, regulate and direct economic activities of the country. The Government should accelerate industrial and economic development by expanding large scale industries in the core sector.

Need to Encourage Research and Development. Instead of importing and buying technology, the governments, in the developing countries should stress on research and development regarding science and technology. The institutions and the researcher should be encouraged to find out innovation technologies which could make the country self-relevant and reduce vulnerability making the maximum use of indigeneous resources. It should arrange for modernization for both equipment and technology. The government should sponsor the Researchers, students and managerial staff to visit abroad and get training, because it will help in bringing the foreign technology at home. It should ensure accessibility of technology to all segments of the society. The Research and Development wing should be established by the government as it could provide vital inputs to both large scale and small scale industry. This wing could help in developing new intermediate technologies according to the nations specific conditions. There is a strong case for developing labour intensive technologies in all labour surplus backward economies.

It can be said that in this age of rapid scientific and technological development technology has a large impact on economic growth. but in the technological race between different countries, the developing countries lag far behind, consequently they are dependent on the developed industrial world for technology required to accelerate their development process. The international technology market is highly imperfect and is dominated by a few multi-national corporations. They follow various discriminatory trade practices to maximise profits and to perpetuate their monopolistic or oligopolistic positions. Therefore, the use and the development of technology must relate to the people's aspirations. Our own immediate needs in India are the attainment of technological self-reliance, as swift and tangible improvement in the conditions of the weaker sections and speedy development of backward regions. Technology must suit local needs and to make an impact on the lives of ordinary citizens, must give constant thought to even small improvements which could made better and more cost effective use of existing materials and methods of work. Our future depends on our ability to resist the imposition of technology which is obsoletc or unrelated to our specific requirement and of policies which tie us to systems which serve the purpose of their rather than out own. Thus the developing countries which having a large reservoir of human and manufacturing capacity can meet parts of requirements for aid, investment and technology through mutual exchange. the harmonization of policies and preferences of third world countries in the sphere of technology can bring about significant revolutionary developments in the economic growth of these countries.

MODES AND INSTRUMENTS OF TECHNOLOGY TRANSFER

Technology is an essential mode for socio-economic development of a country. But as it is well known, the modern know-how and technology is today monopolicy of the Multinational Corporations (MNs). The less developing countries are lacking it and are totally dependent on MNCs for borrowing has sophisticated and costly technology. This recent practics the made essential to throughly study the problems and prospects of transfer to technology.

Modes of technology transfer can be broadly classified in two ways: *(1)* According to the nature of the technology transfer, and *(2)* According to the nature of the instrument used. As far as classification according to the nature of the technology transfer is concerned, Cooper and Hoffman have presented a three-fold categorisation of technology transfer:

(a) 'simple direct' sales of technology, which consist of outright sales of embodied (machinery) or disembodied (specific consulting services) technology by unrelated firms for prices which are more or less competitive;

(b) 'process packaged' sales of technology, where a complete industrial process or plant is supplied by machinery manufacturers, independent engineering firms or final manufacturers of products; and

(c) 'project packaged' sales of technology, where the technology is accompanied by other requirements for the commercial operation of a project— *i.e.*, management, capital, brand names, etc.,—and by some element of continuous link or control by the seller."

The second method of classifying technology transaction is by the nature of the instrument used, *i.e.*, whether technology is sold in the form of equipment, designing of plant, commissioning, supervision, management, licences, direct investment, etc.

Transfer of technology between countries can take place in a number of ways:

(i) by the flow of books, journals and other published information;

(ii) by foriegn investment and the accociated transfer of know-how and equipment;

(iii) by the movement of people between countries, including immigration, return of emigrants, study visits, and other travel;

(iv) by the import of machinery and equipment;

(v) by technical cooperation programmes, multilateral and bilateral, official and private;

(vi) by licensing patent and know-how agreements.

Most developing countries employ all these methods simultaneously. The first method is more important for transfer of fundamental scientific knowledge rather than industrial technology. All other methods are directly relevant for the transfer of industrial technology.

Through technical cooperation programmes with other countries, governments of the developing countries have sought to introduce latest technology in their industrial sector. For this purpose, they send their missions abroad or invite technical missions from abroad. Through the establishment of a network of technical training and research institutions, they have tried to improve the supply of technical services.

However, the chief instruments of the transfer of technology from developed to the developing countries are the multinational corporations (MNCs). MNCs are huge industrial organisations which extend their industrial and marketing operations in a number of countries through a network of their branches or subsidiaries. They bring with them technical knowledge and equipment and also participate in the industrial development programmes of the developing countries by licensing, patent and know-how agreements. MNCs organise their operations in different countries through any of the following five alternatives:

> **Branches.** The simplest form of extending business operations is to set up branches in the developing countries, which bring with them the technology of the parent company and are linked up with it.
>
> **Subsidiaries.**. MNCs also operate by setting up national affiliates as subsidiary companies. A subsidiary in a particular country is established under the laws of the country.
>
> **Frnachise Holders.** This is a special kind of arrangement by which an affiliate firm produces or markets the produce of a multinational firm after obtaining a licence from that firm.
>
> **Joint Venture Company.** At time, MNCs enter into a joint venture with an indigenous firm or agency. Under this arrangement the MNC makes available machinery, capital goods and technological expertise to the indigenous firm.
>
> **Turn-Key Pojects.** Under this orgnisational form, the multinational undertakes to complete the project from scratch to the operational stage. When the project is ready it is handed over to the host country.

Throguh these various methods of operations, MNCs carry their technology to the developing countries. If MNCs set up a branch on a subsidiary company, it is claimed that there is a direct injection of foreign experience and expertise in the developing country. The branch or the subsidiary company can provide a channel for the transmission of the latest improvements from the developed to the underdeveloped countries. However, success on this front depends crucially on how far the recipient countries are able to regulate the activities of MNCs keeping the local interests in view.

Basic Characteristics of Technology Transfer. Technology is transferred by the advanced capitalist countries to the developing countries. There are the two basic characteristics of technology transfer. First the principal instrument of technology transfer are MNCs which either through their subsidiaries or through the contractual transactions made with developing countries bring mechanised processes and equipments not locally available. Very often the terms and conditions are arbitrarily settled under high imperfect market conditions by the technology supplying MNCs. The monopolistic strength of the technology suppliers emanates from the patents protection for differentiated products and processes.

The second basic characteristic of technology transfer is that the large part of the influx of technology in developing countries is in response to the policy of industrialisation through import substitution. In developing countries, due to structural factors and their consequential effects on terms of trade much reliance cannot be placed on exports to transform savings into current investment goods. Naturally a deliberate strategy of creating a tariff wall to overcome the foreign exchange difficulties has to be followed, and this provides an incentive to MNCs to move to developing countries with their unaltered plants and technical know-how to manufacture import restricted goods for sale in local elite markets.

Transfer of Inappropriate Technology. Conditions in developed countries are vastly different from conditions in developing countries. The first important difference is with regard to the relative factor prices. The wage levels in the developing countries are considerably lower than in the developed countries primarily because of their general poverty the relative abundance of labour and scarcity of capital. The conditions in the development countries are just the opposite, this raises the question of the 'appropriateness' of the technology transferred. The technology that is made available by the developed to the developing countries is capital-intensive in nature by the developed to the developing countries is capital-intensive in nature and accordingly, not suitable to the factor endowments of the latter.

Destructions of Indigenous Capital-Goods Industry. Not only is the technology transferred inappropriate, the operations of the MNCs retard the development of an indigenous capital-goods industry. As noted Multinations may stifle the growth of indigenous enterpreneurship, so that the net addition to capital accumulated is such less than the investment provided by the multinationals themselves.

PRODUCTION OF OTHER SOPHISTICATED PRODUCTS

The technology transferred by MNCs is inappropriate also in the sense that it produces commodities which are unnecessary or over-sophisticated in relation to the needs of the developing countries. Moreover, MNCs encourage forms of consumption among the broad mass of the people, particularly in the urban areas, which are inappropriate in the stage of development and often nuritionally damaging. Important examples here are powder, baby-milk and Coca Cola.

These tendencies distort economic structure of the under-developed countries, are wasteful in nature, encourage acquisitiveness, reduce domestic saving and can worsen balance-of-payments by encouraging expensive tastes.

MNCs and Employment Creation. Because of the capital-intensive nature of their technolcgy the employment effect of the operations of MNCs in the host countries is negligible. Moreover, such technology transfer is likely to increase income inequalities. When a multinational corporation sets up a unit in a developing country, it concentrates on employing a few highly skilled labour force of that country. These people are offered higher wages than the incomes of the unskilled domestic labour force. Thus technology transfer fails in increase employment opportunities in the developing countries on the one hand, and promotes inequalities in income and wealth on the other hand.

Some supporters of MNCs have argued that the impact of technology transfer by MNCs on employment position in development countries is positive. However, they take only a partial view of the reality. Almost all developing countries of Asia, Africa and Latin America and labour abundant economies. The transfer of highly sophisticated technology to these countries by the MNCs leads to greater unemployment. The incapability of this technology to absorb labour is simply due to the fact that "it was designed to do the opposite, *i.e.*, to be labour saving and capital using."

Impact on Industrial Concentration in Developing Countries. The penetration of MNCs in underdeveloped countries leads to higher concentration in the long run to the following reasons: *First*, due to their competitive strength the MNCs may force local firms out a business. This may simply by due to the fact that market forces reduce the profitability of marginal suppliers and force them to leave the industry. *Secondly*, a multinational corporation may buy out its local rivals through acquisition. *Thirdly*, the conduct of foreign firms may have an indirect effect on concentration by stimulating defensive amalgamation among local firms. *Finally*, through skillful negotiations with the host government, the MNCs may bargain for themselves secure and influential positions in their industries.

The net effect of these tendencies of concentration promoted by the activities of MNCs is very damaging for the small scale industrialists who find it more and more difficult to exist in the face of increasing penetration by MNCs.

Capital Flows and Balance of Payments. The developing countries are often required to pay high direct costs for technology transfer in the form of profits by many MNCs have been substantial and many more times than their total investment in India.

On account of the above factors, some critics argue that the operations of the MNCs 'decapitalize' developing countries—that is leave them with less capital than they would have had in the absence of MNCs. A related criticism is that outflows of imcome lead to a futher deterioration in the already weak balance of payments positions of the underdeveloped countries and lead to erosin of their foreign exchange reserves. While a loan creates obligations for only a certain number of years, private investment may involve an unending commitment.

The behaviour pattern of MNCs reveals that they do not engage in R and D activities within the development countries. Their R and D efforts are concentrated in laboratories in the home country or in other industrialized countries. However, the developing countries are forced to bear the cost of the R and D activities as the affiliates of the MNCs remit payments on this account also.

Restrictive Practices of MNCs. MNCs impose a number of restrictions in their technology transfer agreements with the developing countries. One of the most common restrictive clauses in contracts of technology transfer is that of export prohibition. In other words, foreign technology using national firms and subsidiaries of MNCs obtain capital equipment and technical know-how on the specific condition that the production will be done only for domestic market. In rare cases MNCs grant freedom to technology consumers in respect of exports. The implications of these restrictive clauses in backward economies are serious. First, by virtue of these restrictive provisions technology supplier MNCs exercise control over the business decisions of the technology buyers in respect of output, market prices, and often this results in creation of excess capacity. Secondly, restrictions forbidding sales in third markets inhibit host country's export promotion drive and thereby prove to be serious obstacle to development.

A large number of technology transfer contracts include obligatory conditions with regard to purchase of equipment and intermediate goods from the same sources as that of technical know-how. For technology supplying MNCs such tie-in arrangements serve an important purpose. They ensure a secure market for their capital equipment and intermediates and facilitate earning of monopoly profits. Tie-in restrictive arrangements in technology transfer contracts take several forms. The most common form is to explicitly forbid the purchase of capital goods and intermediate inputs from other sources. Sometimes in addition to this, use of local material is either limited or even completely prohibited.

International Institutional Structure Biased in Favour of MNCs. The international institutional structure also has a distinct bias in favour of MNCs and against the developing countries. As far as technological transfer is concerned, this bias is reflected at four different levels: *(1)* Institutional arrangements such as international patent system have a negative effect for the interests of the developing countries; *(2)* International mechanisms such as international insurance scheme to cover properties of MNCs facilitate existing relations of MNCs with host governments; *(3)* International efforts as the preparation of codes of conduct has limited effects in favour of developing countries interests; *(4)* Thus, there is an absence of internationally agreed provisions for the disclosure of information and accountability with respect to the activities of the MNCs.

Technological Dependence and Threat to National Sovereignty. Last but not the least is the 'technological dependence' that technological transfer at times introduces in the recipient country. Many developing countries have not paid sufficient attention to the programmes of research and development within their own national boundaries and have continued to depend on the import of technology from abroad. From a long term point of view, the costs of such a policy are colossal as the country becomes more and more passive to the needs of educational, scientific and technical development. Thus the basic infrastructure of 'learning' fails to evolve in the country. However, even more risky than this is the power that such technological dependence confers on the MNCs to dictate terms to the recipient country. As the technological dependence of the developing country increase on the MNCs, the ability of the latter to dictate economic and political terms to be former also increases. At times, the powerful MNCs gain control over local assets and jobs and then exert considerable influence on the political decision-making process at all levels. They may even subvert the very political process in small countries and jeopardize their economic and political freedom.

SCIENCE AND TECHNOLOGY POLICY

India became independent in 1947 after about 200 years of colonial rule. The Government of India from the very beginning adopted a policy regarding the scientific and technological development of the country. In fact, the new leadership of India was very much aware of the national conditions and capacity along with the international condition and the superiority of the west on the fields of science and technology particularly. Hence, with the desire to make India a modern country and a big regional power with an international role, the leadership put more emphasis on the development of science and technology. particularly, Prime Minister, Jawaharlal Nehru realised that to get rid of backwardness, science and technology would be most helpful.

Jawaharlal Nehru was instrumental for the adoption of Scientific Policy Resolution (SPR) by Government of India on 4th March 1958. It recognised science and technology as the key to national prosperity. India is scarce in capital and initial materials. It has to heavily depend on modern technology to overcome such limitations. The aims and objectives of SPR are:

(i) To promote, foster, cultivate and sustain science and scientific research-basic and applied;

(ii) To ensure adequate supply of highly trained and qualified research personnel by recognising their work as an important component of nation's strength; and

(iii) To secure the benefit of science and technology to all the people in the country.

Thus, the SPR acknowledges the cardinal importance of cultivating science and scientific thinking on mass scale by the masses by building large number of scientific institutions, training large number of scientific manpower and applying the science and technology results to the economic cultural development of all the people.

In response to the need for guidance on a wide ranging and complex set of inter-related areas of science and technology industry, economy and trade, the Government of India had announced the Technology Policy Statement (TPS) in January 1983. Its main objectives are to develop indigenous technologies help absorption of the improved ones. Accordingly its main aims are:

(1) To attain technological conscience and self reliance;

(2) To blend a correct mix of technologies of mass production by the masses and for the masses;

(3) To upgrade both technologies and equipment on continuous basis;

(4) To develop essential technologies in the critical areas which are nationally relevant and internationally competitive;

(5) To promote economic efficiency and quality in production; and

(6) To Ensure harmony with environment, ecology and habitant and so on.

Historical Background. The Industrial Policy Resolution (IPR) of 1948 and 1956 was one of the first policy options of Government of India. It aimed at promotion, directional and regulative aspects of economic activity of country. The aim of IPR was to accelerate industrial and economic development by expanding large scale industries in the core sectors through public and co-operative sectors. It emphasized the need for equitable distribution of wealth among the population by the state by promoting basic and strategic industires. Massive import of both capital and technology was considered essential for the industrial development of the country. The Industrial Development and Regulation (IDR) Act of 1951 was considered as an instrument of achieving the objectives of IPR. It allowed grant of licences to select and thrust areas which are considered essential for Economic Development.

Later Developments. The Monopolies Restrictive Trade Practices (MRTP) Act of 1969. extended its scope mostly to private sector industries whose main objectives were, prevention of concentration of wealth, direction of flow of investment and business operations towards select industries needing advanced technologies, and promotion of regional development.

Foreign Exchange Regulation Act (FERA), 1974 extended its scope and covered private sector firms whose foreign equity was more than 40 per cent. Its main objectives were similar to that of MRTP Act. Higher rate of foreign equity was allowed, provided the firms operated in the high technology areas, exported all their manufactured goods and shouldered the responsibility of developing backward areas.

The government provided certain incentives to promote R and D by industries. The Department of Science and Technology (DST) formulated and implemented a scheme in 1973 to recognise in house Research and Development centres of industries by registration. Such centres are eligible for certain fiscal benefits including import of critical materials and equipment under open General Licence (OGL). They are also entitled for a grant of foreign exchange for deputation of experts abroad, allocation of special controlled materials, exemption of excise duties, Income Tax (IT) exemption upto 100 per cent of expenditure incurred on R and D, preferential treatment in licensing for utilization of indigenously developed technologies.

Industries sponsoring research projects with national laboratories under C.S.R.I. are eligible to Income Tax deduction, subject to proper approval of competent authority. There is a provisions of Income Tax deduction on the amount spent on a pilot or semi-commercial plant based on C.S.I.R. technologies and on expenditure incurred as enhanced capacity in the form of plant and machinery.

Depreciation rate higher than 50 per cent is allowed to users of indigenously developed technologies. Central and State Financial Corporation operate several incentive schemes such as interest subsidies to encourage industries who venture to commercialize newly developed indigenous technologies. The subsidy varies between Rs. 20,000/- for small units and Rs. 4 lacs for large scale units.

Interest free personal loans, under Risk Capital Foundation Scheme, limited to 50 per cent of equity share in the project, is available for setting up of medium and large scale projects.

The IDBI, operates a Venture Capital fund created by Government of India 1986-87 budget by imposing 95 per cent cess on all imported technologies Finance Corporation Limited RCTC assistance is available in three forms., *viz. (1)* Conditional loans as an instrument of profit and risk sharing without any interetst bearing; *(2)* conventional loan carrying progressive interest ranging 6—15 per cent per annum; and *(3)* direct equity participation in the company.

A look at the trends in the growth of annual expenditure on Science and technology activities and per cent share in GNP (Gross National Product). shows that though Science and technology expenditure in absolute terms made a 742 fold increase, its relative share in the GNP increased only 50 times. It is obseved world-wide that many developed countries spend 2 per cent of GNP or more on indigenous Science and technology efforts.

However, inadeqate it might be, India's consistent efforts to raise Reserch and development expenditure have created a wide ranging network of Science and Technology agencies and institutions.

Due to inter-institutional competition and changing socio-economic priorities a readily altered pattern of distribution of Research and Development expenditure is seen now. Today Defence related Science and Technology activitives share the bulk of Research and Development expenditure.

Distribution of expenditure by nature of research is experimental development 30 per cent, applied research 30 per cent basic research 14% and other 24 per cent. Likewise, discipline 49 per cent natural science 31 per cent, agricultural sciences 15 per cent and medical sciences 5 per cent.

Development of Science and Technology infrastruture in India has 3-tier activity: *(1)* Agencies for policy promotion and planning; *(2)* Agencies under ministries and departments to implement the policy formulations; and *(3)* Institutions undertaking Research and Development projects and programmes. The Ministry of Science and Technology is the nodal wing of the government. Individual powers are delegated to DST, DSIR and DBT. Besides, there are many state councils for Science and Technology programmes. The chronology of individual Science and Technology agencies set up by government are: CSIR (1942); ICAR (1947); ICMR (1949); DAE (1954); UGC (1956); DRDO (1958); DST (1971); DOE (1971); DOS (1972); DOEN (1980); DOD (1981) and DNES (1982).

Over 100 professional bodies like National Science Academy. Indian Academy of Sciences, National Academy of Sciences, Institution of Engineers. All India Management Association, Institution of Costs and Works Accountans, National Productivity Council, State Productivity Councils. etc. are functioning in the country to promote professional excellence in their respective disciplines.

TECHNOLOGY POLICY STATEMENT OF 1983

Technology Policy statement was issued in 1983 for the development of indigenous technology and efficient absorption of imported technology according to the national priorities and resources its aims to:

(a) Attain technological comeptence and self-reliance, to reduce vulnerability, particularly in strategic and critical areas, making the maximum uses of indigenous resources.

(b) Use traditional skills and capabilities making them commercially competitive.

(c) Provide the maximum gainful and satisfying employment to all strata of society with emphasis on the employment of women and weaker sections of seciety.

(d) Ensure a correct mix between mass production technologies and production by the masses.

(e) Identify obsolescnce of technology in use and arrange for modernization of both enquipment and technology.

(f) Develop tecnhologies which are internationally competitive partcularly those with export potential.

(g) Ensure maximum development with minimum capital outlay.

(h) Reduce demands of energy, particularly energy from non-renewable sources.

(i) Improve production speedily through greater efficiency and fuller utilztion of existing capabilities and enhance the quality and reliability of performance and output.

(j) Ensure harmony with the environment preserve the ecological balance and improve the quality of the habitat; and

(k) Recycle waste material and make full utilization of by prodcuts.

The statement mentioned that in technology development, special emphasis will be focused on food, health, housing, energy and industry with particular importance on agriculture including dry land farming. It mentioned:

1. Optimum use of water resources, increased production of pulses and oilseeds,
2. Provision of drinking water in rural areas, improvement of nutrition, rapid reduction in incidence of blindness, eradication of major communicable diseases and population stabilisation,
3. Development of use of renewable non-conventional sources of energy, and
4. Low cost housing,
5. Industrial development. The Government of India decide to give full attention to the development of indigenous technology to achieve technological self-reliance and reduce dependence on foreign inputs, particularly in critical and

> vulnerable areas and in high value added items, in which the domestic base is strong. The technological potential inherent in this system of interliked capabilities must be fully utilized and in turn provide fill up for further development from within the system. Therefore, incentives will be provided to users of indigenous developed technology and for products and processes resulting from such use.

The technnology policy mentioned about environment too. It referred that:

> To facilitate utilization of natural resources for ensuring a sustainable benefit stream for a better quality of life, it is essential that the technology conversion process must be made as efficient as possible, as this will provide a much higher output of the productive goods and services from the same material inputs. The policy therefore aims at:
>
> — adoption, adaption and promotion of state of the art technologies for waste prevention and reduction by lesser consumption of raw material with special emphasis on indigenous efforts;
>
> — modification of upgradation of the process technologies for optional utilisation of natural resources;
>
> — adoption of preventive approach for pollution control;
>
> — promotion and use of cleaner technologies;
>
> — ensuring access to cleaner technologies available abroad.

The policy mentions a few thrust areas:

(1) Energy related technology including those for alternative fuel, renewable non-conventional source and energy consevation technologies with due weightage to domestic local availability base.

(2) Indigenous industries like those in the small scale sector or based on traditional and household skills.

(3) Technologies for conservation of land, water and energy resources and their integrated management for sustainable development.

(4) Extensive and intensive mapping and exploration of natural resource as well as estimation of reserves.

(5) Agriculture, allied services and agro-based industries including development of non-hazardous pesticides, herbicides and fungicides.

(6) The necessity of protecting vast sections of people against natural hazards like earthquakes, cyclones, droughts and floods.

(7) Technologies to betterment of infrastructural facilities such as transport, communication and housing.

(8) Technologies for provision and maintenance of health services, as well as leading to developing of new drugs/ medical devices and instrumentation, vaccines and their delivery systems.

The tecnology policy statement of 1983 is directed to:

— achieve a greater spread in the use of technological developments;

— ensure accessibility of technological devices to all segements of the society with a speical emphasis on remote and rural communities in order to improve their quality of life;

— enahance infrastructural facilities;

— upgrade traditional skills and reduce drudgery keeping in view the special needs of women and weaker section of society;

— encourage industries for enahancing human skills and upgrade existing technology to comparable international levels as well as to attain such levels for newer and emerging technologies.

Policy has also mentioned about the role of Research, Development and Engineering. It stated as below:

(1) Association of the relevant R and D Elabouratory systems for technology acquisition.

(2) Institution of measures to upgrade the efficiency and productivity of technologies for ensuring quality and enhancing competitiveness.

(3) Enlarged role of R and D E in our economy.

(4) Providing technology support and services for major export oriented areas like leather, textiles, jute, jewellery, handicrafts and agro-products.

(5) Providing support for substantive value addition for export in areas which may emerge due to rapidly changing global mix of technologies and

(6) Development of indigenous clean technoloies which are urgently needed to preserve the environment and ensure the health and safety of our people.

It is also noted that Rand D E could provide vital inputs of enabling small scale industry to grow and successfully compete with large scale industry.

Due to its policy towards science and technology India has made quite a good development in its socio-economic conditions. It is today a recognizable fore in the world and particularly in South Asia. Its leadership and bureaucrats realised that in this age of rapid growth science and technology are important tools. But international technology market is highly imperfect and dominated by a few multinational corporations. They follow various discriminatory trade practices for their own benefit. It was also realised that the developing country depend on them to borrow technology. Hence, Indian government followed a dual policy *(1)* to borrows developed and costly technology; and *(2)* to develop indigenous science and technology for the betterment of society and the nation.

❒

16

Economic Systems and Environment

CAPITALIST ECONOMIC SYSTEM

Economic system of country provides its broadest economic environment. In a capitalist economic system activities of a business firm are by and large market determined. Nearly all economic activities are carried out by private sector. The scope for private sector to operate is wide in capitalism in comparison into any other economic system.

According to G.D.H. Cole, capitalism is that profit-oriented system which is characterized by private ownership of objects of labour, instruments of labour and means of labour. Production is mainly carried out with the help of labour sercies rendered by the working class in returns for wages and the class of capitalists has the right to whatever output is produced within the system.

Cole's definition of capitalism is scientific. It clearly underlines the fact that of the private ownership of the means of production the implication of which is that the capitalist economic system offers ample scope for private business.

FEATURES OF THE CAPITALIST SYSTEM

It is the oldest type of economic system. Presently a large number of countries notably the U.S.A. Japan, Germany, France, the U.K., Itally etc. have the capitalist economic system. The main features of a capitalist economy and the following:

1. **Economic Sovereignty.** In a capitalist economy, producers are free to use their capital in the production of any commodity. Workers are free to acquire any type of skills and choose any occupation: Similarly, consumers are free to purchase any commodity and in any amount they like. These freedoms are also referred to as producers sovereignty' and consumer sovereignty in the capitalist system.

2. **Right of Private Property.** In a capitalist economy every individual has the right to hold and use of property and the means of production such as farms, factories, mines, transport etc. After the death of the owner, his property is inherited by his legal heirs. In this way the right of property perpetutates in the economy.

3. **Private Ownership of Means of Production.** Under Capitalism the means of production such as farms, factories, mines, transport, etc., are owned by private individuals or firms and they use these means of production for their private benefit.

4. **Labour Power as a Commodity.** An important feature of the capitalist system is that under it the labour power of man becomes a commodity and can be bought and sold just like any other commodity. In a capitalist economy the majority of the people own only one thing *viz.*, their capacity to work or their labour power. Whatever the nature of the economy, man has always possessed his labour power. Labour power just like any other commodity commands a price which is equivalent to the cost of those commodites which are essential for the maintenance of the labourers and their family members.

5. **Production for the Market.** One main features of capitalist economy is that under capitalism business firms produce mainly with the aim of selling the output in the market.

The producers forms follow division to undertake the production of different commodities. The development of the factory system renders the division of labour even more complex. As long as the tools required in the process of production were possessed by everybody it was normal practice for all to produce just everything which they needed. It is only when the means of production get concentrated in a few hands that the capitalist system based on commodity production starts emerging.

6. **Price Mechanism.** The working of a capitalist economy is regulated by the functioning of price mechanism. The decisions of producers to produce particular commodities depend on price, demand and costs of production of different commodities. Producers produce such commodities that are priced high, and engage such factors of production that are priced low and contribute relatively more to output. Households purchasers are also influenced by prices of different commodities. Households prefer to buy more of such commodities that are priced low and yield greater amount of statisfaction. Thus price mechanism helps prodcuers and consumers to take decisions about production and consumption.

7. **Exploitaion of Labour.** Workers are exploited under capitalism. Very often due to the freedom granted to the workers at a formal level, many people are wrongly given to believe that the workers by bargaining in the free market are able to get a fair price in return for their labour power. But this is not true, according to Marx, businessmen exploit workers and pay less wages than the goods produce by them.

8. **Growing Wealth of the Capitalist.** In a capitalist economy the wealth of the capitalist class increases in a sustained manner. Under capitalism to earn more profit, generally every firm makes the utmost effort to eliminate every often firm. A firm which losses out in the competition leave the

market and its share is captured by sucessful firm. In this way only a handful of firms manage to survice in every industry and with them large wealth is concentrated. Another may by which wealth is accumulated is the exploitation of workers.

9. **Class Contradiction.** The capitalist system rests fundamentally on class distinctions. As capitalism develops, the society gets divided into two mutually hostile classes. On the one hand are the handful of capitalists with whom wealth as well as power is concentrated. In spite of the enormous power vested in the capitalist class it cannot do without the class of workers. Machines are not self-operative. Therefore the labour power is indispensable for the survival of the capitalists. The workers who through their hard labour create immense wealth themselves remain poor and exploited throughout their lives, while the capitalists by laying a claim to the entire output become richer over time. The class of interests of capitalists and workers takes the form of class conflict. Since the power is with the capitalists they are offered all possible help in their supperssion of workers by the government agencies like the police.

10. **Emergence of the Working class.** The working class in capitalism is totally dependent on the capitalist for its livelihood. The freedom enjoyed by the working class in only at a formal level. Under capitalism the increasing use of machinery leads to widespread unemployment and an increase in the rate of exploitation of workers which implies a decline in the share of workers in the national income over time.

WORKING OF A CAPITALIST ECONOMY

In a capitalist economy neither an individual nor any institution takes decisions in a planned manner concerning its day-to-day functioning. However, the people of capitalist countries know that in spite of all this the producers generlly produce those commodities which they effectively demand in the market. Besides this the producers find it necessary to demand their services on the rendering of which they obtain their income. It is only by spending this income that the poeple can buy goods and services of their choice.

In a free market economy the behaviour of all individuals including causumers and producers both develop the system of price mechanism. This system not only solve the central problems of a economy but also helps in reaching the state of equilibrium. This can be understood with the help of the following figure.

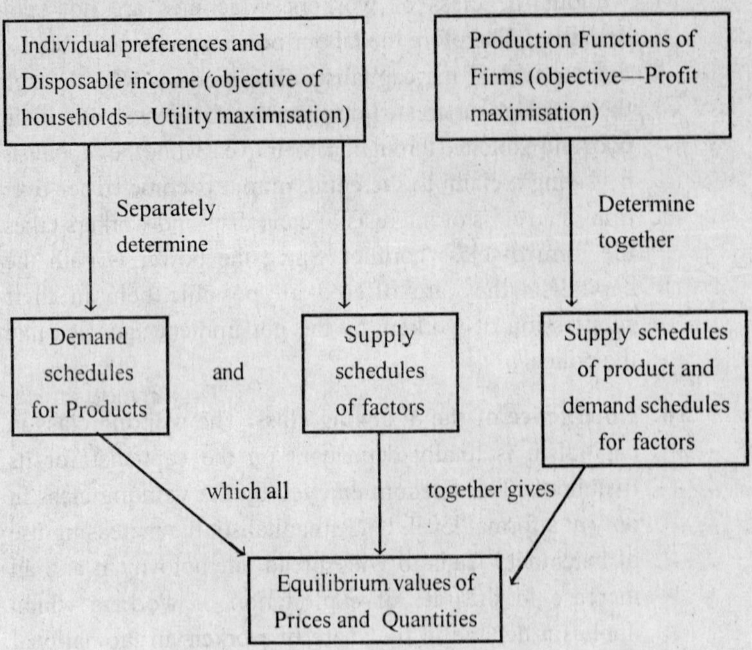

Fig. Working of Price Mechanism

It is clear from the diagram that the preferences of the people with regard to consumption goods and their income which they wish to spend on them will together determine the demand for various goods in the market. The production function or alternatively the quantity and proportion in which labour, capital, land and other factors are used in the productive process determine the supply of products in the market. It is these conditions of demand and supply in the commodity market which determine the prices of all products which enter it. In the various factor markets the wage rate, rent, etc., are determined in more or less the same manner.

Very often the economists of capitalist countries claim that it is through the working of this price mechanism that the free enterprise economy takes decisions regarding the three central problems *viz.*, what to produce, how to produce and for whom to produce in favour of maximum social welfare.

This price mechanism works efficiently under the conditions of perfectly competitive market structure and equitable distribution of income and wealth. But in the capitalist countries of today neither is the distribution of income equitable nor is the situation of perfect competition found to prevail. Therefore, a number of weaknesses can be noted in the way in which the price mechanism regualtes the economy. It is very often seen in capitalist countries that on the one hand there is a scarcity of necessities like wheat and milk, while on the other liquor, motor car, television and other luxuries are freely available. Moreover, whereas the children of the poor fail to get enough of bread, the dogs and cats of the rich live on meat and milk. this is an irrational situation.

Economic Role of the Government

Some limitations of the price mechanism in the context of a present day capitalist economy have revealed themselves and are as follows:

1. If the economy depends solely on the price mechanism to solve its central problems, then given the income and wealth inequalities there is a possibility that a large number of people die of starvation while a handul possess the good things of life very much in excess of what is required by them. Thus, in a Welfare State the government finds it

necessary to curb such inhuman traits in the working of the price mechanism.

2. The growth of monopoly firms in the market has put an end to the consumer's sovereignty. J. K. Galbraith asserts that the giant corporations by spending huge amounts of money on advertisement campaigns distort the demand pattern of consumers. This implies that very often people in response to sales promotion drives launched by producers of non-essentials switch over their demand from basic necessities to luxuries. Thus, the ability of the gaint corporations to influence the pattern of demand which emanates from the market deters the production of right commodities in the market. Given such circumstances, intervention by the government becomes invitable.

3. Generally the price mechanism due to the individualistic orientation of human behaviour cannot adequately provide for education, medical facilities and other social services. If in any society in addition to the above mentioned services, the level of production of such other services of immense national importance, like transportation, communications, water and electricity, is also to be determined by the price mechanism alone, then it is likely to result in a very short supply of each one of them. Therefore, it becomes imperative for the government to participate directly in the production of these services. In the Third World countries like India the regulation of the economy in the past by the price mechanism has been very defective, so much so that the development of steel, heavy engineering, chemical and other basic industries has suffered considerably.

MEANING OF SOCIALISM

Socialism was in fashion till the breakup of U.S.S.R. Though its popularity has declined sharply, still it is approved by most of the economists, social reformers, politicians etc. Socialism is used by different persons in a different way. Socialism is a economic system where private sector does not have any kind of control over production and distribution and all major economic activities including production distribution and consumption are controlled by the state or state-established agencies.

There is no universal definition of socialism. The concept of socialism has conceived in different ways by different thinkers. Thererfore it become necessary on our part to study a few important definitions of socialism. According to Paul M. Sweegy, "Socialism is a complete social system which differ from capitalism not only in the absence of private ownership of the means of production but also in its basic structure and mode of functioning."

According to Prof. H.D. Dicknson, "Socialism is an economic organisation of society in which the material means of production are owned by the whole community and operated by organs representative of and responsible to the community according to a general economic plan, all members of the community being entitled to benefit from the results of such socialised planned production on the basis of equal rights."

There are numerous definitions given by various economists, politicians and socialists. They differ in terminology but the following features are common in all the definitions.

FEATURES OF SOCIALISM

1. **State Ownership.** In socialist economy, there is a social or state ownership of the means of production. Because of social ownership, there is no profit motive to produce goods and services. The production is guided by social and other economic motives.

2. **Equality of opportunity.** Every individual should have equal opportunity to rise in life whether he is born in the poor family or the rich one. One must get equal opportunity to get education and training so that he should enter occupation of his choice. Under socialism steps are taken to ensure that every child whatever his birth and whatsoever

his parental background is provided sufficient opportunities to develop fully his latent talents and potentialities. Health services and free education upto a certain standard and or level sould be made for all.

3. **Equality of Income.** In socialist economy there is perfect equality of income but each person is paid according to work, performance and needs. Thus, the gulf between the rich and the poor is minimum.

4. **Social Welfare Motive.** An important features of socialism is that it is the motive of social welfare rather than private profit which guides production. Under capitalism, luxury goods are produced for their rich as they ensure greater profits while poor go even without necessaries as their production does not bring adequate profits to the producers. Under capitalism profit motive is the driving force of the economy. But under socialism the welfare of the society as a whole is the driving force fall economic activities. The place of impersonal forces of market which work under capitalism (Price mechanism) is taken by a central authority or the Planning commission which takes decisions about all important issues.

5. **Economic Planning.** Economic planning has been most closely associated with socialism. Effective planning cannot be adopted under capitalism because under capitalism means of production are owned and controlled by private individuals and production of goods and allocation of resources are directed by price mechanism. Planning ensures rapid economic development along desired. It granautees efficient and optimum allocating of resources in under developed countries where the level of national income and wealth is very low.

6. **Classless Society.** Socialism believes in a classless society. The existence of caste system is country to the concept of socialism. In a socialist state every body irrespective of his

> caste, class need and religion is provided with equal opportunity in all fit fields of life. A truly socialist state is a secular state. The two main classes of labour and capitalist no longer exist under socialism. Zamindars and capitalists are not allowed to remain under socialism because ownership of private property is strictly restricted every body is rewarded according to his work, and merit. Thus class struggle which is the chief feature of capitalism comes to an end under socialism.

The capitalist manufacturing industries being more developed, can easily be nationalised soon after the revolution. Similarly, the Government may also take over the core sectors such as electricity generation, construction, railways and other transportation.

In agriculture, farming is sought to be carried out on State cooperative farms. Important agricultural inputs like modern implements, seeds, fertilisers and cattle are owned by the State or cooperative societies. Therefore, even in the field of agriculture private ownership of the means of production is abolished and it is for this reason that no one individual can use the means of production owned by cooperatives to exploit other individuals.

In a socialist society farmers, mill workers and the people working in offices are given the right to own privately some amount of property, the ceiling for which is stipulated by the State. Private property which is generally in the form of land is allowed to be used for production of those goods which are required for the personal consumption of the family. In China and the other socialist countries, people apart from growing vegetables and fruits on this on this land also use it for poultry farming and animal husbandry. In order to alleviate the problem posed by the limited housing space, people are sometimes granted permission to construct a house strictly for their own use. Thus, one thing which should be noted is that some means production which individuals can retain for themselves cannot be used for the production of commodities, that is, goods and services which are produced with the intention of sale.

Though, under a socialist set-up the means of production get socialised yet, the consumption goods earned by the workers through their labour become the personal possessions of these people. The incomes earned by the people, their savings, some residential accommodation, furniture and various other consumption goods constitute their personal possessions. Labour is the sole source of personal wealth under socialism and the government under this system does not allow transformation of this wealth into capital which could later on be used as a means of exploitation.

Role of Planning. Planning under socialism plays exactly the same role as is played by the price mechanism in a capitalist economy. The Planning Commission, in other words, is required to solve the basic central problems of what to produce, how to produce and for whom to produce. In order to do this the Planning Commission has to, on the one hand, make an estimate of the entire economic, human and natural resources at its command, while on the other it has to determine the requirements of the nation for various goods and services. To put it more clearly, the Commission has to decide upon the various commodities which the economy should produce with the available resources. There can be many different ways of achieving the output targets. The Planning Commission in a socialist country takes into consideration the social welfare aspect and the development related goals of the nation while choosing the technique of production to be used. The price mechanism in a capitalist economy operates in such a way that production takes place only to meet the demands of all those people who have considerable amount of disposable income. Under this system not much attention is generally paid to the production of those commodities which belong to the poor man's basket. In a socialist economy, however, income inequalities are drastically reduced so that everyone has an adequate amount of disposable income. While determining the pattern and size of output the Planning Commission has to see to it that its decisions in this regard are such that they ensure the availability of commodities for all in the market.

Economists view socialist planning as equivalent to planning for economic development. Therefore, every economic plan of the nation which determines its economy's pace and pattern of development should necessarily incorporate two elements: First, the way in which national income is to be distributed between consumption and accumulation, and secondly, the manner in which investment is to be allocated among the different sectors of the economy.

Role of Prices in a Socialist Economy

Prices play a secondary role in the working of a socialist economy. However, it would be wrong to jump to the conclusion from this that they have no useful task to perform in the economy. They perform the following two functions in a socialist economy. In the first place it is the prices of consumer goods which determine the distribution of these goods amongst the people. Secondly, prices are essential for carrying out rational economic calculations for the nation. In a socialist economy, therefore, two types of prices can be seen to prevail. In case of those goods and services for which a market exists, *viz.*, consumer goods, the equilibrium prices or the market prices are determined at a point at which the demand for each one of them is matched by their respective supplies. On the other hands, for producer goods in the absence of a market, accounting prices are used. These prices are set by the Planning Commission on the basis of historically given prices and thus are not arbitrarily determined. If the price for any producer good happens to be set too high, then at the end of current time period a surplus of it will result. This is because a price higher than what is necessary will compel the State enterprises to unduly economise on that particular producer good. On the other hand, if too low a price is set, then a deficit of the producer good in question will arise. If the Planning Commission is faced with the former situation of a surplus ensuing for some prodcuer good at the end of the planning period, it will raise the price of the resource in question. In this way through a procees of trial and error the right accounting prices can be arrived at. These accounting prices of means of production and the market prices of consumer goods are used for the purpose of economic calculation in the planning process of the country.

MIXED ECONOMY

A mixed economy represents a mixture of features of the two types of economies capitalism and socialism. Under this form of economic system, the ownership of means of production is partly in the hands of privae individuals and partly owned by the society. The public authority usually own public utility sevices like supply of water and electricity, roadways and railways, shipping and air services, hospitals, schools and colleges, defence industries. As regards the distribution the Governments tries to remove disparities and inequalities in the income distribution by various measures such as taxes and their levies and through public expenditure.

According to Samuelson, a mixed economy is characterised by the existence of both public and private institutions excercising economic controls. In this economy price mechanism and partial planning both plays an important role. Indian is perhaps the best example of such an economy and can legitimately be called a mixed economy.

FEATURES OF MIXED ECONOMY

1. Coexistence of the Private and Public Sectors. The concept of mixed economy presupposes the existence of two or three sectors. In the Public or state sector the entire system of production and distribution is managed, owned, controlled and financed by the state itself. Private individuals are not permitted to undertake any economic activity in this sphere. The public sector performs three functions:

(i) it is to provide/create social heads;

(ii) it has to create industrial climate; and

(iii) it has to create a sound industrial base in the economy.

2. Price Mechanism and Government Control and Regulation Work Together. A mixed economy contains the goods features of both socialism and capitalism. Every possible effort is made to make the best possible use of available economic resources.

and Birla—having total assets exceeding Rs. 200 crore each. In 1997-98 there were 10 business houses having assets worth Rs. 14,852 crore or more each.

3. Bureaucratic Inefficiency and Corruption. In a number of developing countries though a large public sector has been created, no serious attempts have been made to develop efficient managerial cadre to run public enterprises. Interestingly in most of the developing countries after they got independence colonialist administrative machinery was retained and, for managing the affairs of public sector economic units, managerial cadre was drawn from this sources. The inefficiency in public sector enterprises emanates partly from this fact. Another factor that may also be mentioned is that even now "bureaucrats carry out their duties in formal structures that are reminscent of the pre-Independence imperialist administration. Rules, regulations, procedures, control mechanisms and basic management practices have essentially remained unchanged." over the years. Obviously this kind of administrative system can neither ensure efficiency in the completion of development projects nor activate high standards of productivity when actual production is carried out.

Introduction of discretion and administrative controls in a mixed economy ereated conditions for widespread corrpution. It has-been observed in a number of mixed economies that corruption impedes the process of decision-making and execution at various levels. Corrpt officials explit the position of public responsibility for private gain by using the threat of obstruction and delay. At the macro level influence of corruption gets reflected in the low rates of economic growth. Corruption may also introduce an element of irrationality in planning and may influence the course of development in a way that distortions develop in the plain itself.

4. Built-in-tendency to Slide Back. Now a days in India the policy of drifting away from economic planning is being pursued. The public sector is criticised for its poor performance and by implication privatisation is advocated for the improvement of the performance of the economy. But this is not correct. However, once in a mixed economy a new capitalised classs grows, often proposed up by the public sector and physical controls, it starts exercising pressures for dismantling the regulating sturcture. This results in a emergence of pure capitalism in which state shows little concern for the poor.

5. Denial of Social Justice. The mixed economy framework generally tends to favour relatively rich on account of their strong economic position. The deprived in the social system expect the government to counte this tendency by regulating the activities in the private sector and through direct participation in extensive areas of economic activities. However, in a class society that is to be found in all the countries having a mixed economy, the government has neither the ability nor the required will to prevent the tendency of the concentration of economic power.

GLOBAL ENVIRONMENT

The business environment has changed radically world over during the 1990s. Economic and political changes have surprised both business analysts and business practioners. Presently there is so much uncertainty that even the most competent corporate executives are not feeling confident about their business strategies. Now we shall analyse the impact of global and national economic environment on business and trade in India.

Presently for the Indian business the global scenaniro is not very encouraging. The global environment can be discussed under the headings of the unipolar world globalisation, economic crises in East and South-East Asia, the wash of Japan, Underdelopment of Russia and East Europe, global recession, regional economic groupings, protectionism and multinational corporations.

1. The Unipolar World. The collapse of Eastern Europe and U.S.S.R. marked the end of a bi-polar world. With the demise of socialism in these countries the USA established its supremacy over the world economy. Though Japan is a second largest economy but it is in no position to challenge the political and economic moves of the USA. The West European countries such as Germany, France, Italy and the U.K. could match the USA collectively but not individually.

The USA now behaves like a big brother and punish all those countries which dare to take independent policy decisions. Recently the nuclear tests by India in 1998 invited the wrath of the USA and it slapped sanctions on our country. The USA has recently threatened South Korea of a trade unless it agrees to import more American cars. This type of environment is not congengial to including India.

On Jan 1, 1999 the European Economic and monetary Unions launched a single european currency '*euro*'. With the euro's launch coinciding with the weakening of major Asain currencies including the Japanese yen and Chinese yuan, the dollar and euro are likely to dominate world economy as reserve and key currencies. This trend may spell doom spell doom for developing economies including India by triggering off competitive devaluation and increasing debt burden. IMF Managing Director however, believes that the world is moving towards a multipolar world in monetary field. However, in immidate future this does not seem to be the possibility.

2. Globalisation. Broadly globalisation implies simply the expansion of economic activites across political boundaries of the nation, states. The word has been used in two ways. When the term globalisation is used in a positive sense it implies a process of integration in the world economy. When the world gloabalisation is used in a normative sense, it prescribes a stretegy of economic development involving a rapid integration with the world economy. In whatever manner one defines globalisation, its fundamental attribute is the increasing degree of openness in a large number of countries. The three important of this process are International Trade, International investment, and International Finance. The openness is not conflined to these aspects only. It often extends to flows of technology, information and services across national boundaries. But it must be recognised that these movements are far more restricted than trade flows, investment flows and financial flows. It is probably this reason why most people consider trade, investment and finance as the core of globalisation.

Rapid globalisation over the past two and a half decades has made profound changes in the world economy. A study of the Top

200 global corporations has revealed that these colossal corporations, most of them larger than many national economies, now control around 28 per cent of the world's economic activity. Their combined sales at $ 7.1 billion surpass the combined economies of 182 countries. The study noted that presently there are 191 countries and if we substract the GDP of the big nine economies—the USA, Japan, Germany, France, Italy, the UK, China, Brazil and Canada, the combined GDP of the other 182 countries is $ 6.9 billion. Moreover, over half of the sales of the Top 200 corporations is in just five economic sectors, *viz.,* trading, automobiles, banking, electronics and retailing. There is also a growing concentration of a few firms in each of these sectors. In automobilies the top five firms account for almost 60 per cent of the global sales. The top five firms also have over 30 per cent of the global sales in personal computers, steel, oil, airlines, aerospace, chemicals and media. Finally, 186 of the Top 200 corportations are headquartered in seven countries, *viz.*, Japan, the USA. Germany, France, the UK, the Netherlands and Switzerland. Brazil and South Korea are the only developing countries to join the group of the Top 200 global corporations.

3. Economic Crisis in East and South-East Asia. For about two decades since the mid-1970s certain economies of East and South-East Asia Malasia, South Korea, Indonesia, etc., registered high rates of economic growth. Since these economies are basically markt economies, the IMF—World Bank functionaries aggressively marketed their model to other developing countries. In India, since we had registered only a modest rate of growth until 1990, we developed a great fancy for these economies. In fact, by adopting the liberalisation policy and pursuing greater opennes in the matters of trade flows, investment flows and finance flows we had hoped to repeat the performance of thse economies. When the Indian government was contemplating along these lines, the 'miracle' economies of Asia almost collapsed in 1997-90. The crisis engulfing these economies of was as harsh as unexpected.

The Asian crisis is relevant to India business in two ways—first, it may have some impact on the Indian economy and second, it may influence the policy makers in this country and they might opt for a reversal of the liberalisation process. Bhalla and Nachane are of the view that there are three likely channels through which India can catch East and South-East Asian economic meltdown contagion. These are as follows:

(1) the direct and indirect impact on India's exports due to the downturn in the Asian economies and the spread of the contagion to other markets for Indian goods;

(2) the imapct on the inflow of foreign capital; and

(3) the impact of contractionary domestic policies initiated in response to the crisis.

Presently there is a sharp decline in the world demand and prices for such products as electronics, semi-conductors and petrochemicals. Hence, chances of recovery are dim in East and South-East Asian economies. India should thus be cautius about fast spreading contagion.

4. The Crash of Japan. Performance of the Japanese economy was simply spectacular during the 1960s and 1970s. However, it considerably slowed down during the 1980s and its GDP growth rate was as low as 1.4 per cent per annum between 1990 and 1997. Never since the Great Depression of the 1930s a developed country has been cought in an economic crisis of the dimension Japan faces presently. It is interesting to observe that Japan continues to amass a large trade surplus, as against the unprecedented US deficit on external account. These phenomena, however, do not strengthen the yen and cause the slide of the dollar as certain analysts surmised. According to Frederic F. Claimont, "Far more crucial is the capital account of the balance of payments. Here Japan is in the deepest of quagmires with the return on yen assets woefully uncompetitive on international capital markets, and becoming more so daily. The public debt in Japan stand at 127 per cent of GDP and the non-performing loans of the banking system hovering around $ 1.6 trillion hence loans that will never be repaid.

There are also serious problems of growing unemployment, falling real wages and wholesale prices, and slump in housing construction. *The Financial Times* describing the situation wrote, "This is an economy from which confidence is being drained by the minute." This is reflected in the daily outflow of dollars from Japan. The real source of Japan's current difficulties lies in the major economic crises in the East and South-East Asian countries. This has cut down demand for Japanese exports in these countries drastically and the value of assets held by Japanese investors has fallen sharply. From the point of view of the India business, malaise in the Japanese economy is of great relevance as Japan accounts for about 6 per cent of exports from this country.

5. Underdevelopment of Russia and East Europe. Ever since the East Europe and Russia abandoned socialism and opted for capitalism, the economies of these countries have been caught in deep crisis. The reform measures adopted in these countries have failed miserably and the GDP has been falling at the rate of 10 per cent per annum or even more.

Now it is well known that the IMF and the World Bank had designed the package of reforms for Russia and East Europe. They are still calling the shots without realising that their short sighted policies designed from extremely narrow economic standpoint of industrialised countries do not serve anybody's interest. It has to be understood that an impoverished Russia or East Europe will not provide large markets for the goods produced in the Western countries. This fact is as much relevent for the Indian business which until the 1980s had large exports to these countries. Inability of Russia and East Europe to import from the West in a big way at a time when economies in Asia are caught in deep crisis in helping to accentuate the recession in the developed countries of the West. This phenomenon obviously will have adverse effects on the demand for the Indian exports as well.

6. Global Recession. Free markets and the IMF-World Bank experts did not think till recently that their activities would inevitably push the world economy towards recesion. But what was not suspected has happened. The world is now in the grip of recession.

At present two-fifths of the global economy is already in the grip of recession; and another two-fifths is on the brink. Leaving aside a few hardcore free marketers now everyone else seems to the convinced that there is a great likelihood of the repeat of the Great Depression of the 1930s. So far India and China have not caught economic melt-down contagion but the rates of growth have certainly declined. How long these countries will remain insulated from global recession will depend on the economic policies of these countries.

7. Regional Economic Groupings. Developed countries had become aware of their interdependence even before World War II, but after the War when reconstruction began in West Europe they realised the need for having a permanent system whereby it could be possible for them to cooperate with each other. As a result, organisations like OECD (Organisation for Economic Cooperation and Development), EU (European Union) and EFTA (European Free Trade Association) came into existence. The European Union (EU) was organised as a customs union.

The following regional groupings of the less developed countries have come ito existence over the years:

1. The Latin American Free Trade Association (LAFTA) formed in 1960 and consisting of eleven Latin American countries—Argentina, Bolivia, Brazil, Chile, Colombia, Ecuador, Mexico, Paraguay, Peru, Uruguay and Venezuela. It was later replaced by the Latin American Integration Association under Montevideo Treaty of 1980.

2. The Central American Common Market (CACM), comprising Costa Race El Salvador, Guatemala, Honduras and Nicaragua was formed in 1960. CACM functioned like a customs union.

3. The Caribbean Free Tade Area (CARIFTA) formed in 1968 and consisting of twelve Caribbean nations. In July

1973 this free trade area was converted into a full-fledged Caribbean community.

4. The Central African Customs Union (CACEU) formed in 1964 and comprising Cameroon, Central African Republic, Congo and Gabon.

5. The Andean Group was forme in 1969 consisting of Bolivia, Chile, Ecuador, Colombia and Peru. It operated in a more liberal trading atmosphere.

6. MEROSUR came into existene on January 1, 1995. This is a major free trade agreement originally signed by Argentina, Brazil, Paraguay and Uruguay. Chile and Bolivia joined it more recently.

7. Economic Community of West African States (ECOWAS) was formed in 1975 consisting of fifteen West African countries.

These regional groupings have bestowed benefits on business firms of the member countries in a number of ways. Yet their achievements are rather limited. This is due to the fact that the regional spirit has yet to grow. Most of the participating countries are guided by narrow national interests and nurture a feeling of suspicion towards other member countries. It is partly due to the fact that Western industrialised countries constantly try to sabotage such efforts at economic cooperation by giving military aid to some member countries of these regional groupings. It is this kind of sabotaging by the industrialised countries that the concept of Asian Common Market (ACM) could never become a reality though most countries of the region accept the advantage of creating such a common market. The Association of South East Asian Nations (ASEAN) founded in 1967 is the oldest grouping in East Asia. It comprises Brunei, Indonesia, Malaysia, the Philippines, Singapore and Thailand. This arrangement started as a preferential trade zone but new initiatives are afoot to convert the block into a free trade zone.

8. Protectionism. Since the mid 1970s the industrialised countries of the West have been increasingly resorting to protection. The success of Japanese exports and then of exports from the newly industrialising countries produced pressure on the USA and the West European countries for pursuing the protectionist policy. The older industrialised countries want to avoid competition from newly industrialising countries in their domestic markets and thus create non-tarriff barriers (NTBs). During the past two decades trade in textiles, leather goods, footwear, steel, ship-building, cars and consumer electronics has been subjected to blantant protectionism by the western countries.

Tariffs are now low and thus not used for protection. The main instrument of protection during the past two decades has been the non-tariff barrier (NTB). It violates widely accepted principles of non-discrimination and transparency in trade. Recently European Union has imposed anti-dumping duties on Indian export of stainless steel products while the EU countries continue to heavily subsidies their steel industry. This is obviously a case of blatant protectionism. It amply clarifies that it is not easy for the business firms of the developing countries like India and Pakistan to penetrate the markets in development countries.

9. Multinational Corporations. At present the global economy is dominated by 40,000 corporations. The activities of these enterprises cross national boundaries. These firms operate in overseas markets through some 2,50,000 foreign affiliates. According to the letest estimates of the Washington based Institute for Policy Studies (IPS) the top 100 of these global firms account for a growing share of the world's economic activity. Illustrating the growing economic clout of the global gaints the IPS report states that out of the 100 largest economies in the world, 51 are corporations; only 49 are countries. Wal-Mart the number 12 corporation is bigger than 161 countries including Greece, Poland and Israel, Mitsubishi is larger than the fourth most populous nation on earth, Indonesia, Toyata is bigger than Norway, General Motors is bigger than Denmark and Ford is bigger than Portugal.

The giant corporations with massive resources at their command, in the face of falling demand are engaged in ruthless competition with relatively smaller companies. Peter F. Drucker has rightly pointed out that medium and small businesses also operate in the world economy and they are not always visible. These firms in the prosperity phase of the business cycle grow and generate substantial revenues. However, with the onslaught of global recession their existence is threatened. In this period no goal setting, no vision and no strategy will help these small corporate enterprise in their growth pursuit.

The National Scenario

The national scenario at present is not as much encouraging as it was a few years ago. The country nevertheless lacks political stability. It seems that for some time the country can hope to get only coalition governments at the Centre which means that economic policies may not have a clear cut long-term perspective. The coalition governments which are likely to last for sort periods may follow adhocist economic policies. However, there is not much dispute on liberalisation and globalisation.

1. Liberalisation. In response to the economic crisis of 1991 the government embarked on a wide ranging reform of the policy regime. Prior to 1991 the Indian economy was a highly regulated economy. In July 1991 a beginning was made to dismantle controls which had over time become a major obstacle to industrial growth. Policy changes made to unshackle the economy from controls and to orient it towards the free market are known as the liberalisation measures. These measures are related to *(a)* the industrial sector, *(b)* the trade region, *(c)* foreign investment and technology, *(d)* the public sector, and *(e)* the financial sector.

In the industrial sector, barriers to entry for new firms and limits on growth in the size of existing firms have been removed. Industrial licensing has been abolished for most of the industries irrespective of the levels of investment. The MRTP Act has been amended to remove the threshold limit of one billion rupees on the assets of large business houses. The prior approval from the government is no longer required for capacity creation, amalgamation, merger or acquisitions on the part of such companies.

The abolition of controls in the sphere of investment decisions was necessary and desirable. However, deregulation by itself does not reduce the degree of monopoly. It may also fail to increase the degree of competition among the firms. Some recent developments in India suggest that mergers acquisitions or takeovers by firms in the industrial sector have enabled the enlarged corporate enterprises to capture larger market share. There are so many examples which one can cite, but some cases are worth noting: the merger of Brooke Bond Lipton with Hindustan Lever, acquistion of Goa Electrical by Crompton Greaves, the merger of Parle with Coca Cola and the merger of Ponds India with Hindustan Lever. In these cases either the established competition has been eliminated or potential competition has been pre-empted.

The policy regime for foreign investment and foreign technology has been liberalised at a rapid pace. The government now wants to enlarge non-debt-creating inflows. Hence, prior approval for foreign investment is not the rule. It may be required in excepted cases. The liberal access to imports of technology aims at facilitating technology upgradation which is a necessary condition for increasing international competitiveness in industry.

The trade policy reforms have eliminated quantitative restrictions on imports and exports. Further, there has been a substantial reduction in tariffs on imports alongwith abolition of subsidies on exports. The exchange rate changes have led to a sizable depreciation of the rupee. It is hoped that the exposure of domestic firms to international competition in this manner will compel them to become more efficient. In this relatively open environment domestic firms will have to upgrade technology, reduce cost and improve the quality of products. The assumption of the trade policy reform introduced in the country is that internationally competitive good products can always be exported. In practice, this may not always be true export surplus. Some countries in any case must have matching import surplus. This implies that it is not easy for Indian firms to raise exports unless certain countries choose to cooperate with them.

Till recently the commericial banking system and the domestic capital market were over-regulated and under-governed. Over the past few years an attempt has been made to improve the health of the financial sector through deregulation. With the reductions in the statutory liquidity ratio and the cash reserve ratio resources received by the banks in the form of deposits are not pre-empted by the government but are made available to the private sector. Interest rates in the domestic capital market have been deregulated. Now prior government approval regarding the size and price of equity issues in the primary capital market is not required. Market forces are now expected to discipline the capital market. The Securities and Exchanges Board of India, however, establishes rules and regulations to government the stock market and intermediaries.

As a result of liberalisation the activties of the public sector have been reduced. Now the focus of public sector is only on those sectors which are strategic and high-technology or constitute an integral part of the infrastructure. Chronically sick public enterprises are being referred to the Board of Industrial and Financial Reconstruction which decides whether these units are to be revitalised or simply closed down. Further, disinvestment of government equity in government enterprises is creating greater space for the private sector in industries.

2. Globalisation. Over the past eight years the Indian economy is being integrated into the global economy. The three policy measures initiated to realise the objective of globalisation are:

(a) Exchange Rate Adjustment and Rupee Convertibility. Since July 1991 rupee has been allowed to depreciate more or less freely. It is argued that the depreciation of the rupee increases international competitiveness of Indian products. However, the fact remains that over the years India's exports have not increased significantly in spite of a steady faill in the external value of the rupee. The value of external debt in rupee terms has nonetheless increased substantially. In 1992-93 the rupee was made partially convertible. The 1993-94 Budget introduced full convertibility of the rupee on trade account. Full convertibility of the rupee on current account was achieverd on August 19, 1994. India has adopted a cautius approach about the capital account convertibility, and most experts are now convinced that his country has managed to avoid South-East Asian melt-down contagion precisely on account of this reason.

(b) ***Import Liberalisation.*** There are two aspects of import liberalisation. First, the quantitative controls on imports have been dismantled and second, import duties have been cut drastically. Import liberalisation is expected to make Indian industry efficient and internationally competitive. Over the years Indian industries had become rent earners and did not consider it necessary to become efficient. With import liberalisation either they will have to become competitive or else perish.

(c) ***Foreign Capital.*** The Indian Government now sees merit in foreign capital. It is now widely believed that foreign direct investment accelerates the industrial growth. Therefore, in a bid to attact foreign capital, the government has offered various incentives and facilities to foriegn investors. Now foreign institutional investors also have access to the Indian capital market. Over the period August 1991 to October 1998 the government approved 5,874 fogeign technology collaborations and 8,396 foreign direct investment proposals amounting to Rs. 1,75,032 crore. However, the actual inflow was only Rs. 51,558 crore. Hence, the inflow of foreign capital has been far less than what was expected.

Apart from opening up the economy to foreign goods, capital and technology, it is necessary that the Indian firms penetrate foreign markets. In December 1995 the number of Indian joint ventures abroad was 592 of which 70.0 per cent were concentrated in just thirteen countries.

Now globalisation is a reality. It definitely offers opportunities to Indian business. But in the existing global situation it is doubtful that Indian firms will manage to penetrate foreign markets in a big way. Indian firms are presently too small as compared to major players in the global market. In the domestic market itself Indian firms are now uneasy at the threat that foreign capital poses.

The Indian corporate business does not consider the presence of foreign companies in India beneficial to them. In fact, many Indian companies now find that they are the target rather than the beneficiaries of the increased activity of foreign MNCs. It is aruged that under the circumstances one need not become defeatist about foreign MNCs. The correct approach is to create our own MNCs. This, however, is easier said than done. The less developed countries have failed to create major players in the global economy. Indian business at the most can hope to survive only in those industries in which major global players have little stakes.

❐